BLACK FREEDOM FIGHTERS IN STEEL

D1562765

Black Freedom

Fighters in Steel

The Struggle for
Democratic Unionism

Ruth Needleman

ILR Press
An imprint of
CORNELL
UNIVERSITY
PRESS
Ithaca & London

Copyright © 2003 by Cornell University

All rights reserved. Except for brief quotations in a review, this book, or parts thereof, must not be reproduced in any form without permission in writing from the publisher. For information, address Cornell University Press, Sage House, 512 East State Street, Ithaca, New York 14850.

First published 2003 by Cornell University Press
First printing, Cornell Paperbacks, 2003

Printed in the United States of America

Library of Congress Cataloging-in-Publication Data

Needleman, Ruth, 1945–
  Black freedom fighters in steel : the struggle for democratic unionism
/ Ruth Needleman.
    p. cm.
Includes bibliographical references and index.
  ISBN 0-8014-3741-5 (cloth : alk. paper) — ISBN 0-8014-8858-3 (pbk. :
alk. paper)
  1. African American iron and steel workers. 2. Iron and steel
workers—Labor unions—United States—History. I. Title.
  HD8039.I52 U5744 2003
  331.6'396073—dc21

                                                    2002151189

Cornell University Press strives to use environmentally responsible suppliers and materials to the fullest extent possible in the publishing of its books. Such materials include vegetable-based, low-VOC inks and acid-free papers that are recycled, totally chlorine-free, or partly composed of nonwood fibers. For further information, visit our website at www.cornellpress.cornell.edu.

Cloth printing   10 9 8 7 6 5 4 3 2 1
Paperback printing   10 9 8 7 6 5 4 3 2 1

To
George Kimbley,
Bill Young,
John Howard,
Curtis Strong,
and
Jonathan Comer,
for dedicating their lives
to the fight for freedom
and
in memory of
Jonathan Jacob Levin
(1966–1997)

Contents

Acknowledgments

I am indebted to many workers, scholars, archivists, and foundations for support of this book.

First, I acknowledge the extended commitment of two of the freedom fighters, Jonathan Comer and Curtis Strong. For the past fifteen years, they have worked with me on this project. In addition to participating in repeated interviews, they reviewed each draft of the manuscript and assisted with photos and contacts. It is an honor to have been entrusted with their stories. Although my time was more limited with George Kimbley, William Young, and John L. Howard, each opened his home to me and recounted his experiences in great detail.

Their families and coworkers were equally generous. Nell Comer, Jonathan's wife, sat in during many interviews and provided a lengthy interview of her own. John L. Howard's son, David Howard, helped with additional information, materials, and photographs, and reviewed the manuscript for accuracy. Other people, labor pioneers themselves, not only agreed to interviews but have responded to my questions and requests many times over the past two decades. I regret that I could not include their stories, which are no less remarkable: Walter Mackerl (USWA Local 1066), John Mayerick (USWA Local 1014), Frank Perry (USWA Local 1011), William Gailes (USWA Local 1010), Joe Gyurko (USWA Local 1010), Al Samter (USWA Local 1014), and Leon Lynch (USWA Local 1011).

The United Steelworkers of America and its leaders and activists have provided me with inspiration, information, and a home in the labor movement. The following steelworkers, identified by local union, provided interviews, research help, and contacts. USWA 1010: Jim Balanoff, Mary Elgin, Jim Fleming, Bill Hoggs, Nick Koleff, Nick Migas, Tommy Mills, and Eugene Sufana; USWA 1011: Jim Baker, Sidney Dent, Chuck Fizer, Basil Pacheco, Bill Payonk, Henry Rowsey, Bill Scoggins, and Fred Stern; USWA 1014: Hubert Dawson, Chris Malis, and Oris Thomas; USWA 1066: Glen Dowdell. Former USWA District Director Jack Parton helped me obtain access to files at the USWA's archives at Penn State. Vice President for Human Affairs Leon Lynch, the first African American to serve on the USWA's International Executive Board and its most senior member, shared his experiences as well and provided me with important insights. I also received extremely helpful observations from USWA leaders and staff, retired and active: Josephine Brooks, Scott Dewberry, Oliver Montgomery, Fred Redmond, and Jim Robinson, the current district director.

My coworkers in the history department at Indiana University Northwest have provided continual encouragement. Jim Lane, in particular, checked historical facts and edited the text. Steve McShane, historian and archivist at the Calumet Regional Archives, duplicated materials, scanned photographs, and assisted in many hours of excavation. Elizabeth Balanoff's thorough study of the African American community in Gary greatly enriched my work. She interviewed some of the same labor activists as I, but twenty years earlier, enabling me to balance memory, perspective, and facts. Mike Olszanski's interviews, research, and personal experiences in USWA Local 1010 served as an invaluable resource.

Through a summer faculty seminar, organized by Melvin Dubofsky and funded by the National Endowment for the Humanities, I found my historiographical legs and began serious work on the manuscript. All of the seminar participants provided invaluable, sometimes daily, feedback; colleagues Paul Mishler and David Witwer continued to offer their support and guidance long after the seminar had ended.

I especially want to thank Alexander Saxton, a historian whose work and friendship have greatly influenced my own. Bruce Nelson's help and knowledge strengthened my writings considerably. I received critical guidance and support from Herbert Hill, who challenged me to refine my political analysis. Jack Metzgar's detailed comments on the manuscript saved me from digressions, exaggerations, and generalizations.

For comments and assistance, I am equally grateful to journalism professor Carol Polsgrave, union and civil rights leader William Fletcher Jr., historian Joe Trotter Jr., labor educator Charley Richardson, my labor studies colleague Thandabantu Iverson, my freedom-fighting friend Clernest Moore, and Nicole Morse, organizer, taskmaster, and friend. When possible, I turned to colleague Cathy Iovanella to check on the clarity of my writing, and colleague and friend Gayle Gullett read tirelessly. Without the constant support of my office manager, Velma Rucker, I would not have had the time to complete this book.

Without the patience and support of my editor, Fran Benson, the book would never have been completed. She saw me through difficult delays and some unnecessary whining and walked me through the hardest steps of writing and preparing a book for publication. Karen Hwa from Cornell University Press worked with me to the end.

I am extremely grateful to the foundations that helped fund my work. The National Endowment for the Humanities provided a stipend and two fellowships. In addition, I received a Henry J. Kaiser Grant for research at the Walter P. Reuther Library; the American Association for State and Local History Grant-in-Aid; a research award from the Project Development Program, School of Continuing Studies, Indiana University; and from Indiana University Northwest, a small grant for research, transcription, and supplies. The Division of Labor Studies at Indiana University has supported my research for many years, through aid for travel, duplication, and interviews, and helped to make possible the inclusion of so many photographs.

Finally, I come from a family of fighters and educators. What greater inheritance is there than a passion for social justice! My great-grandmother's sister, Rayzi, arrived on America's shores at the turn of the century; her daughter, Leah, joined the Ladies' Garment Workers' Union, studied at the Bryn Mawr School for Women Workers, and became a union organizer. My sister, Carol Levin, raised three remarkable children who, like their mother, chose education as a calling, not as a profession. My youngest nephew, Jonathan Levin, brought hope and self-respect to high school students in the South Bronx as an English teacher and advocate. He lost his life trying to help someone who had given up hope. His murder inspired my sister to teach in the South Bronx. My niece, Laura Levin, served as my very first research assistant, and both she and my nephew Lee Levin carry forward the family tradition of standing up for fairness. Finally I pay tribute to my mother. She took pride in my accomplishments, including my defiance in the face of injustice. Her support has made possible the many photographs in this text. This book is part of my own contribution to the fight for social justice.

BLACK FREEDOM FIGHTERS IN STEEL

Introduction

Black Steelworkers Fight for Unionism

"Twenty-five miles of steel mills!" Walter Mackerl called up this image from stories he had heard about the Calumet Region in Indiana. After a childhood spent sharecropping, Mackerl could hardly wait to see it. "I figured there had to be a job for me." Raised in Pine Bluff, Arkansas, Mackerl figured right, along with thousands of other African Americans who arrived in northwest Indiana in the 1920s. They dreamed of decent-paying jobs and a world without Klansmen, chain gangs, and cotton. They found jobs, but the mills were an industrial hell.

Fleeing Mississippi, Bill Young discovered that "slavery hadn't ended, at least not at the Inland Steel Company." George Kimbley lasted less than four days in the blast furnaces at U.S. Steel; he had survived six months in the trenches during World War I. Oris Thomas was "scared to death" by the shifting overhead cranes and walls of fire. "Wish'd I hadn't got that mill job," he recalled.

When the new industrial union movement came to the Calumet Region in 1936, these men were ready. They had been organizing for years among themselves in the mills and their communities. "An industrial union with no discrimination! That's what I was told," confirmed Walter Mackerl. "If your organization mean what it say," he told Nick Fontecchio, spokesman for the Committee for Industrial Organization (CIO) in Indiana, "then we'll organize steel." Fontecchio gave Mackerl an enthusiastic hug, and the campaign was on.[1]

Grassroots African American organizers in northwest Indiana spread out through the region and signed up thousands of workers within months.

Their efforts turned the call for interracial unity and working-class solidarity into a reality. One by one, they convinced skeptical black workers to set aside memories of discrimination and exclusion in the interest of building an integrated movement. African American organizers worked hand in hand with immigrants, the radical left, and the breakaway leadership from the American Federation of Labor that had established the CIO. Without the resources of the CIO, its commitment to organize all unskilled workers, and the practical experience of radical activists with interracial organizing,[2] they would not have been successful. It was, however, African American initiative and far-sighted leadership that guaranteed black-white unity at this decisive moment in labor history.

What black unionists did to gain representation for themselves had a lasting and major impact on workers' rights and union democracy in the United States. African Americans fought unrelentingly for the establishment of seniority over favoritism in job assignments and promotions. They pursued the principles of equal pay for equal work and equal access to training and apprenticeships for all workers, because anything less locked them in at the bottom of wage and occupational hierarchies. Their struggle for fair treatment on the job and representation in the union provided leadership in the struggle for union democracy. This book examines the movement for democratic unionism from the bottom up, through the lives and experiences of grassroots African American steelworkers in northwest Indiana.

Black Freedom Fighters in Steel focuses on five African American men who labored at the heart of this country's steel industry, in Gary and East Chicago, Indiana, to build a union for all workers. Their collective story began in the post-Reconstruction South, involved active participation in two world wars, and climaxed during the tumultuous years of the black power movement in the late 1960s. Their persistence and vision helped to create safer and decent-paying jobs in steel. Challenging social and institutional barriers of race and class, these workers adopted organizing and coalition-building strategies that laid a foundation for interracial and democratic unionism.

The biographies and stories in this book document an essential phase of the black freedom struggle, as it moved from the South to the urban, industrial North. Northwest Indiana was the destination point for tens of thousands of southern black migrants hoping for a new life as blue-collar workers.[3] In fact, this area, known as the Calumet Region, had the highest density of black workers of any urban center in the North. Their experiences included the hardships of the Great Migration and the battle to enter industry and survive in the most degrading work environments.[4]

The oldest union man represented here, George P. Kimbley, was born in 1897 in Kentucky, the youngest, Jonathan Comer, in 1921 in Alabama. Kim-

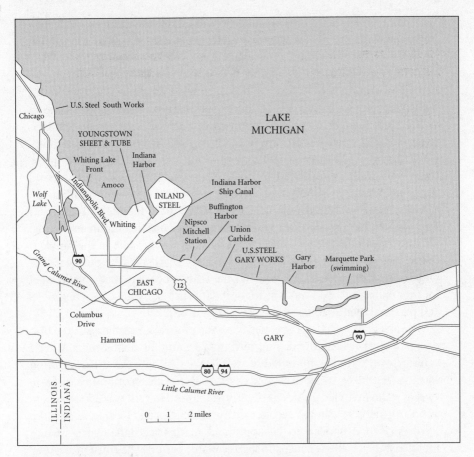

Map of the Calumet Region shows the three integrated steel mills discussed in this book. Youngstown Sheet and Tube stood just west of Inland Steel in Indiana Harbor, East Chicago. Further east, in Gary, was U.S. Steel (formerly Carnegie Illinois Steel). Map courtesy of Calumet Regional Archives, Gary, Indiana.

bley fought in World War I, Comer, in World War II. William Young, born in Mississippi in 1903, fled the South for a job at the Inland Steel Company in 1922. John Howard grew up in Gary, although he was born in Alabama. His father had moved north to take a job during the 1919 steel strike. Curtis Strong left Mississippi with his family when he was four. They settled in Dixon, Illinois, in 1919, and Strong hired into the steel mill in Gary in 1939.[5] Kimbley, Young, Howard, Strong, and Comer spent most of their lives in the mills and the union. Each fashioned a distinct approach to life and work. Each favored different ideologies and activist strategies and developed a different philosophy for handling racial conflicts and individual prejudice.

George Kimbley, William Young, John Howard, Curtis Strong, and

Jonathan Comer played instrumental roles in establishing a union in steel, in implementing seniority agreements and workplace standards, and in forging alliances with community, civil rights, and women's organizations. They spent their work lives in the Calumet Region and gave their union years to the United Steelworkers of America (USWA) in what was known as District 31. Four of the five eventually served on the International Steelworkers Union's staff; four of them held top local union offices. All five were still alive and actively engaged when I began my research in 1985. I chose the five men because they covered three generations of labor activism and worked in the three main mills in northwest Indiana, Inland Steel, Youngstown Sheet and Tube, and Carnegie Illinois, or U.S. Steel. They held leadership positions in the four basic steel local unions (USWA 1010, 1011, 1014, and 1066), and four of them were promoted to international staff positions. William Young, the only one of the five who never went on staff, was a leader of the Amalgamated Association of Iron and Steel Workers (AAISW), the Steelworkers' Organizing Committee (SWOC), and the USWA Local 1010 at Inland Steel for over half a century. I was able to meet with each of them, view scrapbooks and personal memorabilia, and meet family as well.

On various fronts, these five men were the pioneers. Kimbley was the first to sign a Steelworkers organizing card in Gary and the first African American steelworker to be appointed to staff in the Chicago area district. Young was the first black to serve as vice chair of a grievance committee in basic steel and the first vice president of his local. John Howard was a first-generation northerner, was the second vice president of his local, and was the third African American to be appointed to district staff. Curtis Strong founded the first black caucus in a coke plant, became the third vice president of his local, was a founder of the National Ad Hoc Committee of Black Steelworkers, and was the second man to be appointed to the International Civil Rights Department. Comer became the first African American president of a basic steel local and the third to be appointed to the Civil Rights Department. They are not typical African American workers, but they are surprisingly representative of the diverse circle of black activists who chose the union as their primary organizational vehicle. All of them made the union central in the fight against racism and injustice and carried forward the civil rights struggle into the U.S. labor movement.

Their lives and stories cover many of the watershed events and turning points in working-class African American history. The men made the shift from South to North, from agricultural to industrial labor. When they hired into the mills, they were assigned to the dirty, dead-end, and dangerous jobs reserved for black workers. Every one of them stood up to his employers, took on a steel corporation, and then confronted his own steel union over issues of discrimination. Even so, the men never wavered in their belief in the necessity of unions for workers—above all, black workers. Each in his own way demonstrated the inseparability of class and race in this nation's history.

At the same time, the five knew each other and argued continually over how best to organize African Americans into the union, and then over strategies for promoting black representation within it. Political backstabbing and infighting among African American unionists were as common and as destructive as among white trade unionists. Black unionists' ideological conflicts were, in many ways, representative of the debates in the black intellectual community throughout the twentieth century, championing black nationalism at one point, socialism at another, favoring economic self-sufficiency and separate organization, or calling for complete integration.[6]

Each one of the five men was branded an Uncle Tom at some moment in his union career; they labeled each other as Uncle Toms, black hillbillies, or black nationalists. Some opposed separate black organization and special positions for African Americans in the union; others believed there to be no way to break down discrimination in plants and unions except through independent black organization and an affirmative action policy based on quotas. They all had a slightly different approach to balancing race, class, and gender as components of their struggle, but none of them argued for the isolation of one from the others. Most found lifelong friends and allies on the left, although all of them put space between themselves and left organizations in order to carry forward the fight against racism during the cold war. The four oldest had been drawn to the antiracist campaigns of the 1930s and 1940s led by communist and other left groups. Their first friends among white union activists were often radicals.

Given the racism of their world, it was inevitable that these men would be pitted against each other, compared to each other, and used to maintain tokenism and white supremacy. Their accounts of surviving in this environment, finding common ground, and collectively advancing the interests of black workers in labor provide important lessons and models for trade union work today. Perhaps most instructive is their reliance on coalition building within the union, first to carry out the mass unionization drives of the 1930s and later to advance the civil rights struggles of the 1960s. Black workers participated in the dominant political caucuses of the union but maintained sufficient alliances and organization among themselves to exercise leverage in union politics.

From their perspectives, the achievements of the Steelworkers' Organizing Committee (SWOC) would not have been possible without the self-organization of distinct groups, from racial minorities to ethnic immigrants, from specific departments and occupations to separate community organizations. The triumph of industrial unionism in northwest Indiana relied on extensive networking among existing organizations long before the CIO sent in its first organizer. The CIO facilitated connections among the networks but did not create them. Many workers, white and black, native-born and immigrant, had already engaged in systematic efforts to coalesce the various groups, respecting the autonomy and issues of each. Their efforts were successful, and their strategies worked to bring African American workers and concerns into the union's leadership and program. Multiracial organizing relied on organizational and not just individual relationships.

The diversity of approaches used by the five men facilitated black unionization and representation and contributed to the advancement of black rights in the union. At different historical junctures, one method proved more effective or appropriate than another, but each of the five men discussed here pushed organized labor one step forward. Each showed courage in breaking radically with the norms of society and with the mainstream black community. Each man had to negotiate compromises in order to hold leadership positions in the union. Each one overlooked hundreds of abusive comments and mean-spirited acts throughout their union years. They were not naive or idealistic; they knew that change would come only with risks and sacrifice. Their stories show in realistic and sometimes painful detail how unity was built.

Truth in Storytelling

The narratives in this book also contribute to an understanding of working-class formation and the complex interactions between race and class. Oral historian Alessandro Portelli has emphasized the importance of looking at individual lives in order to understand the working class. "Class exists in relationships" he noted, "and implies a multiplicity of oppressions. You cannot talk about class as if it were one thing or made of steel."[7] He advises us to turn to individual lived experience to document history. I have taken his advice, although I do not claim to have captured historical realities through these narratives.

Even though I have relied on what Kimbley, Young, Howard, Strong, and Comer told me, it is impossible to tell someone else's story. Even though I spent many days, sometimes years, getting to know each of these five freedom fighters, it is our conversations more than definitive narratives that I offer in this book. I recorded hundreds of hours of the men's words and tunneled through archives trying to validate their accounts. I have also grieved over the deaths of three of them, and developed deep friendships with the remaining two. I listened carefully to the stories they shared with me but recognized that there were many more they chose not to tell. I might have heard their words clearly but misunderstood their meaning. "Stories," Alessandro Portelli writes, "is what history means to human beings." The interviewer's interpretations "co-exist with the interpretations imbedded in the quoted words of sources, as well as with our readers' interpretations of them."[8]

My information and my interpretations reflect more than two decades of collaborative work with steelworkers and with their union, the USWA. Over that time, I interviewed formally more than a hundred rank-and-file workers, union activists, and top leaders, from five mills and seven union locals. I examined local and national union and civil rights records and unearthed new documents from the basements and garages of my subjects. I have been a labor educator in the Calumet Region since 1981, and I work with thousands of steelworkers. They are my students, coworkers, and friends. I have lived through long bus rides to Washington for demonstrations, handed out leaflets at picket lines, and stood in downpours at rallies. In collaboration with other committed educators and unionists, I created a special college degree program just for steelworkers, known as Swingshift College, in 1994.[9]

I came to northwest Indiana for a job in labor studies at Indiana University Northwest from Detroit, where I had been a labor activist. I began my professional career as a traditional university professor in romance languages and literatures and Latin American studies at the University of California in Santa Cruz in 1969. Four years later, I left the university to work as an editor of the United Farm Workers Union newspaper, *El Malcriado*. Since then, I have held a minimum wage job as a plastics fabricator in a New York sweatshop and unloaded trucks part-time for the United Parcel Service in the Motor City. All of my work—professional as well as blue collar—has been done in multiracial environments. In every case I found myself embroiled in battles against racism.

In 1984 I began collecting stories about how workers benefit when they oppose discrimination and unite across racial lines. I included examples of these stories in all my classes. As I spent more time in conversation with African American labor pioneers, I came to question many of my assumptions. Although most workers I met had derived benefits from black-white unity and unionization, white workers had benefited more than black workers, and often at black workers' expense. In addition, African American steelworkers repeatedly told me that they had a harder time working with many northern, white so-called liberals than with southern, white bigots. They explained that they knew where they stood with the southerners but became confused by the hypocrisy of the North, the gap between what people said and what they did.

The most difficult form of racism, they argued, stemmed from the reluctance of white workers to acknowledge the dominance—sometimes even the presence—of racist attitudes and practices. White leaders and workers would often insist that they and their union were color-blind. This denial undermined the efforts of black workers to fight discrimination. White workers accused blacks of "playing the race card" when they pointed to examples of discrimination, because what was clearly visible to African Americans proved invisible or inconsequential to many white union members.

Racism's intransigence was caused by twin demons: white denial, on the one hand, and systematic institutionalization, on the other. By the time civil rights legislation prohibited discriminatory hiring practices and occupational segregation, these practices had defined and limited labor markets in the United States. Racial inequalities, therefore, had become self-perpetuating, without discriminatory intent or racial bias. Union cultures, everyday assumptions about skills and qualifications, word-of-mouth communication systems, all favored the union insiders, those already at the top and in the know. It had been easier to battle outside, identifiable enemies such as Jim Crow segregation than it was to change accepted patterns and practices within organized labor.[10]

African American workers in northwest Indiana's steel mills fought harder for unionism and under more difficult conditions than most of their coworkers. Facing exclusion, discrimination, and even segregation within organized labor, black unionists struggled consistently for working-class unity; in the face of racism and violence, African American leaders pleaded for solidarity. Yet the American labor movement time and again pressured black workers to set aside their quest for equal rights in the name of working-class unity and to abandon their demand for representation in the name of union democracy. These realities shaped the basic structure and life of organized labor in the United States.

No organization in this country, however, has done more to raise the living standards of black workers than unions. Even today, unions are often the only integrated organization in workers' lives. Yet inequalities among workers have proved to be remarkably persistent. Labor's most important weapon—working-class solidarity—continues to be the major challenge facing the U.S. trade union movement.

Black Freedom Fighters in Steel is organized into three parts. Part 1, "Five Freedom Fighters," includes biographical chapters on all of the men profiled in this book, covering their lives from childhood through their careers with the United Steelworkers as leaders. The chapters are in chronological order, beginning with the life of George Kimbley, the oldest of the five men, and trace the emergence of the African American community in northwest Indiana from the turn of the century to the 1970s.

Part 2, "Civil Rights Struggles in the USWA," recounts the efforts of black workers to organize for equality within the USWA. Chapter 6, "Change This Segregated System!" describes the history of independent black organization, zeroing in on the National Ad Hoc Committee, a black power caucus formed in the mid-1960s. Chapter 7, "Between a Rock and a Hard Place," explores the experiences of the four activists once they were appointed to union staff as representatives. Chapter 8, "Diplomats and Rabble-Rousers," provides an overview of their role in shaping black radical thought and practice in the union movement.

Part 3, "The Longest Struggle" brings the story up to the present. Chapter 9, "Upheaval in Steel," describes briefly the events in steel from the 1974 Consent Decree to the present, with its restructuring and widespread unemployment. The Consent Decree, agreed to by the industry and union, introduced affirmative action procedures into mill hiring and promotions. Chapter 10, "Fire in the Belly," captures in a roundtable discussion the views of five black labor activists today. Two pioneers, Curtis Strong and Jonathan Comer, participated in the exchange. The final chapter, "Ask Harriet Tubman!" analyzes the roundtable and draws attention to the main lessons of the African American struggle in steel: the importance of coalition building within the union as well as with outside groups and the necessity of independent organization for African American representation.

George Kimbley, William Young, John Howard, Curtis Strong, and Jonathan Comer never underestimated the importance of the fight for unionism or the power of racism to resist them every step of the way. The United Steelworkers of America belonged to them as much as it belonged to any other worker, and they fought for shared leadership and ownership. This book tells their stories, from our combined perspectives, highlighting the immense contributions African American workers made to both the labor and civil rights movements. Their efforts demonstrate the centrality of the antiracist struggle to a strong union movement.

Part One

FIVE FREEDOM FIGHTERS

CHAPTER I

"Oh, That Kimbley, He's Union Crazy"

George Kimbley

George P. Kimbley arrived in the Calumet Region in February 1920, shortly after his release from the U.S. Army. Shaken by his World War I experiences in the trenches in southern France, Kimbley looked to settle down in Gary. Like so many other returning and dislocated veterans, he hoped to find a decent job; the steel industry seemed promising. He found a place to live in central Gary, an overcrowded section of the city known as the Patch, where European immigrants and African American migrants lived side by side in shacks and tenements. The Patch sat right below the South Shore railroad tracks, downwind from the giant mills. Kimbley landed his first job within a few days.

George Kimbley could never have predicted that he would become the first Gary African American to sign a membership card with the Steelworkers' Organizing Committee (SWOC) in 1936, nor that he would be the first black rank-and-file steelworker to be appointed to the SWOC staff in the Chicago/Northwest Indiana District in 1938. Kimbley had come of age in the Jim Crow South; his greatest dream was to work hard and be left alone. His life, however, took a dramatic turn when he discovered the power of organization. Unionism would transform George P. Kimbley, and he, in turn, would transform unionism.[1]

When I met George Kimbley in 1989, he was living in Frankfort, Kentucky, where he had been born ninety-two years earlier. A long life of hardship and struggle had grayed his dark skin, but had not dimmed his memory. Although age had shaved a few inches off his height, he carried himself with surprising strength. For six hours without a break, he shared the story

of his life, with unparalleled detail and epic drama. Mr. Kimbley—even his peers used the title—had a gift for storytelling.[2]

Growing Up in the Old South

"I was born in Frankfort, Kentucky, July the 14th, eighteen and ninety-six. My mother's name was Ella Kimbley and my father, Luther Kimbley." George was the first Kimbley born outside slavery. He grew up in a small house across the street from the family that had owned his parents.[3] "We were just thirty years this side of slavery," he reminded me. His mother did housework for a number of white families until later in life, when she found a job as "chore woman" at

George P. Kimbley became the first black worker from the mills to be appointed to USWA District 31 staff in 1938. Photo courtesy of Calumet Regional Archives, Gary, Indiana.

George Kimbley with the author. The interview with Kimbley took place in Kentucky in 1989; he was ninety-two years old. Photo courtesy of Ruth Needleman.

the post office. His father combined jobs, working as janitor and cook at a saloon. By the age of six, Kimbley had also joined the labor force; he received fifty cents a week and two meals for helping a white family after school. Later he worked on area tobacco plantations.

Growing up in a white neighborhood, Kimbley rarely played across town with other black children. He hardly knew childhood. He relished occasional game-playing hours, but in his neighborhood, he had to address children younger than he was as "miss" or "mister." Perhaps he grew accustomed to his isolation; Kimbley remained something of a loner throughout his life.[4] He knew his grandparents but neither they nor his parents chose to talk to him about slavery. "Slavery was a bitter pill," he said flatly. "Sometimes I think it is just better to forget it because it was cruel. Reconstruction was as cruel a period as was slavery," he added. "The KKK was in brutal control. Negroes were flogged, beaten, lynched, and burned at the stake."[5]

Slavery and the post-Reconstruction world of Jim Crow, the world of his parents, molded George Kimbley, his outlook on life, and his relationships with white people. It was by observing his mother that Kimbley picked up what would become his "survival strategies." Kimbley avoided symbolic protests against racism; he viewed them as fruitless and dangerous. He saw value not in "stating his mind," but rather in speaking and acting with great caution, with an eye toward those behaviors that would keep him safe. Ella Kimbley, raised as a house servant, maintained many of her prewar manners through Reconstruction. She made a practice of assisting poor whites, especially those who had once had money and status. To help them preserve their public image, she would provide them—always secretly—with food, clothing, and other assistance. She would go through the neighborhood begging for welfare handouts that she would then pass on to her white neighbors. Because she never betrayed their trust by telling anyone else of her work, she was privy to their most confidential secrets. They trusted Ella Kimbley, confided in her, and treated her with respect.[6] Under the conditions of the plantation South, this was a form of power. George Kimbley would adapt this approach in his work and union life.[7]

"I went to the Clinton Street School and I often think about it," he recounted. "The first day I went to school I had a fight and it looked like the rest of my days in school it was always a fight." According to Kimbley, he remained in school only until the eighth grade. "I quit. I had some problems and I just decided that I didn't need an education. I figured if I had plenty of good work—if I could get a job—and maybe if I would be honest, I could make it, because I didn't see where education was doing too much for black people at that time." Kimbley, however, prided himself on his intelligence. During his years in school, he told me, "There wasn't an examination of what I didn't get the first, second, or third honor, and I didn't have to study either. I could read my lessons over once, and it would be sufficient. I had an extraordinary good memory. Never forget anything."[8] He continued, "My biggest ambition at that time, and I can recall it, was to never let anybody beat me in examinations."[9]

"We Are Not What We Seem"

After he left school, Kimbley made plans to move north. "I felt mistreated," he said, "and lost faith in blacks ever being totally free. . . . I believed my people would always be half free, so I made up my mind to live the best I could under the system."[10] As a teenager, he traveled to Indianapolis with five friends to look for work. From there, two years later, he took off alone for Detroit in hopes of finding "better money."[11] There he obtained a job in an icehouse and had his first contact with a union. He was not eligible for membership, just the peddlers and helpers; they most likely belonged to a teamster, hod-carrier local.[12] "When there was a shortage of labor, around 1916," he continued, "they pulled me out of the icehouse and gave me a job on the ice wagon as a helper. And it was on the ice wagon as a helper that I was pretty much disgusted with some of the northern people who I'd heard were so liberal when all day long I heard the word 'nigger.' " Throughout his life, Kimbley found it easier to handle race relations with southern whites than northern ones.[13] The southerners were more predictable and direct. Many of the northerners, in his opinion, were hypocrites, talking one way but acting another.

Kimbley dwelled on his icehouse experience because this was his first prolonged encounter with northern racism and it was during this job that he began to work out his strategy for handling race relationships. The white folks he grew up around did not use the word "nigger," and he was taken aback by the language of the northerners.

"They got a nigger on the ice wagon." And the kids would say, "See the nigger. See the nigger." Well, it hurt but I never heard that much in the South, as bad as some of the people were in the South. I never heard that word "nigger" used a whole lot. . . . I made up my mind I was going to break that down and did break it down. Well, there was a rule of luck that you mustn't sell ice on credit and you couldn't give it away. If you did, they fired you. So the fellow I worked with, named Adams, would take an ice in the house . . . and if the people didn't have money, he'd bring the ice out, and I could see it. I'd go right in behind him, when he'd go in another house. I'd go in there and the lady would say, "Well, the other man was in here; he wouldn't leave the ice, because we didn't have the money." And I says, "Well, I can't take it back. Oh, I know how hot it is and all, and if I let you have this ice and they find out, they'll fire me and I don't want to be fired." "Oh, I won't tell anybody." And I'd leave the ice.

Kimbley thought he could use his humanity to show those around him that character and not race makes the man. Working in a world of strangers, however, he recognized that kindness alone would not necessarily educate people. He continued his story:

> The people began to realize that I had a different nature than the man that I was working for, because he was pretty cruel. Even the kids'd get up on the wagon, he'd throw his tongs at them. As soon as he'd go into a place, I'd grab a chunk of ice and cut it up and give it to the kids and tell them, "Take it and run." One day a gang of them was sittin' on the sidewalk and I just picked out one of them. I said, "Oh yes, you're that little guy that called me that bad name." "Oh no, sir. Mister, I didn't call you no bad name." I said, "Yes, you did. I'm not going to give you any ice." And that's how I broke that "nigger" stuff down, see. The people got to the place where I didn't never have to buy any beer. I didn't have to buy any lunches. And somebody was always giving me something.

Kimbley had learned to work within a profoundly racist system. When he wanted to teach white folks a lesson, he did it through indirect ways, usually by making them uncomfortable by playing along with their stereotypes. If he found what he considered uneducable whites—which he did throughout his life—he set out to embarrass them before their peers. He had an extraordinary ability to stand back, think through a situation, and figure out how to manipulate the whites into behaving themselves just a bit better. He used their negative energy against them by pretending that he was unaffected by their degrading comments or actions. He expressed hurt and anger during our interview, but to protect himself in those early years, he buried his private self and feelings deep inside. Throughout his years in the union, he functioned through a persona, a controlled, public self. He manipulated the white folks to limit their racist behaviors, to save himself from further insult and injury by getting them to treat him better. He neither blamed nor cursed their attitudes, because he never expected white people to act any differently. Like Malcolm X in his performances as a shoe shine boy in New York, George Kimbley used tricks to shape white folks' behavior.[14]

Kimbley told a number of remarkable stories about his interactions with white people during his ice helper days. Some southern whites, newly migrated to Detroit, would run out of their houses to greet "the negro" because they hadn't "seen no colored for some time," recounted Kimbley. He, of course, did not take offense. But when they cast him into a stereotypical role, he fought them with the weapon of embarrassment.

> After leaving [the house of a white woman from the South], hot on my wagon, getting ready to drive off, she comes out with a slice of watermelon that long [stretching his hands two feet apart]. I knew exactly what she wanted. I says, I'm going to entertain her. It was a hot day. I took the watermelon in both hands and bit right down in the center. I knew that's what she wanted. Every time she'd get ready to walk back in the house, I'd start a conversation. I held her there until I licked the rind and threw it away.

The next time Kimbley delivered ice to that woman, she invited him into her home to have some watermelon at the table, which she had set with a knife and fork. "That's how I learned about working with people," he stressed. "I knew [racism] had to be broken and couldn't be all done with my fist. So I won a lot of people over." One immediate result of his good relations with the icehouse superintendent was that two of his friends were given jobs. Later on, Kimbley's attitude helped him keep his job in the steel mill when the majority of workers were being laid off during the depression.

The War Changed His Life

In November 1917 George Kimbley was drafted into the U.S. Army to fight in World War I. "There was no integration at that time," explained Kimbley, so he was assigned to a "colored unit." According to his memory, he was placed in the 372nd Infantry and trained in Texas and Alabama, preparing to go overseas.[15] In March of 1918, Kimbley and his unit landed in France. He had studied up a bit on the French language, so he could talk with people when he got there. "We were all on the decks, and I saw a Frenchman, waved and I hollered 'Bonsoir, Monsieur,' and he hollered and everybody hollered."

"We were among the first fighting black troops in France," he said, smiling with pride. "The 369th, the 371st, and the 372nd, my regiment." Welcomed as liberating troops, African Americans such as Kimbley "found the French people to be a loveable people." Interactions between the French and the black troops impressed him greatly. The French talked with and treated them as equals, if not heroes, which contrasted sharply with the treatment the black troops got from the American military leadership. "They wanted to make stevedores out of us," Kimbley commented bitterly. "We let the world know we came over there to fight. If we wasn't going to fight, we wasn't going to work. They saw we meant it, so instead of taking us, Pershing let us go into the French army."[16] Kimbley fought in the south of France. "The black troops won quite a bit of decoration and glory," he said. Kimbley insisted that his six months at the front were the defining moments of his life.

"It was about October the 4th or 5th that I was under heavy bombardment. The Germans had cut loose what you would call a boxcar barrage on my section of the trenches. . . . To tell you the truth I prayed so hard that I couldn't say anything but 'God,' being a religious person to begin with. And the next day, praying to God, I say, 'Lord, if you get me out of this, there's certain things that I'm going to do.' " He promised to return to his birthplace in Frankfort, Kentucky, and carry out work for the church. At that point Kimbley stopped his story, looked me in the eyes, and said, "I've just about completed the promises that I made God."

On his release from the military, George Kimbley returned to Detroit and married. His ability to survive trench warfare had convinced him he could endure anything, with God's help, even degrading treatment from northern whites.[17] The French had given Kimbley a glimpse of social acceptance and equal treatment. Although he never expected to be treated equally back home, he did know what it was like not to be patronized.

Kimbley's wife urged him to move to Gary so she could bring her mother, who wouldn't live in Detroit, up to join them. Kimbley went ahead alone to find work and a place to live and then brought his family to his residence in the Patch. "I lived in a neighborhood where there were foreigners," he noted. "There wasn't a whole lot of racial feelings. People made friends. The foreign element was very friendly, but it wasn't a whole lot of mixing other than among the lower classes for sex."[18]

Across the tracks on the segregated North Side, however, stood the stately homes of the so-called Americans, white families whose breadwinner was a foreman or a skilled craftsman in the mill. On the South Side, tar-papered shacks stood back to back. Rows of tenement housing lined the unpaved streets, with barely three feet separating one row from the next. Nine units shared a single privy and water pump, and each unit included multiple boarders.[19] "The [shacks] were built out of little thin wood with tar around them," described black worker Oris Thomas, who settled as a child in the same neighborhood.[20] Housing in the Patch was scarce and inferior but very expensive.[21] Black migrants paid up to 200 percent more for a rented room in the Patch than they would have in other sections of the city. According to one local social worker, "Europeans, Negroes, and Mexicans frequently occupy apartments in the same building, the Negroes, perhaps, being the only ones conscious that there is anything unusual in such an arrangement."[22] "You could go anywhere on the South Side," Kimbley recalled, "Restaurants there served blacks and immigrants."

Gary, Indiana

Kimbley arrived in Gary as part of a major migration of African Americans to the North. Between 1920 and 1930 the black population in Gary jumped 238 percent, from 5,299 up to 17,922. Over 93 percent of the blacks living in the city when Kimbley arrived had been born outside the state of Indiana.[23] Most of the African Americans in the region before 1920 had settled there after 1910. The city of Gary, in particular, became a magnet for migrating black families.

From its founding in 1906, Gary was a company town, a creation of Carnegie Illinois Steel, run by Judge Elbert Gary. Along a seven-mile stretch of Lake Michigan, the new Gary mill overshadowed the surrounding dunes with towering structures of steel: blast furnaces and coke ovens spreading dense clouds of white, yellow, and black smoke over the lake. Most of the African American workers who had done heavy labor on the original construction crews were gone, chased out of town by a series of campaigns between 1909 and 1911 against unemployed blacks and immigrants.[24] When production started at the Gary Works in 1909, there were only sixty-six African Americans working in the mill.[25] There was, in fact, very little employment for black workers in Gary at that point, and the remaining families consisted largely of small business owners and professionals.[26] Prewar Gary lacked resources for poorer African American migrants. The Urban League had not yet formed, and no settlement houses existed until after 1920.[27] A network of small organizations had emerged, dominated by families, church groups, political clubs, and mutual aid societies.[28]

By the time Kimbley took up residence in Gary, the black working class was gaining influence. Severe labor shortages during World War I had translated into growing black in-migration, so that working-class families for the first time outnumbered the middle class by a significant margin. Steel had become the largest employer in the region, hiring an overwhelmingly immigrant workforce, primarily from eastern and southern Europe. Had Kimbley arrived one year earlier, he would have found a dramatically different community.

The Great Strike

In 1919, while Kimbley was recovering from his months in the trenches, northwest Indiana was locked in a fierce struggle between workers and steel barons. War production demands had created intolerable conditions in the mills. Workers were forced to labor seven days a week, twelve hours a day, producing steel at the expense of their lives. Accident rates had soared, leaving many families without a wage earner. Despite record profits, the steel companies had decided to impose across-the-board wage cuts on the workers.

The newest, most advanced mills in the nation stood on the shores of Lake Michigan. Steel-making technologies enabled these facilities to outproduce the eastern mills, and they required fewer craftsmen. The companies hoped to take advantage of the reduced importance of skilled labor and the overwhelmingly immigrant nature of the workforce to undermine the upcoming campaign for unionization. Almost 85 percent of the workers in the Midwest were new immigrants, from the poorest European nations, including Poland, Rumania, Hungary, Yugoslavia, Greece, and Italy. Few workers spoke English, and they had not yet been acculturated or "Americanized." Back east, the workers were first and second generation. They had lived through the early battles for unionism and had already buried family in the hills of western Pennsylvania and eastern Ohio. They were more settled, and perhaps more cautious.

When war production ended, organizing efforts escalated in the Calumet Region. Special events, advertised in local papers, drew hundreds and later thousands of workers together, first by ethnic or racial identity, later in huge pro-union rallies in the parks and streets near the mills. In the months leading up to the Great Steel Strike of 1919, the communities of northwest Indiana debated union issues.

Beginning in February of 1919, labor organizers held special meetings regularly in the black community to recruit workers into the union campaign. Out of a workforce of thirty thousand, there were less than one thousand black men in the region's mills. Two of the most prominent strike leaders, members of the Lake County Strike Council, were African Americans, Louis Caldwell and C. D. Elston. These two men helped turn the promise of interracial unity into a reality in Gary, at least for a while.

Louis Caldwell, born in Mississippi, received his college degree in 1903. After working for a number of years as a Pullman porter, he settled in Chicago and worked his way through law school. He then moved to Gary in 1915 and worked labor in the American Sheet and Tin Plate Company, until he received his legal certification from the state. He specialized in injury lawsuits against the steel industry on behalf of black workers and involved himself in community activism as a voice for the newly emerging working class. When the Gary Iron and Steel Council set up operations in 1918, he took a leadership role. He had firsthand knowledge of work conditions and a fairly extensive network of contacts among the workers. C. D. Elston was the first rank-and-file steelworker to quit his job to work full-time in the union campaign. He had hired in at Carnegie Illinois Gary Works, shortly after migrating north to Gary. In 1918, he accepted a leadership position on the council along with Caldwell. Together, they built support for the strike in the African American community among workers and professionals. As a result of their efforts, a majority of black workers would honor the strike lines.

In the period prior to the strike, both men addressed mass gatherings of white as well as black and Latino workers, and the call for racial unity marked every event. In contrast to Chicago, for example, where the summer South Side riot deepened racial hostilities, northwest Indiana remained peaceful and focused on strike preparations. Blacks, especially in Gary, were demonstrating some of the same kind of fighting temperament that had characterized Kimbley's army regiment overseas.[29]

When the national labor leaders called the strike on September 23, 1919, demanding an eight-hour day, higher wages, and union recognition, over three hundred fifty thousand iron and steelworkers walked off their jobs.[30] The strike in the Calumet Region had overwhelming community support; more than 85 percent of the workforce honored the picket lines at the three major mills—Carnegie Illinois in Gary, and Inland Steel and Youngstown Sheet and Tube in East Chicago. According to local sources, the African American community in northwest Indiana backed the strike efforts. More black workers left the mills than crossed the picket lines. The Northwest Indiana Steel Council called on Elston and Caldwell to speak at every major rally during the months of the walkout.

In other steelmaking areas of the country, skilled workers proved ambivalent toward the strike, and many returned to work to protect their jobs. Strike-breaking by skilled workers and police repression enabled eastern mills to roll some steel. Violence was also widespread. In addition, of the thirty-five thousand African Americans brought north as strikebreakers, the vast majority entered the mills in the East. Fewer than one thousand black men were sent into the Calumet Region. The lack of racial hostility or violence among northwest Indiana's steel workforce undermined the efforts of the steel barons, particularly Judge Elbert Gary, to end the strike quickly. Pressured to break the strike, local political forces provoked confrontations in order to justify calling in twelve units of the state militia, followed immediately by federal troops. Gary's mayor imposed martial law in October and prohibited pickets, rallies, and marches anywhere in the city. He even outlawed the wearing of army uniforms by World War I veterans.[31]

The racially charged environment and deeply demoralized workforce that George Kimbley found in Gary in February 1920 had been created by the repression, race-baiting, and red-baiting unleashed by the U.S. Army between October and January. According to local newspapers, military intelligence reports, and steel industry reports, black strikebreaking and Bolshevik agitation had doomed the strike effort. This version of events reflected the elite's determination to ward off future union organizing by isolating labor

Federal troops occupied the Gary Commercial Club during the 1919 steel strike when martial law was declared by the city's mayor in October. Industry leaders frequented the club. Photo courtesy of Calumet Regional Archives, Gary, Indiana.

radicals and planting distrust among the workers. Business and government together blamed black workers and socialist radicals.

Postwar patriotic hysteria, stirred up by the Bolshevik revolution in Russia, made radicals an easy target. Bitterness among the largely ethnic workers was redirected by a growing white supremacist presence in the region, with black workers serving as a convenient scapegoat.[32] To this day, many people in the region believe that the racial polarization of workers in the 1919 steel strike was responsible for institutionalizing racial tensions. The Gary *Post Tribune* still describes the strike as the event "that pitted whites against blacks."[33] The unusual interracial unity built during the strike, owing in large part to the role of black working-class leaders, was forgotten. Nonetheless, interracial organizing and black leadership reemerged in northwest Indiana with each upturn in the mass movement.

George Kimbley did not discover Gary's tradition of black activism until the depression years. In 1920 what he heard about the strike and its aftermath was the usual second-hand story about racial tensions and black strikebreaking. He explained that hardly anyone talked about the strike, and that people seemed to keep their views on it to themselves. He mentioned only that "the blacks were used as strikebreakers and they got some pretty good jobs down in the mill." Of course when Kimbley tried to get one of those jobs they had disappeared. When he looked around for those skilled black workers rewarded for their company loyalty, he never found more than a handful.

Over the next decade, the foreign-born were moved out of the Patch and subjected to a process of Americanization that stressed segregation and black inferiority.[34] William P. Gleason, plant superintendent at Gary Works from 1906 to 1935, was a staunch segregationist, as were other mill officials who controlled Gary's parks, hospitals, and other institutions. Together they hired a school superintendent, William Wirt, who shared their segregationist beliefs, despite having a national reputation as an innovator and reformer. Gary's power elite made sure that the city became a completely segregated community during the 1920s, and that the school system not only established but perpetuated segregation. There was only one integrated school in the central district, Froebel, and even there, black students had to attend separate classes, labeled chain gang classes by some of the whites. Blacks were not permitted to participate in extracurricular activities, dances, or other social events, and their pictures did not appear in the school yearbook.[35]

"Nothing was there. All around the school, nothing but sand," observed Walter Mackerl, who arrived in the Patch in 1927 and became Kimbley's coworker at the Sheet and Tin, and later his closest union associate.[36] "There was bushes and sand, and sand was the worst thing I'd ever seen." All recreational facilities were segregated, and Gleason made it clear to black workers at his mill that if they or their family used those white facilities, he would fire them. The only park facility for blacks was named after Gleason himself.

Working in the Mills

Kimbley's first job-hunting stop was the big mill, owned by the Carnegie Illinois Company but known as Gary Works. For black job seekers, the months after the strike provided a window of opportunity. Many workers had been blacklisted, and the mill had a lot of catching up to do on steel production. Kimbley was sent to the blast furnaces, where he quickly succumbed to the heat, fumes, gas, and filth. He lasted only four days working twelve-hour shifts; in contrast, he had withstood six months on the battlefields in France. He quit and found employment at the tin mill a few days later. "I wanted one of those big-paying jobs," laughed Kimbley, "a job up on the pickler. But it was just too much for me. I couldn't stand that work either. So the man let me go into the tin house. I stayed there seventeen years."

Kimbley valued his job at the Sheet and Tin Mill. "I imagine about a third of the workers in the tin mill were black," he recalled. "The tin house had all kinds of bad conditions. I worked in the white-hot furnace. They had what they called bagging machines where those plates run through . . . all that dust. Guess I'm about the only one living out of the tin house," he added. Kimbley said he secured himself a niche at the tin mill by never turning down a job his foreman asked him to do, no matter how hard, dirty, or low paid.

"If you got a week's worth altogether, you done a marvelous job. We were there three or four days out of the week and sometimes two days . . . but there was always extra work needed to be done in keeping those pots hot, metal pots. They didn't want that metal to freeze. I always took that extra work; all of that work, I got it. Others wouldn't take it, because you only got $3 and something a day. Common labor was $3.49, I think. Well," he went on, "my mind was shook up from the war, and my wife and I had separated, and I'd rather be working than laying around the house, so I took all the work I could get." Kimbley had figured out how to make it up north: work hard, be honest, and, like his mother, get folks to like you and rely on you.

During the 1920s in Gary, a series of recessions made work unsteady. Blacks were more likely than whites to be laid off, but not the George Kimbleys, who had made themselves as indispensable as they could. Between shutdowns in the auto industry and downturns in the economy, blacks could no longer depend on the mill for a job.

Gary Works had put a 15-percent ceiling on the number of blacks it would hire. Now to get a job, workers would crowd into fenced areas at the Virginia Street gate, day after day, hoping to get lucky. "The bullpen had a big fence around it with five or six hundred guys inside," explained Walter Mackerl. "The hiring guy would come out and stand out there and look over the crowd and point: you, you, you, and like that. One of the foremen out of the mill was looking for someone one day, and he saw me, but wouldn't take me. Said I was too light."[37] Other workers would be turned down because they were too dark.

By the late 1920s George Kimbley had made a life for himself in Gary. He had a number of friends in the tin mill and some other associations he had made at various events sponsored in the community by the NAACP and the Universal Negro Improvement Association (UNIA). The UNIA, headed by the Jamaican black nationalist Marcus Garvey, rallied African Americans under the banner of black pride.[38] Kimbley met Walter Mackerl in the mill but saw him also around the UNIA. They lived near each other, and shared some common views on the black condition. In particular, they believed black workers had to get organized, and even though neither of them was interested in social integration, they both thought they would need to stand with whites to get anywhere in the workplace.

When the Great Depression hit Gary, most workers lost their jobs, but unemployment among African Americans was much higher than among whites. Kimbley had been smart: "When nineteen and twenty-nine came around, let me tell you, I fed a lot of people off of that extra day's work." He went on, "People helped each other, and a guy would come up to you and ask you for a dime or a nickel, and if you had it, you'd give it to them, white or black." That extra day was more often than not Kimbley's only day at work in a week. But no one else was working more than a day or two a month.

As work disappeared and city resources dried up, the city's politicians started to look at its minority populations as unnecessary competition for white workers. First the city rounded up Mexicans and, through a series of "repatriation drives," returned them to Mexico.[39] Then in 1932 the city floated a proposal to send African Americans back to the South. The black community had developed an extensive network of organizations that rallied together to stop these efforts. From ministers and professionals to iron- and steelworkers, the community resisted the relocation plan, and then launched a series of job campaigns involving churches, clubs, masonic lodges, the YMCA, and the NAACP.[40] "Don't shop where you can't work," became a familiar slogan on the streets of Gary's black sections. Growing numbers of unemployed and injured black workers joined together in suits against the industry, hoping for some compensation for their sacrifices. As in other African American communities, people took initiative to build co-operative movements in order to share scarce resources.

Kimbley admired the militant action of the Unemployed Councils. "During the depression, they did a lot of work turning people's gas on, turning on the electric lights, and organizing protests to the Welfare Department to get food. I was amazed at the things they did do! There was a very good feeling existing back in those days," he added, "and that's where I learned about the Communist Party."

Kimbley was not an ideological convert to the party, but he found its methods effective and was drawn to its integrationist approach, both in fighting evictions and in holding social events. Some of his peers argued that he was, in fact, a party member, but in those days supporters and "fellow travelers" were hard to distinguish from cadres. Kimbley and Mackerl began to focus more and more on building working-class unity within the African American community. They developed informal networks among black steelworkers and their families, whom they had met through work, church, and community struggles.

One of Kimbley's and Mackerl's mutual friends, Jesse Reese, would connect them directly to a small group of organizers sent to the Calumet Region to establish the Steelworkers' Organizing Committee (SWOC, pronounced as one word). Reese worked over at Youngstown Sheet and Tube in Indiana Harbor, but lived in the same building as Walter Mackerl and played cards with George Kimbley. Reese was a spokesman for the Communist Party in Gary, one of the few African Americans to identify himself openly with the party.[41] Reese, Mackerl, and Kimbley talked about many things, but most conversations led back to the steel mill and the prospects for a union.

Steelworkers' Organizing Committee

George Kimbley claimed to be the first person in Gary to sign a SWOC card, on July 9, 1936. It was his friend Jesse who signed him up: "There was a fellow by the name of Jesse Reese," began Kimbley. "Jess was a likeable sort of fellow. Very much so, and I stopped by his house one Sunday afternoon. We had a way of playing cards. He had just left a meeting and he came in and said, 'Brother Kimbley, here's a union card. Sign it!' I took it and signed it. He said, 'Gimme a dollar.' And I gave him a dollar. And to this day I have never seen any card that predated this card."

According to Kimbley, Jess then signed up Stanley Cotton—whose dollar fee Kimbley paid, since Cotton had a family and Kimbley did not—followed by Walter Mackerl. From that point on, Reese would deliver the union cards and materials to Kimbley, Mackerl, Cotton, and Ted Vaughan, all black workers at the Sheet and Tin. They, in turn, spread out through Gary to re-cruit for the union. The tin mill had the strongest union base among blacks and, according to Kimbley, the tin workers were the first to set up a local union. They would be the first, as well, to put an African American, Walter Mackerl, into the vice president's position.

"Oh, I signed a lot of them after we got this thing going," Kimbley said proudly. "We had a fellow by the name of Hank Johnson. He was a mar-velous speaker, and let me tell you what; under his leadership we set up a volunteer organizing committee, and we just raked the town." Hank John-son, son of a union organizer and mine worker in Texas, became a well-known Congress of Industrial Organizations (CIO) leader; he associated with left advocacy organizations throughout his life. John L. Lewis, the charismatic leader of the mineworkers and first CIO president, sent Johnson and two other alleged communists, Jack Rusak and Joe Webber, into Gary to assist in the campaign.[42] Johnson's father had been a Wobbly, and Johnson had spent the previous four years as an organizer for the International Workers' Order (IWO), a militant rank-and-file organization established through the initiative of the Communist Party.[43] Johnson's job of coordinat-ing a volunteer organizing committee turned out to be relatively easy; he re-lied on the networks that already existed in Gary.[44] Kimbley praised Johnson as "an outstanding speaker and organizer. He was black and well educated."

The Gary community offered substantial support to the campaign. Un-like the *Chicago Defender* and the Negro Press Association, the Gary black papers backed the union drive.[45] The U.S. Steel Corporation made an appeal to black workers who had remained loyal during the 1919 steel strike, calling on them to aid the company once again, but few black steelworkers did so.[46] SWOC cards started pouring in from the black community; white SWOC organizers and leaders were stunned by the response. The black organizers were not.

The volunteer organizers knew the black community well, and developed a strategy of outreach designed to bring about broad community participa-tion. They relied, in part, on the foundation laid in 1919. A handful of African American workers were already participating in the chapters of the Amalgamated Association of Iron, Steel and Tin Workers.[47] The organizers also drew on a tradition of community-based organizing that had sustained their people in Mississippi and Alabama, the states from which most of Gary's blacks had migrated.[48] Whole communities had re-rooted themselves up north, carrying with them church and family ties. The volunteer organ-izers divided labor among themselves, enabling them to orchestrate a broad campaign. They worked the churches, the saloons, and the streets, and relied almost completely on face-to-face recruitment methods. Ted Vaughan and Stanley Cotton had been involved in the old Amalgamated Lodge as well as

Kimbley and other black workers recognized that the CIO was committed to organizing all workers. This float moved through central Gary in a Labor Day parade in the late 1930s. Photo courtesy of George Kimbley/Ruth Needleman.

the U.S. Steel company union, and had contacts with foreign-born and native union supporters.

To increase the pool of organizers, Kimbley, Mackerl, Cotton, and Vaughan used a method they called chain recruiting.[49] An organizer and his wife, according to Mackerl, would set up an evening dinner affair with a friend and his wife. Organizers only went to the homes of people with whom they already had close relationships. The two couples would spend the evening talking about family, community, work, and the union. The organizers, husband and wife, explained why they supported the union and described the benefits it offered black workers. They represented the labor movement as a collective struggle with many individual advantages. Once the couple expressed interest, the man was handed a union card to sign, and then both were asked if they would be willing to help out. Then, for example, Walter Mackerl would take his friend's wife, and plan a visit to her best friend's house. Edna Rose Mackerl accompanied the new member to pay a visit to another of his friends. The organizers built on preexisting relationships and targeted people they already knew and trusted.

Using such methods, the black volunteer organizing committee was targeting networks rather than individuals.[50] This joint visiting resulted in family support for the SWOC campaign throughout the black community, and black workers' wives played a central role in building the union organization.[51] African American women had carved out important activist roles for themselves in Gary, from membership in clubs to the ownership of the black newspaper, the *Gary Sun*.[52]

George Kimbley had primary responsibility for working with Gary's black Ministerial Alliance. He spent many long hours in discussion with the ministers. According to him, most ministers had already been turned against the union by the company. Kimbley appealed to their collection plates. "Let me tell you," he said to the gathered ministers, "the union is an organization that goes out to get more money, and if your members get more money, you're going to get more." Always a practical man, Kimbley did not hesitate to say or do whatever he thought would best serve the interests of unionization.

"The only thing that saved me in this Ministerial Alliance," Kimbley declared, "was the fact that there were working ministers in the mill that attended the ministerial meetings. I would have to beg to get in those meetings. When I started telling them about problems in the mill, those working ministers would get up and say, 'Mr. Kimbley's right.' " But then Kimbley would confront them with their own cowardice: " 'If you think I'm right, when you're down in the mill you don't open your mouth about conditions at all. You just take it, but you come back here on Sunday and preach brotherhood.' I was a little hard on some of them," Kimbley admitted, "so they stopped me from coming and meeting with the ministers."[53]

When the union opened its drive publicly, Kimbley warned Hank Johnson not to hold openly advertised meetings in the central district. "We'll do our work in the hotels, the saloons and in taverns, in barber shops, on the streets, in the mills. Don't put out any handbills," he advised. Hard as they tried, laughed Kimbley, "the ministers couldn't find us! And when they woke up, they found they had more blacks in the union than they had whites."

It seems Kimbley was most comfortable talking to people down on their luck or short on hope. He could start a conversation with just about anybody on the street or in a bar and move it over to the union. He met three of his wives doing his outreach work. He definitely understood the reluctance of many older black workers to join a "white man's union." Likewise, he cautioned SWOC organizers not to organize black and white together in the same room, because southern whites especially would not enter a union if they thought it had too many blacks.

He brought out this lesson in his story about Victor Chemical. It was a very large, segregated workplace, an early SWOC target. Hank Johnson had told another white organizer that he could use Kimbley for the campaign. When he was approached, Kimbley laid down the terms of his involvement:

"We can organize this plant," I said, "but we have to do it separately. You take the white, I'll take the black, and we'll gradually get them together." "Oh no, we can't do that, we can't do that," he repeated. "I'm not going to become part of no discrimination of black workers." So the white rep called a big meeting and the blacks showed up. When the whites come by and saw all those Negroes sitting in the meeting there, they just turned around and went on home. They never did organize that plant. It ain't organized today.

Of his skill in organizing Kimbley said, "It didn't require a whole lot of education, just a lot of good hard common sense and experience. I never had any problems."

Kimbley as a Full-Time Organizer

"It looked like everything I got into, I'd have to stake my life in it to get it done, and I didn't mind," confided Kimbley. "I had been through some rough living during World War I. Six months of it. I was ready."[54] When he swore the oath to build SWOC, Kimbley was in his forties, had no family, and had begun thinking of returning to Kentucky to fulfill the promise he had made to God during the war. He worked for a year as a volunteer organizer, and when the opportunity for a staff job came his way, he took it. George Kimbley became the first African American worker out of the mill to hold a full-time union staff position.

According to Kimbley, however, he was third choice on the district director's list. He claimed that the district director, Nick Fontecchio, first approached Stanley Cotton and then Walter Mackerl. "They said to me, 'Kimbley, you don't have a family. If the thing goes down, it'll just hurt you, but if it goes down and I take it, it'll hurt my family.' So I didn't mind. I took it, 'cause I'd just about made up my mind I wanted to go back to Kentucky. So I said, 'Well, I'll work here until they fire me or I'll dislike it and I'll quit and go on back to Kentucky.' "

From 1937 to 1958, George Kimbley served as the first, and for ten years the only, black staff rep in District 31 of the Steelworkers Union, covering the Calumet Region. Despite his version of the story—that he volunteered for the job when no one else would take it—the district did the picking, and the district carefully screened workers before promoting anyone to staff. Mackerl confirmed that he and Cotton had urged Kimbley to take the job because they did not want it. Mackerl turned down the offer because he did not think he could fight for black rights on staff. The district director knew

Staff rep George Kimbley (left) participated in a press conference with USWA Subdistrict Director Orval Kincaid, Gary, c. 1940. Photo courtesy of Calumet Regional Archives, Gary, Indiana.

Kimbley was the man. "I could speak their language. And they understood me," he explained, referring to southern white staff especially. "They felt like I was one of them. I didn't have any place to go. I didn't have no ambition to climb up because I didn't think I'd be staying with the labor movement."

Later in our discussion, he added, "I knew what to put my nose in. I knew when to keep quiet. I knew when to speak out." Kimbley's approach to negotiating race relations was rooted in the example of his mother; this approach was a perfect match with what the union was willing to accept at that time. SWOC went out of its way to recruit outspoken, militant rabble-rousers to build the union, but it did not want boat-rocking black organizers on permanent staff. It needed someone who would not make his white coworkers uncomfortable.

"My mother she worked in the dark," he stressed, meaning that she worked behind the scenes, and did not ask for any recognition. "I knew then that was one of the ways of getting things done. A lot of people don't mind helping you, but don't go about bragging about it. That was in me. You've got to make people like you," he insisted. "There's something about making people like you. You ain't going to get anywhere unless you make people like you and accept you. I learned that," he stressed, "before I left the South."

The next generation of black steelworkers did not share Kimbley's view. They would be more impatient and confrontational.

Kimbley's southern socialization, his limited expectations, and especially his unshakable faith enabled him to survive on staff without internalizing all the degrading attitudes and behaviors he faced over twenty years. On one level, Kimbley clearly grasped that racism was imbedded in the institutions, and did not hold individuals responsible. He let a great deal of abuse slide by him without any acknowledgement. It was his decision to ignore it, and that gave him some element of control over his life and feelings. "I knew how to take care of myself. I could live by myself very nicely. I never felt alone."[55] Kimbley did not try to make the union an instrument of liberation or equality, but recognized that through it blacks workers would have the opportunity to advance economically. "I didn't think much of racial equality. It just wasn't no question in my mind. All I wanted was an opportunity. I'd been accustomed to going to separate everything, churches and medical organizations and clubs. It didn't bother me."

His first staff organizing experience tested the strength of his beliefs and commitment. In 1938 Kimbley was assigned to help in the organizing drive at Blaw Knox in East Chicago. The union had managed to sign up a good number of white workers, but had not been able to reach the black ones. Kimbley, along with another black worker, talked one-on-one with the black men in the plant and convinced them to come together for a meeting. Kimbley asked Director Fontecchio to come over and address the group. "Nick got up and was making this big long speech like he does and he made this statement: 'We've got some of the best niggers in any union!' And I'm on the front seat there and I just fell out in the floor and just opened up. I laughed and laughed and laughed that thing down. That's the way I saved Nicolas Fontecchio."

Kimbley figured he had scored twice in this situation. The blacks had signed the cards instead of walking out of the room, and Fontecchio began to rely more and more on Kimbley.[56] Kimbley recalled:

> I never opened my mouth about it. He just got closer to me. Everywhere he was, he wanted me with him. And I got an idea there too. I'd see some of these white boys that wanted to move up in the union. They could all talk to me, because I wasn't easily insulted. I was almost forty-two when I was appointed to staff. Wasn't any place for me to go. So I'd tell them, "Listen, you want to get somewhere in the union, you get you a couple of black fellows to support you. Let them help you. You'll move." And then I'd go to the black fellows and say, "Listen, if you want to break down some of this racial prejudice, you get behind some of these white fellows

and you push them up. But you'll have to know everything there is to be known about the union, so you can tell him. Protect him." And where I got the cooperation, success came about and we were able to break down a lot of hard prejudice.

Kimbley spent most of his early staff years engaged in outreach to unorganized black workers or on diplomatic excursions to represent the union at special African American or minority events. Kimbley had joined the National Negro Congress (NNC) before he went on staff, and attended many of its Chicago-area meetings, including its founding convention in Chicago, February 14 to 16, 1936.[57] Other black individuals and organizations played a more visible role than he did in the congress, among them, Walter Mackerl, Bill Young, and Stanley Cotton. A number of Gary professionals served on the NNC Executive Board.[58] Philip Murray, the national director of SWOC and assistant to John L. Lewis, was in regular communication with the leadership of the National Negro Congress. Henry Johnson, the SWOC staff organizer in Gary, maintained close ties, as did Leonides McDonald, a black SWOC organizer based in East Chicago.

Kimbley learned quickly that he was a token African American on the SWOC staff. When Van A. Bittner, the leading CIO staff organizer in the Midwest, announced Kimbley's staff appointment at a mass meeting in Gary, he pledged: " 'He will be assigned local unions just like the rest of [the staff]. No difference,' he said," recalled Kimbley. "Well, that sounded good, but it just didn't happen."[59]

In 1940 Fontecchio left SWOC along with his leader, John L. Lewis, and Philip Murray, now CIO president, appointed Chicagoan Joe Germano to be district director of 31, the largest and most powerful district in the union.[60] During the war years, Kimbley was in no position to affect the struggles within basic steel against segregation or unequal pay scales. He was marginalized from workplace battles and local union initiatives against Jim Crow. The fight in the mill was carried forward by rank-and-file workers, mainly black, but often with white support. Kimbley assisted in organizing drives, but found the district an increasingly hostile environment as white southerners were added to the staff and soon dominated the union culture.

Kimbley's experiences, beginning in the shadows of slavery, and reaching through SWOC to the United Steelworkers of America, made his loyalty to the union unshakable. The union, in his lifetime, had improved the status of black workers visibly. Kimbley went from having no dreams to a life that had, perhaps, for him, a dreamlike quality. Kimbley was not treated equally on staff but he was treated better than he had ever expected to be. He had a full-time job with the union. He had escaped the dirt and dust in the mill. He received a higher salary and more perks than he could have imagined, trips across the country, and a chance to meet union and African American dignitaries. Nobody in the union called him names to his face, and he sat at the district decision-making tables in rooms full of white staff men. He did not understand the younger blacks coming up in the mills, demanding equality, criticizing the union, and denouncing him as a sellout. Kimbley had no problem with his peers' characterization of him as an Uncle Tom. "I don't mind being Uncle Tom, but I says these Uncle Toms is what saved you during the days when your grandparents were in deep slavery. It's many an Uncle Tom saved you. We misuse the word."

Kimbley saw himself as a radical, a black who dared to take on the black ministers and the white company men, and stand side by side with white workers against oppression. He thought many of his black peers were too impatient and shortsighted. He opposed the idea of blacks organizing separately in the union; it was understandable that blacks should be handled separately during organizing, he reasoned. But once blacks were in the union, he thought, any step toward separate organization threatened the tenuous unity that had been built between whites and blacks. He also opposed as unfair special positions or promotions for blacks in the plant and in the union. Kimbley argued that "democracy in the union" prohibited special positions for and special organization among blacks.

In his own way, George Kimbley taught lessons about the dignity of black workers and exposed the blatant racism of many white workers. He gave his final years to his religion and to his people, although he never lost touch with the union freedom fighters he had known. Kimbley and Mackerl, in fact, talked by phone the day after my trip to Kentucky. Kimbley prepared Mackerl for my interview, encouraging him to set up his own video and tape recorders.

Kimbley never was as crazy about any organization as he was about the Steelworkers Union. "As long as there are rich people that are helping the rich people to get richer," he explained to me at the end of our interview, "poor people are going to get poorer. Poor people need something to protect them and that something is the union. . . . I have just as much love for the Steelworkers Union as I had when I was in it. Folks just say, 'Oh, that Kimbley, he's union crazy. That man's goin' crazy. He's nuts.' I don't mind it because I knew what the union was doing for black folks."

CHAPTER 2

"Slavery Never Ended at Inland"

William Young

In Bill Young's view, slavery didn't end until the union came to Inland Steel Company in 1937.[1] Employed by Inland for more than half a century, William Young dedicated forty-five of those fifty-one years to the
union. He joined the Amalgamated Association of Iron, Steel and Tin
Workers in the 1920s, was a founding member of the SWOC lodge and then
of USWA Local 1010. Beginning in 1937, Young held positions of union
leadership continuously and served on almost every kind of committee the
union established. "You can't live without unions," he still argued in 1989.
"You'd go right back to twenty-eight and a half cents an hour, seven days a
week; Inland worked you like dogs then and still would, if they could."[2]

William Young was an "impressive-looking man, very distinguished," according to those who knew him.[3] Whether or not he was sporting his three-
piece suit, Young stood tall, spoke well, and carried himself with dignity.
Born in 1903, Bill Young was seven years younger than George Kimbley. Dependent on a cane to get around at eighty-nine, when I interviewed him,
Young still gave the appearance of a self-confident, powerful man, the kind
of person you would want standing next to you if you had a battle to fight.
He was living with his brother Lamar in Atlanta, Georgia.

Back in the Calumet Region, Bill Young had already achieved legendary
status because of the number of years he had remained active in the union
fight. One of his peers insisted he was 110 years old, and said it only half jok-
ingly. No one was sure how old Young really was, since he sheared a few
years off his age every time someone brought up retirement.

Despite serious health problems, Young had not lost his passion for the union, his sense of humor, or his deep, resonant voice. No doubt these attributes had served him well as the first African American to sit across the negotiating table from Inland management, and the first African American to serve as chair of a basic steel grievance committee in the United States.[4]

Young's tenure with the union spanned so many decades and so many social, political, and economic changes that it would be impossible to speak of one Bill Young. Certain of his views and beliefs held constant, but others changed as the union and the country moved to the right, and also as he aged and grew more attached to his union job. It is indicative of Young's complexity that different coworkers viewed him very differently. He was both praised and condemned for being a socialist. Held up as the model African American leader for decades, he was later denounced as an Uncle Tom. His approach to organizing, so effective in building the union, brought him under attack as a radical in the 1940s and 1950s. His oppositional consciousness and union beliefs identified him with the left, the radical pioneers who gave USWA 1010 its nickname, the "red local."[5]

When the cold war and the Taft-Hartley loyalty oath led to a frenzy of red-baiting in the region and his union, Young opposed it actively. He never turned his back on his former comrades. The next generation, however, both white radicals and more militant African Americans, came to view him as a "union hack," even a traitor to the cause. He became embroiled in the corruption of a conservative leadership, and even involved himself at one point in a controversial all-black slate.[6]

Bill Young, however, was a union stalwart when there were no more than eight members in the Amalgamated, in the 1920s. His name appeared among other members' on the lodge's original charter. He never spoke about the local union in a negative way; in fact, he was convinced there was no better union anywhere in the United States than Local 1010. And he attributed its special character to rank-and-file militancy and control.

Escape from the South

Young's grandparents were slaves; his parents, however, started their lives under Reconstruction. William Young was born in Winona, Mississippi, on July 1, 1903. He described Winona as a small, southern town in the most backward state of the union. He lived in a black community with his extended family, including his grandparents, who were too old to work by then. He had one brother, Lamar. His grandparents had shared many stories with him about their life under slavery, but Young was reluctant to pass them on. "The only difference between slaves and animals," he observed sparingly, "is that slaves could talk. They were treated just like animals,

Above: The USWA Local 1010 Grievance Committee in 1963. William Young served as vice chairman of the committee beginning in 1938. Seated in the front row, from left to right: Joe Gyurko, Pete Calacci, Cecil Clifton, William Young, and Les Thornton. The other three men in the row are unidentified. *Left:* William Young after thirty years in the mill. Photo courtesy of USWA Local 1010, East Chicago, Indiana.

worse. As a form of punishment, they would starve them to death, whip them. They wouldn't do that to their animals."

Bill Young grew up knowing that he could not live under someone else's control. He constantly fought the Jim Crow South, stood up to Inland Steel Company, and even bragged about his independence from the International

Steelworkers Union. "I don't want nobody to pick on me. That's why I left the South and never wanted a staff job. I know who I am and I know how I am," he stressed. "All of my life from childhood in the backwoods of Mississippi, I always objected to being buckled down. I was buckled down, but I objected to it. I was shot at about a dozen times because I couldn't take the way I was treated."[7] His family had raised him with a strong sense of self-worth and a spirit of rebellion. It is not surprising, then, that he left Mississippi as soon as he could and joined the union the very first day he found it.

His father was a bricklayer, and moved north to work in the mills. According to Young, his father had been beaten in the streets of East Chicago during the 1919 steel strike. Young spoke very little about his parents.[8] At five, he attended an all–black, one-room schoolhouse just two blocks from his home. Laughing, he confided that he probably would not have gone had it been any further away. His education would serve him and the union well down the road. "The neighborhood was all black, couldn't be otherwise," he said. "Mississippi was and still is the most backward and poorest state. It was always my desire to leave Mississippi, even as a child. That was my dream, to leave and get a good job. There were no good jobs in Mississippi, and if there had been, blacks wouldn't have gotten them anyway. I wanted to learn, start at the bottom and learn, but then I wanted to make it to the top."

After finishing school, Young got his first full-time employment in a local hospital. "My job was to fire the furnace to keep the steam going in the winter, to heat it up and also to furnish steam for the operating room, to sterilize the instruments. That was my main job. In the summertime I also mowed the yard." As soon as he could, he left Mississippi; he didn't go back until he was over seventy.[9] He settled in East Chicago, Indiana, because his father had been told there were jobs for blacks at the Inland Steel Company. Bill Young found employment there in May 1922.

The Inland Steel Company

"I can remember my first day like it was yesterday," recalled Young. "I was working with a pick and a shovel, scraping scales off the red-hot steel, and then shoveling them into a scrap car. It wasn't the job I had dreamed of, but it was the only job I could get at that time. I had never seen the inside of a mill. I didn't know how dangerous it was. I should have been afraid." Young decided to look for greener pastures and quit that job; he traveled to Pittsburgh hoping for a better opportunity in an eastern mill. Two years later, however, in 1924, Young was back at Inland, making rails for the transportation industry. He worked in the twenty-eight-inch-rail mill; he would be employed there until his retirement in 1973.

Conditions were intolerable. "From what I read about slavery," Young noted, "there was very little difference between it and working at Inland." He continued:

> You could be fired for asking how much a job paid. You could be fired for anything. The foreman could just look at you, not like you, and drive you out of the mill. They paid me twenty-eight and a half cents an hour, working twelve hours a day, six days a week. In my history lesson back in school, I can easily remember my lesson about slavery; they said it ended in 1865 in the United States. That was one of the biggest lies that ever was put on paper. Slavery hadn't ended yet, not at Inland.

When Young arrived in East Chicago, he found a room at a boarding house in the Indiana Harbor area. Two other black workers resided there as well. He lived near Block and Pennsylvania, the only place blacks could find housing in a very tight housing market.[10] Indiana Harbor was an integrated neighborhood surrounding Inland Steel and the Youngstown Sheet and Tube mill. Over fifty different immigrant nationalities had settled in Indiana Harbor between 1900 and 1920; by 1920, an increasing number of rural and southern migrants were flowing into the community for jobs in steel. In this section of East Chicago, as in central Gary, African Americans and immigrants lived side by side for some time.[11]

There were very few blacks at Inland when Young hired in. Almost all the workers "imported" during the strike in 1919 had been Mexican Americans. Inland placed them in labor gangs with Spanish-speaking supervisors. The majority of the workers, however, were European immigrants. Young was the only black in his department. "For the first five years I was in the mill," he said, "I wasn't around not one black." The company preferred Mexicans because they worked hard, did not speak English, and lacked the community support that already had been established for most ethnic groups.[12] Among the European immigrants, according to Young, the company preferred Polish workers, because they came from the poorest regions in Europe and were most desperate for work.

Young figured out immediately that a black worker could keep a job at Inland if he learned the equipment and did whatever the foreman asked. Like Kimbley, he kept quiet and listened carefully. "I learned more from foreigners than I did anybody," he volunteered, laughing. "We had people who had union experience, people who had worked in the coal mines, who knew about unions. I learned from the Germans, the Polish, the Greeks, and the Mexicans, too. I used to speak pretty good Spanish."

The foreman relied on Young to train newer workers for positions he himself could not get. "I was forced to teach people jobs they wouldn't give me. I could operate five or six different kinds of machines. I could operate cranes. I had taught three people to do the straightener job. When the I beams and rails rolled out of the mill," he explained, "they were crooked. It took skill to straighten them." Shortly after the union came into Inland in 1937, Young got that job for himself.

Some of the men in his department whispered about unions. A few had been part of the old Amalgamated that led the 1919 steel strike. About two years after Young returned to Inland from Pittsburgh, one of his coworkers invited him to a meeting.

> One night I was passing a building on the corner of Clark Avenue. A white fellow, a Polish fellow I knew, told me to come on in and hear the meeting of the union. "Hear the union people talk. You might like it." So I went in and I liked it from then on. You didn't have a union in the mill then, just the remnants of the old union from the 1919 strike. There was still people who would get together. They didn't break up the union completely. The company didn't recognize them, but they were still sticking together. I joined that group in 1926.[13]

The core group of eight people gathered secretly in the basement of an undertaker. Young estimated that no more than thirty workers ever attended a meeting in the early years. He was the first and only black among the original eight members who went on to form SWOC 1010 in 1936.[14] Up until 1934, they remained an underground organization. Yet the workers found ways to act like a union when they could. Young recalled a time when his aunt died and he wanted to go to the funeral. "They [Inland] wouldn't let me, but I took off anyhow. When I came back, they told me I didn't have a job. I went to the locker room and took my time, standing around. Soon plenty of white guys were standing beside me. I wasn't out of a job fifteen minutes before I went back on."[15]

The depression years were tough. Young worked infrequently, like everybody else. "They cut down low to keep from laying off, cut down to three days a week or no days a week. Sometimes I worked no more than three days a month. There was no relief whatsoever, not until when Franklin Delano Roosevelt got elected. I remember parades and protests for cash relief." Young also recalled the repatriation drives. He estimated that close to one thousand Mexican workers from Inland were shipped back to Mexico during the early years of the depression.[16]

To get by, Young hauled trash, collected and sold bottles. "I was selling scrap and everything like that, anything that I could do to make a dollar. . . . The worst years of the depression," Young continued, "was when we started doing more organizing, from about 1932 through 1934. We began organizing groups among the unemployed, meeting in churches, Masonic halls, and places of that kind. I was one of the first involved."

Young did not do very much recruiting among black workers at Inland. Where he lived and worked, his contact with blacks was limited. In addition, given how few blacks were employed at Inland, many felt that loyalty to the company and hard work were a better job guarantee than involvement in any union. "Participation was poor among blacks in the beginning. They didn't know what the union was about," Young suggested. "I had black friends who told me I was crazy. If we join, the company is going to fire us. But I didn't pay it any attention." The small numbers and isolation of African Americans at Inland affected the approach SWOC and Young used to organize blacks into the union. At Youngstown Sheet and Tube and Carnegie Illinois Gary Works, African Americans had high visibility among the first organizers for SWOC, and were able to bring blacks into the union in larger relative numbers than whites.[17]

"All Members Were Organizers"

Even before the passage of the National Labor Relations Act (NLRA)—the 1936 federal law known also as the Wagner Act that gave workers the rights to organize and bargain collectively—steelworkers acted boldly to organize. They isolated the Employee Representation Plan (ERP), a company union, by urging workers not to participate. At U.S. Steel, in contrast, the labor organizers joined the company's ERP and took it over, forcing it to act more like a union.[18] Young told this story of how their Amalgamated lodge, led by William Thomas, who would become the first president of the 1010 SWOC lodge, used the so-called insurance plans of the company to intervene on behalf of a widow.

> One of the first meetings I went to, I was shocked. Shortly after the chairman opened the meeting, there was a woman got up and raised her hand. He told her to sit down. She was a white woman. She wasn't what we would call American. You didn't have many of those in East Chicago at that time. I don't know what nationality she was. She finally got the floor and told how her husband had been killed in the open hearth. There were two open hearths; he was in the big one. There were fourteen furnaces.[19] He was working on scaffolding. When the scaffold broke, he fell into a ladle of hot metal. That was it. No fumes, no body to be buried. Inland didn't give her a single penny. Well, we didn't think much of it because we had knowed other people that got killed in the mill and didn't get a penny. We didn't have a union then but he got her some money. William Thomas did get her some money.

By the time SWOC arrived, the organizing committee had been on the job for years. "There was no fair treatment at Inland. Workers knew they needed protection and we were all organizers. Not staff people. All members were organizers, getting people to join the union. We carried cards everywhere we went." Some workers were more eager to join than others, observed Young. "Immigrants were much easier to recruit. The bottom people joined. Before SWOC we were afraid even to ask anyone to join the union because we were afraid they'd tell the boss and we'd be fired." In 1936, the union advocates held an open mock funeral for the company's "independent" union.

Nothing Young experienced seared his memory more than the Memorial Day Massacre in 1937.[20] "Oh yes," he said, "I was there. Most certainly." Republic, Inland, and Youngstown had gone out on strike. Workers had been locked out of the mills, and Republic, more than any other, was turned into a fortress. The Thursday before Memorial Day, Young and a few other Inland workers went to the gates at Republic to find out what was happening. "There were children outside the gate, calling for their fathers to come out. Women with babies in their hands walking around. We could see guards inside the mill walking with rifles on their shoulders and pistols around their waist." Young could not have seen guards in the mill from the gate; his memory must have superimposed these images from secondhand information or the police riot a few days later.[21] The union called for a protest outside the gates for Sunday, a Memorial Day picnic.

"It was one of the most brutal things I've ever seen in my life. That was Memorial Day of 1937. I can't even talk about it now. When I talk about it, I cry." His face contracted in pain.

> I was standing within a few feet of a neighbor of mine (Lee Tisdale), a black man just like me. He had a wife and five children. The oldest was only ten. An automobile rolled up with three policemen. One got out with a machine gun; I looked back but he didn't. They shot him in the back six times, and then drove off. Ten union members were killed that day and one newspaper reporter. There were more than a hundred beaten to the ground. They were hauling people off in ambulances for over two hours. I was clubbed over the head and still have the scar to show it. I saw a woman that I know knock down four Chicago policemen with a nine bar before they knocked her down and beat her. The next day we went back to the picket line. There were more than a thousand people there.

Young described the difficulties they had in Little Steel—Republic, Inland, and Youngstown were known as Little Steel—compared to Carnegie Illinois Gary Works, the largest U.S. company. Carnegie Illinois had signed with John L. Lewis, head of the CIO, without a strike in March of 1937. "They had privileges, even before they had a union," asserted Young. "Peo-

INDEPENDENT
UNION INC.

FUNERAL SERVICES OF COMPANY UNION
INLAND STEEL CO.

SWOC supporters at Local 1010 held a mock funeral for the company union in 1936. Bill Young is seated left of the speaker, Manuel Trbovich. Photo courtesy of USWA Local 1010, East Chicago, Indiana.

ple in Gary had rights and privileges we couldn't even think of."[22] In the aftermath of the massacre, Inland signed an agreement with the governor of Indiana on wages but would not recognize the union. Grassroots work would have to sustain SWOC organization until 1942, when the National Labor Relations Board (NLRB) would force the Little Steel companies to allow a union election. In the meantime, constant in-plant and gate actions were necessary. All that militant rank-and-file activity also ensured an overwhelmingly pro-union vote in that 1942 NLRB election.

During the 1937 strike Inland had operated the mill with supervision and some scabs.[23] SWOC had allowed the company to use a few pro-union workers, because the mill provided power for the city. In an effort to weaken the union after 1937, Inland reestablished many of the welfare plans that had been eliminated during the depression. The company set up a credit union, brought back picnics and the Inland Athletic Association, and inaugurated a twenty-five-year club for old-timers. Inland's efforts to revive welfare capitalism did not have a chance of success. Despite the lack of official recognition, by 1939 Inland management was meeting regularly with union representatives on departmental problems.[24] The general minutes from 1939 through 1942 describe labor-management sessions, union membership drives, dues pickets and inspections, and unauthorized strikes taking place on a regular basis.[25]

Building the Union from the Bottom Up

With the dissolution of the old Amalgamated and the formation of the SWOC lodge at Inland in 1937, Bill Young assumed the lodge vice presidency. He was also the griever in his department. For a majority of his time in Local 1010, Young presided as vice chairman of the Grievance Committee. He preferred that job over local union president, he explained, because "that's where you do your fighting." He acknowledged, nonetheless, that in the early days no black man could have been elected president. I doubt that any one man went to more union and committee meetings, conventions, and conferences than Bill Young.[26] Week after week, in the early days, Young participated in union meetings; his name appeared frequently in the group minutes, the Grievance Committee minutes, and the general meeting minutes. At the union hall, if anyone had a question, they were told to "ask Bill Young; he remembers everything."[27]

Between 1939 and 1942, when SWOC became the USWA, Young demonstrated his commitment and militancy. He led nine unauthorized or spontaneous strikes, called wildcats, in his department alone, over various issues, including demands for weekly paychecks and equal pay for women.[28] "In some cases," he noted, "we had to call departmental strikes. In my department, the twenty-eight-inch rail mill, we had more strikes than anywhere else. If we applied for something and didn't get it, I'd call them out. I'd stand by the gate and call out to the men in my department. 'Stand over there; we're on strike.' And they'd stand aside, even some of the ones we called scabs, those who didn't pay union dues; they wouldn't go in either."

Without a contract, Lodge 1010 settled problems through direct action on the shop floor. Under the union recognition agreement at U.S. Steel, in contrast, workers could not strike, and only those who had already signed up for the union could be represented by it. At Inland, strikes were frequent and effective. During these years of contract limbo, Local 1010 gained its reputation as the most militant local, the "red local," the anti-International local. It was a well-earned reputation.[29]

As a leader of the Grievance Committee, before there was any contract, Young saw his job as that of an organizer and rabble-rouser. In 1939, Young tried to get the local to bring the office workers into the lodge as members. He was told it was not appropriate.[30] In the 1940 union elections, Young was the second-highest vote-getter, after president Virgil Smith. In April of 1940, Young urged the local to take on an organizing drive among "the new men." And in August of that year, he tried to persuade the Grievance Committee to represent temporary employees.[31]

Once Inland agreed to a contract in 1942, Young's job became contract administration, making sure the company abided by the provisions of the contract. Very little got by Bill Young. He knew every inch of the contract, and was a stickler on the issues of proper procedure, seniority, and wage equity. A vast majority of the early grievances had to do with seniority, discrimination, and favoritism. After all, Inland foremen were used to awarding jobs to those who paid the biggest kickbacks, who showed their gratitude with gifts of liquor, or who volunteered to do construction on the foremen's homes. Since Young served on the first Wage Policy Committee[32] and most negotiating committees thereafter, he was an expert on the contract and what went on in negotiations. Young's excellent memory meant that the company could not make things up in front of him.

Young also had a sophisticated understanding of politics; he called himself a socialist in the early days. He knew how to build alliances and protect his own base of power in the local. His popularity among white workers was rooted in his willingness to fight Inland every step of the way, his pioneer status, and his extreme caution in not presenting himself as a spokesman for his race. Young rarely characterized any issue as a specifically black issue, although he fought discrimination just the same. By making seniority, for example, the standard for promotion in departments, Young could make the fight against favoritism a cover for his fight against race discrimination. He strongly advocated equal pay for equal work, first for women and blacks during the war, and then afterward based on job evaluations.[33]

Young took particular pride in his local's record on supporting women workers and including women in leadership positions. He took the women's side during the war period, when Inland tried to set up separate seniority lists and establish separate wage scales for women. He opposed every effort of Inland after the war to lay off women without regard to seniority, to make room for veterans. "More than any other union in the United States, our local had more active women. I don't think we ever had a convention that Local 1010 didn't send a woman, at least one or two women delegates."[34] Young's inclusive, egalitarian approach came out of his experience as an African American. His oppositional consciousness drew him to socialist ideas, which in turn provided him with a coherent ideology for his class-conscious beliefs.

Fighting Racism in the Red Local

During the first decades of USWA 1010, Young associated very closely with the radicals: John Sargent ("Wildcat Johnnie"), Bill Maihoffer ("Wildcat Willie"), Nick Migas, Hugh McGilvery, Stanley Rygas, and others.[35] They would remain his staunchest supporters and closest friends. Young openly defended them against red-baiting in the postwar years. He shared the left's view on the primacy of working-class unity and class struggle. At Inland,

Bill Young (far left) sat on national and district Contract and Wage Policy Committees. Here he took part in contract negotiations, c. 1956. On the right, with white hair, is Sam Evett, District Director Joe Germano's right-hand man. In the center, in a dark suit, is Ted Rogus. Photo courtesy of Calumet Regional Archives, Gary, Indiana.

that translated into a commitment to integration, rank-and-file democracy, militant action, and community involvement. At the "red local," the left activists were the most outspoken opponents of racism and job discrimination from the 1930s through World War II.

Given the newness of the union and the vastness of the mill, struggles broke out and were settled primarily on a departmental basis, and the griever was the most powerful union man in the department. From 1943 to the war's end, Bill Young held the top union job as chairman of the Grievance Committee. The steel companies established segregation through their pattern of hiring; blacks and Mexicans were channeled into the worst jobs in the coke plant, open hearth, and blast furnace, or into the labor gangs in predominantly white departments.

In the mills, the worst jobs were in steel-producing, the areas where the steel was made. Steel-producing—the hot end of the mill—involved the making of coke, iron, and steel by heating the raw materials to blistering degrees in giant furnaces to separate, purify, or forge the final products. In the coke plant, for example, workers cooked the coke in batteries of ovens in order to drive out volatile chemicals, such as benzene gas. No matter where someone worked in the coke plant, at the end of the day everyone looked black because of the bellowing black smoke.

The open hearth turned iron into steel. Workers threw scrap, pig iron, and a few other ingredients into a huge furnace for cooking. When the mixture melted and boiled, workers used a small dynamite charge to unplug the furnace. Clay had been forced in to seal the furnace. When the dynamite knocked out the plug, the steel poured from the furnace into ladle cars that ran on railroad tracks. This process was called tapping the furnace. The blast furnace produced the iron, by heating iron ore, limestone, and coke to several thousand degrees. Then huge amounts of hot air were blown into the furnace through the molten metal to remove impurities. A kind of scum called slag floated to the top and the iron remained on the bottom. Workers would tap the furnace at the top to remove the slag and at the bottom to drain out the iron. These were almost all nasty jobs. The finishing end of the mills, where workers rolled and shaped and coated the steel, were not as dirty and dangerous. Steel mills overall are very dangerous workplaces.

Even the coke plant and open hearth had some good jobs, skilled and higher-paying jobs, such as heater, melter, millwright, and pipefitter. The company, however, arranged jobs into sequences or groups, segregating the better jobs from the worst ones. Where the company placed a worker when he hired in determined what kinds of jobs he would be assigned and what promotional opportunities would be open to him. A worker could only promote in his assigned sequence.

No African American was placed in the craft or mechanical sequences and few even worked labor in the finishing mills. The company opposed intramill transfers, unless it was on the company's own initiative. There were white jobs and black jobs in the same department; the ones held by African Americans were all hard labor and grouped into dead-end sequences.[36]

In most departments where minorities were locked into the worst jobs, for example in the open hearth and blast furnace, they did not have the numbers to elect a minority griever. The coke plants at all the mills were the first departments to have African American grievers elected. White radicals often chose departments with the highest number of minorities, especially the coke plant, open hearth, and blast furnace. They used their racial advantage to secure griever positions and then fought racism by pressuring the company and coworkers to accept the promotion of blacks into semiskilled sequences. That was the case at Inland.

In the early days, the strategy was to destroy the segregated sequences within departments and demand that blacks be promoted into previously white jobs and sequences, based on their departmental seniority. Black grievers such as Bill Young and later Buster Logan in the coke plant followed the same tact: make seniority count by department. The Grievance Committee set up a special task force on seniority, because so much of the union's work focused on establishing seniority as a basis for promotions.[37]

The resistance was strongest where white workers, often with less seniority than black or Mexican workers, saw their privileged positions as threatened. They spoke in favor of seniority rights but not plantwide, not even within the departments. They argued for seniority within sequences, because they wanted to maintain the all-white sequences and better-paying jobs for themselves. As a result, radical grievers such as Nick Migas and, after him, Joe Gyurko in the number one open hearth, faced severe backlashes when they forced the company to promote minorities into semiskilled sequences—for instance as helpers on the open hearth. These battles began in 1942, once a contract was in place; by 1943 the changes were visible. Young had moved up to straightener, and Mexicans and blacks were working as third and second helpers in the open hearths. Blacks were bidding on jobs that had been previously denied them, even though the company and some of their coworkers tried to talk them out of it.

According to Young, the company had developed its own special method for preventing black promotions. He saw through it immediately and began to warn his coworkers about the company's "false front on discrimination."[38] Inland foremen used deceit to get black workers to withdraw their bids on a promotion. If a black man expressed interest in a job, for example, the foreman would call him into the office and persuade him not to apply. Young described the foremen's methods: " 'You can get a better job than that,' the foreman would say. 'If you just wait, the opportunity for a better one will come.' So the guy would walk back out and never get another job. Whenever the boss could get someone into his office alone, without the union, they'd do that. That's why we always instructed our workers, 'Don't go into the foreman's office alone, have a union representative with you.' "[39]

In those departments that Inland reserved for whites—the cold mill, the tin mill, and all the craft and mechanical sequences—the struggle was much harder because the union faced challenges from both management and coworkers. First, the union had to take on management's right to hire and assign as it pleased. The company continually argued that it put men where they fit best or kept them in jobs for which the men were already trained. It was very common for a foreman to refuse to promote a black worker into a better job, claiming he was the best qualified or too valuable in the job he held.[40]

The second, more stubborn, resistance to integrating the lily-white departments came from the white workers in those areas. Young contended that even the grievers in some of the all-white departments defended the exclusion of blacks, arguing that the men were not ready for integration. Few white workers anywhere were ready for integration in the 1940s, and whites often protested the introduction of blacks through hate strikes. Inland, Youngstown, and Gary Works all had incidents of hate strikes, although nowhere near the number in the auto plants.[41]

The Grievance Committee had to intervene over the heads of the grievers, who feared losing their next election if they personally forced their members to work with blacks.[42] The committee leadership, including Young, made sure that protesting workers knew that they had only two options: work with blacks or go home. Bill Young recalled numerous visits with departments that had resisted minority promotions, such as yards and transportation and the blast furnace. The white women in the tin mill inspection department also wildcatted when the first black woman came into the area.[43]

Postwar Upheaval

By the end of the war, the battlefront had become the lily-white departments. Returning black veterans and younger black workers had much higher expectations for change and much less patience than the previous generation. Young at first opposed their radicalism and confrontational style, fearing they might destroy the black-white unity that had made the union possible. He was convinced—and would be to his death—that black people needed unions more than anyone else, and that there would have been no union without interracial alliances. Young also knew how easily interracial unity had been shattered in the past.

The postwar period tested Bill Young's commitment to everything he believed in; he would feel compelled to choose between so-called race issues and union issues, between black coworkers and red allies. He fought to hold on to a unionism based on class struggle, community involvement, and direct action. He tried to resist hierarchical forms of union leadership and a business approach to union affairs. In the postwar period, the labor movement wrestled with opposing conceptions of unions, commonly referred to as social versus business unionism. Although Young strongly supported social unionism, he was drawn into the bureaucratic structures set up in the union to deal with an increasingly complex corporate structure. He attempted for a time to walk a tightrope, cautioning the younger African American activists not to push too hard and urging the union to move more quickly on integration and pay equity issues. Within a few years after the war, however, USWA Local 1010 would be torn apart by red-baiting and racial conflicts. These battles set back the fight for racial equality and interracial unionism for decades.

Much of Young's grievance time in the years right after the war was taken up with job evaluations and classifications, which served as the basis for identifying and eliminating wage inequities between jobs, departments, and even mills in the Calumet Region. The contract did not allow him to tackle pay inequities based on racial or gender segregation, because the jobs held by women and blacks were not identical to those held by white men in terms of skill and responsibility, as calculated by the time-study experts. Inland hired time-study engineers to study and rate jobs. "There were repetitive jobs and complex, diversified jobs," Young pointed out. "Some people went in and did the same thing every day. Others had to do different jobs, and had more decision-making responsibility." Bias within job evaluation systems historically undervalued the work of women and minorities. Young worked to counter that discrimination.[44]

In conformity with International USWA and CIO policy after the war, the local established a special Anti-Discrimination Committee.[45] Its task was to investigate and remedy inequalities on the job, and work in the political arena for progressive legislation, including a law to establish a National Fair Employment Practices Commission, an antilynching law, and an anti–poll tax law. CIO unions also involved themselves in community battles over fair employment practices, open housing, and school desegregation.[46]

At Inland, the Anti-Discrimination Committee undertook a survey of the status of African Americans throughout the mill. This group brought the following recommendations before the Grievance Committee in 1946: "a.) a minimum % quota for each Dept., 10%; b.) Negro workers in plant now to be given privilege of transferring to other Dept.'s that need new workers; c.) Newly hired Negroes to be placed in Dep'ts that have not reached their 10% quota of Negro workers."[47] According to Young, the union never expected to win these demands, but used the report to push open the door to the integration of additional departments.

The Grievance Committee continued to be the main forum for race-based complaints related to jobs. Other civil rights issues, such as school desegregation and support for public housing in East Chicago, went to the Anti-Discrimination Committee. Young continued to be involved in most workplace investigations and settlements because of his position as vice chairman of the Grievance Committee. The younger generation of black activists, however, gravitated to the Anti-Discrimination Committee. Initially, a succession of white radicals held the chairmanship of that committee, with black and Mexican workers included as members.[48] New names of African American activists began popping up regularly in the general minutes by 1947: Eugene Blue, Al McClain, Bill Gailes, Eugene Jacques, Clarence Royster, and Glover Gary.[49] By 1951 black workers controlled the committee, shifting its focus back into the mill.

In 1946, in an early issue of the *Labor Sentinel*, the first Local 1010 newspaper, Civil Rights Committee member Clarence Royster penned an article on "The Negro Worker." In it, Royster emphasized "the awakening of the Negro to the realization that he, too, must accept his share of the responsibility in fostering union principles." At the end he referred to the article as "a poignant plea to our laggard members to come forward." In the same piece, he paid a double-edged tribute to Bill Young. "Mr. William (Bill) Young has pioneered the Negro interest from the days when the union was in its embryonic stages. Mr. Young has fought a noble and uphill battle of which all Negroes are proud. He fought diligently, without active support, but now he has been joined by other able leaders to form a nucleus of men dedicated to the task of gaining the full rights and privileges to which the Negro is so rightfully entitled."[50] Bill Young did not necessarily want to be joined by other "able leaders" with a different agenda and approach to union work.

Young's union career was still far from over, but his work with the new insurgents took him on a roller coaster ride. This group of new leaders was becoming increasingly outspoken on racial discrimination in the workplace and union and refused to be diverted by resolutions supporting civil rights legislation or school integration in the community. The white progressives no longer served as the point men in the fight against discrimination. The radical culture at Inland had not allowed any faction or caucus to ignore racial complaints or run a slate of officers that was not integrated. The opposition caucus, supported by the district leadership, saw an opportunity to take over the local if they could attract more black votes by breaking the alliance between blacks and progressives.

The left carried the civil rights banner from 1937 until 1947, fighting for promotions and speaking out in the newspaper and at meetings.[51] Beginning in 1947, African American steelworkers took to the floor and then established independent leadership. Disagreement over tactics led to divisions among African Americans. To promote their agenda and sometimes themselves, some black activists took whatever slot was offered, coalescing at times with the pro-International, anticommunist forces in Local 1010.

Conflicts and Divisions

Between 1948 and 1950, union meetings began to take on a circus atmosphere, as the trade union conservatives became bolder in their bid for power. The culture of the local underwent a visible change. Workers spoke openly against efforts to reduce discrimination or promote more minorities, saying that such efforts themselves were discriminatory. For example, president Bill Maihoffer, "Wildcat Willie," requested funds to set up a special Mexican youth organization in September 1950. He argued that the local had to make special efforts to bring the new Mexican workers arriving in East Chicago into the union. Since many of the Mexicans did not speak English, he thought a separate group would be the best way to proceed. Opposition was widespread. The recording secretary noted:

Bro Powell agrees with Bro Mamula that the Union cannot afford to support a group which would foster discrimination of any kind. Sister Kelley [the recording secretary] also states the opinion that a Youth group of Local 1010 would be a good thing if it were open to all, because it would be a good place to break down nationality, race and language barriers. Bro. Powell [also] objected on the basis that he feels local 1010 is not a charitable organization and cannot afford donations to any and every group seeking such.

Maihoffer brought up the issue at the next meeting, arguing that it was "his opinion that our first job is to get the people into the hall, so that they can be shown that there is no class or race barrier. . . . When you see a chance to organize," he continued, "you do so, welding small groups into larger ones."[52] This time the membership voted down the proposal. At the same meeting, however, the local voted to send two white officers, Financial Secretary Tom Conway and International representative Joe Jeneske, to an American Bowling Congress dinner with unlimited expenses. The purpose of the dinner was to celebrate the success of a suit against the Bowling League for excluding "colored fellows." Throughout these debates, Bill Young took no public position.

Another telling debate developed over discrimination in the union's Club Bar, downstairs from the union hall. In addition to causing various financial and staffing scandals, the club refused to serve black members. The issue became a focus for discussions on discrimination, detracting from what many African Americans felt was the more important issue of racism in the mill. One member commented: "There is too much fighting amongst ourselves. . . . We should fight discrimination out in the mills instead of in the Club Bar." According to the minutes, Brother William Gailes took the floor, agreeing "that our Negro and Mexican members are more interested in fighting discrimination where it should be fought than they are in a glass of beer or whiskey and that it should be fought in the community and the mills instead of a Bar."[53] Increasingly Bill Gailes and not Bill Young would take center stage in the debates. Young consciously avoided contentious discrimination issues, which might force him to take sides with either his black peers or his white coworkers.[54]

The most serious incident—a political firestorm—occurred in January 1952, and Bill Young was dragged right into the middle of it. An African American worker, Jesse Godwin, was promoted into power and steam, a previously all-white department. This was the third attempt to integrate the department. During the war, under pressure from the federal government to increase minority hiring, Inland introduced black workers into power and steam, but the white workers ran them out. A contemporary report detailed the actions. "They broke into their lockers and destroyed their clothing, stole their tools, and generally made it uncomfortable."[55] In 1951 Inland tried again, this time hiring a graduate of Michigan Law School. Again the white workers said "they didn't want any colored," and the union griever agreed, arguing that it was bad timing, given the number of "hillbillies" in the department.

On January 9, 1952, shortly after Godwin's promotion, workers threw three gallons of torch oil on Godwin while he was smoking a cigarette. The oil ignited. After dousing the flames, the griever brought Godwin down to the union hall to meet with top officers. Everyone was equally outraged, but they butted heads over a remedy. Inland filed charges against the instigator but not against the other two men involved in the attack. Inland later dropped even those charges for lack of evidence. The local president, still Bill Maihoffer, took an unusually cautious approach. He had always denounced racist acts within the union, but in 1952 he faced a serious challenge in upcoming elections from the conservative opposition. He feared a white backlash would result if he took on the racism in power and steam too energetically. Urging moderation, Maihoffer recommended following the company's lead and prosecuting the instigator but not all three men involved. Don Lutes, his opposition and chairman of the Grievance Committee, saw his opportunity and grabbed it, declaring himself chief prosecutor for the African Americans in the local.

Bill Young got trapped in the middle. The local leadership leaned on Young to promote its position among black workers. Maihoffer worked first to convince the chair of his Civil Rights Committee, Eugene Blue, to back off and agree to one charge only, but he failed to convince the committee members. Clarence Royster, a member of the union committee but also chair of the East Chicago Fair Employment Practices Committee (FEPC), refused to back off the demand for a thorough prosecution. According to Royster, "The president [Maihoffer] accused me of wanting to start a big fight on the local floor and said that I was just being obstinate, and he wanted me in an act of unity to sign the majority report."

At that point, Financial Secretary Tom Conway interceded with Bill Young and Buster Logan, griever in the coke plant, and asked them to talk Royster out of his position. Royster was angered by what he termed "the betrayal" of his black brothers, who, he said, "told me that my attitude was too harsh and that the white people might rebel against finding three white men guilty of discrimination. . . . If I persisted, they warned, in going for three, I might lose all three as well and commit political suicide personally." It is impossible to know whether Young spoke his own mind when he went to Royster or just carried Conway's message. Regardless, it was the messenger Royster shot down as a traitor.

This incident led to one of the first mobilizations of Africans Americans by African Americans in the local. Bill Gailes and Clarence Royster packed the union meetings in February 1952, and used the political rivalry between Lutes and Maihoffer to their advantage.[56] Royster recognized that Lutes "was primarily concerned with establishing a 'good reputation' as a friend of the Negro people, in view of the coming biannual local union elections." So many African Americans turned out for the trial meeting that only five workers voted against prosecuting all three wrongdoers. Lutes emerged the champion and won the next election. Maihoffer, having chosen an opportunistic retreat to save his control of the local, was defeated. Bill Young found himself not only discredited but defeated. Clarence Royster opposed him in that election for the vice presidency and won.

At the March 6, 1952, general meeting, Young began the long trek back toward redemption. He spoke on behalf of a black brother "to thank this Local Union for their attitude and action on Civil Rights, citing the case of this Negro who was able to obtain a job through the efforts of Bro. Don Lutes and has since been advanced with the help of the union and is the first Negro ever to hold a machinist's job in the mill." At the same meeting, Eugene Blue asked for local approval to send three delegates to the National Negro Labor Council meeting, which was given without discussion. Lutes and Royster would team up, Young would vacillate, and African Americans would run against each other in future elections, divided by slate.

Despite the internal conflict, it is important to note that Local 1010 remained united in the major battles against Inland and the steel industry. Beginning with the 1946 contract and continuing until 1959, the USWA brought its basic steel membership out on strike over economic issues on every contract. The union had remarkable national participation in the strikes; none of the internal issues wracking the union interfered with solidarity on the picket lines. The strength of rank-and-file strikers had its rewards; workers won annual wage increases, cost-of-living increases (COLA), paid vacations and holidays, and pension and healthcare benefits. The last national strike, held in 1959, lasted 116 days; in the face of great hardships Local 1010 membership gave its full support.[57]

McCarthyism: Labor Takes Aim at Itself

Red-baiting in the local, the district, and the International succeeded in driving a wedge between blacks and radical whites. The loyalty oath provi-

Gary workers gathered at mill entrances for picketing during one of the many strikes between 1949 and 1959. Photo courtesy of Calumet Regional Archives, Gary, Indiana.

sion in the USWA constitution required by the Taft-Hartley Act served as a divisive weapon. Many blacks saw the handwriting on the wall and distanced themselves from the beleaguered left. The USWA cleaned house, firing radicals on staff, removing officers who refused to sign affidavits, and supporting anticommunist, pro-International slates in local union elections.[58] Local 1010, being the most militant and independent, was a main focus of the district and International's red-baiting campaign.

The result for someone like Bill Young was increasing isolation as he tried to steer a course through the storm. Younger blacks already distrusted the paternalism of the left and wanted to fight their own battles. Many followed labor leader A. Philip Randolph's advice to "form your own organization." In 1959, at an NAACP convention, the president of the Sleeping Car Porters Union called for the formation of a black labor organization. In a meeting of 75 black labor activists in May of 1960, Randolph founded the Negro American Labor Council.[59]

The Negro American Labor Council provided leadership and a home to militant black workers at Local 1010. On the one hand, the cold war produced some strange bedfellows and opportunistic alliances that slowed the fight against workplace discrimination. On the other, the move to strengthen black organization within labor created the leadership, the momentum, and the national networks necessary for the emergence of black power in the union a decade later.

Attacks on radical leadership in USWA 1010 escalated in 1948, backed by District Director Joe Germano and the International. At the 1948 convention, Nick Migas, griever and former 1010 president and staff rep, challenged the leadership from the floor as an open communist.[60] Bodyguards carried him out of the hall, beat him up, and left him in the gutter. The story made front-page headlines in the Boston papers.[61] Then the International removed Migas from all local union positions and recommended his expulsion from the union.

In 1948 the left still controlled the local and selected a trial committee clearly on Migas's side. As a result, the local voted to reverse the International's decision and reinstate him as griever. Over 250 workers in his department, the number one open hearth, signed a petition stating: "We, undersigned members of Local 1010, USA-CIO, working in Open hearth #1, Inland Steel, declare that the highest authority of this union is the rank-and-file membership. It is the expressed wish of the rank-and-file . . . that Brother Migas be our Grievance Committeeman. It makes no difference to us that he is a communist. He is a strong union man, a good fighter for us men here."[62] Bill Young put forward the argument for re-instatement, relying on the USWA constitution, which declared all steelworkers, "regardless of race, creed, color or nationality . . . eligible for membership."[63]

Local union cold warriors, headed by Don Lutes, filed an appeal to the International, demanding the Trial Committee's ruling be overturned. Bill Young again volunteered to represent Nick Migas as his advocate, even though Migas had hired an outside attorney not subject to union pressures. Bill Young's defense of Migas before the International Executive Board reflected his integrity and courage:

I am co-member for the counsel for the defense of Nick Migas and I have had the privilege of working with Nick Migas for a long period of years as shop steward, grievance committeeman, executive board member and as a rank-and-file member. . . . Nobody asked me to defend Nick Migas. I sought the privilege of defending [him] . . . based upon several factors among which is, I'm a Negro, one of the persecuted, and I'm opposed to persecution, whether it is based on the color of a man's skin, his religious beliefs, or political faith. I stood side by side, surrounded by more than 150 people in the Conference Room of No. 2 open hearth in the month of November 1944. Among these men was Superintendent Fred Gillies, and I heard Nick Migas and a Negro, Al McClain, branded and called every name you could mention. Nick bravely stood his ground . . . to place a Negro on the floor of the No. 2 open hearth which made history in the union against discrimination. I have made a study of the names of the accusers in the affidavit signed against Nick Migas. . . . Not a single solitary among them ever lifted up his voice at any time against discrimination in this Union. . . . I believe that this Article in the Constitution purported to deny a Communist to hold office in the Local Union or to serve on committees in the Local Union conflicts with not only the spirit but the wording of the Constitution itself.[64]

In Young's view, Migas and other leftists were "just good union people. They didn't do anything to try to break up the union. They would brand anyone a communist who would stand up and fight for workers' rights in the union. I have been branded a thousand times," he told me, "but that didn't make me a communist, you see. Anytime you got up and spoke against discrimination, you were branded a communist, because number one they always opposed race discrimination. They were good people and they were my friends."[65]

Young's loyalty to his friends made him a constant target of the opposition. A few years after Migas's hearing, Young was called before another International Executive Board (IEB) committee to defend himself and his local against charges of corruption. It was guilt by association; Young had had nothing to do with Lutes's leadership of the local in those years. In 1955 Local 1010 was taken over by the IEB because of serious financial misconduct. Such an arrangement was called an administratorship.

In his testimony Bill Young stood on his record.

[I am] Vice Chairman of the Grievance Committee and I might say for the record I am "ex" because I was not suspended, I was fired.

I don't know very much about these things. . . . The financial circumstances of our Local would be hard for me to explain, because when I was elected to office in June I had been in the hospital 14 months.

I say this one thing in behalf of the members of Local 1010 who sent me down here, that if there has been anything wrong the guilty people should be punished. I don't believe that the people of our Union should bear the brunt. I am a charter member of Local 1010 and I was a dues paying member of 1010 long before the CIO ever came on the scene. My name was written on the Charter issued by the Steelworkers' Organizing Committee, and I don't like my name branded in the newspapers as a thief, and I came down here to clear my name. I am not begging for a job or any of the International Union's money. I wear a service pin here for 35 years of service, and still I am not begging. Still I don't want to be called a thief, and I want my name to be cleared by this Executive Board.[66]

During the closed-door proceedings, the general counsel of the USWA, Arthur Goldberg, asked, "What about this fellow Young, my law student?" Another committee member, a district director, explained that Lutes had tried to make a deal with him outside the room, saying he would approve the

International's budget if he [Lutes] could remain president and if the IEB would "recommend the discharge of Bill Young and John Sargent." "He wanted Young out of the way," read the transcript, "but he wanted the International Union to assume responsibility of getting Bill Young out of the way, and John Sargent also, both of whom were fulltime men."[67]

Bill Young survived this incident, only to be called before the House Un-American Activities Committee (HUAC) hearings in Gary in 1958. He was the only African American subpoenaed. He was never called to testify because of an incident that occurred within earshot of the HUAC. When Joe LeFleur, the government's witness, completed his testimony, Bill Young walked up to him with an outstretched arm, as if to shake his hand. Bill Young was a very large, very unforgettable man. LeFleur, flustered, asked, "Do I know you?" Young responded, "No, you don't but you named me anyway!"[68]

Bill Young remained griever in his department and vice chair of the Grievance Committee until he retired in 1973. In the mid-1960s, John Sargent and other old friends and radicals once more took control of the local. By that time, however, Bill Young had lost his influence. He never got involved in the black power movement, including the National Ad Hoc Committee in Steel. Other activists from his local, such as Bill Gailes, took the lead. In fact, Bill Young never wanted any other organization in his life than Local 1010. He never had a bad thing to say about his local union. "The local started off number one," he stated proudly. "When it started off there was no room for discrimination. We stuck together closer than any other union. I got a lot of friendship and a lot of respect from the union," he concluded. "Friendship is one of the best things in the world. You need a lot of friends, and I had plenty of them."

Bill Young's contribution to the union and to his black brothers and sisters was extraordinary. He led the union in establishing fairness as the fundamental union principle. Through his persistence and dedication, seniority, job posting, and departmental bidding became the rule of law in steel mills throughout the country. No one knew the contract better than Bill Young. No one enforced it more rigorously. The Inland Steel Company never did "put one over" on him. Bill Young lived and breathed union, and his personal history was inseparable from that of USWA Local 1010.

CHAPTER 3

"The Only Race That Mattered Was the Human Race"

John L. Howard

Johnnie Howard grew up in a multiethnic community in central Gary during the 1920s; his neighbors and playmates were first-generation immigrants, primarily from eastern Europe.[1] Most of his childhood experiences led him to believe that he would have the same opportunities as any other kid on his block. He had occasional run-ins with prejudice but did not identify these incidents as part of a larger racist system. Later in life, when he left his community in search of a job, he would be forced to confront the Jim Crow institutions of his society. His approach would be to defy discriminatory barriers and deny the power of racism to limit his life chances.

John L. Howard dedicated forty-two years to active involvement in the steelworkers union, from its founding in 1937 to the eve of the restructuring that changed the face of the U.S. steel industry in 1980. He began as a departmental representative, enforcing the contract, and rose to local union vice president. In that position, he assumed leadership in community and political affairs, standing up for the causes of his time, from school integration to support for Henry Wallace and the Progressive Party in 1948. In 1958 Howard assumed the position previously held by George Kimbley: International staff representative with District 31. By the time he retired in 1979, Howard had achieved the American dream of success. He had reached the top echelon of his profession, and, equally important, he had raised ten children on his union wages and sent eight of them through college. Johnnie Howard knew what the union meant to black workers.

An optimist and humanist, Howard focused primarily on what was best in people and events. He valued honest, straightforward communication,

John L. Howard, 1986. Photo courtesy of David Howard.

and, as a coworker said of him, "His word was good."[2] Throughout his life, Howard resisted racial stereotypes, refusing to look at the world in terms of black and white. In his own mind, the differences that mattered were those that divided right from wrong. John L. Howard believed in and fought for a color-blind society. "The only race that mattered," he liked to repeat, "was the human race."[3] His philosophy of life reflected the character of his experiences and determined his leanings and alliances through the years.[4] His childhood among immigrant children instilled in him the pride and confidence of a first-generation American. His depression-era struggles brought him into close association with the left during the 1930s and 1940s, when, according to his son David, "it was easier to tell the good guys from the bad guys." Struggles against segregation, evictions, and unemployment fostered a militant, often rebellious spirit, which Howard carried with him into the mills. During the 1960s his long and close association with ethnic, white workers caused him to look with suspicion on his African American peers who sought to build independent organization within the union. For Johnnie separate would always be segregated. As he explained, "You either integrate fully or segregate fully. I don't see the sense of separate caucuses." Although his loyalties changed as his circumstances evolved, he never turned his back on former friends. In the aftermath of the red scare, for example, Howard continued to express as much respect for the radicals of his early union days as he did for the union insiders of his later staff years.

Although he was born in Alabama, John Howard saw himself as a second-generation black northerner. His father, Johnson Howard, brought him to Gary as a very young child. When I first met John Howard, he was seventy-five going on thirty. He walked with a bounce, as if he could not contain his energy, and had only a thin dusting of white covering his hair. Like so many of his peers, Howard did not take retirement sitting down. In January 1989, he was appointed to the Gary Employee Relations Commission; two years later, he was designated chair. He served as a director of Goodwill Industries, and took active leadership in the Gary Urban League. At his retirement dinner he opened his remarks with these words, "When I was much younger, I read about Ponce de Leon's search for the fountain of youth and I scoffed at his quest. Now that I am older, I wish he had found it!"[5] The truth is that Howard drank from that fountain of youth when he joined the union in 1937.

Howard led me through his house to the basement, where he pointed with excitement to the photographs and memorabilia of a long, prestigious life. "I considered myself a pioneer," he explained. He took immeasurable pride in his accomplishments and spoke without regret about good times and bad. In every photograph, from an early shot of him in a baseball uniform with other steelworkers to a picture of his retirement from the International staff, Howard wore a broad smile, so broad that his cheeks puffed out like a child's, giving him an appearance of enduring youth. "I always looked younger than I was," he acknowledged as we sat down to talk. His attitude and posture, the way he moved his hands and swung his arms as he recounted his life story, all made him look like a much younger man.[6]

He clearly enjoyed storytelling and laughed as he recalled each memory. "Oh yes," he repeated often, leaning back, perhaps envisioning the moment: "I saw that"; "I was there." Like George Kimbley, he took great delight in remembering the names of neighbors, childhood friends, and coworkers.[7] It was as if he were paying a brief tribute to the individuals, conjuring up their image by naming and identifying them. It was clear Howard had shared the narrative of his life before. He had a repertoire of stories that flowed one into another. His voice shifted to play different roles, rising and falling with the drama of events.[8] When I questioned him about details or feelings, he hesitated thoughtfully, and usually came up with a more personal observation. He had to dig to get behind the tales he had constructed over the years.[9]

Howard selected his words carefully, and often paused to find the right descriptive phrase. A reporter who heard Howard speak in 1949 compared his oratory to that of CIO president Philip Murray. "His voice and gestures conveyed the quality of Murray himself, as is the great orator's hypnosis that purified and endured beyond the normal expectations."[10] Howard's voice evoked atmosphere as his words drew images.

Growing Up a Garyite

Born in 1914 in Union Springs, Alabama, Howard, known to his friends as Johnnie, moved north to Gary when he was four. His father had obtained one of the better jobs available to blacks in the South; he was a miner for Tennessee Coal and Iron (TCI), a subsidiary of Carnegie Illinois Steel. In 1918, as part of its preparation for the big steel strike, the company requested that Howard's father transfer to Gary to work at the big mill. John-

Johnnie Howard and his mother in front of their residence in Union Springs, Alabama, 1918. Photo courtesy of David Howard.

son Howard belonged to the older generation of African Americans who gave their loyalty to the company. He had been promised job security and a promotion if he moved north. In exchange for his working during the 1919 strike, Carnegie Illinois promoted Johnson Howard to shear man. No black man would be able to bid into such a high-paying skilled position for another quarter of a century. When he helped his son hire into Gary Works in 1935, John entered at the very bottom.

One of the first African Americans employed in the newer Midwest steel mills, Johnson Howard valued his position, especially for what it meant for his family. The way Johnson Howard saw it, Johnnie grew up without the fear of lynching and with access to a decent education because of the Carnegie Illinois Steel Company. John Howard's first impression of unions reflected his father's attitude. "My father had told me they were only organizing whites; they didn't try to organize the blacks or the Mexicans."

Johnnie heard the story of the steel strike many times, because 1919 turned out to be a very tough year for his family. A flu epidemic killed his mother in the spring. "You didn't have a black mortician in Gary," explained Howard, "but Burns and Williams embalmed the body and we went back to Alabama. My father buried my mother at the Mount Pleasant Grove Baptist Church, where she had grown up." Johnson Howard left his two sons and a baby with his wife's parents and returned to Gary in September, shortly after the strike had begun. According to John, his father entered the mill on an ore boat from the Lake Michigan side to avoid the picketers at the front gate. Within a year Johnson remarried and brought his family back to northwest Indiana.

Howard's few childhood memories of Alabama centered on his grandparents' farm. He chuckled describing a big dog, "maybe a Newfoundland, that we younger fellows would climb on and ride." Both sets of grandparents owned the land they worked, so in some ways young Johnnie was insulated from contact with the racial violence taking place throughout the South. He painted the picture of an idyllic South.

> My cousins would take care of the chores on the farm, and when they wanted to water the stock, they'd take them to the watering hole, the little creek. I cried to ride the horse to the watering hole like my cousins. So one day my cousins put me on the horse, and I grabbed the mane. You know it had no stirrups; it was bareback. I was unaware that when the horse got to the water, he'd lean over to drink. Over I went into the water, and they had to get me out of that.

"Yes, I remember the Mason-Dixon line," Howard affirmed, recounting his second voyage north in 1920. "All the blacks had to sit in the front of the train behind those steam locomotives, because all the smoke hits the first coach. The whites were way in the back where the smoke didn't reach them."[11] As the train approached Chicago, Johnnie Howard pressed his face against the gray window. He had never seen anything like Chicago. Howard grew up from age five on in Gary across from the school he would attend for twelve years, the Froebel School, near Fifteenth and Jackson. Froebel was the only "integrated" school in Gary. Black students, however, made up a very small minority; most African Americans attended the all-black Roosevelt School.

> Froebel was a big edifice with a chicken fence around it, and the grass was about knee-high. There were frogs, garter snakes, and all that on the lawn; my parents didn't allow us to go there. There was only two or three black families in our neighborhood then. There were a few black and lots of white children of first-generation immigrants. Some couldn't speak English too well, but we got along. Most of them went to the parochial school, including one of my best friends, Albert Rodinski.
>
> We had Serbians, Polish, Italian, Greeks and Russians. And we children, we would go into each other's house; we would sleep there. Like Albert Rodinski. We would be studying our lesson, it would get late, his mother would go to my mother and tell my mother, your son is going to stay with Albert tonight. That was the kind of association we had together. It was nice.
>
> There was twenty-six nationalities at Froebel, a regular melting pot. But every ethnic group except blacks could swim in the swimming pool as class work during school hours, and they could play in the band and orchestra. We couldn't and I couldn't understand it.

Howard recalled spending many afternoons at the public library. "We read a lot, and I dreamed. I believed that someday I would get an education and make something out of myself in the professional field." He never imagined a life in the mills.

Gary's black population almost tripled between 1920 and 1930.[12] In contrast, the white population grew by only 68 percent. Mexicans had also begun settling in Gary, though compared to in East Chicago, their numbers were small.[13] The influx of foreign-born immigrants that had swelled population figures in the region between 1900 and 1920 had been cut off first by the war and then by restrictive immigration legislation in 1921 and 1924. For newly arrived black families limited to housing in the central district, the overcrowding created serious health threats. In 1923, for example, the Gary Health Department demanded that some three hundred shacks south of the Wabash, housing fifteen hundred people, be vacated for sanitary reasons. The Howard family, however, had taken advantage of the higher income of a skilled job to buy a home in a better neighborhood.[14]

My father never talked to us about his work. Back then, they worked twelve hours, six in the morning 'til six in the evening, or six in the evening until six in the morning.[15] I can remember seeing my father only at certain times with the exception of his off day. He would either be coming from work, going to work, or sleeping. He would come home, have his supper, and then he had an ointment he had made for himself that he would rub on his arms, shoulders and his legs. I asked him, "Why do you do that, Pa?" He said, "Just keep living, you'll find out." So I've found it out.

Employment for most African Americans in Gary could not be measured by Johnson Howard's experience. Right after the 1919 strike, U.S. Steel hired additional black workers, but their numbers peaked at 3,181 in 1923, when they accounted for 20 percent of the workforce. Once the industry was forced to drop the twelve-hour day in 1923, black employment declined for the next decade, to a low of 14 percent in 1932.[16] As Gary's African American population became larger and increasingly working class, housing and jobs became scarcer. Gary's black alderman, A. B. Whitlock, criticized U.S. Steel for breaking its pledge to the black worker. "The Negro has not been promoted in the degree that his loyalty has warranted. White men and white foreigners," he noted, "are in a big percentage of the cases given priority over the colored men."[17]

The black community responded to shrinking opportunities by developing networks of organizations and a penchant for activism. The Universal Negro Improvement Association (UNIA) attracted widespread support in Gary; people especially loved its flamboyant parades. "I used to go to UNIA meetings," Howard recalled.

They were located on Twenty-third and Adams, but I didn't fully understand. I saw Marcus Garvey, yes; he would come occasionally, and they would parade with their swords and their uniforms and all. I saw that. And it kind of made me proud to see someone who had guts and nerve enough to buck the status quo, and that's what they did. Some of my playmates played in the UNIA band. I couldn't play in it because I couldn't play an instrument at Froebel.

John Howard narrated his personal story as if each memory encapsulated the period; in his description of the UNIA marches, for example, he blended all the marches into one snapshot.[18] He drew as much from the stories he had heard as from his own experience. He also tended to adopt the standpoint of an observer. His repeated use of phrases such as "yes, I saw that," and "yes, I was there" suggest that he saw himself on the margins of the activity. For example, although he had access to better schooling at the integrated Froebel School, he had been denied, as a black student, access to band. Not being able to play a musical instrument left him standing on the sidelines of the UNIA parades. Kimbley, too, had spent many of his early years on the margins of black community life, on the white side of the tracks in Kentucky. From that position, Kimbley had analyzed the white society around him. Howard, in contrast, felt a part of the immigrant society in which he grew up and tended to describe the major events in the black community more as an outsider than as a participant.

Howard finished high school in 1933, the grimmest year of the depression. His father worked at most one day a week, sometimes fewer than three days a month. According to Howard, the Gary Heat, Light and Water Company turned off their utilities, forcing them to seek relief elsewhere.

They set up a spigot on the corner and we'd go there for water. The whole community would go there to get their buckets of water. We had no heat. We'd climb on the dune and dig the roots of old scrub oak, and chop it for fires. Living in close proximity to the school, we would go there at night, and they would let us swim in the pool, and sometimes on Saturdays and Sundays we'd go over to take showers. The janitor was a nice guy, John McKennis. He would have the soap and towels for us, and that was the way we kept clean.

It was rough. The steel corporation would give employees plots of land they owned. They gave plots in these low-lying areas close to the Little Calumet, all the way down to Burns Ditch. They would give you seed. I was the oldest, and I'd walk some five miles with my father to our little plot. We had to turn that land over, and we planted all kinds of vegetables. And being a city-bred boy I thought cantaloupes grew on trees like oranges. I saw these things on the ground like watermelons, and I didn't know what they were.[19]

Unemployment in Gary and East Chicago reached all-time highs, with some seventeen thousand families in northern Lake County on relief. More than one out of four African Americans was unemployed in Gary according to the U.S. Census for 1930.[20] The steel industry had been running hot up to that point, and had broken production records in 1929. Johnson Howard's job had been steady and had paid well. His faith in U.S. Steel had probably led him to trust the company's varied welfare programs, including its stock option program, as a way of saving for future hard times. But when the stock market crashed, workers lost everything. Howard rarely worked, depleted his savings, and, like every other employee at the big mill, he lost most of his insurance and benefits.[21]

> Boy were there evictions! But this is where the people kind of took over. They would put families out; the sheriff would come and put their furnishings in front of their house and leave. The people would wait until those sheriff's deputies left, and they would put all that furniture back. Yes, I saw that. I saw people climbing poles to reconnect the electricity.

Howard said many of those activists were "left-wingers." He went on, "They believed all men were of one race, the human race, like Paul Robeson. They helped people do humanitarian things and I still have a lot of respect for them 'til this day." Because Howard ignored stereotypes and judged people one at a time, he held his communist acquaintances in very high esteem. "These people who were accused of being communist," he later reflected, "were the militant color-blind individuals who were concerned about the welfare not only of individuals who worked in the plant but their families as well. These were the people who put people back in their houses. They were dedicated people. They would give you the shirt off their back."

He was critical of the older generation of African Americans in the community, whom he described as "placid." "They had a kind of slave mentality to me," he observed. "They wouldn't fight the powers that be; they wouldn't question the powers that be. And that's another thing that caused me to have my militant attitudes in later life. It was terrible how some people suffered."

Joining the Black Experience

After graduation, Howard told his favorite math teacher, Ms. Stewart, that he was going to college. He remembered her telling his class: " 'Choose for your life's work what you would rather do than play.' That went to my heart," he explained, "and I took it under advisement." But when he told her he was interested in college, she replied, " 'No, you're not college material.

My advice to you is to get a job in the mill.' And I took that as 'Christ, maybe I'm not qualified to go to college.' " He would worry throughout his life that people thought less of him because he lacked those initials after his name.[22]

Not wanting to be a burden to his family, and unable to get a job in Gary, John walked with a good friend, Hosea Rasberry, from Gary all the way to the Great Lakes Naval Station on the north side of Chicago.

> We waited in line. Hosea's over six feet. I'm short, five foot seven, and I'm standing in front of him. This guy says, "Now what can I do for you fellows?" "We want to join the navy." "Oh," he replied, "you want to be officers' orderlies or cooks?" "No, we want to be sailors." He told us to wait, goes off, and when he comes back he said, "The Congress of the United States does not allocate money for the training of Negroes." That's what they called us in those days. That stuck with me. I'm seventy-five today and it's still a scar on my heart.

This experience began Howard's education on racism in America. He had glimpsed Jim Crow at Froebel, but only in the school's band and swimming pool policies. He had not yet connected the dots. Starting with his journey in search of employment, he began to develop a black awareness. In his youthful world, blacks and whites had done most of the same things, and done them together. He could not understand what had changed.

Rebuffed by the navy, John and Hosea went to the Calumet Township Trustee Office in Gary for help in finding a job. "They were recruiting for the Civilian Conservation Corps (CCC)," he remembered. "They told us to go home and pack—we didn't have much—and then they took us in a truck to the National Guard Armory. They fed us sauerkraut and wienies, and that was the first time I had a full meal in several months. Bread! I bet you I ate fifteen!"

Along with dozens of other young men, John rode the train to Fort Knox, Kentucky. Despite his air of independence, John had never been away from his family. "I was looking back as the train pulled away, and tears were welling in my eyes, and I'm trying to disguise it. I look around and everybody was crying." He continued:

> Army officers met the train, and lined up the new recruits. Those army officers called us niggers and black boys. One day an officer said that, saw our faces and added, "If you don't like what I'm saying, take two steps forward and I'll give you a one-way ticket back!" The guy next to me had to grab my arm to keep me from stepping forward.
>
> We stayed in Fort Knox for over a month, and I learned something [about racism], being a neophyte. They had us segregated four ways. One area you had blacks from the North; another area had blacks from the

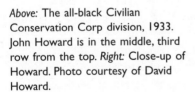

Above: The all-black Civilian Conservation Corp division, 1933. John Howard is in the middle, third row from the top. *Right:* Close-up of Howard. Photo courtesy of David Howard.

South; northern whites were in one place; southerners, in another. Now the most friendly group with respect to being a northern black were the northern whites. We were real close. The southern whites, oh if they caught you in the canteen, for example, trying to get a bar of soap, they would beat you up. We'd go for help. Whites from the North said, "We're with you." We'd go to the blacks from the South and they'd say, "Oh, we're not going to have anything to do with it." It was ingrained into their psyche, you see.

Well, one time we almost had a riot there. We were going to fight, when all at once the regular army came up marching. The officer told the southern whites to go back to their barracks. They refused: "We're goin' to get those niggers!" Then the officer ordered those army guys to put their bayonets on their rifles. He gave another order and they showed them. When they started marching on the southern whites, they broke it up. I had never seen anything like that. It was really a shock to me.

The CCC paid thirty dollars a month; they sent twenty-five to Howard's parents, leaving him with five. After his initiation in Knoxville, Howard was transferred to Bloomington, Indiana. He worked in the Monroe State Park planting trees. "We had to plant up to a thousand trees a day," he asserted. He described an assembly line method of tree planting that allowed teams of ten men to dig, seed, plant, and water like clockwork. On December 31, 1934, Howard shipped home, still penniless. Shortly afterward, the CCC sent his honorable discharge in the mail. To Howard's great surprise, he read that he had "brown eyes, brown hair, and was as black as coal." It had been tough for him to accept the implications of being black; now he had to digest the next nuance of discrimination, based on the darkness of his skin.

"All We Have Is Chipping"

Back in Gary, Howard spent days walking from one mill to another trying to find work. Every morning, he huddled in the Illinois Carnegie bullpen—the employment office at First and Virginia Streets—hoping to be one of the few picked for work. The foremen favored the big, stocky workers who looked like they could handle a double workload. Howard was not only young looking but relatively small and slim. "I'd keep my eye on the employment agent. One morning he pointed at me and said 'what are you doing here?' I was twenty-one but I looked very young. 'I want a job,' I said. 'Do you have relatives working here?' he asked. I told him my father had been there for almost twenty years. He told me to come back with my father."

Johnson Howard was working midnights, so Johnnie waited for him at the gate and brought him over to the agent. The agent examined Johnson's brass badge, with "shear man" pressed across the top, and told John he could go in and fill out an application but warned him not to jump to any conclusions about a job. Since he had taken years of drafting, machine shop, and foundry in high school, Howard noted on his application that his top three job choices were machinist, pattern maker, and any other skilled work. " 'All we have is chipping,' they told me. 'I don't know anything about chipping,' I said, because the boys had told me to stay away from chipping, that it was too rough.' " The person at the counter repeated in a slow monotone: "All we have is chipping." Realizing he had no choice, Howard quickly interjected, "I can learn."

The first day I went in there, I went through the viaduct under the railroad track to the foundry. There's the electric shop, a pattern shop, a boiler shop, and a machine shop. I walked into the rail mill; it was like another world. I see the cranes, I see guys burning with acetylene torches. I was all eyes. But the watchman took me along to the foreman's office, a Mr. Griffin, who explained about safety and everything. He said, 'You have any problems, my door is open to you.' I believed him; I believed that grown-ups didn't lie.

On March 5, 1935, John Howard went to the thirty-six-inch and forty-four-inch blooming mill, where he joined other black, Mexican, and European immigrant workers as a chipper. The job was worse than he had ever imagined. Howard's job was to remove scales or impurities from the surface of red-hot blocks of steel called blooms. Molten steel was poured into molds known as ingots, and then, depending on the final uses, the ingot was rolled into blooms, slabs, or billets. Blooms were not as flat or as long as the slabs sent to the hot and cold rolling mills. Billets were closer to squared blocks, usually rolled and cut for rails. To remove or surface the impurities, the steel was sent through a bath of sulfuric acid. The chipper had to remove the surface scales while the steel was still fiery red from heat.

They gave me a hammer, a pneumatic hammer with some 150 pounds of pressure. It was the strongest one they had. The slab was five inches thick, and I wrestled with that hammer, but my arms cramped, and just gave out. I lay on the floor 'til the feeling came back in my arms. The older blacks wouldn't show me how to do it. I'd put that hammer on the steel, pull the trigger and . . . *vroom*! The older black guys, they would stand back and laugh at me. Older black men resented us, I think.

Even this other black, a lot younger than my father, told me he wasn't going to do any of my work. He borrowed a tape from the inspector and drew a line down the middle of this pickled bloom—they were making blooms for boulder dam—and in ten minutes he had finished his half. I was still only a few inches from the edge. I didn't know you had to find a special angle. It was men of foreign extraction and a Mexican who took my hand and showed me. Once I was proficient an older black came to me, saying he'd work with me. I told him where to go.

They pickled these big blooms in sulfuric acid and that would expose all the surface defects. I was paid $4.28 to chip the surface, and when they put me on labor, they paid me $3.78.

I asked John Howard about his worst memory of those early days. Grim-faced, he recalled how in the stifling heat of summer, his foreman assigned him to be a water boy.

I'd be told to get the water. They didn't have refrigerated fountains then. I'd have to put a yoke around my neck with two buckets hanging at either end and go up and down steps, about half a mile, to get water. By the time I'd get back half the water would have spilled out of the buckets on my pants. I'd pour the remaining water into a container with ice chips. Five minutes later they'd come get me to go again. How'd they drink all that water so fast? This time, I watched them after I poured the water. They waited until they thought I was gone and then poured the water on the ground. Well, I got mad and went to the washhouse.

The foreman came for me and told me to go get more water. I told him to hide and watch like I had. When he saw them pour the water on the ground he told me to go back to the washhouse and wash up because they didn't need any damn water. But then I'd get my paycheck. Even though I was chipper most of the week, job class seven, I'd be paid as a water boy, a laborer, job class two. When I went to the foreman, before I could open my mouth, he told me, "If you don't like it, stay home." We had no union then.

Not surprisingly, John Howard began to question his father's views on unions. What young Howard saw was a small group of older black workers, such as his father, with a handful of good jobs that they had been given during the 1919 strike—a shear man here, a crane man there. But the average black worker had the "hot, dirty, low-paying jobs. And where I worked was the most filthy place you'd ever seen. There were no women then, so the men would wear old work clothes until they practically fell off their body. You could buy overalls for fifty-nine cents, gloves for a quarter, but who could afford it? I've seen men chipping and a chip fly and stick in the flesh, and he'd just pull it out."

Howard's view of the mill shifted from it being a "place of opportunity" to being a man-eating monster. "The worst thing I saw was a young man, working the midnight turn, and his job was to pull the slag. As the butt conveyor would bring the ingots up, red-hot ingots, and dump them on the roll line, the slag would fall off of it, crusts and all, red hot. His job was to take a long hook and pull them off, and they would fall into the pits, or scale hole, as we called it." One night Howard heard the whistles blow, and he knew there had been a fatal accident. "I ran over to the billet mill. The worker had tried to pull one of those scabs off that ingot and the hook got stuck. He didn't have the presence of mind to turn it loose, and it pulled him through the roll. You looked around and saw parts of his body, smelled that burning flesh."

Howard's high school shop training had made him a master chisel sharpener. Anytime he'd go into the machine shop to sharpen his chisel, his coworkers lined up behind him: "Hey John, you do mine next?" One day, a friend played a practical joke on Howard that sent him to the steel infirmary, a place as dangerous as the mill. The coworker swiped his chisel out of his pocket as a joke, and waved it at Howard when he returned to the job site.

"Throw it to me!" I yelled. He threw that chisel, but not far enough; it hit a steel slab and then my leg. We were all laughing. When I looked down, a few minutes later, blood was running out of my shoe. That chisel had hit an artery. I went to the infirmary, and the doctor told me he'd have to put a stitch in there. I thought he was going to deaden it. He got that catgut and crooked needle and he just grabs my skin. I could feel the thread coming through the raw. Whooo! Then he tied it and told me to go back to work! I can imagine how other workers got treated! My hands were so callused, you could stick a pin in my finger, and I wouldn't feel it!

Shortly after hiring into the mill, John L. Howard met Jewel Corrine Crockett at the Campbell Friendship House in Gary. She was born and raised in Tennessee and later moved to Chicago with her family. Jewell had three sisters, two of whom took jobs as domestics in order to survive the depression years. Howard married her soon after they met, because "she was the only one I could trust." She would support John Howard through all the twists and turns of his union career, although she never got personally involved. Her family and the church were her life.

"The Unions Got More Brazen"

It did not take Johnnie Howard very long to jump on the new union train. As he recalled:

Late in 1936, there was talk about a union. If the supervisor found out you were talking, you were fired on the spot. The union had buttons. I think you paid fifty cents and they gave you a little button. You couldn't wear that button out; you had to wear it inside your shirt or under your work cap. They began to talk about what unions could do. They were telling me, "Oh, you'll get vacations; you'll have insurance." The guy talking to me was of foreign extraction, a first-generation individual. He was a nice, hard-working fellow. He was the type of individual who treated everybody good; color didn't mean a thing to him. His name was Mike, and he was a chipper too.

Well, I bought that union idea. We would have seniority, a right to promotion, all that. So I paid, and he told me to go down to the next meeting. We met at 560 Broadway; that was our headquarters in those days. So I go to the meeting and there's a guard outside the door. He asked me where I worked and what the password was. I didn't know any password. He cracks open the door and says, "You see anybody you know?" I pointed out this guy. He went and got him; Mike told him I was OK. He told me to go up to [Nick] Fontecchio, he was in charge. And Nick says to me "Now I'm going to give you the password. You don't write it down, you don't verbally give it to anyone." He whispered in my ear, "Expansion." Expansion. I never forgot it to this day, you see.[23]

The union raised Howard's expectations, and he decided to sign a union card and wear his union button inside his shirt. Just knowing that the union was there encouraged him to speak out. He started to raise questions about the arbitrary commands of the foremen and the company's discriminatory practices. "Why, they'd bring in white guys, younger than me, and they would put them working with us, and we would show them the job. A month later, the foreman would say, 'This is your new supervisor.' 'What the devil is going on here?' I'd say to the union, and they would try to give me excuses. 'To hell with that,' I said and threw the button away. But then they'd come back and talk to me, and they'd get me back in the union." Howard fairly quickly lost the naive belief that the union could magically change conditions and began to take an active role. His ambivalence, however, was not uncommon among black workers, given the union's past history.

Howard saw in the CIO what he had seen in the Unemployed Councils and later in the CCC camps. He saw workers building alliances and standing up for each other regardless of race. As in the CCC, northern whites, especially the immigrants, stood with the minorities and advocated for equal rights. Although southern whites displayed more outward hostility, there were not yet very many of them in the big mill, and even some Klan members were joining the CIO, knowing its stand on racial integration.

Howard's northern socialization among progressive immigrants and

John Howard (center) never missed union meetings and always sat up front, c. 1940. Photo courtesy of David Howard.

more conservative, older African Americans had shaped his attitudes toward blacks and whites. He had little tolerance for the "slave mentality" of the older generation of black workers, and he strongly distrusted southerners, both white and black. Howard assumed that foreign-born and second-generation northerners would be his friends and allies. The Jim Crow practices that Howard faced in his first decade in the mill, however, led him into coalitions with other black workers. He could see the advances blacks could make when they worked together. His primary union mentor in the mill was another African American named Pat Riley.

Howard developed a circle of pro-union black friends during the SWOC years. He knew George Kimbley, Walter Mackerl, and Jesse Reese; but his closest buddy in the early days was Riley. Talking about Pat, John's face stretched into a huge grin. "You know he got a promotion once, because they saw his name and not him. Thought he was an Irishman!" Howard first met Kimbley in 1937 in the basement of a local fraternal order, where Kimbley was signing up new members. Howard explained:

> The biggest supporters of the union were the first- and second-generation whites and the second-generation blacks. The first-generation blacks—like my father—were a little skeptical. Kimbley was an exception. Walter Mackerl was an exception. With the others, it was the life experiences they had growing up in the South. They were afraid. If you had a difference with a supervisor, you got blackballed. Then you couldn't get a job at Inland, Youngstown, or anywhere, because U.S. Steel was the kingpin. These older blacks were afraid of being blackballed. Us younger fellows, we didn't give a damn. If they had fired me, I would have gone to college!

At U.S. Steel, Myron Taylor, the CEO of the company, recognized the union voluntarily in 1937, after a series of secret meetings with John L. Lewis. The 1937 agreement, however, gave SWOC representational rights over only the workers who had already signed cards, and were members of Lodge 1014, the Rubicon Lodge, or 1066, the New Deal Lodge at the Sheet and Tin.[24] Many of the union supporters who had taken over the company "union," the Employee Representation Plans (ERP), in the early 1930s now shifted their allegiance to SWOC.[25] The ERP became a bastion of procompany stooges, used by U.S. Steel to attract workers and undermine the bargaining power and leverage of SWOC. For that reason, the struggle in the Carnegie Illinois mills after 1937 focused on new organizing. The emphasis would shift during the war, when the Roosevelt administration agreed to "maintenance of membership" clauses for unions in order to gain their full cooperation.[26] These clauses secured a worker's membership in the union for the life of the contract, once a card was signed.

Fighting on the Home Front

Even more than the union had, the rhetoric of the war against fascism raised Howard's expectations for fair treatment on the job and democracy in the union. John Howard did his wartime chipping in the long-bar storage area, surrounded by structures filled with bars awaiting processing. There he worked with the outspoken Pat Riley. "He was a world adventurer. Pat had worked on ships and knew all about unions. He was my prime tutor. We raised hell. There was agitation everywhere, at Inland, Sheet and Tin, and Youngstown. New hires came into the yard, and we'd give them a card to sign up with the union. If workers wouldn't join, well we'd have a little session and agree to ostracize them. We'd refuse to start work; we'd turn off their air."

Howard recalled one particular instance when all the union men in his area stopped work.

> The foreman, Stetson, would try to talk other workers into working, but they'd say, "Talk to Pat Riley or Johnnie Howard." Finally the foreman come yelling in our face, "What's going on here?" "We're not going to work with these fellows who won't join the union!" We'd point them out, and the foreman would call them into his office. "C'min here," he'd say. "There's a war going on and I'm not going to send home fifty workers to keep two working!" Turning to us he'd say "Give me the cards."

Laughing, Howard finished, "[The foreman] would take them and make them sign. 'Now go to work!' "

With the wartime demand for steel skyrocketing, workers made a habit of refusing to work in order to settle a problem.[27] Wages were frozen, and the accident rate kept climbing. Workers fought for what they could get—fairer treatment, access to better jobs, and shop floor control. Stoppages over safety and health were the most common. According to Howard, the conditions for the chippers during the war deteriorated quickly, as speed-ups and shortcuts were imposed to bolster productivity.

> All the steel we chipped was pickled steel. We had to take brushes and brush the dust off the steel onto the floor. Then when we picked up our pneumatic hammers, in ten minutes there'd be a pall of dust. You couldn't even see the crane men in the cranes, and the men were breathing that stuff.
>
> I raised hell and got myself a respirator. Most men I worked with are dead already; inhaling those fumes and dust did it. And when they would die, the diagnosis was always the same, heart failure. Every man that died, company called it heart failure. U.S. Steel controlled the doctors. Hell, it wasn't heart failure; it was congested lungs, and hardening of the arteries

from inhaling those toxic fumes. Plus my gloves, my coat, everything to protect me from the heat was made of asbestos.[28]

A strike in the long-bar storage area put Pat Riley in a crane in 1943. That was an early breakthrough. Increasingly, African Americans were demanding promotional opportunities by seniority and challenging the segregated units and separate lines of progression. The coke plant became a frontline of the struggle.[29] Even though SWOC as a whole had little power face-to-face with the steel industry, on the shop floor, workers staged a fierce battle over control.[30] The efforts of African American workers to open jobs for themselves established the basic practices of job posting, bidding, and promotion by seniority. As at Inland Steel, grassroots activists were making the rules. "During the war, unions got more brazen.[31]

In a conspiratorial whisper, Howard described how the workers organized to press their demands. "All the employees would meet," Howard explained.

> The Latin American, the Slovak, the Polish, Italian, Greek, whoever, we would meet and make our plans. Sometimes in the basement of taverns or in someone's house. When a job opened, I'd go in [to the foreman] and say "Look, I want to be broken in as a loader." "You get out and go to work," they'd answer. "No. Why is it you're breaking that guy in? He just got hired yesterday." "Well, you don't like it, I'll send you home."
>
> He wrote me a pass and I'd go to the washhouse and start changing clothes. "What's the matter?" the guys would say. "He's sending me home!" Well, it was all planned. They would all line up, demanding, "Send us all home!"

Once the USWA was established in 1942, and Roosevelt issued his executive order to end segregation in war production industries, the struggle escalated. In August of 1944, for example, John Howard joined five members of the Central Mill Discrimination Committee to file a complaint with the East Chicago Fair Employment Practices Committee (FEPC). Referring to the bloomer and forty-inch billet mills at Gary Works, the complaint noted: "It is almost an impossibility for Negroes to obtain promotions or any type of advancement, no matter how qualified they are."[32] A National Urban League study reported similar barriers: "While some upgrading has been achieved by Negroes in the steel mills, there are still obstacles which have frozen the largest proportion of Negroes in unskilled jobs." The same report noted that black workers "had been upgraded but in most cases only after union intervention." "Discriminatory policies of management and labor," the report concluded, "have limited job opportunities."[33]

Promotion and integration of black workers into better jobs and previously lily-white departments often led to hate strikes by resistant white workers as noted in the previous chapter. A government report on interracial issues and strikes, covering January 1943 through December 1944, listed several strikes by blacks over failure to be upgraded, and more by whites resisting integration; only a small minority of the actions occurred in steel.[34] U.S. Steel had problems back east, but none were reported in Gary. The War Manpower Commission investigated only one hate strike in northwest Indiana, at Youngstown Sheet and Tube in Indiana Harbor in December 1944. Protests occurred with some regularity, but the union, in general, moved quickly to support the minority workers.[35]

Howard told one story that highlighted the retaliation often directed at white grievers who supported upgrades for African Americans.

Frank Wright worked as a bottom-maker, rebricking furnaces in the pits. The crane men, now that was a lucrative job, would come to work four to twelve or midnights and get sleepy. They trained Frank to run the crane for them, and the supervisors never knew because you couldn't see who was up there in the crane. So a job vacancy comes up for pit crane man, and Frank signed the posting.

Now I was assistant griever, and Lambert Schoon was the new griever. Management was threatening to give the job to a younger [white] worker, contending that he had more experience than Frank. He didn't know that Frank had been running the crane off and on for a couple of years. Schoon threw the contract on the superintendent's desk, shouting, "That's the Bible!" Foreman says, "You mean that?" Well, he put Frank up there. All the white crane men ran their cranes against him and pushed him into a corner. The [whites] climbed down from their cranes and went into the office, declaring, "We're not going to work with him."

Schoon is there and he says to them, "Any of you don't want to work with Frank Wright as a pit crane man, give me your name and badge number. I will turn it in to the time department, where you can go and get your money." One guy quit. Everyone else went right back up in the cranes. Frank Wright ran that crane for years.

Not long afterward, Lambert Schoon paid a visit to Howard's home. According to Howard, he was very shaken. " 'You know what those guys told me? What the hell are their kids going to do if the niggers get all the jobs. They called me a nigger-lover.' Now he was only carrying out the proper terms of the contract. All those pioneers caught hell. There were about four or five grievers who went out on the limb like that."[36]

Without the support of progressive whites, African Americans could not have succeeded in their battle. Nonetheless, African American activists carried out the decisive organizing. Walter Mackerl informed government investigators in 1943 that "everywhere they had been able to activate the Negro workers, old policies and barriers have been broken down."[37] Breakthroughs occurred in coke plants, open hearths, and furnace areas led by Howard, Young, and others like them.[38] By the time the war ended, the local union at Gary Works had developed strong departmental organization based on solidarity among European immigrants, African Americans, and Mexicans in those departments where they worked side by side.[39]

Postwar Radicalism

"During the war we broke the mold, and some blacks were able to exercise their seniority. But in the late '40s and early '50s, we brought changes." Howard explained that many more African Americans were able to transfer into better jobs during this period. He told his own story as an example. He had been trying for years to snag a loader's position. The long-bar storage area closed when the war ended, and Howard went to work in the forty-four-inch billet mill. "I hate to say this, but it's the truth. I asked my grievance committeeman, 'Leo,' I says, 'why can't some of us Negroes get these loading jobs and control men jobs?' You know what he told me! 'Negroes aren't capable of doing those jobs.' Well, we not only got the jobs but we replaced him in the next election!"

Howard started to shadow his foreman, Frank Irvin, after his transfer into the billet mill, demanding a chance to train as a loader. The loader had to keep track of the steel as it was loaded onto rail cars. The job was easier and paid more. Time and again, Irvin pushed him away, telling him to "come back tomorrow."

> I was burning one day when I saw those shiny shoes coming by. After the war, the mill was like a Nazi concentration camp. Every time a foreman walked by, you'd find something to do. This time, late 1946 or '47, I turned off my torch, raised my hood and cut him off. "I want to talk to you now!" Well, he started walking faster, so I ran after him, snatched him by the shoulder and turned him around. "You tell me something today!" He looked at me and said, "By God, as long as I'm assistant superintendent here you'll never load in this department." "You finally gave me the answer I've been trying to get," I told him. "What do you mean?" he asked. "There are people above you!"

When Howard went home that evening, he picked up the telephone directory and called the superintendent of Gary Works, Steve Jencks. "The maid answered—she was black—and I told her I was John Howard and needed to speak to Mr. Jencks. She put him on." Howard laid out his years of service, and asked politely, "What I want to know is why Negroes can't get better jobs?" Jencks offered to meet with him the next day an hour before work in the main office. When Howard arrived, Jencks was waiting. "I thought Negroes were satisfied with what they had," Jencks told Howard. " 'Hey, I'm serious,' I said. 'Well, I'm serious,' he answered. 'Let me tell you something. If there are Negroes in this plant who are dissatisfied with the jobs and the status they have, they want better jobs, tell them to ask for it! You go back, one more time, and ask Frank Irvin and Tom Connors for the loader's job.' "

Howard knew that blacks had been asking for years, but he took the man at his word and went back to the billet mill. The foreman met him, asking if he wanted to break in as a loader. Howard said, " 'Oh, you think it's funny!' I started to give him hell. Then he says, 'Go out there; Bill Davenport will break you in.' " Jencks had already phoned Irvin. Howard followed Davenport around for a few weeks, but Davenport would not show him anything. Howard did not expect him to cooperate. "One day, I followed Davenport into the loaders' shanty and I took a handful of loading sheets. 'What are you doing?' he asked. 'I'm making them out. You won't show me anything so I'm doing them and I'm going to put your name down.' " The next day, when Howard arrived at work, the foreman told him Davenport had quit, and that he now had a full-time job as a loader.

Howard's inability to get his griever to take up his struggle pushed him further toward individual activism. He figured out ways to fight his own battles in spite of union procedures. When Howard got from the plant superintendent what he had not been able to get through the union grievance procedure, the union paid a price. It was easy for Jencks, in this case, to play the good guy by overruling the foreman. But the policies that blocked promotions for black workers remained intact, while the company looked good at the union's expense. Whenever the union failed to confront and challenge discriminatory practices, it lost some of its positive image and power, because other workers would also seek individual solutions to collective problems. Howard, despite his union affiliations, often led by individual example rather than by organizing a collective action. That was his style.

From 1945 to 1954, John Howard served as vice president of USWA Local 1014 under president John Mayerick. In April of 1945, Pat Riley and a few coworkers had come to Howard's house to ask if he would run for the position. The timing was not right; John was still mourning the loss of his father. The previous month, Johnson Howard had been killed in a terrible mill accident, cut in half by an oversized plate.[40]

"I turned them down," Howard recounted. I wasn't ready. A couple of days later, they're back again. They're almost pleading with me to accept the

"The union was my university," said John Howard (first row, second from left, c. 1946). USWA Local 1014 sent its rank-and-file activists to the University of Illinois for a week each summer for union education. In the second row are three of his radical coworkers: Chris "Cash" Malis (second from left), Sylvester Palmer (third from left), and Curtis Strong (fourth from left). Photo courtesy of Fran Malis.

nomination, because people knew me. I grew up in Gary; everybody knew me. Reluctantly, I said OK." Howard won the vice presidency that year and for the next eight years. He was able to play a very outspoken and visible role in many of the struggles that took place in the union and in Gary in the postwar period—from the 1945 Froebel School strike against integration to the movement to integrate Gary's main beach at Marquette Park. Howard ignored the first outbreak of cold war red-baiting and continued to support the program and activities of the left.[41]

Howard did not want to be seen as the "black vice president," as a token vice president. He went out of his way to demonstrate his competence and authority. He inserted himself into the grievance procedure and would call supervision directly when members came to him with unresolved complaints. At one point, Mayerick was going to be away and recommended that Howard cancel a regularly scheduled union meeting. Mayerick knew there were white men who would challenge Howard at the meeting. Howard refused to cancel, and confidently prepared for battle. When he opened the meeting, a number of white workers in the front continued talking loudly; one had kept his hat on in the hall.

I opened the meeting, requesting, "Would the brother with his hat on, please take it off." He ignored me, so I said, "I'm going to ask you one more time to take your hat off." When he didn't move, I called for the inner and outer guard to lead the brother out of the hall. As they approached him, the brother took that hat off his head. Then I had another guy feign drunkenness, a guy who was working his way through Valparaiso Law School. He kept trying my hand on parliamentary procedure. Well, he ended up apologizing. Another member came forward afterward and told me I was a first-class person, that I handled the meeting better than Mayerick.

As vice president, Howard represented the local in many community coalitions, especially on issues dealing with race. In 1945, during his first term, a racial strike erupted at his alma mater, Froebel School. President Mayerick sent Howard to the Gary Unity Council, the organization created to fight the parents and students who backed the strike.[42] Howard started as vice president of that organization and the following year became president. The Froebel strike was triggered in part by a policy that allowed blacks, for the first time, to sign up for swimming, band, and orchestra.[43] Under Howard's leadership, the Steelworkers maintained a strong presence throughout the campaign, even though many striking parents were also union members.

Howard welcomed public exposure, and the radical groups behind many of the rallies and marches welcomed his presence. He spoke at antilynching rallies, helped organize a Paul Robeson concert in Gary, and spoke strongly in favor of Henry Wallace's presidential campaign.[44] Most African Americans continued to support Henry Wallace's candidacy, long after the CIO withdrew its endorsement. Henry Wallace, a long-time New Dealer, had served as FDR's vice president in the forties until the southern Democrats, known as Dixiecrats, knocked him off the ballot in 1944 for his strong stand on civil rights. Although Harry S. Truman and Henry Wallace differed on many political points around foreign policy and the cold war, it was Wallace's advocacy of civil rights that won him loyalty among black activists. Paul Robeson's active participation in the Wallace campaign certainly influenced Howard.[45]

A year later, in 1949, John Howard took on an important role in the Beachhead for Democracy struggle to integrate Marquette Park beach on Gary's lakefront. Mainstream papers denounced this campaign as a red plot. The Communist Party did take a leading role, but the Urban League and the CIO were also involved.

Howard described himself as the hero of one very publicized action. The Beachhead for Democracy group planned a march on Marquette Park in late August 1949, followed by an integrated swim, as a response to confrontations between black families and white teenagers. The previous day, African American militant Ted Vaughan from Local 1066, Sheet and Tin, had been attacked when he entered the lake. As vice president of 1014, Howard asked all the black grievers, including Curtis Strong, Oris Thomas, Joe Carlisle, and Sylvester Palmer, to join him for a swim. Howard claimed that only Strong showed up and that when they got to the beach house, Strong begged off, claiming his trunks were too tight. (Curtis Strong, of course, told a different story.)

Howard plunged alone into the deep and was soon confronted by a rowdy group of white bathers. Howard did not retreat. According to his account, when he emerged from the water, local beachcombers offered him a towel and a sandwich. In reality, those two locals were left activists Chris and Fran Malis, primary organizers of the event. Again the mainstream papers called the action "communist-inspired."[46] An editorial in the black-owned *Gary American* noted, "We do not know whether the sponsoring group is communist, socialist, progressive, liberals or what they are, but we are certain that the movement is a step in the right direction." It took another few years of agitation before the beach was integrated.

Mainstreaming His Image

When John Howard lost the election for vice president of the local in 1955, he blamed the African American activists in charge of the recently formed black caucus, the Eureka Club. Curtis Strong, Arthur Adams, and Sylvester Palmer created the Eureka Club in 1952 as a black power base. They believed that without organization, blacks could not exercise any political power in the local or in the city of Gary. Neither John Howard nor George Kimbley trusted Strong and his cohorts; they opposed the idea of separate black organization designed to build political leverage within the local. Kimbley thought it would upset the white-black unity in the union. Howard understood that it was a political instrument to advance a set agenda, but it was not his agenda. Howard believed, for example, that promotions in the union belonged to the most qualified, not the most organized or the most senior. He resented the group's maneuvering, which left him out in the cold.

When it came to promotions in the mill, most African Americans agreed on seniority as the determinative factor. In the union, however, claims of competence vied with seniority, and African Americans who could advance more quickly individually wanted to protect that option. This kind of stepping "out of turn" angered other African Americans, who did not think determinating competence should be left up to the union's white leadership. They argued that some African Americans courted white acceptance in exchange for appointments. These differences opened the door to bitter competition and divisions among black activists. These men, so uniformly committed to the union, fought each other from this point on for the few positions held out to them by the union leadership.[47]

In his account of the controversial 1955 election, Howard explained, "Mayerick usually ran unopposed, whereas I had challengers. The competition between me and an opponent brought out more votes for me. Strong argued that since I was getting more votes than Mayerick, I should run against him [Mayerick]. I was satisfied with the vice presidency, and said no." Howard then explained that Strong went ahead and told Mayerick that Howard planned to run against him. "Strong went behind my back. So I ran." Howard's logic is hard to understand, because he did not have to run for president and could have easily stepped down at any point. Nonetheless, Howard held Strong responsible for his defeat. Strong ended up supporting Oris Thomas for vice president on the opposition slate, and Mayerick decided to support a white, Joe Chestovich, as his running mate. "Joe became the first white vice president of Local 1014," added Howard bitterly.[48]

Johnnie Howard and Curtis Strong saw most things differently and had already had a number of fallings-out. Howard had always remained on the sidelines of the Eureka Club because of his suspicion of segregated organizations. He felt double-crossed by the club's leadership after the election fiasco. "I was a charter member of the Eureka Club," he said. "It was a means of drawing [African American] people together, from the east to the west end of the plant. We all became acquainted, socialized together, and talked about our problems. The purpose was to aid and abet minority workers seeking better jobs." Howard withdrew when "some people in the leadership wanted to make it a political organization and run for municipal elections. I was disappointed," he explained, "because I thought it should work to improve our status on the job site." In Howard's view, leading caucus members advocated separate organization in order to promote themselves. He resented what he described as manipulation by the caucus. "The way they put it, 'we decide who the next black to go on staff; we decide who the next black to go there, we decide.' Well, I don't buy that. I didn't buy that. I don't know who in the hell made them kingmakers and kingkillers! They would use the influence of an organization to either make a person or kill a person." Howard was directing his anger at Curtis Strong in particular.[49]

After Howard lost the vice presidency, the local leadership ran him in the Calumet Township Advisory Board elections, which launched Howard's own political career. It would not be long before the USWA district leadership would select John Howard for a staff position. When George Kimbley announced his upcoming retirement in 1958, the political sparring began among black activists. According to Howard, his subdistrict director, Joe Goin, took him aside one day and told him that District Director Joe Germano wanted to see him down at the district office. A few days later Goin repeated the message, and Howard decided to make the trip over to East Chicago.

" 'Come on in,' Germano told me. 'Take a seat. You know that Kimbley's retiring, don't you?' " Howard nodded affirmatively. " 'Why haven't you made application? Aren't you interested in being on staff?' 'Sure,' I said. 'I've been working all these years with the hope that eventually I could get on staff.' " Then, according to Howard, Germano pulled three long sheets of paper out of his top drawer to show Howard, saying, "President McDonald sent me copies." Howard described them as legal-size petitions with about 150 names, each one calling for a different African American to take Kimbley's place:

> "We the undersigned want Curtis Strong and not John Howard to be staff. We want Oris Thomas and not John Howard. Sylvester Palmer and not John Howard." According to Germano, President McDonald asked, "Who the hell is this John Howard guy?" Germano told him I was the guy at the Philadelphia Convention in 1952 who gave the Community Services presentation. McDonald immediately told Germano that he wanted John Howard for Kimbley's position.

Howard chuckled when he added, "To this day, Curtis Strong, Sylvester Palmer, Oris Thomas don't know how I got on staff!"[50]

A Union Man to the End

When John L. Howard was appointed to the District 31 staff in 1958, he had been an assistant griever for thirteen years, a vice president for nine, chairman of the Community Services Committee for six years and a Calumet Township Assessor since 1954. Unlike his predecessor, George Kimbley, Howard had years of union experience when he was hired onto staff. He had used his position as vice president to intervene in settling grievances and had taken responsibility for running the local. Howard characterized the two African Americans who preceded him as vice presidents at USWA 1014, Ellis Cochran and Henry Johnson, as "ceremonial." He saw Kimbley in the same way. When Howard accepted Germano's offer, he made it clear he wanted real responsibility, not just status and a paycheck like the black staff before him.[51]

Reflecting on the union's role in bringing fairness to steelworkers, Howard used the term "marvelous." He meant literally that it had been a marvel; the steelworkers union had transformed the steel mills and communities of northwest Indiana in his lifetime. It had also transformed Howard himself. His personal achievements as a union leader and staff representative confirmed his belief in the American dream. Howard saw his own life as proof that his generation had conquered institutional barriers, not only for African Americans but for the working class as a whole.

Toward the end of his union career, Howard became somewhat disillusioned by changes in the union, ranging from the conviction of Local 1014 officers for embezzlement to what he saw as the indifference of younger black workers. He never was able to understand the commercialization of life, the union, and basic principles. The union, he reasoned, should not be driven by market laws or personal ambition.

John Howard stood for individual integrity and the rights of all workers. He always characterized himself as a servant of the downtrodden, the left out, and the underdogs of society. He had grown up in the class-conscious milieu of the CIO and would always believe that solidarity meant "black and white, unite!"

CHAPTER 4

"Get Your Horses"

Curtis Strong

"**A** little firestorm" is how one of Curtis Strong's coworkers described him. "He'd go out front and fight and fight and fight. He'd start it, and we'd end it up!"[1] More than any of his steel mill peers, Curtis Strong proudly wore the label of rabble-rouser. He was quick to anger, quick to denounce, and always willing to stick his neck out and take the heat. His black peers viewed him as everything from a hero to a demon. He aroused strong emotions, because once he set his mind to something, he advanced—in fact—like a firestorm.

Curtis Strong still has the tall, lanky build of an athlete. In high school, he was the track, basketball, and football star. He was popular with his teammates and with the girls. His self-confidence always carried with it more than a touch of arrogance. Strong stood out among his peers in high school. Not only was he gifted and outspoken but he was one of only a handful of African Americans in Dixon, Illinois, where Strong grew up in the 1920s. Dixon was a small town in northern Illinois, with a southern culture and maybe a hundred black residents out of ten thousand people. "Very small black community," Curtis mused. "Most of us were related."[2]

Curtis Strong normally spends little time reminiscing. Still enmeshed in Gary politics and union intrigue, Strong has no time for the past. Although his memory often fails him on dates, he recalls the tumultuous events of his life down to the details. He painted clear and dramatic images of his "outlaw" union life. He was—and still is—an infidel and a rebel. Strong instigated walkouts and wildcats, local and national protests. He battled with words and fists, depending on the situation. At the 1956 Steelworkers Con-

Curtis Strong's high school graduation picture, Dixon, Illinois, 1933. Photo courtesy of Curtis Strong.

vention in Los Angeles, Strong was thrown out of his third-floor hotel window by a couple of "union goons" for his leadership among dues protestors.[3] During the hotly contested race between I. W. Abel and David McDonald for International president in 1965, Strong spent a night behind bars with his local's ballot box. He described these rough times with a sense of pride. In our many conversations, he alternated between reliving and reflecting on his past. Only recently has he taken more time to think about the impact of his actions over the years. He has few regrets when he looks back over the choices he made.

Despite his eighty-eight years, Strong still likes a good fight, whether it involves getting his church to support labor or getting his union to stand up against the Klan. He is an outspoken member and vice president of his local chapter of the Steelworkers Organization of Active Retirees (SOAR), a leader in his church and in various community and civil rights organizations, and a mentor and agitator among younger generations of steelworkers. "Damn the cost of speaking out," he declared passionately.

As a result of his intense involvement, Curtis Strong has been labeled an opportunist, a black nationalist, and even a Mussolini[4] by union leaders and coworkers, African Americans included. Strong, of course, was no slacker in handing out labels to those who disagreed with him: "Oh, he was an Uncle Tom," Curtis proclaimed, characterizing one of the pioneer black leaders of his union. "That one," he said in reference to another coworker, "he was a black hillbilly and a quisling." In response to my raised eyebrows, though, he added, "Maybe I was a bit quick to judge people." After hesitating, he confided, "But I was young, hard drinking and a rebel. I had had it with 'colored brother' this or that. I wasn't no 'colored brother.' "[5] "Looking back over it," he commented, "I often wonder why blacks take so damn much of that before they rebel. I realize, though, that we had been conditioned for untold number of years that you did have a place."

Strong inherited what he called his "father's low tolerance for discrimina-

Curtis Strong ran for Gary city councilman when he was in his forties. This was his campaign photo. He lost the election. Photo courtesy of Curtis Strong.

tion." He was not used to closed doors and limited opportunities. "I would speak out. . . . I know now it sometimes wasn't the right thing to do. It didn't pay off sometimes. But, you couldn't look in the mirror if you let something go unsaid or done."

The Strong family had a long history of challenging traditional attitudes and practices, although Curtis did not talk much about his family until I asked him for photographs, more than fifteen years after our first interview. He mentioned a family portrait hanging on his bedroom wall, and I expressed great interest in seeing it. He retrieved a beautiful and carefully posed family portrait from 1918, with his parents flanked by the first five of seven children. Sit-

Curtis Strong at a meeting of the Steelworkers Organization of Active Retirees at his union hall, Local 1014 in Gary, 2001. Photo courtesy of Ruth Needleman.

ting straight and proud, his father looked out over a thin nose and drooping mustache. "Your father's white?" I asked, thinking that perhaps he was one of the many blacks who could pass easily for white. "Oh yes!" Strong nodded. "My father's grandfather was a big plantation owner and owned all of my mother's family back in slavery."

For the next hour or more Curtis Strong charted his family history with me. His father, Scott Strong, and Scott's two sisters and brother had interracial marriages. Curtis's grandfather's sister, Corey, married a black man in her third marriage. Scott's brother married Eliza, also descended from family-owned slaves. According to Curtis, in Westpoint, Mississippi, mixed marriages happened all the time. The Strong family just had no tolerance for racism.

The Beginnings of an Attitude

Curtis Strong was born in Westpoint, Mississippi, in 1915. His mother died in Saint Louis when he was four; his father had moved the family there for economic reasons. After her death, the family moved to Dixon, Illinois, where Scot Strong's aunt lived.[6] Scot Strong found a decent-paying job in a construction plant soon after the family arrived. Curtis Strong's stepmother, a nurse, cared for a Spanish American war veteran. A few blacks in Dixon were homeowners; they lived in the southern, working-class part of town. "You had integration on the South Side," Strong recalled, "but not on the North Side." Although the Klan was popular in town, Strong had few run-ins with racism. He remembered attending KKK rallies with his elementary school buddies; it was, he said, "just a parade."

Given his athletic stardom, Strong "had the run of the town." His high school girlfriend was white. "We didn't realize how discriminatory the town was," Curtis added. "I use to pick up my girlfriend at her house, which was a no-no for a black to pick up a white girl." Occasionally an opposing sports team refused to play against his school because of Strong's participation, but his team members wouldn't play without him. They resorted to hand-to-hand combat with the other team. Strong was confident, assertive, and smart. He knew about discrimination, read books and the *Chicago Defender*, and had joined the Rockville youth branch of the NAACP, forty-two miles north of town. But in his own early life, he had always gone after what he wanted and got it, until he entered the job market.

"I got such a raw deal when I was kid," remarked Strong, referring not to his school years or to the Great Depression but rather to his first encounter with Jim Crow segregation in the job market. He had his heart set on being a pilot. When his high school counselor explained that he could not be a pilot, because the air force had no facilities for black recruits, Strong was

Family portrait, c. 1918. Curtis Strong's parents, Scott and Fanny Lee, are seated on the couch. Children, from left to right: Fanny, Scott Jr., Curtis, Lawrence, and Lee (standing). Curtis's youngest siblings, Kate and Arch, had not yet been born. Photo courtesy of Curtis Strong.

shaken. "It was a hell of a shock. . . . I had a teacher who tried to soften the blow. He tried to get me to go to Tuskegee, but I didn't want to be a farmer or a carpenter or a mechanic or anything. I wanted to be a pilot. That was quite a shock."

The depression did not immediately affect Strong. Although his father lost his job, his mother kept working. An older brother and sister were already employed in Gary. "There were no protests in Dixon," Strong recalled. Neither was there any township relief or welfare. When the war veteran his mother had cared for died, "that took away the breadwinner." Curtis went out looking for a job in Dixon. The only work he could find was as a bellhop at the local hotel. According to Strong, he couldn't "stand having to be subservient to anyone. I didn't want to carry anybody's suitcase. I wanted them to carry mine! . . . Menial work," he explained, "was just not my cup of tea."

Shortly after graduation, in the mid-1930s, Curtis Strong joined his brother and sister in Gary. He had spent summers in Gary before and liked being in an African American community. "I couldn't wait to find a girl-friend," he said, laughing. He moved in with his sister and planned to return to school, still hoping to become a pilot. His brother Lee Strong worked at U.S. Steel's Sheet and Tin and helped him get his first mill job. Lee was a union rep with the new SWOC Lodge 1066 when Curtis Strong hired into the Sheet and Tin Mill in 1937. Lee warned Curtis in no uncertain terms that unless he signed a union card, his "brothers" would not allow him to work. Reluctantly, he signed, but Curtis Strong didn't believe unions had ever done much for the black worker. "The union was highly discrimina-tory," he observed, "and although you had unions, blacks could not belong to certain unions. When they organized the AFL, way back then, blacks were not a part of them. So you had this 'anti' feeling. Sure you knew the com-pany was wrong . . . but you're going to have to take on the union to take on the company. No sooner than you beat the company in line, then the next thing is they're going to kick the blacks out. That was the history of the labor movement."

Strong's first job in the mill was as a tin opener. "The sheets of tin were rolled in four to eight layers. The sheets had to be rolled hot to certain lengths and sizes," he explained, "and then we opened them up [separated them]. Back then it was a comparatively good-paying job," and available to blacks. The department had blacks, Greeks, and Mexicans. Mexicans held the worst jobs in general labor. In the rolling mill, blacks were laborers and openers. Greeks were shear men and shear helpers, but the rollers," Strong stressed, "were all WASP." As the war in Europe shifted production toward weapons, the Sheet and Tin cut back production in light-gauge steel. Strong worked in light gauge, supplying steel for refrigerators, but there was more money in arms. It was 1939. Strong was bumped back to labor and put on a three- to four-day workweek. He quit and found a job in a munitions plant, losing recall rights at the mill.

Strong married Willa Dean in 1939, less than two years after he arrived in Gary. Together they had three children in three years, two girls and a boy. In 1941, Strong's wife died of pneumonia, and he was raising three children alone. He decided to leave the munitions plant in 1943 and returned to U.S. Steel. This time he sought out work in the coke plant at Gary Works with the clear intention of becoming an activist. He knew if a black man were to be elected to union office, it would be in the coke plant.

"Fight Our Way to Acceptance"

Strong remembered entering the coke plant during the war. "My first day I said, 'To hell with this.' Can you imagine you pull a lid off of an oven, lid about the size of a dining room table? You get flame thirty feet up in the air—an explosion. It was hot. It was dirty. It was unhealthy. It was unsafe. But it was my choice. I mean I decided to go there, because I wanted to be in union leadership." African Americans had some voice in the coke plant, because they held most of the worst jobs on top of the batteries, a line of fiery ovens where coke was forged. There was no ventilation and no safety equipment—no masks, safety clothing, or protective shoes. On the battery, Curtis noted:

> You were charging cold coal into a hot oven and shit comes back up and all that coal dust, whew, and you had the gases. All this was hard on the lungs. And breathing that coal dust, that's hard on the lungs. The heat itself was a killer. People would fall out. You work in the summertime; it's one hundred degrees out in town, two hundred degrees on top of the battery. It just wasn't fit for humans to work in.

Strong had friends in the coke plant, and they saw a chance to organize an opposition. "The blacks were getting the shaft," he said. "The leadership we had at the time with the exception of two men, or maybe three, weren't speaking out. They were willing to accept the status quo. I couldn't see that. I couldn't see in the coke plant where a white man should be a Grievance Committeeman."[7] There were other experienced African Americans in the coke plant who had already come to similar conclusions, in particular a veteran activist named Arthur Adams. Adams was a fighter and a philosopher, according to Curtis. Philosophically, he was a Marxist, and had worked earlier with the left-led Mine, Mill and Smelters Union. He became Strong's mentor on the job.[8]

"[Arthur Adams] had a lot to do with shaping my ideas. He was left as all get out, but he educated me on it. We realized that whites are not going to treat you right, and that we're going to fight our way to acceptance. First you have to start with the union," Strong stated, "and then you realize it's the capitalist system. Maybe I shouldn't use that term," he added with a grin, "but it was the capitalist system that was anti-union and antiblack."

> We needed a union because the working class was being exploited. No question about it. And given the conditions under which we worked, a union was a necessity. But the company wasn't going to give in to you, unless you united in a force. Now that wasn't the end. As far as I'm concerned, that was just the beginning. Some blacks thought it was the end, and that's what made us so mad at the blacks.

Strong was referring to the continuing battle among African Americans over whether or not separate black organization was necessary in the union.

A number of the earliest African American SWOC members, such as John Spillers, Jacob Blake, Pat Riley, and John Howard, cautioned against all-black caucuses, although they supported special work among African Americans. Pat Riley, along with Johnny Howard, had forced a wildcat in 1943 at the long-bar storage area to get the first black crane man in the mill. Many thought that, once the union had accepted blacks in leadership or on staff, the need for separate organization no longer existed. The left at USWA 1014, in contrast to the left in 1010, the "red local," did not oppose the black caucus concept; they supported it and took leadership from black activists such as Strong and Adams.[9]

"We got to be friends," explained Strong. "Adams was older and more experienced. We would talk for hours and hours, just discussing different philosophies. You know at that age you think you know things, so you sit down and discuss philosophy, and how blacks had suffered." Adams convinced Strong that there were allies among progressive white workers, and that they had to build alliances within the local. Under Adams's tutelage, Strong transformed his outrage and impatience into a strategy for activism. Strong agreed that an integrated union was essential, but he never assumed a white-led union would fight for African American workers. He and Adams advocated independent black organization as a prerequisite to building alliances and sharing power with white-dominated groups within the union.

"*We* had to coalesce first," Strong said with great emphasis. "If the other side is stronger than you, to hell with coalescing. Coalesce as equals or you don't coalesce." This was the fundamental lesson to be observed in any interracial organizing, according to Strong. Many years of effective coalition building confirmed the viability of his approach. "My philosophy was that we will organize blacks and then we will coalesce with the whites, but if we go into the black and white together, unless we have strength, we'll always be at the bottom."

The coke plant, with the largest concentration of black workers, became a focus for the struggle for black rights. Shortly after Strong arrived in the coke plant in 1943, Arthur Adams and he spearheaded the formation of a black group known as the Sentinel League. Adams was president; Strong, secretary, with Denver Lee and James Scott as the other two officers. "We were all coke plant. We got together so we could elect us a griever," Strong recalled, chuckling.

When Strong hired in, George Morphus, a white skilled worker, was griever in the coke plant. When Morphus went on staff, he appointed Moses Brown as the first black union rep in the department. Brown always held his ground against the company but lacked education. He would wave the contract in the foreman's face and beat on the desk, but he had someone else write up his grievances. According to most of his peers, Brown was a great union man. According to Strong, his lack of education made him too dependent on white workers. Strong wanted that job for someone more educated, namely, himself. When Brown retired in 1952, Curtis Strong ran and was elected griever in the coke plant, with the support of the Sentinel League. His opponent was also African American.[10] Curtis would retain this position for the rest of his years in the mill, and would be elected to higher office as well because of this power base.

The Sentinel League did not present itself as a political lobby at first. It followed in the tradition of earlier mutual aid societies; it became a support system in hard times and a center for card playing, drinking, and talking. Every Friday night, the Sentinel League sponsored social get-togethers. "We were young and wild," said Strong. "We drank and talked and got to know each other." According to Strong, "You cannot organize and work with people you do not know. Our first organizing steps were carried out on a social basis."[11]

From the beginning, however, the *leaders* of the Sentinel League had a specific political agenda: to gain control of the union in the coke plant, and then to use the coke plant as a base from which to win power in the local. They demonstrated remarkable skill.[12] Strong emphasized the value of trust in speaking to a group of active steelworkers in 1996. Awed at his success at bringing people together, a woman electrician from Inland asked, "How did you do it? How did you get people to work together?" "It takes time," Strong responded. "You can't trust someone you don't know. You gotta get to know each other first; socialize together. When was the last time you had lunch with the white brother there or your black sister over here?" Strong inquired, pointing to other steelworkers in the room.

In the Sentinel League, joking over cards developed into strategizing over union elections. From the coke ovens, the organization grew, by the early 1950s, into a plantwide caucus, known as the Eureka Club. African Americans from other departments joined, and a base for "coalescing with whites" unionwide took shape. "We thought this over," Strong recounted. "When we sat down, [Al] Dority, [Sylvester] Palmer, [James] Ward, [Ben] Coleman, and others, we thought this over for months. How do we win? The only way you can win is to take over this damned local. The only way you're going to take this local over is to have a black base. So we got a black base, took over and integrated the local." The Eureka Club met in Gary on the first Saturday of each month. The connections that were built lasted for lifetimes. The Eureka Club still holds regular meetings in Gary.

"We took the position," Curtis continued, "that if other groups were going to get together, for example, the Poles in a Polish National Association, then there should be a Black National Association. There was always a group of us. It wasn't Curtis Strong by himself." Strong's belief in independent black organization within the union set him apart from many others. "That was where [Walter] Mackerl and I differed, [George] Kimbley and I differed. [John] Howard opposed it. . . . Jake [Jacob Blake] and me were from different schools. . . . That's why we differed from the NAACP, too." Nonetheless, almost every black activist went to Eureka Club meetings—to be part of it, to keep tabs on Curtis and the caucus, or to stay off their enemy list.[13]

With the support of his activist base, Strong was elected division chair in the coke plant in the late 1940s. There were thirteen divisions in the mill, and each had a Grievance Committeeman and a division chair. The chair conducted all the meetings; the griever handled workplace problems. Many African Americans had more education than the immigrants and were tapped for positions, such as chair, that required writing skills. In the largely white merchant mill, for example, African American Oris Thomas was selected division chair in the late 1940s.

Despite the concentration of black workers in the coke plant, the jobs were completely segregated. There were five or six seniority units within the division, each with its own closed promotional sequence. There were white jobs, immigrant jobs, and black jobs. "Maintenance was a seniority unit," explained Strong.

> That was a no-no as far as blacks were concerned. The heating department on the coke batteries was a no-no for blacks. Distillation was a seniority unit; that was a no-no. Then you had parts of coal producing, where they brought the coal in from the mine and started pulling it into the coke plant. It had to be processed before they put it on the batteries. Now that was an integrated unit with the exception of three jobs: bridge crane operator, dumper, and one other. They were all white.[14]

The seniority units were set up so that a worker could not move from one to another. Blacks were assigned to the lowest-paying, more-dangerous units and could never promote to the better jobs in other seniority units.[15] Strong remembered bitterly that, when he challenged the segregation through a grievance, even his union president told him, "Now Curtis, you know that's a white man's job." "White man's job" was not part of Strong's vocabulary; when he heard it, his father's low tolerance for discrimination kicked in. "There's no such goddamned thing as a white man's job, and I'm not your colored brother!" His coworker, Sylvester Harris, had bid on the crane man's job, and when the president rebuffed Strong, Harris had to hold Strong off the president.

"Primarily," Strong said, "the way we broke down discrimination in the coke plant was we had wildcats. Blacks walked out. Whites walked out too. Although it was the dirtiest, the coke plant was the most important department in the mill." Curtis Strong understood power and that it took power to

The Eureka Club, c. 1962. Top row, left to right: Curtis Strong, Oris Thomas, unidentified, Hubert Dawson, Sylvester Palmer (second from right), and W. B. Brown (far right). Bottom row, left to right: Albert Campbell, unidentified, Fordrey Cody, and Henderson Majors. Photo courtesy of Curtis Strong.

make change. "Without coke and gas, you couldn't operate the rest of the plant. At that time, [U.S. Steel] made their own gas; the blast furnaces ran on coke gas, and without it you couldn't operate the open hearth. Even the rolling mills relied on coke gas. When we shut down the coke plant, we shut down Gary Works. Even the city depended on coke plant gas. It gave us quite a lever."[16]

Curtis Strong took advantage of this leverage often. The first wildcat he took part in during the war, in October 1943, before he became griever, "was purely racial." The way he remembered it, a black female employee, Lillian Crawford, went into the canteen for food; a white female worker called her a "black bitch," triggering a fight. The foreman fired Crawford and "told the other girl to go about her work. When the word hit the batteries, all the blacks walked off."[17] They waited in the segregated washhouse for the next shift to arrive and told them what had happened. The men on that shift then refused to work, and waited for the eleven o'clock crew to arrive so that they could pass on the information. "The company offered to go out and bring her back on midnights," Strong continued. "By then the rest of Gary Works was shut down. The midnight turn said, 'we didn't shut it down, the day turn shut it down, so you deal with the day turn. We're not going back to work unless the day turn goes back.' " Everything went back to normal once the day shift showed up in the early morning.

Well-Planned Actions

According to Strong, there is no such thing as a spontaneous action. The caucus had plans, signals, and unity. When the members wanted something done, they'd tell each other, "Get your horses." When Strong needed a wildcat to convince the superintendent to negotiate, he stood at one end of the coke batteries, removed his hard hat, and walked down the line. Work stopped.

In the late 1950s, Strong used this dramatic action to integrate maintenance jobs in the coke plant and to give plant workers preference over new hires. To control job assignments and maintain segregated units, the company relied on its Virginia Street hiring office, which used a special number coding to identify the race of applicants. If the coke plant needed men for an apprenticeship, the superintendent called Virginia Street, indicated the job title and class, and the hiring office would send an "appropriate" worker. For maintenance, it sent only white applicants. Apprenticeships in the mill represented a bridge to the skilled trades, the best jobs with the best pay. An apprentice would receive extensive training as an electrician or a millwright, for example. For the majority of white as well as black workers, these programs constituted the most valuable opportunity for advancement. When the mill hired someone off the street, all the mill workers lost out.

Curtis Strong was determined to stop this practice. On a selected day he walked into the coke plant office and made his position clear. He insisted that U.S. Steel allow coke plant employees to apply for apprenticeship openings before any new hires could be called in. When the superintendent refused, as Strong knew he would, Strong stalked out of the office, pulled off his hard hat, and began the long walk down the batteries. The men stopped working. As a result of the protest, for the first time, workers in the coke plant were allowed to bid on craft jobs and apprenticeships and were considered before new hires. Both white and black workers had scored a victory for fairness, long before the union won bidding and promotion rights across seniority units contractually.[18]

There was no question that independent black organization created the power that drove workplace and union change at Gary Works and at USWA Local 1014. It also made rank-and-file accountability possible. Strong was accountable to the men who had elected him; he held his position only as long as he represented their interests. He could snub his nose at the leadership and the status quo, when he judged them wrong or racist, and still get reelected. In contrast, most African Americans in positions of authority in the union served at the behest of and reported to the higher-ups. White caucus leaders slated them for certain positions, and their job was to represent the union's majority views to their black constituency. The security of their positions depended on their organizational loyalty.[19] They served as tokens, regardless of their skills and seniority. "The blacks they would put on the slates," observed Oliver Montgomery, a black labor leader out of Youngstown, Ohio, "were not active in the movement; they weren't active in the struggle. They were people that we usually didn't agree with and they were fighting us as much as they were fighting the company."[20]

When Strong got out of line, at the local or later on at the International, the white leaders went to the African American above him to complain, and then that black leader passed the reprimand on to Strong. "I never aspired for the vice presidency. I never aspired to be president. I never wanted a full-time job. I wanted to be second."[21] According to Strong, it was always preferable to "go under some other black." It allowed more elbowroom. His secondary position turned out to be a form of job protection. His relative autonomy from the union leadership was a constant source of aggravation to the United Steelworkers' hierarchy. He was feared and hated; but he was also respected, because he could not be controlled from the top.

Support Systems and Radical Alliances

The great challenge was to win the support of mainstream white and ethnic workers. Strong succeeded in getting broad support in the coke plant, because he delivered results. When he challenged the company on discrimination, he fought for the rights of every worker in the department. When he stopped the company's practice of placing new hires off the street into apprenticeship positions in the coke plant, he opened up opportunities for all department workers. When he put a stop to favoritism in job assignments and promotions, and demanded respect for seniority, white workers as well as blacks received fairer treatment. He was rarely challenged as griever and became a top vote getter in localwide elections. Workers who claimed to hate him for his arrogance and bully tactics voted for him nonetheless.

Strong did not give all the credit to black organization. "You have to remember" he stressed, "we're talking about a time when we had some extreme leftists in the plant. We had some members of the [Communist] Party in the plant, and progressives. Back then we had a saying: 'Black plus white makes red!' Because I had a white man as my assistant [griever]," Strong added, "one of us had to be a communist!" Al Samter, the assistant, was militant and outspoken, like Strong. Samter had hired into Gary Works in 1948

Curtis Strong and Jeannette Buchanan at a USWA constitutional convention, c. 1956. Photo courtesy of Curtis Strong.

and by 1952 had teamed up with Strong. He had been a union activist in New York, accustomed to interracial union work. As a young jazz enthusiast, Samter had spent endless hours at music spots in Harlem. One of his first friends in Gary was Jacob Blake, who played the saxophone when he wasn't organizing in the mill. Samter supported and often followed the lead of the Eureka Club.

Al Samter understood that black rights stood at the heart of working-class issues. When the International tried to force Strong to dismiss Samter, who had been called before the Gary House Un-American Activities Committee (HUAC), Strong refused.[22] If someone was willing to "walk the walk," Strong walked with him. In the late 1960s, Al Samter would be the first white candidate to run for local union vice president under an African American presidential candidate, William "Buddy" Todd. Strong considered Samter and other union radicals to be "natural allies."

Besides having the Eureka Club at work, Strong had an equally important support system at home. After the war, Strong had begun regular visits to the union hall, where he met Jeannette Buchanan. Buchanan was the first African American woman on the office staff of Local 1014 and served as a CIO convention delegate as early as 1944.[23] In Strong's words, "She knew more about organizing than I ever did." Her father had been an early leader

Curtis Strong helped pack groceries for the NAACP to deliver to a tent city in Tennessee during a southern voter registration drive in the mid-1960s. Photo courtesy of Curtis Strong.

in the Gary community, including in the Gary chapter of the Universal Negro Improvement Association (UNIA). She grew up with Marcus Garvey's message of black pride and attended the large, working-class rallies and events held in Gary in the 1920s.[24] Jeannette was a union member as well as office secretary. When she ran for convention delegate in the 1940s, "she led the ticket." Jeannette was even more involved in civil rights activities in the community. She became the president of Gary's NAACP, then of the Indiana State NAACP, and served on the National Executive Board. Respected as one of Gary's most effective civil rights leaders, Jeannette Buchanan could bring people together and set them into action.[25]

"I kept going out to the union hall because she [Jeannette] was there, and she kept me going in the union," Strong admitted. When Jeannette and Curtis married, their home became a civil rights think tank. Strong might have been one of the boys out in the mill, but he rarely made a decision without talking it over with Jeannette. She imposed long-term strategizing and careful reflection on his rambunctious and unpredictable behavior. Strong viewed their relationship as a political as well as a personal partnership, an advantage shared by few others. They built the NAACP together, walked precincts for political candidates, and went to Mississippi in the 1960s to help with voter registration. Jeannette's advice and wisdom helped build a stable foundation for Curtis's union success. Even today, when people talk about Curtis Strong, they add, "But you should have known Jeannette."

Race and Class: Two Fronts, One Struggle

Perhaps Curtis Strong's greatest strength was his refusal to separate class issues from civil rights issues. The structure and culture of the union promoted an artificial division between race and class issues, a distinction institutionalized throughout society. Unions tended to regard class issues as issues everyone could support, by which they meant ones that concerned the union's majority constituency of white men. The industrial workplace had always been racialized; the skilled jobs were white jobs and the worst ones were for black, Latino, and immigrant workers. The compartmentalization of jobs into separate seniority units preserved the white advantage. Wage classifications shadowed the racial divisions, with a majority of black jobs at the bottom of the scale. Most mills also maintained separate seniority lists for layoffs and recalls. The USWA was effective in eliminating separate seniority lists and took consistently strong public stands against racism in the workplace. But the union balked at confronting the advantages of its white membership. Union democracy reflected a "one man, one vote" standard, which gave the majority the deciding vote every time. Similarly, fair representation reflected majority rule, not diversity.[26]

In the union's early years, all workers claimed to support seniority, but most white workers opposed plantwide seniority in favor of unit or departmental seniority, in order to protect their cleaner, better-paying status. They would label black groups as divisive if they organized around what were considered to be "their own issues." The union, in contrast, never criticized craft workers for holding separate meetings for electricians, pipe fitters, or machinists.

Even in their best years, with a clear antidiscrimination program and interracial approach, the CIO unions, including the United Steelworkers, relied on a compartmentalization of race, class, and gender issues. Blacks were hired as organizers but assigned to win the support of black workers. For visibility's sake, African Americans and women often sat on conference welcoming committees and handled community relations. Leadership was committed to including a black at the top at the local level, usually as vice president, but not in the top decision-making circles. Unions opposed lynching and school segregation, fought for equal pay for equal work, and fought for a national Fair Employment Practices Committee, but they rarely challenged job segregation in the workplace. They kept overall control in the hands of white leaders and preached gradualism. Integration for most leading white unionists meant opening the doors to African Americans one at a time.[27] The result was that blacks in leadership often felt compelled to focus on economic issues, and leave civil rights matters to white allies or special committees. Bill Young followed this path.

Unfortunately, Local 1014, just like Local 1010, tended to rationalize certain in-house "traditions." As discussed in chapter 2, Local 1010 had a bar under union headquarters that refused to serve black members until the integrated women's auxiliary forced its integration. At Local 1014 there was the Subway Club, a drinking establishment that drew crowds of union members after every meeting. This tavern was frequently denounced by the *Gary American* newspaper as well as by radical steelworkers. "They drew the line at Negroes in the crowd," reported one very skeptical columnist.[28] He commented on the participation of some white workers, whom he called "a few rocky reformers willing to make the drive on general principle." He viewed the support of "rocky reformers" as an effort by some union stalwarts "to persuade Negroes that the union was good for them." Curtis Strong refused to go along with "traditions" that kept Jim Crow alive.

Efforts to discredit Strong in the union by labeling him a black nationalist never worked, because he had such productive working relationships with white activists.[29] He picked his battles and his allies based on politics and ideology, class politics wrapped in a nationalist philosophy. When members of his black circle ran in elections, he supported those with seniority and experience. But he always made sure blacks were on the ballot. Strong refused to subordinate his interests as an African American to so-called workers' interests in general, because he viewed them as the same. His class interests depended on black liberation, and vice versa.

Strong gave an impression of inflexibility and he was stubborn. Yet, as a strategist, he was extremely resourceful. He could handle contradictory attitudes and practices. For example, he understood the dual nature of his union and its leaders, often schizophrenic about fighting racism. Strong advocated unionism as essential to every working person, yet never overlooked day-to-day discriminatory practices. He embraced the union, fought for leadership, and took advantage of every contract rule and union procedure to better the conditions in the mill for blacks and everyone else.

Curtis Strong made the USWA *his* union and forced it to accept him as he was. He did not relinquish his sense of ownership to the white leadership. He accused many of his black peers of being apologists for the racist leadership, because they echoed the "go-slow, be patient" urgings of those in power. Strong rejected gradualism as a strategy, just as he rejected second-class citizenship for African American steelworkers. Independent black organization, for Strong, was neither a tactic nor a negotiable issue. It was integral to his strategy for building a better union and a just society. "If we fought the company by day, we fought the union by night," he stressed. Strong dismissed those who charged him or any black caucus with dual unionism. He saw himself as loyal to the union. He would not, however, pledge loyalty to individuals who confused their own self-interests with the interests of the union.[30]

It was common for black workers who wanted to be civil rights advocates to focus on legislative or political action work in the union or to join community-based civil rights organizations. Walter Mackerl, for instance, became the first state political action representative for District 31. At Local

1010, with the exception of Bill Young, the African Americans sought control over the Civil Rights Committee and the local NAACP. Strong always did both union and community work in support of workplace and civil rights. He brought his class issues into the NAACP, where he served as chair of the Industry and Labor Council, and he fought racism in the plant and the union as part of the class struggle. His confrontations with the dominant, white caucuses over slating provide an interesting example.

The Eureka Club generally coalesced with the progressive slate in the local. Known as the Green Slate, it included the majority of second-generation immigrants. From the establishment of the SWOC Lodge in 1937, there had been an agreement to slate African Americans, usually in the vice presidential slot. As the Eureka Club grew stronger, it wanted additional slots for black workers and, even more important, felt that the club should get to choose the African Americans for the slate.

Deal making in local politics, especially at 1014, did not always follow agreed-upon rules. In 1962, the Green Slate president, Steve Bazin, crossed the Eureka Club. He had promised a certain number of black appointees in exchange for support for his slate. After the election, he changed his mind. Strong decided that in the next election, the club would support the opposition caucus, predominantly southerners, led by Mark Tencher. Strong referred to them as the rednecks. A few Eureka Club members already leaned toward the Tencher group, seeing it as another avenue for getting slated. Oris Thomas, for example, the USWA 1014 griever in the largely white Merchant Mill, supported the southerners' slate. Strong had labeled Thomas a black hillbilly because of his support of the southerners' caucus. Thomas maintained that he had played middleman in getting the Eureka Club to back Tencher, and in exchange, Tencher had offered him the position of chair of the Grievance Committee.

Strong had his own version of the story. According to him, he initiated the negotiations, and formed an alliance with Tencher in exchange for positions for black steelworkers. Strong said to Tencher, "There will be a black chairman of the Grievance Committee in 1962." Since Oris Thomas had the most seniority, Strong proposed him for the chairmanship. Strong was able to negotiate a number of Executive Board positions, including treasurer, so the Eureka Club went all out for Tencher in the next election, paying back Bazin and the Green Slate in the process. Having lost the election, many of the progressives on the Green Slate accused the Eureka Club of opportunism.

There was always a hefty amount of maneuvering and mudslinging at Local 1014. Strong and the Eureka Club realigned with the progressives, but only after teaching Bazin the importance of honoring an agreement. At the same time, Oris Thomas turned his back on the Eureka Club to keep his position as chair of the Grievance Committee under Tencher. Curtis Strong began calling him quisling instead of black hillbilly. Oris Thomas argued that Strong tried to take credit for everything, and that he, Thomas, had brought Strong and the Eureka Club onto his slate "against their will." "I brokered the deal for the 1962 elections," claimed Thomas. Referring to Strong, he went on: "He's a son of a gun. But I knew how to work with him. You see I got him over on our side . . . and then on my side he was instrumental in getting me elected chairman of the Grievance Committee. I worked with him. I let him go ahead and say what he wanted to say. Not my concern. I'm going to get my little bit in one way or the other if I can go behind in the back and do it. I learned the game of politics."[31] Thomas used the opening to promote himself. Curtis Strong also seized opportunities for himself, but he linked his fortunes more closely to those of the black freedom struggle.

In some situations, such as the Bazin election, Strong found it harder to work with the so-called progressives than the southerners. As he put it:

The foreigners wouldn't give us chairman of the Grievance Committee.[32] They wanted to still consider us "colored brothers." The hillbillies may call you a nigger, but you sit down at the table and deal with them. . . . That's why we worked with the hillbillies. We could sit down at the table and say, "Why are you saying that? It's racial. Well, we can carry as many votes as you can or more." The Polish group had a better philosophy. They were more liberal, when it was dealing with someone else. Just like liberal northerners during the civil rights movement. They go south; they were some hell-fired liberals, but you come to Chicago, "Don't come in my neighborhood."

Strong didn't mind the labels attached to him. "What's wrong with being a nationalist anyway?" he questioned. In demonstrating the Eureka Club's power to exact accountability, Strong played politics and won. Strong did not think it was opportunist to protect black representation in the union. He did argue that it was opportunism on Bazin's part to betray his promise to the caucus. Was Strong self-serving in his flip-flops, or was it Thomas who was self-serving? Or Bazin? Was the Eureka Club nationalist, or was the Green Slate discriminatory?

To the degree that white coworkers, regardless of their philosophy, separated race and class, they were blind to the hypocrisy and contradictions in their policies and practices. They insisted that class unity came first but put attempts to win white support ahead of antiracist issues. Many progressives maintained that the "best interests" of black workers should be identical to their own; if not, they were minority concerns and not really class interests.

That's why, Strong emphasized, "sometimes we had an easier time with the company than we had with the employees, our members."

Strong did not hold grudges against his white allies, but he never forgave Thomas's betrayal. African American unionists on all sides judged and were judged more harshly for their shortcomings. They were, in the end, harshest with each other.

The battles over integrating washrooms demonstrated further some of the contradictions among the progressives. Because of widespread resistance among white workers, the local union tried to avoid taking a stand on integrating the washrooms. Individually many of them supported integration, but they were not willing to risk losing votes in the next election.[33] All the washrooms and shower rooms were segregated, until, as Strong said, "We started raising hell about it, threatened to shut it down."

Strong found his allies among the leftists in the mill, who openly advocated integration in the face of ugly threats and attacks. In many ways, white unionists such as Chris Malis and Al Samter took more heat from white coworkers than Strong did but continued to fight with integrity and courage. Strong confronted the resistance with the antidiscrimination language in the contract. He forced the company to build a new washhouse.

Before then, all byproducts [a particularly unpleasant work department composed mainly of Mexicans and blacks] had their own. The maintenance had their own, and batteries and production had their own, all except the heaters. The heaters went with maintenance, because they were all white. We were raising so much hell they built an all-encompassing bathhouse. When they got ready to assign lockers, I sent one of my assistant grievers to help the company assign lockers.

Strong entrusted the job to Al Samter, who made sure that black and white lockers were interspersed.

In response, according to Strong, the white workers "come down to the union hall and raised hell. But who was going to file their grievances. I was the griever," Curtis explained, laughing with great satisfaction. The reaction was similar when it came to job integration at Gary Works.

When we put the first black in with the pipe fitters, they walked out. The division superintendent called me; I was at the union hall. He said, "We got a problem." Now we had been talking about this situation. He was from Alabama; we got to be fairly good friends. I did him a favor once, and I kept picking up that IOU every chance I got. Anyway, I came on out there, and the [white pipe fitters] were all in the shop. They said they were not going to work. Superintendent said, "What are you going to do with them?" I said, "Fire 'em. Send 'em home. Anyone don't want to work, come get your card. The union says fire you."

All but one returned to work. A similar situation occurred among the machinists. Ironically, in the paint department, the Eureka Club backed off its demand to promote an African American worker. Strong explained: "Eureka ended up dropping the issue. All the workers, including the subforeman, spoke nothing but Greek. How the hell was he goin' to tell this black what to do?" Strong raised his shoulders in a questioning shrug.

Strong used similar tactics to force U.S. Steel to hire black foremen around 1964. "A black foreman at 1010 or 1011 at that time was a no-no," Strong said. "We told them [the company], we'll give you until July 4th to give us a black foreman. If we don't have a black foreman, we'll shut this son of a bitch down! We'll shut her down now just for a trial run. We shut the plant down just to prove that on July 4, this is what was going to happen." Strong made sure he was in Milwaukee on that day. "We were cocky. We were crazy. We had them by the tail. And we twisted them. Maybe we were wrong," added Curtis, "but we integrated."

Black Power—The Ad Hoc Committee

The bridge that carried Curtis Strong from the local to the International was the Ad Hoc Committee, a nationwide black steelworkers caucus that he helped found in 1964. The USWA had taken advantage of good economic times during the 1950s and early 1960s to negotiate long-overdue wage gains and expanded benefits, from pensions and health care to supplemental unemployment pay. But twenty years after the first black was promoted to crane man at Gary Works, almost all the nation's steel mills maintained occupational segregation and discriminatory hiring and placement practices. Most of the craft workers were white, as was most of the union leadership.

Strong recalled a trip he made to Pittsburgh for a rank-and-file meeting. "In that whole valley was only two black maintenance people. Almost no black union leaders." In fact, as Strong remembered it, "We had about twenty-two black employees out of fifteen hundred [on union staff.]"[34] There were no black representatives on the International's Civil Rights Committee and no black leaders on the Executive Board either. With the creation of the Ad Hoc Committee, black workers unionwide moved from informal invitational meetings in hotel rooms, or small caucuses in certain districts, to a national level of mobilization.

It wasn't just the absence of blacks in union leadership that propelled the committee; it was the absence of more democratic representation within the union as a whole. Since its founding under Philip Murray, the United Steel-workers had always been a top-down, centrally ruled union. When Philip Murray died, David McDonald, Murray's personal secretary, took over the presidency. No steelworker had ever headed up the steelworkers union. No International election had ever been seriously contested. And whereas Murray had been a workingman, McDonald wanted to be a Hollywood star. McDonald courted the wealthy, sought out connections with high society, and postured for the media. He wanted to be "discovered." Through periods of major strikes and battles, McDonald was often hard to locate.[35]

The blacks were not alone in building a national network during the sixties. Women began organizing, and a broad rank-and-file organization for union democracy began to form. "One of the ways they controlled blacks and other rank-and-file movements," Strong explained, "was by saying that the union would never be destroyed from without. If it's destroyed, 'it'll be destroyed from within. What you guys are doing is going to destroy the union.' I think," Curtis added, "they used this [argument] against every-body. That's how they kept down rank-and-file movements. That's why you didn't have any big rank-and-file movements before the mid-sixties."[36]

In 1964, with twenty years of black organizing under his belt, Curtis Strong sat down with his peers from around the country, and said, "To hell with you, Junior [McDonald]. Let's form us a group."

CHAPTER 5

"Plain Old-Fashioned Discrimination"

Jonathan Comer

Jonathan Comer went from picking cotton in rural Alabama to the presidency of a large, basic steel local at Youngstown Sheet and Tube, the first African American to hold that position. Although he favored behind-the-scenes persuasion, and conducted his affairs with great dignity, his persistence was legendary. "Me and my big mouth," he joked, shaking his head and laughing. He liked winning his battles with words, but when words failed, he found other means to be heard. "You can always cuss and fuss," he advised, "but that should be the last thing you do." In August 1968, he realized the time had come to raise hell. Jonathan Comer led the first insurgent black power demonstration against the United Steelworkers at their international convention in Chicago.

A tall, slender man with close-cropped white hair, Jonathan Comer seems never to tire. Comer's schedule, which includes early-morning exercise, political and civic meetings, and endless church work, keeps him out and about until late evening. His energy—like his smile and laughter—is contagious. As a young mill worker and union leader, Comer was built more like a farmer, broad and strong. His hair turned white at an early age, setting off his dark complexion and attentive eyes. He still drives a battered car, known as Old Bessie, from one end of the state to the other, as active as ever in the fight for freedom. "We should not forget," he told me, "we are still in the longest struggle."[1]

Growing up in the heart of the black belt South, Comer learned to choose his words carefully. He knew the repercussions for speaking his mind could be severe. "My own mother and father would have killed me. They did that to preserve your life." Comer learned to question the world he was born into, but not out loud. "I wondered why I had to call this young white girl my age 'miss.' I wondered about that, and it bothered me quite a bit, but I dare not say it around my mother and father. I knew which color I was, and I knew what color white people was, but I wanted to know how come society and everybody else felt that they was so much better than I was, or why I was less than human."

By the time Jonathan Comer received an honorable discharge for his World War II service, he had found his voice. From that point on, he could not be silenced—not in the mill, the union, nor the community. "I have to tell it like it is, and let the chips fall where they may," he insisted. His straightforward honesty was disarming. In a recent visit to my labor studies class, Jonathan was asked to comment on the differences between what some leaders say and what they do. "Some folks' actions are so loud," he laughed, "no one even hears what they say."[2]

Comer's actions reflect his character and dedication. Just a year ago, he agreed to head up a special task force to guarantee that construction trades that worked in Gary found room in their union apprenticeship programs for young blacks. Comer continues to play a leading role in the NAACP statewide. Unable to say no, he coordinated the get-out-the vote efforts for the NAACP throughout Indiana during the November 2000 presidential elections. He is deacon of his church and chairs the board responsible for church business. At seventy-eight, still lacking his high school diploma, Comer enrolled part-time in the labor studies program at Indiana University Northwest. Imagine studying social movements with a man who was neck deep in quite a few of them! With a 4.0 grade point average, Comer is working toward a college certificate in labor studies.

Despite more than fifty years living up north, Comer still wears his southernness on his sleeve. His knack for storytelling, always with the drama of a Sunday morning sermon, his never-ending homilies and folk wisdom, and especially his modesty make him irresistible. Even when he delivers a blow, he does it with charm and an apology. Many have disagreed with Comer's views throughout his life, but virtually no one I spoke with saw him as an enemy. He has received awards and honors from labor, civil rights, and community organizations, and in 1995, the governor of Indiana gave him the state's most prestigious honor, the Sagamore of the Wabash Award.[3]

Learning Psychology in the South

"I was born March 21, 1921, in a place called Old Springhill, Alabama; it was known as Comer, after the plantation owners. Our slave masters gave

Jonathan Comer, c. 1970. Photo courtesy of Jonathan Comer.

In front of Jonathan Comer's childhood home in Comer, Alabama, c. 1957: Comer's father, Jesse; his youngest brother, Arthur; and his mother, Beatrice. Photo courtesy of Jonathan Comer.

that name to my people. Compared to other slave owners, well, I guess we were blessed. They weren't as bad as most." The plantation still dominated the farm community of Comer's youth, although his parents had land of their own. His father was a farmer and also ran a country grocery store, filling station, and gristmill. "My mother was a housewife," Comer remarked. "She always looked out for our welfare and was a strict disciplinarian. If you violated her rules, you paid a heavy price. She raised ten children, eight boys and two girls, out there in the sticks." The closest town was eighteen miles away.

"My childhood was extremely wonderful," Comer said, talking about how close his family was, how much love they shared. He remembered talk about lynchings and violence, but his early years involved limited contact with white society. It wasn't until later in the depression years that Comer left his protective black community to work for a plantation owner.

Jonathan and his siblings attended a local segregated school. "There were big yellow school buses taking the white children past three black high schools to a white one, twenty-eight miles away," he remembered. Not much was integrated in Comer, Alabama. "All blacks in the South," Comer argued, "should have got doctorate degrees in psychology, because they had to learn exactly how to deal with white folks, what to say and what not to say." He continued, "You'd be standing talking with some white children your own age, and you'd say 'Yes, John.' And they'd come back with, 'What did you say, boy?' The next thing you knew, your mother slapped you in the face and told you to call him Mr. So-and-so. That would satisfy and soothe them somewhat. . . . Mothers, black women in particular," Comer said, "were extremely instrumental in saving black males, because a black woman would slap you down. Because if she didn't, you could get into some big problems, beaten or lynched." With his mother's guidance, Comer studied the art of resistance.[4]

The Comers squeezed through the beginning of the depression by working their own land, but as the hard times dragged on, the Comer farm could no longer produce enough to sustain the family. They could eat but they had nothing to sell and no money to buy anything. By the age of eight, Jonathan had already mastered the plow; when necessity called, in the early 1930s, he and his brothers went out to work the fields at the old Comer plantation. "I believe I picked cotton at twenty-two or twenty-five cents a hundred pounds. I would pick cotton, chop cotton, pull corn, gather velvet beans, and [do] other types of chores to make a little cash money." Hard work did not bother young Comer.

Throughout this period, Comer observed:

> Blacks began to travel a little more and to see beyond their own horizon. A few people would go to the cities and to the North and talk about it. We loved to say "the North" and we saw some kind of utopian situation in the so-called North, where people worked and made, oh my goodness, they made more money in one hour than there was in our whole world. I worked for forty cents a day for fourteen hours' work in Alabama.

Comer harbored dreams of a better life. He thought he would leave home and make his millions. "As a teen, I wanted to have a farm, and I wanted to have the proper equipment to work with. I wanted to make lots of cotton and corn and for those to be turned into cash, so that I'd have some money." As he grew older, his dreams changed. "I began to dream about other things. I went to a trade school. I went to Tuskegee for a short while in a summer program and studied carpentry. But secretly," he smiled, "one of my foremost dreams was to become a conductor on a train. My father did not discourage me. My father did not tell me, and I didn't know, that the only black people on the train was waiters, porters, and firemen on the wood and coal-burning engines used in those days. Now that was the height of my ambition." That his father did not crush his dream of being a conductor strengthened Comer's faith in his own abilities. His optimism made him a fighter.

As soon as Comer began working away from home, he had to put aside dreams and think about realities. "Early in my life, I became race conscious," he recounted. At the age of sixteen, he joined the National Youth Administration. "It was a type of junior WPA [Works Progress Administration] for poor youth on a part-time basis," he said, "because you had to attend school to qualify. We were building an airport some twenty miles from my home. It was about 1937 or '38. I was the night water guy. I'd work all day rolling the dirt, and then I'd fill the tank with water and sprinkle the dirt down, to pack it into a hard surface for landing aircraft."

One morning, Comer and a few coworkers were crouched on the ground, fixing a leaky hose, when his supervisor, Charlie—"His name actually was Charlie"—said, "We're looking for some rain today." Comer automatically responded, "No, I don't think it's going to rain today." "This was all quite innocent," he added. "Charlie took his foot and put it in my rear part. He didn't kick me or anything; he just put it there, to let me know it was there. He said, 'Boy, are you questioning me? Are you calling me a liar?' I said no, because I just thought it wasn't going to rain."

Comer's father had arranged for him to stay with another young man, named Milliken, at the house of an elderly woman. Milliken's father happened by that night, heard the story, and went immediately to find Jonathan's father. "They came back a few hours later, and my daddy got me from down there, and he lectured me. 'Don't you get involved with them anymore,' he said. I didn't know what was going to happen to me, or if anything was going to happen to me." Comer recognized, however, that the time had come to leave Alabama.

Shortly afterward, Comer journeyed to Florida. He knew a lot of Alabama field hands who had gone there to work the citrus industry after the local crops had been harvested. "I had no intention of coming back. I didn't want to see the dirt, trees, or farm anymore. I went to Leesburgh and worked the citrus industry and also sold wood in the community. Finally I got with a truck and delivered small bundles of wood." Word of job openings at a new naval station in Jacksonville lured Comer and many others further north. He landed a job laying pipe, work done by both white and black workers. "The young whites were making about a dollar per hour more, more than twice as much as we were," he recalled. "We were doing the same job, only they were doing less work than we were."

Comer leaned back and added, "Let me tell you the story of my big raise. . . . I saved that superintendent's job," he chuckled.

We were putting giant drainpipes into a ditch, and the next day the clay soil would raise up those pipes, making them unusable for storm water drainage. So I devised a scheme that you drive timber and pilots down, put tracks on the pilots, and then laid the pipe on the track. "You got me out of a problem," my superintendent told me thankfully. And I got a great big raise. I got ten cents a day raise and now I was making fifty cents. I'm making the big money now!

Nell, Comer's wife, listened to the story attentively, although she surely had heard it a hundred times before. Jonathan and Nell have been together for over sixty years.

Jonathan met Emma Nell Mount in Jacksonville, Florida, although she too was born in Alabama, fifty miles south of Montgomery.[5] Jonathan took his meals at a cousin's house just across the street from Nell's. They were drawn together by their shared background; their rural, respectful ways; and their religious faith. "He was very fun loving, easygoing. He didn't drink, had a good upbringing, and was good-looking," Nell Comer added coyly. "We were great companions." Most of all, they had fun together—"We talked silliness," she said—and laughed a whole lot. Jonathan could confide in Nell; "She was the smart one!" he said. They still laugh easily, and both enjoyed reminiscing about Jonathan's picaresque youth. Nell, though, took exception to his courtship story. "Oh, I knew Nell was special," he began. "I knew we were meant for each other, so I just slowed down so she could catch me." "No, no, no," interjected Nell. "It wasn't that way at all. You chased me and you know it!" Comer married Nell on July 18, 1942, and in November of that same year he was inducted into the military.

Fine-Tuning His Awareness of Racism

Comer felt it was his duty to go fight for his country, although he did not speak in terms of patriotism. Six of his brothers and sisters also entered the armed services during the war. Comer began training in Florida and then was sent up to Fort Benning, near Columbus, Georgia. "Oh yes, there was discrimination in the military," Comer stressed. "They had separate units, and what a difference between them! The white units had better equipment, better housing, better food, better everything."[6] Comer remembered one violent incident when a black soldier got stranded and began walking back to camp. "He was beat up," Comer said, "and we went to the commander. They said they would investigate, but I don't think they ever did." It was during his wartime experiences that Comer developed the habit of, in his words, "telling it like it is." He talked with others openly and often about what he saw.

Overseas, black soldiers got together regularly and examined racism. "There were people from lots of parts of the country. You're not talking about little green Jonathan Comer from Alabama; you're talkin' about guys from New York or D.C., Indianapolis and all around." Over time, the discussions became more organized. "We started having meetings. Myself and several other guys began to meet at night and talk. We'd say, 'Did you see where they had the colored guy up there last night?' Or, 'Did you hear about what happened to that colored soldier who went to the wrong Red Cross?' They had two separate Red Cross centers, and they told this guy: 'You go back there in the alley, that's where you folks do the jitterbug.'"

These discussions sparked a restlessness in Comer. His northern friends "talked about eating in the same restaurants as whites and riding on the bus or train wherever they could find a seat, front or back. Some went to school with white kids. It is hard to describe my feelings," Comer wrote, "about such a wonderful condition opposite from what I was accustomed to, being in a Jim Crow army with conditions so unequal. Something within me just haunted me," he continued. "I looked for any opportunity to do something, to act, to bring attention, and shed light on the conditions that I had to live with through the years. My reasoning was that if I was fighting for freedom, why then should I not enjoy freedom, too?"

Then the letter-writing began. The soldiers wrote letters to the army brass, to their congressmen, and to the president to complain about the discriminatory treatment they faced. "We wrote letters just about every day. White service clubs had many things we didn't have, such as books, movies, games, and different types of food and entertainment." Comer was stationed at the time in Hull, England; it was 1943. "White soldiers could intimidate black soldiers with the blessing of white officers and white policemen. I guess most of the letters never left the European Theatre of Operations. However, some action was taken." To reduce the random violence against black soldiers, in response to their letter-writing protests, the military decided to add one African American to each police patrol team as an auxiliary military policeman (MP). Jonathan became one of the first provisional MPs; their title and status was, of course, second-class.

Comer's position as a provisional MP opened up informal opportunities for exchanges. "People started talking more about their ideas about the blacks or colored as they called them then. This one guy, a nice guy from Mississippi named Hogan, we patrolled together. One night as we patrolled, an English girl said to Hogan, 'You told me all black soldiers had tails and that they just hid them.' As more people realized how ridiculous some of this prejudice was," Comer added, "well, they just opened up. You'd get invited to their homes or out to a restaurant. All this talking helped to fine-tune what I already knew. I knew something was wrong, but in the military we learned from each other. I'd call it fine-tuning my awareness of racism."

An incident that took place in 1944, after Comer was transferred to Cherbourg, France, lit a fuse that never stopped burning:

It was three A.M. in the morning and we were awakened by a loud whistle and were given orders to line up outside our barracks. Large floodlights were turned on, and military policemen brought a French girl to look at each soldier in the line-up. We found out later what we suspected then. She claimed that she had been raped but had never said the person was white or black. But they came straight to the black camp and stood us in line like criminals. Now we talked about that and I asked, "Why did they come to the black soldiers first?" I was told to keep my mouth shut. I wrote a letter.

Comer understood that it was now his job to mouth off, to protect black soldiers from being singled out for punishment.

I don't know if this letter got through, but I know one did. I wrote to generals, to Congress, to everybody. One Sunday afternoon in Cherbourg, in November 1944, they called my name over the loudspeaker: "Jonathan Comer, report to the office." There were three very distinguished-looking white men sitting in the room, one of them a general in uniform. At least I thought they were all white. These men just asked me a lot of questions. "You got a problem with the food?" "Nope," I answered, "Food's okay." "You got a problem with this or that?" they kept asking. So I told them some of the problems I saw. It turns out—and I found this out months later—the brigadier general was black, the only black general in the military at that time, Brigadier General Bill Davis. He looked as white as the others. I didn't even know I had a brother in the room or I might have opened up a little more.

"Disillusionment II"

Like so many thousands of other African American soldiers, Jonathan Comer was transformed by his overseas experiences in the armed forces.[7] "It is doubtful," editorialized the *Gary American* in 1946, "if this country has known a tragedy more depressing than the Negro's disillusionment at the conclusion of World War I. . . . Then came World War II."[8] The article describes the plight of returning World War II veterans, "rebuffed on every side. The doors of job opportunities are being slammed in the faces of our brave sons who have a just right to expect better things of their country. . . . Negro veterans are left suspended between the things they want to do and the things they have to do to earn their daily bread."

In that same year, Jonathan Comer, released from the army at Fort Dix, New Jersey, joined his wife in New York City and began to hunt for a job.

Nell had moved with her mother up to New York in 1944, hoping for industrial employment. In Jacksonville, she had had a job waiting tables in a small, black-owned restaurant. Nell secured a job in the garment industry in New York, making panties and slips on a machine. This was her first contact with unions, as a member of the International Ladies' Garment Workers' Union. As Jonathan settled down in central Harlem, he wondered if he could handle the urban North.

> My memory of the South collides with all of its harsh restrictions and hatred of black people, with promises of the North, with its glittering lights of democracy that helped me dream a new dream. A dream where I could call myself a man and feel and act like a man. I had not made up my mind where I would live after I was discharged from the army. I considered several options, going back to Jacksonville, Florida, to Alabama where I was born and become a successful farmer or a job of some kind. There was always this thought in my head: what about the promising North with its unions; eat in any restaurant you wanted, ride on public transportation wherever you could find a seat. But there was also some caution. You are not smart enough to make any change from country to city life. It could be too much for you. You may not be able to fit in. I would sometimes have to shut down my thoughts about where I'd live after the war. After being discharged, I began to get some courage to try and live in the North.

Comer had never seen a black city neighborhood like Harlem. Nell already felt at home, but her husband was all eyes. Jonathan expected he would have no trouble getting work, given all he had heard about the North. The only jobs he could find, however, were in the garment industry, in nonunion shops doing irregular work. "These recessions kept coming along, and I'd be out of work. A few months here, and then out of work."

The unemployment among African American veterans was a national problem, serious enough to alarm federal bureaucrats. The United States Employment Service (USES) launched a series of employment surveys in one urban area after another to get accurate counts of black unemployment and to identify possible remedies.[9] They feared the storm of anger that would erupt when black veterans' expectations bumped up against shrinking job opportunities.

Comer, in fact, resented his postwar status. He spent more time on layoff than working during the two years after he arrived in New York. In time he realized that the North was not as different as he had been led to believe. "Now I ápplied for this one job as a shoe salesman for three New England states," he recounted.

I knew I could sell shoes, and figured it would be steady work. After I filled out the application, one of the men took me aside in his office to let me know I wasn't going to get that job. That was no colored man's job. What I discovered was that relations between whites and blacks wasn't all that different in New York. Sure, I could go in a restaurant and sit down, eat where I want to eat. But when it came to jobs, and associating with white people, well it wasn't there.

Nell's work was steady, so she was bringing in more money. Jonathan decided to take a short vacation and visit his sister and cousins in East Chicago, Indiana. Many Comers had settled in the Calumet Region and were working in the mills.[10] Jonathan's sister's husband had a job at Youngstown Sheet and Tube in Indiana Harbor, and told Comer he could get him hired in a minute.[11] He took Jonathan over near the mill, and showed him all the "help wanted" signs.[12] Comer looked at the size of the mills and all the smoke and figured, "No, no, no. No steel mill for me!" But what stuck in his mind were the vacant land and the "Hiring now!" signs. "My brother-in-law talked about the union benefits, seniority, job security, promotions, and more. I could not erase that invitation from my mind!" On the bus ride back to New York, Comer kept thinking about that empty land and those jobs. "Not a concrete jungle like New York," he thought to himself. "I could have a garden. I got the yearning for a garden, for some dirt."

After returning to New York, Comer felt torn. "Now I was faced with making a critical decision, understanding that I had to consider the welfare of my wife and son. I then discussed the decision with my wife. The reception was not good. She became almost bitterly opposed to the idea. She felt that to relocate would not be good for the family.[13] The truth is she wanted nothing to do with Indiana, not after having lived in New York. She said straight out, 'You can go without me.'" Nell had relatives in New York; Comer's family was in northwest Indiana. "We continued to talk about the move, because I did not feel I could demand that she agree. I feel blessed because she finally agreed to try it." She left her son with her mother and moved to Indiana. Over the next decades, living in East Chicago and then Gary, they would raise three children together and have six grandchildren, two great-grandchildren, and, so far, one great-great-grandchild.

"I Had a Good Feeling about the Union"

On May 9, 1948, Comer arrived in East Chicago; on May 11, he was hired at Youngstown with the help of family. Like the vast majority of blacks, Comer was sent to the dirty end of the mill, the old open hearth. The mill had developed a variety of ways of blocking the advance of black workers, locking them into the worst jobs. Comer requested work as a plumber, since he had done some of that work in the South, but the office girl—"What the heck did she know about jobs in the mill!"—told him there was no work like that for him. "The open hearth—all that fire," Comer recalled. "It was fascinating, and it was scary. I looked around and said those aren't people; they must be robots. Human beings can't work in all this heat. I threw up my hands, 'Oh Lord,' and went to work as a laborer, lifting manganese. Now that's the heaviest stuff I ever lifted. Right away I started looking to see what other jobs I could do. I wanted to get off that job the day I was put on it." "He'd come home," Nell said, "and his hands be curled. He couldn't even open them up, they were so sore from grabbing that manganese."

Comer knew he would have to start at the bottom, but what he discovered almost immediately was that all the black jobs were at the bottom. Just a few weeks after he hired in, he was offered the job of chipper. Comer welcomed the opportunity to escape the manganese. He saw it as a promotion. "I was blessed with a promotion to chipper in the open hearth a few weeks after I began. I felt good about making more money and that the union was responsible for my promotion." There were nine units in the open hearth, but most of the units where blacks worked were one-man or two-man units. That meant dead-end jobs. After a month of chipping, Comer began to ask about his next promotion.

"I received an unexpected shock. I was told by fellow workers that the job of chipper was a one-job unit—nowhere to promote to. I asked my union rep, 'How can I ever get a promotion?' He told me that I had to go back to the labor gang as the bottom person." In order to bid on a better job in a different unit, workers in dead-end units such as Comer had to return to the labor gang first. In doing so, they would lose whatever bidding seniority they had. They would be the "newest" man with the lowest seniority in the gang. "I was angry and disappointed. I could not believe that the union would be a party to such an injustice. My rep tried to explain to me it was just the unit system. I felt it was plain, old-fashioned discrimination."

Comer soon decided that any job in a larger unit was better than a lifetime of chipping.

Now the chipper had been a white man, but he bid on a maintenance job and he moved up. That's how I got the chipper job in the foundry. You made castings in sand. They poured the metal in the sand, so when it comes out, it has sand baked on it. You have to chip that sand off and clean it down to the metal, and that was my job. Quite a dangerous job! You were inhaling the silicon sand. There were no respirators at that time when I was chipping. Sometimes I would take an old handkerchief or rag and put it over my nose, when the wind was blowing the wrong way.

Well, that job really ate at me. I'm thinking about my contribution during the war. I was no hero but I could have got killed like everybody else, and I'm wondering why can't I have one of those other jobs that pay well. From day one I said, "I'm not going to stay on this job." And, boy, I began to just talk to everybody I could about it. And this guy John Nolan, he knew how I felt and he said to me, "These things happen. What you have to do is just organize." John was a white union rep.

Man, I began to talk like nobody's business. Then, I went to the union hall. They told me we have union meetings twice a month, and we're goin' to take out your dues whether you come or not. So I went to a union meeting. I didn't know when you stand up and when you sit down. I got up on the floor, me and my big mouth. Wow! I didn't even know what I was talking about, but I knew one thing. I was in this unit that was a one-man unit. You got this big department and nine units. Why should I be in this unit. I can't get promoted or anything else. I was just popping off at the mouth.

After that first meeting, Comer was disillusioned. "They made me feel foolish and stupid. Other guys were yelling, 'Sit down, you are out of order!' Just about everyone by now was laughing at me. When he finally let me talk, I was told I would just have to live with that condition. I decided not to attend any more union meetings. A few days later, I changed my mind! I began attending every meeting that I could."

Standing up and telling it like it was at union meetings brought Jonathan Comer some new friends. After one meeting, Frank Perry, a black leader in the local, walked over to Comer with his hand out. Perry had already been involved in the union for a few years. He had become a union representative in 1947 and then one of the first black grievers in 1949.[14] Perry saw it as his personal mission to recruit black workers into union activity. He had hired in at Youngstown immediately after the war, in 1945; during the war, he had worked in a series of defense plants from East Chicago to Oakland, California. Born and raised by his mother in a small college town in Alabama, Perry knew how to take care of himself. He also recognized Comer as a southern brother.[15]

Youngstown Sheet and Tube was the smallest of the three mills in northwest Indiana. It sat across the canal from Inland in the Indiana Harbor area of East Chicago. Unlike Inland, which hired very few African Americans, Youngstown hired blacks, whites, and Mexicans in almost equal numbers. Like Inland, the local had a vocal, identifiable group of radicals.[16] The president of the Amalgamated Association just prior to SWOC's formation, Jesse

Frank Perry embraced the union soon after he hired in. Taken in the late 1940s, this photo shows a very young Perry proudly wearing his union jacket. Photo courtesy of Frank Perry.

Reese, was an open black communist. Reese had come to the area in 1929 and agreed to work in the Amalgamated at the Communist Party's request.[17] Reese also served as the first vice president of SWOC Lodge 1011, starting in 1938.

By the time Comer came to Youngstown, black workers, many of them veterans of World War II, had already established themselves as union activists. Besides Perry, the group included Jim Baker, Hank Rowsey, Bill Scoggins, Leroy Love, Frank Breckenridge, Ben Coleman, Clelon Hobson, Eli Poindexter, Chatman Wailes, Bill Sims, Joe Wilcher, Hosea Hill, and Lawrence Hall.[18]

Soon Frank Perry, Jonathan Comer, Leroy Love, Jim Baker, and Hank Rowsey became known as the Big Five.[19] They never identified themselves as a black caucus, but they became the center of black organizing in USWA Local 1011. Frank Perry, according to Comer, "was the lynchpin." The five acted like a magnet drawing in other African Americans. The white political caucuses in the plant realized they had to contend with this informal group. The leadership started checking with the Big Five before slating any African American. When the union leadership wanted black support, they turned to the Big Five to decide who would represent them. Like the Eureka Club of USWA Local 1014, this network of activists exerted influence because it had widespread African American support throughout the mill, and many of the members held positions as union officers and grievers.[20]

Impressed by his performance on the floor of union meetings, Comer's griever asked him to be a shop steward two months after he entered the department. The Big Five agreed it was a great idea, and Comer accepted. The problem was that Comer did not know the first thing about filing grievances and union procedures. "I thought maybe he gave me that job to shut me up. 'You want to mouth off so much,' he probably figured, 'then take care of yourself.' . . . If it hadn't been for this guy Nolan I don't know how I would have learned the ropes. John Nolan explained everything, how to do this, how to write that." Nolan was white, with a reputation as a left radical. He became Comer's mentor and a good friend on the job.

The first chance Comer saw to dump the chipper job, he put his new authority to the test. A few months after he became union steward, another job opened in the maintenance department, where the previous chipper had gone. Maintenance included crane machinists, welders, and riggers—all good-paying craft positions. The maintenance group at Youngstown had what they called a "molehill." To enter the white inner sanctum, a worker had to find his way through the molehill. "They'd hire a white guy as what they called a grease monkey. He would grease railroad cars and other machinery. Then one day he'd be gone, and someone new be in his job." Comer went on:

> Next thing you know, you see him over there with a belt around his waist in the maintenance, going out to this job or that job. Now I tried to get in through that hole, and they were really put out. But I was a union griever by that time. I was using my mouth in the department, down at the hall, everywhere. Even black workers were telling me, "They put you on that job and you mess up bad enough, you know you're out of here; you're gone."

Contributing to the workers' fear was the understanding that a failure by any African American would be used to judge them all. Comer, however, was not deterred.

> As soon as they posted that job in maintenance, I figured that's where I'm going. I went right up there and signed that cotton-picker [the bid]. Yeah, I signed it, and all 'H' broke loose. Let me tell you everybody was wondering why I would sign for that job. The superintendent came over and said, "Why would you sign that?" My Grievance Committeeman came over, and said, "Why did you sign that posting?" I said, "Why the heck you ask me that? You know why I signed it." Everybody was just amazed; it brought out a lot of furor. Well, I signed it because I wanted to go in maintenance. I had already worked as a plumber with pipes.

Comer continued, "The superintendent said, 'You can't get in there that way.' 'What do you mean I can't get in there that way? He got in there that way' [referring to the former white chipper]. 'No,' he shouted, 'that was different.' They had palace guards, as it were, at the door to prevent us from moving anywhere," Comer explained. He knew the established system would always be different when it came to promoting a black worker. The superintendent had overall authority of the mill but worked the day shift. On the other shifts, his assistant, the senior melter, had authority and could decide who would work what job. The melter was in charge of maintaining the temperature in the furnace and acted like a subforeman. Even more than the superintendent, the melter in the open hearth was opposed to blacks taking helper positions. "He didn't want colored on his turn," Comer said. "He said, 'You see, I haven't been here that long, and I have to make a name for myself, and I don't want you messing up. Colored people just don't think keenly enough like white people do in this type of work. Maybe someday they will, but I just don't want you on my floor.' "

Comer mused:

> I shall never forget that young man. The superintendent over him never said a word, and he just kept up his harassment of me. "I worked at TC & I," he told me one day. This is a U.S. Steel installation in Birmingham, Alabama. "You say you're a deacon of a church, but you don't act like the boy I knew down there. That boy used to shine my shoes and keep my clothes clean." Then he looked around nervously and added, "He didn't do it for nothing, now. I paid him." I said back to him, "I have mine shined. OK. That's number one. And number two, just so you understand, I am looking to have your job! I'm looking for a job that pays as much as your job."

In 1948, shortly after Comer hired in, white switchmen on the railroad in the transportation department organized a strike against the first black put in that job.[21] They walked off the job and crowded into a union meeting to protest. "They had a stormy meeting at the hall. I was there," Comer said. Bill Christy, then president of the local, told the protestors: "Tomorrow morning, if you're not back on that job, you got a problem. I'll tell you that right now. Because if the company fires you, we're not going to do a thing about it." Comer recalled that they stayed out two days, but then returned to work alongside the African American switchman.[22]

Harassment was a common response to what white workers saw as encroachment on their jobs or departments by blacks.

> Blacks go on a job and he be tricked. This is documented a million times over throughout this country where a black would go to work, and the chain be cut, or something be snipped. Then he'd go to his lunchbox and there'd be a dead rat in his lunchbox, grease on his chain, that type of thing. A man could get seriously hurt by these actions. And we had leaflets. A noticeable one was hunting season, you know, "open season on niggers." A crew would write on a bench in the chain house, "Why don't you go home nigger and raise watermelons." All kinds of filthy rotten things they'd say. Then sometimes they'd put blacks on jobs and show them the wrong thing to do. It was quite an experience for me; I wouldn't take nothing for this journey that I made.[23]

The most common obstacles to promotion for blacks at Youngstown Sheet and Tube were rooted in departmental seniority, lines of promotion, and incumbency rules, just like at Inland and U.S. Steel Gary Works. The advantage belonged to white workers assigned to the better-paying jobs in departments that had promotional opportunities available inside the unit. Jonathan Comer was in one of the many black ghettos of the mill, and he would watch a stream of younger white workers enter the mill and pass by him into the better jobs.[24]

Comer learned early on to use the grievance procedure to help him fight his battles. Frank Perry served as his mentor. Comer recalled, "I was sold on the union, but I still had misgivings. After all, the union sat there and let those guys set up those one-man units; they was a party to them. And they set those darn units up to discriminate against blacks." In 1952 Comer contacted his own griever, Tommy Pasko, who, in turn, talked to the chair of the Grievance Committee, Dan Kokot. Comer said, "I just kind of figured these guys aren't going to do anything. I didn't expect them to come out and get me on the job, but at least I wanted to be represented."

Comer described the meeting that followed in the foreman's office:

I was working three to eleven when I got called into the office. Dan Kokot, chair of the committee, and the local president, Al Roadruck, both white, they were there. Let me tell you when that meeting was over, they performed so beautifully, that I was bound to the union for life. The foreman had got up and read the riot act, and he was running at the mouth. Kokot jumped up. Man, he used some Sunday school language! He told him to set right down. "I don't want to hear your mouth anymore." I'm bracing up now, ready for anything. You know they did not give me that job. But another one came open very shortly. I signed for it, and I got it.

The reaction to Comer's second and successful effort at promotion was just as dramatic. Neither workers nor management could believe that he would sign a bid for a "white man's job."

"I signed a job posting again for first helper. You'd thought I had robbed a bank from management's reaction and from the response of my fellow workers." The assistant superintendent and a melter, a working foreman of sorts, went down to the number eight furnace, where Comer worked, to try one more time to talk him out of the bid. Comer would not budge. "I want to tell you something," the assistant superintendent said. "I'm not going to hold your hand." Comer continued:

I knew what that meant. Every other white worker came in, the melters stood there and helped them. When I went into number one open hearth in 1948, the blacks working there had told me that the superintendent said there would never be any black first helpers, charging car operator, or pit crane men, because those jobs paid extremely well. There was jobs for blacks and jobs for whites. But I have to say after I finally got that job, the white first helpers on the floor, every one of them, helped me. Now maybe it was because by then I was their union griever and we were in a tough battle over bonuses, but they went out of their way to help me. They'd walk over from another furnace and say, "Hey, Jon. I think you ought to do it this way."

Sticking with the Union

Jonathan Comer spent most of his working life as a union activist. The outspoken advocacy of his grievance chairman and local union president during his battle to escape job segregation had completed his conversion to unionism. It did not, however, blind him to union discrimination or close his "big mouth." "I just felt that 'union' meant, literally, togetherness, and I saw some togetherness. Although there were certain things I didn't like, I thought my fortune would be better cast with the union."

Comer started as a shop steward and was elected Grievance Committeeman in 1954.[25] He had been convinced to run against griever Tommy Pasko in 1952 but lost miserably. When workers begged him to try again in 1954, he refused, for a while. As an increasing number of white as well as black workers approached him to run, he decided to consult with his chief adviser, Nell. She told him to go for it "and let the chips fall where they may." Nell's support was strategic. At first, she explained, "I resented the union because they was taking him away. But then I started to read the books, and he [Jonathan] started to fill me in. Soon I'd take that small book and I'd write the grievances for him while he was sleeping. . . . We always did everything together," Nell added. "I found out that the union was just as much a part of life as living." Comer held that griever's job for thirteen years, and Nell took on an increasing amount of work. She helped organize meetings and Comer's election campaigns, not only in the local but also in the precinct for the Democratic Party.[26] His election support became so strong that eventually he ran unopposed.[27]

At one point, Nell accompanied her husband, against his advice, to a local caucus meeting. Comer asked her to sit out in the car, since only members could attend. By three A.M., however, Nell was banging on the door to get him out and home. "The busier he got with the union," she went on, "the busier I got with the children. But the truth is, the deeper I got into politics, the better I liked it. I could turn out a lot of people." Then too, she observed, "I never had room in my heart for bitterness."

Nell Comer organized this party at her home to promote her husband's political work as precinct committeeman, c. 1965. Left to right: Jonathan Comer, Jesse Mae Williams, Gary mayor Martin Katz, Nell Comer, and Alberta Vaughan, precinct committeewoman. Photo courtesy of Jonathan Comer.

Jonathan Comer still downplays his effectiveness as a griever, pointing to a lack of technical skills and attributing his success to his "big mouth." But what brought Comer increasing support from white as well as black workers in his department was his skillful negotiating approach. He did not turn every issue into a confrontation, although he never failed to mention ongoing discrimination. He always acted as if the company and some of the less-welcoming union workers would eventually see it his way and change. His belief in people's ability to change, his general reluctance to stereotype or write off anyone, enabled him to move people out of the past. Comer caught his opponents off guard, and turned them around so that they would be looking at a problem from his perspective. His flexibility combined with his tough moral character not only made Comer a man of remarkable integrity but also made him easy to approach. He left his adversaries with a way out.[28]

Comer recalled one instance when he had prejudged a coworker, an older white man he had known only in passing. "I always thought this guy was a racist. He never said anything, like he hated everybody, although he never did anything to me. You know what he told me one day? He sidled up to me one day in the late sixties and says, 'I hear you guys [black workers] are having a demonstration.' I say, 'Yeah.' And he answered: 'So what took you so long?'" Comer leaned back, laughed, and added, "Well, that really surprised me! And taught me a lesson or two!"

One of Comer's favorite stories involves the integration of the mill's clerical staff, which was lily-white.

> I think they had seventy odd people in the employment office, and not one of them was black. Now I had a meeting with industrial relations every month as long as I was Grievance Committeeman. Every time I went in to talk to the superintendent, I said the same thing. "Why don't you people have somebody black in the employment office? Wouldn't it look better if you did?" But they never did. Toward the end of my tenure at the local, when I was president, I went to talk to the superintendent about some problem. Before I got in the door, he said, "Jonathan, I know, here come your old thing again." So when I started off bringing up the clericals, everybody started grinning, just laughing, breaking up. I'm smart enough to know these guys got something cooking down around the creek. They got some moonshine going. They had put a black person in that office, finally put a black person in there. Now that was way in the late sixties.

Comer deserved that degree in psychology he claimed every southern black had earned. He would speak out, and then apologize for his lack of knowledge. He would expose racist behavior but not engage in individual blame. He saw racism as an institutionalized phenomenon, not as a character flaw. So when the superintendent and melter, for example, denied him the first helper bid for lack of experience, Comer knew it was because he was black. But he would agree with them, catch them off guard by admitting that he had no previous experience. "I knew I didn't have experience," Comer explained. "But then I would ask them about several white guys—we called them floaters—who come in the mill and had no experience either but had been given the job. That's how I let them know that I understood their lies."

Comer's approach was rooted in his dual socialization: first, in Alabama, where he learned how vindictive white people could be, and second, in the military, when he learned that water dripping on a rock long enough can make a mighty hole. He used his sense of humor along with his outspokenness to educate those around him. He would smile in a friendly way as he reminded the union and the white leadership that they were changing at a glacial pace.

Comer remained a griever until he moved into the union's vice presidency in 1967. His attitude toward his job was "straighten out problems with no nonsense." And despite his insistence that he "didn't know nothing," he won everyone in the department a bonus, higher incentive pay, and, most important, fair treatment, including promotional opportunities by seniority. "I gained the respect of white workers as well as black workers," he said. "Of course at politicking time, some would run against me. I had no problem. They didn't come close." Eventually they stopped trying. Comer attributed his electoral victories to the pragmatism of his coworkers. "The white workers in that plant," Comer explained, "knew that to support their Grievance Committeeman was in their own interest. And that proved to be fact. And one thing I want to say that gratified me," Comer added, "I didn't do it myself. People joined me."

By the time Comer left the open hearth, he had gone from laborer to chipper to third helper and finally to first helper. It was not the same department he had entered years back. He recalled:

> One night, a young man by the name of Ramón Ramírez, Mexican American, was on number three furnace, and I'm on number two. So he called me up on number three. "Hey Jonathan, come up a minute if you've got time!" So I went there. He said, "Now what do you see there on the floor?" "Ramón, what do you mean?" I answered. I would tease him. "You've been drinking tequila again," I joked. "I see furnaces, that's what I see." "No Jonathan, look again!" And then he reminded me. "Jonathan, on number one furnace, Bennie Douglas, black; on number two furnace, Jonathan Comer, black. On number three furnace, Ramón Ramírez, Mexican. On number four furnace, Bill Horner, white. On number five furnace, Jesse Jones, black." And so on. Then he said, "Look at the cranes." There were three cranes high above the shop floor, two controlled by black operators. Two charging operators, two blacks. That really struck me. I'll tell you the truth, I praised the Lord for that. And that accomplishment alone was worth all of the things I went through, and I went through some things. But that's nothing compared to the improvement.

Comer did not take personal credit for the change, nor did he fall for the view that the company had made it happen:

> I don't think the company had any intention of doing it. But the civil rights movement, the organization of blacks within the plant, in the open hearth and other departments, allowed us to say to the local union leadership, "Listen, man, we're going on the theory one for you and one for me. Now all we're saying is, you guys, you straighten this thing up, and you guys support what we're about here." And they did. They supported the Civil Rights Committee in meetings with the company to get some type of working agreement whereby we can integrate those all-white depart-

Comer took union training opportunities seriously, although he downplayed his intellectual abilities in his dealings with white coworkers, c. 1965. Photo courtesy of Jonathan Comer.

ments. It's because black people were saying to white leadership, "It's time now. It's time now for us to get together and try to cooperate with each other."

Comer described black organization in the mill as taking place in small groups, such as the open hearth group or the coke plant group.

We would get together after work and talk. Sometimes at somebody's house. And then we had organization, the Steelworkers Improvement. It was kind of loose knit, but we would get together and talk.[29] "Yeah man we don't have any blacks over in that department. Or this department." Then we'd bring the issue back to the Civil Rights Committee and confront the company. The company would give us that old cliché: "Oh, you want us to fire white people so you can hire blacks?" "Well, don't be stupid," I said. "Don't insult us with that stupidness." Both the union and then the company realized they just had to deal with this problem; it's not going to go away.[30]

African American workers such as Comer used their voting power to secure representation on union slates. "The unions had political caucuses," Comer said. "We knew we had to get near the water hole in time." Caucuses always met to put together slates before the election, and Comer knew the importance of being in the room when the slate was drawn. "I remember we'd go to the caucus meeting. I went to one on the other side of St. John out there, and we met at six P.M. I'm not kidding you, when we got out of that thing the sun was breaking." ("The other side of St. John" was southern Lake County, usually closed to African Americans.) Every caucus put aside slots for blacks, because the black vote was strong, and could swing an election. "Blacks tended to vote pretty good," added Comer. "And they tended to vote in a block."

According to Comer, when he arrived on the scene in 1948, most of the positions reserved for minorities were "ceremonial." "The vice president," he recalled, "was Clelan Hobson, and that position was ceremonial. No question about it. And Joe Welch, a young man, was treasurer. You had possibly three on the Executive Board out of eleven positions, sometimes four. When you talked about vice president, you're talking about somebody black. It was ceremonial.[31] The president go away, you chair the meeting. My situation was a little different," Comer added. The district office pulled his president out to handle negotiations as a staff rep, first on a temporary and then on a permanent basis. "One day, the subdistrict director, Joe Geneske, called me down to the office and said, 'Jonathan, you're going to have to assume the presidency now. Mike Flood is going on permanent staff.' And so I wake up one morning and I'm head of a local union of almost eleven thousand people. It was not my cup of tea at the time. But praise the Lord, I said 'I can do this,' and I went to it."

Comer was the first African American to be full-time president of a basic steel local. He had been promoted into the job, not elected directly, but that would not stop him from exercising the power of the presidency in the local and, months later, nationally. Despite threatening letters and racist phone calls, Jonathan Comer used his leverage as president to lead a national black power protest in Chicago at an International Steelworkers Convention in 1968. He agreed to do it reluctantly, recognizing the consequences for himself and his union career. In retrospect, Comer would admit that it was possibly the hardest decision of his life. Overnight, he went from diplomat to rabble-rouser in the eyes of the district leadership. The time to "cuss and fuss," as he put it, had arrived. For the first time in his life, Jonathan Comer stepped into the national limelight.

Part Two

CIVIL RIGHTS STRUGGLES IN THE USWA

CHAPTER 6

"Change This Segregated System!"

The National Ad Hoc Committee in Steel

In 1964, African American steelworkers came together to form the first nationwide black protest organization in the United Steelworkers Union: the National Ad Hoc Committee.[1] Aaron Jackson, a black activist from Detroit, suggested the name at their first meeting.[2] Out of this gathering came a report, issued nationwide, that read:

> Growing unrest among the Negro-steel workers over 25 years has caused him to think for himself. From Platforms and Rostrums all over the nation where Steelworkers get together; loud voices ring out. "There is no discrimination in this union because of race, creed, color or nationality." In 1964 a Group of Concerned Negroes called a spontaneous meeting to talk over their problems and find out why they could not get above a Local Union office.... They discovered that [the Negro] was discriminated against because of the system. A Committee was formed and titled Ad Hoc. It has chosen for its mission: "CHANGE THIS SEGREGATED SYSTEM."[3]

"We had given our industrial lives to the union," Curtis Strong said emphatically, sitting forward in his chair, "and when they rejected us, we had to do something to change the union."[4] After decades of local black action, dozens of caucuses and convention sidebars, African American steelworkers decided the time had come to storm the citadel. Throughout the nation, civil rights protests were adopting the cry for black power. In one union after another, African American workers began to demand black representation in top decision-making positions.[5]

"It was my union," stressed Oliver Montgomery, a seasoned steel activist from Youngstown, Ohio. "My father, my grandfather built this union. I am fourth generation. We needed to fight a war right here to get our rights."[6] Rayfield Mooty, a leading African American militant out of Chicago, had held every post in his local union "from shop steward to local president" since joining in 1937. "This in fact is a Black revolt within the unions," Mooty told the press. "We've been paying the freight for 32 years, and we feel that after so long a time, we should be *in* the union, not just *on* the union."[7] Thomas Johnson, a longtime fighter from District 36 in Fairfield, Alabama, had put up with Jim Crow unionism too long. "The sad fact is," he wrote, "that the local unions have schemed and thought of every way possible to draw up lines of promotions in order to circumvent and exclude Negroes from them."[8] Aaron Jackson from Detroit could no longer tolerate "the injustices the black man is facing, not only in the unions but also in the community."[9]

The Ad Hoc group defined their mission by developing a three-point program; it called for the establishment of a civil rights department as well as the inclusion of African Americans on staff and in top leadership positions internationally. The activists drafted a constitution, prepared a slew of resolutions, and then took to the battlefield. "We had to use the same tactics against the union that we had used against the company," explained Curtis Strong. "We remembered a few years earlier when George Meany said to A. Philip Randolph that he did not speak for blacks. That not only got us angry; it got us moving.[10] So when [International President] David McDonald gave us his three minutes and indicated that we did not speak for anyone, well we started organizing."

Curtis Strong, of course, had been organizing for a long time, but now he meant nationally.[11] It was early 1964, and the first serious, coordinated challenge to David McDonald for president of the International United Steelworkers Union was in the works. I. W. Abel had key support from other Executive Board members and was known throughout the country and in Canada. He had a good chance at the International presidency.[12] No candidate for the presidency had ever slated an African American to run on his ticket. No African American had ever been elected to a national office. Out of fifteen hundred union employees, fewer than a hundred African Americans occupied staff positions of any kind. Out of the fourteen International departments, only two included a black employee. There was not a single black department head or assistant.[13] Out in the districts, there was only one black subdistrict director.[14]

A Look at USWA Policy and Practice

From the days of the SWOC through the founding and development of the USWA, union leadership had made clear its commitment to equal rights for its black members. What that meant, however, in 1937 was far different from what it meant in 1964.[15] Times had changed; the union had changed, but not sufficiently in the eyes of black rank-and-file members. The CIO and SWOC's stand in 1937 represented a radical break with the Jim Crow practices of the American Federation of Labor (AFL). SWOC hired black staff organizers such as Hank Johnson and Leonides McDonald, and deputized local African Americans such as Jesse Reese, George Kimbley, Walter Mackerl, and Stanley Cotton as district organizers. Perhaps most important, SWOC reached out to black workers in practice and on principle in all its organizing campaigns. Almost every basic steel chapter or lodge in northwest Indiana had an African American vice president by 1938.

At the USWA's founding convention in 1942, President Philip Murray appointed a special assistant to advise him on racial issues, a black staff representative named Boyd Wilson.[16] Throughout the war years, the USWA took public positions in support of a fair employment practices law, against lynching, and against Jim Crow segregation in the military as well as in defense industries.[17] When white steelworkers resisted the promotion of African Americans into semiskilled jobs in the mills, the local union leadership in the Calumet Region took a tough stand. Generally, local union officers told protesting white workers that if they did not want to work with African Americans, they could resign and go home.

The gap between policy and practice, however, began to widen in the 1950s, especially as the union and the CIO as a whole moved to the right to accommodate McCarthyism and the cold war. Increasingly workers and organizations that called for social justice and racial equality were red-baited and driven out of existence.[18] The International USWA played a part in attacking white leftists in the union, men such as Nick Migas (Local 1010), Al Samter (Local 1014), and Chuck Fizer (Local 1011). Migas was forced to resign from his position as president of the union, and then he was put on trial by the International and expelled from the union, despite his immense popularity with the membership.[19] All of these leftists had made the battle for equality in the mill a cornerstone of their activism.

In addition, workers had just emerged from two decades of really tough times, from the intense poverty of the Great Depression to the wage freezes, speedup, and forced overtime of the war production days. Most workers were simply exhausted from the conflicts, and wanted to collect their share of peace and prosperity.[20] There was tremendous pressure on unions from many sides to focus on economic benefits and job security issues. Throughout the 1950s, the United Steelworkers continued to be militant in its fight for economic fairness, striking year after year until a 116-day battle in 1959. The union won pensions, cost-of-living increases, health benefits, and job security protections that benefited every worker in the mill, white and black.

But none of these strikes challenged the exclusionary practices of the skilled crafts or the general segregation throughout the mills. Very few African Americans sat at the major negotiations tables. Most benefit packages were negotiated on a percentage basis, so that black workers who earned less continued to fall behind their white counterparts in terms of wages and benefits. Neither could they buy homes in the suburbs or send their children to college. Their wives had to work, because a second income was needed for household essentials. Even black workers' pensions were smaller.

As civil rights protests swept the South, the USWA provided funds to bail out protestors and passed resolutions in support of the movement and its demands. The USWA established a Civil Rights Committee in the late 1940s and entered into alliances with national civil rights organizations. But changes in the union and the workplace were not keeping up with national developments. USWA Local 1010, for example, fought school segregation in East Chicago but balked at taking on the white workers in power and steam. Local 1014's Eureka Club had forced some promotions, but the locker rooms and welfare buildings at U.S. Steel were still segregated.

The purges that accompanied the red scare, including those resulting from House Un-American Activities Committee hearings in Gary in 1958, went a long way toward discouraging demands for equality and social justice. Internal trials against radical members, executive board takeovers of local unions' administrations (trusteeships), and the inclusion of Taft-Hartley anticommunist restrictions in the USWA constitution changed the union culture, including its antiracist character. Some unionists who had supported a candidate alleged to be a communist or communist sympathizer were being denied the right to seek office under the USWA constitution. At USWA Locals 1010, 1011 and 1014, red-baiting intensified in the late 1950s, encouraged by the district leadership.[21] Many of the most outspoken antiracists became targets of attack, people such as Jim Balanoff, John Sargent, and later Ed Sadlowski. "Black plus white equals red" is how Curtis Strong characterized the International's view. African Americans who had worked closely with white leftists had to step back from those relationships in order to protect their cause.

Black membership saw a growing divide between policy statements and practice, between union talk and union walk. As the union's forcefulness in the antiracist struggle declined, the African American activists turned to civil rights groups and separate black organization in order to push forward their demands. The alienation of many African Americans from their union began during the 1950s.

The union's reluctance to take on racism inside the local unions or the mills dates back to its founding, but it became less tolerable in the years after the war. Special Assistant Boyd Wilson issued reports that minimized problems. For example, in a March 29, 1946, report to the National CIO Committee to Abolish Discrimination (CARD), Wilson summarized the USWA's progress on race relations in these words: "Let us say our policy has at times found itself in conflict with so-called local community patterns," wrote Wilson, referring to both de facto and de jure segregation. And even though he claimed that "the United Steelworkers of America has and will continue to vigorously resist such local patterns when found inconsistent with our national policy," it was not a promise he could enforce. Social mores and institutionalized racism kept even the most committed unions from eliminating racism in their ranks. In the 1940s and 1950s, before the civil rights movement and the Civil Rights Acts of 1964 and 1965, there was no federal or popular mandate for union initiatives dealing with racism. Wilson's report went on:

In cases of wage differentials, based on minority group identity, circumstances forced concessions from some of our District and Local officials. Only rare cases of disregard of seniority rights of minority group workers have been called to our attention. . . . While there may be a trend toward downgrading of minority group workers, it is our intention that this action does not interfere with the seniority rights of our membership.

Our records show that minority groups participat[e] in all phases of our union, including Local Union Presidents and other Executive Officers and also Shop Stewards and Committeemen in appreciable numbers. While there is room for improvement, even in this respect, we do not find too much cause for complaint.[22]

Acceptance of racial inequalities had become standard practice; only blatant instances of racism received union scrutiny. A more disturbing analysis by Boyd Wilson placed the responsibility on black members to reverse deteriorating race relations. "I am today of the opinion that better race relations in C.I.O. Unions will depend largely, but not entirely—with the colored workers." Wilson insisted that "the colored worker must understand that he and he alone must win and hold through work and activity in his local, the support, loyalty, and good will of the other members of his union." He told a long story about a fictitious Johnnie Jones who started out active in his local but then stopped attending meetings. As a result, Wilson concluded, the local failed to pass a seniority agreement that would have eliminated some of the discrimination in Jones's plant. In Wilson's view, it was Jones's inactivity rather than the white supremacist practices of the company or the local that left segregation intact.

Wilson also charged black workers with overreacting. "Discrimination is oft times the results of an unfounded sensitiveness born of past unpleasant experiences. Perhaps some unjust act on the part of a misguided or ill in-formed supervisory or fellow worker. Such acts," he observed, "contribute to a 'mental attitude' which sometimes inspire the questionable charge of discrimination." This characterization of black responses as unfounded, oversensitive, or questionable, and the widespread charge that African Americans "played the race card," more accurately reflected the white denial throughout the labor movement. Whenever the dominant group did not de-tect racial overtones or discriminatory practices, their response was to blame the victim for making everything into a race issue.[23] At the same time, the white majority's insistence on color-blind policies trivialized the impact of racism on union appointments and elections.

In some circles, Boyd Wilson symbolized the union's refusal to take on racism seriously. He was labeled an apologist. "The blacks that they put on staff or slated," explained Oliver Montgomery, "were not active in the move-ment; they weren't active in the struggle. They were people we usually didn't agree with and they were fighting us more than they were fighting discrimi-nation."[24] Besides Wilson, the International used its black staff rep out of Philadelphia, Jimmy Jones, to pat itself on the back. Jones not only de-nounced Ad Hoc from the beginning but argued that the union was right in restricting membership on the Civil Rights Committee to Executive Board members (all white men) and right to promote only those who "deserved" a promotion. Jones went so far as to accuse Boyd Wilson of "build[ing] up false tension among certain members and groups of members . . . creating an anti-David McDonald feeling among as many Negroes as possible." Wil-son had made it a practice to host gatherings of black steelworkers during conventions.[25]

At the 1948 convention, the USWA established a Civil Rights Committee made up entirely of white Executive Board members and chaired by Thomas Shane. When Shane decided he needed help in administering the work of the committee, he ignored Wilson and hired his brother Francis Shane as secretary. Together they kept the work of the Civil Rights Committee fo-cused on legislative initiatives and liaison work with civil rights organiza-tions. Boyd Wilson became the committee's gopher. Thomas Shane particu-larly discouraged Wilson and the committee from interfering in local union issues. For example, in the Civil Rights Committee meeting of August 27, 1957, Shane postponed for the fourth time the discussion of a complaint from District 16, arguing "it is still within the confines of being a local union problem." In this case, it took over four years to correct a local agreement that limited job advancement for black employees in the labor pool.[26]

In 1950, the committee carried out a survey of local unions to identify the nature and extent of racial problems. The report was glowing. "Approximately 99% of all locals participating in the survey report a wide range of jobs open to any worker, regardless of race, creed or color, the only qualifying factors being seniority and ability to perform the job." Wilson glossed over the fact that not all locals were surveyed and that among those surveyed, many did not respond. Jonathan Comer's local, for example, must not have mentioned the dead-end sequences set up for most African Americans.

"Of all the locals surveyed," the summary continued, "71 per cent report they have never been confronted with a serious racial discrimination problem. . . . Several locals indicated no problems of a discriminatory nature were brought to the attention of the union."[27] In response to complaints from black workers about racial discrimination in the handling of their grievances, the report explained: "Through the process of education, these local unions are gradually demonstrating that all grievance cases are won or lost on merit and not on the racial characteristics of the member involved."[28] In his reports, Wilson was speaking for local and national leaders when he placed the burden of proof on the black workers, dismissing their unsettled complaints as lacking in merit.

The report concluded: "Your union, particularly through its Civil Rights Committee, is today engaged in an all-out, steady and unceasing drive to break down racial and religious hatreds." Decades later, this unceasing drive had still failed to promote any African American into a decision-making position in the union.[29] There was nothing subtle about the racist practices in the workplace or the union. For example, in August 1957 Boyd Wilson received a telegram concerning a picnic given by a local. The telegram informed him of "disgraceful, discriminatory picnic arrangements at Rainbow Garden Park. Swimming pool denied Negro members through arrangements by picnic committee." The same communication complained of a similar situation at the Irwin Works, "where Negro members were paid five dollars not to attend" a union picnic.[30]

Civil Rights Activism Targets Organized Labor

Black awareness throughout the country had reached a high tide by the 1960s. Civil rights legislation was pending before Congress, and many of the former CIO unions were supporting it. The AFL-CIO as a whole, however, was very much opposed to being included as an employer in the proposed bill, because it meant that the unions would be subject to the same scrutiny under the law as any other employer. The industrial unions fought the old craft unions within the AFL-CIO over their support—or lack of support—for the civil rights movement and its legislation.[31] The USWA had not rallied behind the 1963 March on Washington, as the United Auto Workers (UAW), led by Walter Reuther, had. Some district directors and top leaders did join the demonstrators and sympathized with their charges of discrimination, still so widespread in the industry, especially in the South. A good example was Howard Strevel, district director for the southern region, based in Birmingham. Strevel responded to racial pressures for the long-term good of the union and intervened from above; without leadership support, grassroots efforts would have been slower and less effective.[32]

As many more black workers formed caucuses and national networks to challenge discriminatory treatment within the labor movement, even the "progressive" unions such as the UAW and the USWA began to denounce black activism as anti-union.[33] Once the 1964 Civil Rights Act became law, more and more black workers turned to the courts and the NAACP Labor Department to go after their own unions. Herbert Hill, the head of the NAACP Labor Department, fought many of the workers' legal battles himself, and came under attack from the unions targeted in the NAACP's suits, including the USWA and the International Ladies' Garment Workers' Union (ILGWU).[34]

Black steelworkers had been a force for change within many locals, and they had met informally at national conventions and other events from the first SWOC national gathering. In 1964 a group of black steelworkers decided to bring the black power movement into the heart of their union and use whatever means necessary to be heard.[35] Activists such as Curtis Strong had learned not to underestimate the resistance they would encounter. They realized that they would need a base of power in order to "persuade" the International to change its ways.[36] They saw the contested International elections scheduled for 1965 as an opportune point for exerting pressure. They planned to use the black vote as leverage against both candidates in order to force a shift in the union's racial politics.

A group of African American activists called together a meeting at the International Convention of the USWA in Atlantic City in the summer of 1964. They were all local leaders attending the convention as delegates. They decided to organize a national committee and set up meetings with the presidential candidates. Curtis Strong was at the founding meeting, along with Rayfield Mooty from Chicago, Aaron Jackson from Detroit, Hugh Henderson from Youngstown, Thomas Johnson from Birmingham, Carl Dickerson from Duquesne, and others.[37]

Forging unity among African American activists did not come easy. "We

USWA President David J. McDonald (left) with Herbert Hill, labor secretary of the NAACP, in 1964. Union leaders met with Hill in Washington, D.C., regarding the NAACP's plans to sue to enforce Title VII of the Civil Rights Act. Photo courtesy of Herbert Hill.

had infighting. We didn't agree on what to do or how to do it," noted Strong. "Both McDonald and Abel [the two candidates] had blacks at our first organizational meeting in Detroit. Alex Fuller was Abel's man, and he wanted us to endorse Abel for president without any discussion."[38] Most participants, however, had not joined in forming a black organization to serve the electoral interests of either candidate. They decided that an endorsement would not be given without a candidate's clear support for their three-point agenda. They had agreed that their purpose was "to work for the elimination of all discrimination within the International Union, United Steelworkers of America, and the mills and factories where the Union have [*sic*] Collective Bargaining Rights."[39] The demands the group presented to the candidates were: 1) the reorganization of the Civil Rights Committee into a civil rights department, under the leadership of an African American; 2) more black representation on staff in the districts and nationally; and finally, 3) the inclusion of an African American on the union's International Executive Board.[40]

Working the International Elections

Representatives of the group set up the first meeting to explain their program with incumbent David McDonald on September 25, 1964, in conjunction with the International Convention.[41] McDonald put off the meeting until December 18. The meeting was over in a blink of an eye. "We were given 15 minutes for discussion," the leaders reported to the group.[42] McDonald trivialized their demand for an elected representative by arguing that he would then have to appoint Polish, Italian, and Greek representatives as well. Then he ushered them out of the room, claiming that "they didn't speak for anyone." In fact, the group spoke for an increasingly large number of black steelworkers.

Soon after the McDonald fiasco, Curtis Strong, Rayfield Mooty, and Aaron Jackson piled into a car on a stormy winter night and drove from Chicago to Indianapolis to meet with I. W. Abel, Walter Burke, and Joe Maloney. They were behind closed doors for over four hours. I. W. Abel and his slate recognized that the black vote could swing the election one way or the other. Abel was prepared to deal. He would commit to the reorganization of the Civil Rights Committee; he would make it a full department and appoint an African American director. He also promised to bring more blacks onto the International staff. None of the three International leaders thought the union was ready for a black executive officer. They argued that it would require a constitutional amendment, which could not be accomplished easily.

Signing the first leaflets as the Negro Steelworkers Leadership Committee, the group voted to endorse I. W. Abel and played a decisive role in getting him elected.[43] They put out their own literature explaining why black steelworkers should vote for Abel. African Americans made up 20 percent of the union membership at that time. If Ad Hoc succeeded in convincing blacks to vote as a block, they could affect the outcome of the election between Abel and McDonald.

District 31 Director Joe Germano headed up the Abel election committee.

Germano assigned Curtis Strong to coordinate the campaign for Abel in District 31. In all the major steel centers with substantial black membership, the Ad Hoc worked feverishly to deliver the African American vote.

Meanwhile, David McDonald realized that he had to address the issues being raised by the black leadership. His strategy was to consolidate his white support and rely on his southern allies to keep the southern black vote in his camp. He added a couple of black steelworkers to his staff, and then opened up a racist propaganda campaign against Abel. In the South, the Mc-Donald people described Abel as "anti-Negro" and a member of the Ku Klux Klan. A black staff representative in Birmingham explained, "I'm told this fellow Abel is anti-Negro and a Ku Kluxer. You know how my people feel when you tell'em he's a Wallace supporter."[44] When George Wallace, the outspoken white supremacist governor of Alabama, appointed a white southern steelworker, John Nichols, as assistant secretary of labor for the state, the McDonald campaign put out flyers in the North announcing that Nichols was an Abel supporter.[45]

In the end, the northern black vote helped put Abel over the top in a very close election. He carried almost all of the northern and eastern districts; McDonald swept most of the southern ones. District 31 went for Abel by an embarrassingly small margin, despite Germano's chairmanship of the Abel campaign.[46] Without the black vote, Abel would not have carried District 31.[47] Curtis Strong and Ad Hoc had secured some bargaining chips with the new administration.

Ad Hoc Shortchanged

One of I. W. Abel's first actions was the appointment of African American Alex Fuller to head the newly organized Civil Rights Department. He then added other African Americans to staff, including Curtis Strong, who was assigned to work for Fuller. In May 1966, Abel addressed the national conference of the Negro American Labor Council, A. Philip Randolph's organization.[48] Abel and his team, however, underestimated the determination of the black activists and what it would take to satisfy the Ad Hoc Committee. H had selected a few of Ad Hoc's top leaders for staff, but the committee wanted integration of all decision-making leadership bodies. In June 1966, Ad Hoc picketed the Pittsburgh headquarters of U.S. Steel, arguing that discrimination was not just a southern phenomenon. By this time, the group had the active backing of the NAACP and its Labor Department, headed by Herbert Hill.

At Abel's first convention, in September 1966, the Ad Hoc openly criticized his leadership. The Ad Hoc had prepared resolutions for the conven-

Top: USWA District 31 leadership campaigned for the I. W. Abel slate. From left to right: Joe Maloney; John Howard, District 31 staff; Tiny Krantz, Local 1066; I. W. Abel; Curtis Strong, Local 1014; Walter Burke; Joe Germano, District 31 director; unidentified. *Bottom:* I. W. Abel and Curtis Strong. Photo courtesy of Calumet Regional Archives, Gary, Indiana.

tion urging the USWA to restore the position of second vice president on the Executive Board and "support a Negro for the position." Another resolution called on the union to negotiate civil rights language and committees into all basic steel contracts.[49] By the time the resolutions came to the floor, unfortunately, three-quarters of the delegates had gone home. After passionate comments from a few African Americans at various microphones, Samuel Stokes, a black leader out of Ohio, took the floor. "Who are we talking to?" he asked angrily of the chair. "Most of them who ought to have heard the 'beautiful things' are out of earshot." The chair had characterized the comments made by black workers as "beautiful things said." Civil rights, Stokes concluded, still occupied "the low place on the totem pole."[50]

Ad Hoc convened before the end of the 1966 convention to elect national officers and then agreed to call their first national meeting, to be held in February 1967 in Youngstown, Ohio.[51] The committee met again in July in Birmingham.[52] Out of these gatherings came letters of protest, demonstrations against steel companies, and lawsuits against the industry as well as the union for racial discrimination. The Birmingham chapter, for example, filed over one thousand discrimination complaints with the U.S. government against the union in one year. In District 31, Joe Germano accused Curtis Strong of organizing secret cabals.[53] Rayfield Mooty, acting as Ad Hoc's secretary-treasurer, sent the International a stream of correspondence, which he claimed was never acknowledged.[54]

By early 1968 Ad Hoc had run out of patience. It had tried repeatedly to set up a meeting with Abel to discuss the union's civil rights work and the need for higher-level appointments. Ad Hoc requested that Alex Fuller send a personal letter to Abel requesting an audience.[55] He did, but it was ignored. Ad Hoc then put out a call to black workers in every district to arrange meetings with their own district directors to get support for a constitutional amendment that would enable African Americans to run for Executive Board positions without being district directors.[56]

Jonathan Comer, particularly dissatisfied with Abel's track record at his own Local 1011, requested in writing a special meeting with Director Germano for February 2, 1968. In the letter, he argued that Local 1011 was the only large basic steel local in District 31 to vote for Abel. Yet, Comer complained, the local had been neglected in terms of staff appointments. "Negroes are concerned about the lack of representation. We will make recommendations to you and the heads of the union. We feel that trouble is in the making, but if something is done," he indicated, "this could be allayed."[57] Comer then warned Germano that "the writing is on the wall. Corrective measures are only taken after disturbances. And the District has only one black staff." He observed: "Young Negroes are calling us Uncle Tom." Rayfield Mooty and Sylvester Palmer attended the meeting, along with the

USWA 1011 representatives, to explain the demands of Ad Hoc.[58] Mooty echoed Comer's advice. "There must be some way we can get above L.U. President," pressed Mooty. "Throughout the years we have said we don't want any violence and demonstrations—but the only things getting done now are by these means."

Germano skirted their arguments. "I don't believe that you are asking that someone should be fired to put on a Negro. Don't be hoodwinked," he continued, "by someone putting you on a slate and promising something." He maintained that qualified men got on staff by seniority. Then he added, "Have a little patience. The top officers are trying to do a good job in this area. I don't forget that in the old days our Negro friends were there when the going was tough. What is bothersome to you," he finished, "is bothersome to me."[59]

"Put a Picket Line around Them!"

After months of silence and dismissals, the committee agreed to set up a picket line at the International convention scheduled for August 1968 in Chicago, the first International convention ever to be held in Joe Germano's home district. In the words of Rayfield Mooty: "By then, we thought we should be somewhere. Abel was refusing to meet with us, so we figured the only way to make them understand was to put a picket line around them." Over the months preceding the convention, Curtis Strong, Sylvester Palmer, and Rayfield Mooty crossed the country organizing support for the demonstration. Strong's advocacy work put his job as a staff rep at risk. "I didn't care," he explained in his usual assertive style.

The Ad Hoc Committee began planning the demonstration at meetings on April 27 and 28 in Detroit. More than forty African Americans participated from Ad Hoc chapters around the country, including Jonathan Comer from USWA 1011 and Sylvester Palmer from USWA 1014. The committee had laid a strong foundation for the protest. It had active local chapters in Detroit, Chicago, Philadelphia, Cleveland, Baltimore, Youngstown, and Birmingham. District 31 had an active and broad-based chapter, cochaired by Rayfield Mooty and Sylvester Palmer. Jonathan Comer began attending chapter meetings in 1967.[60] According to Comer, the Ad Hoc was already being charged with "threatening the director with burning down the [International convention] theater."[61] Accusations of being anti-International were leveled at any group offering dissent.

The Chicago picket line protest—Ad Hoc's first action targeting the union directly—stunned the International. Its visibility and timing showed the political astuteness and power behind the Ad Hoc. The group's demands had been updated for the convention: "1) To eliminate all discrimination within the United Steelworkers of America; 2) Full integration on all levels within the various Districts and National offices as department heads, and policy-making; 3) Revise the Civil Rights program."[62]

Ad Hoc wanted the person leading the demonstration to hold a high position and carry some weight with the International. No staff person could assume that role without jeopardizing his employment with the union. The Ad Hoc turned to Jonathan Comer, elected vice president and acting president of USWA Local 1011, the first and only black to preside over a basic steel local at that time. Mooty convinced Jonathan to go to the meeting in Detroit and hoped he could persuade Comer to be the point man at the protest. According to the minutes, Comer took the floor early in the meeting. The minutes noted that

> he [Comer] was attending his first national meeting of the Ad Hoc; he was very impressed by the fact that there were other people in the union fighting for the same principles he has fought for, for many years. Being a Steelworker and vice-president of Local 1011, gives him an opportunity to know what goes on upstairs in this union. . . . Since he has been accepted as temporary chairman of District #31 Ad-Hoc Committee, it was inspiring to him to see Negro steelworkers taking a stand against the segregated system that have dominated this union from its inception. He stated that Negroes can no longer accept less than what the Constitution provide for them as a union member. He stated that this union extends further than the plant gate, many candidates seek and get labor's support in their bid for election; these politicians have many patronage jobs. These he describes as juicy plums. Just as the Negro is denied his share of these appointments in the city, county, and state and government . . . He stated that Negroes must demand his share, using every method at his disposal, even if picketing is required. . . . Many people accept him as a thing, rather than a person. They try to give him what he need rather than find out what he want.[63]

Comer went on to recount the meeting he had arranged with Director Joe Germano. "Negroes are tired of being short-changed in jobs promotion," he said. He expressed his disappointment in Germano's response, adding, "The director had been ill advised." He ended by emphasizing that "in order for the Negro to know what is happening and when it happens, he must be behind the policy-making doors in every walk of life where his welfare is at stake. He can no longer wait outside the door for his answer."

The following day, the committee worked on resolutions for the convention and plans for the picket line. Comer played an active role despite being

Black delegates to the USWA national convention gathered to coordinate plans, 1968. From left to right: Aaron Jackson, Detroit; Leander Sims, Baltimore; Jonathan Comer, East Chicago; Curtis Strong, Gary; James Baker, East Chicago; and Bernie Parrish, Baltimore. Photo courtesy of Jonathan Comer.

a newcomer.[64] Agreeing to head the protest in his own district under his director's nose was not an easy decision. Prodded for hours by Mooty to accept, Comer knew he would face hostility and perhaps violence in his own local from the white membership.[65] At the same time, Comer's role in the protest would give him his first major national exposure. "Mooty jumped on me with all four feet," Comer said, laughing. Once committed, Comer worked relentlessly to make sure the demonstration and picket would be successful.

When Germano found out that Comer had agreed to head the demonstration, he began putting pressure on him. Various white staff reps took Comer aside, warning him not to involve himself with the protest. They hinted that he would be rewarded with a staff job if he acted as a team player. Finally, Germano called Comer into the district office. Comer recounted: "He told me that if I would call off the picket line at the convention that he would personally join me on a picket line at the International the day after the proceedings. 'I'll be the one behind you carrying a sign,' Germano told me." Comer badly wanted that staff job, but he could not have lived with himself if he had walked away from his commitment. What good, he thought, would a staff job be if it came at the expense of black workers? Comer would make many deals in his life, but not this one. He told Germano it was too late, and went about his business of organizing.[66]

In an effort to undermine the demonstration, Abel invited Ad Hoc Chairman Hugh Henderson to join the International staff just a few months before the convention. Henderson resigned from his position with Ad Hoc at a meeting on May 28 but assured his peers that they could still count on his support. "They thought you skin the top off the animal, then he died," observed Rayfield Mooty afterward. "They thought if they put our leaders on staff there would be no continuity of black leadership. That we'd disappear. They were wrong."

Rayfield Mooty and Jonathan Comer took responsibility for getting the demonstration permit and reserving a room for the Ad Hoc meeting in the hotel where a majority of delegates would be housed.[67] Given Germano's political clout in the city of Chicago, they anticipated trouble. A few days before the convention, the hotel canceled the room reserved for the committee, claiming they had made a mistake, that there was no available space. Comer knew Germano had intervened. He left a message for the hotel managers alerting them that the Ad Hoc would meet in the hotel or in the streets in front of the hotel. The decision, Comer added, would be theirs to make. Then, with his flair for drama, he stopped answering his phone. "It was ringing off the hook. The hotel was in a panic, desperate to reach me. Everybody in the press had heard and was calling me. But I wanted all the publicity we could get, and I knew putting them off just made them hungrier for news."[68]

Ad Hoc had enlisted the help of Gus Savage from Chicago for public relations.[69] In a press event held on Saturday, August 17, Jesse Jackson, president of Bread Basket, helped to publicize the Ad Hoc cause. Ad Hoc obtained clearance from the police for its picket line before the convention opened on Monday. It held a 10 A.M. press conference which, according to the minutes, "attracted world attention through radio, television, and news media. This was the first time they had a chance to look behind the closed doors of this International Union and see the discrimination and segregation that have existed for 31 years."[70]

At 8 A.M. Tuesday morning, Comer led a rather short picket line of a dozen black steelworkers in front of the entrance to the Stockyard Inn at Forty-fifth and Halsted. The many dozen others who had promised to join them fell victim to a collective attack of cowardice. Still, their placards made the picketers look more imposing, flanked by the pushing hordes of reporters and impatient delegates trying to get through the line. Comer knew that none of the recently appointed black staff would loiter outside; the International would be watching them closely. Yet, according to Comer, Alex Fuller, on his way in, shoved a hundred dollar bill into Comer's hand with an invisible nod of support. Abel had to delay the start of the convention, and the media ignored the general proceedings, highlighting the black protest.[71]

The debates on the convention floor were heated, despite Abel's efforts to

Protestors gathered at the USWA national convention, 1968. Jonathan Comer (the tall man in the center) led the picket. Photo courtesy of William "Buddy" Todd, Calumet Regional Archives, Gary, Indiana.

overshadow the picketers. He had invited Bayard Rustin and newly elected black mayor Richard Gordon Hatcher to address the convention. Rustin was a close associate and assistant to A. Philip Randolph. He also became the first director of the AFL-CIO–sponsored A. Philip Randolph Institute (APRI), an integrated organization dedicated to black civil rights. Bayard Rustin could be relied on to discourage public dissent within the house of labor. Rustin cautioned black steelworkers "to fight discrimination in the trade union movement where it exists . . . as a family problem to be solved within the family among allies and brothers." Hatcher felt compelled to speak at the convention because of Joe Germano's support for his election. He praised Abel as well as Germano but added, "As a matter of conscience I cannot stop at the border of the internal union controversy: every group should be represented at every level of this organization."[72]

On the central issue—black representation on the Executive Board—the International controlled the floor debates. Vice President Joe Maloney labeled the suggestion "a form of Jim Crow in reverse." Black staff rep Jimmy Jones from Philadelphia defended Abel from the floor and denounced the black picketers outside. "If a Negro gets on this Executive Board by appointment," he railed, "he will be merely a figurehead for somebody else. And you will be the first ones along with me to call him an Uncle Tom."[73] Abel concluded the debate, stressing that "our good Negro brothers don't want 'separate but equal' privileges in this union." The question was called and the resolution defeated by an orchestrated voice vote. The Ad Hoc held a mid-

Demonstrators in front of a USWA District 31 office protested against Joe Germano and the union for not fighting discrimination, 1968. Photo courtesy of William "Buddy" Todd, Calumet Regional Archives, Gary, Indiana.

Staff rep Curtis Strong (left) led Gary mayor Richard Hatcher to the podium during the USWA national convention while demonstrators picketed outside, 1968. Photo courtesy of Curtis Strong.

night caucus to discuss the rejection; they planned to escalate their fight "until the black man takes his rightful place."[74]

The International undoubtedly got the message. Abel could not have mistaken the fire under his feet for the dog days of August. As soon as he returned to Pittsburgh, Abel started finding more blacks for staff positions. Jonathan Comer was among the first. Leon Lynch, also from USWA 1011, was sent to Memphis. Other Ad Hoc activists such as Sam Stokes were promoted to staff. The International again skimmed off the leaders of the Ad Hoc. "They didn't think we blacks were going to stick together and keep up the pressure. The picket line was the only language they could understand," recounted Strong. "We needed to put lots of pressure on them."

Second-Generation Ad Hoc Activists

The 1968 demonstration convinced a new, younger generation of activists that there was power in organization. The Ad Hoc opened a recruitment drive and planned actions at the next two conventions in Atlantic City (1970) and Las Vegas (1972). Increasingly, women were among the new activists entering the mills. The 1964 Civil Rights Act included a section on employment known as Title VII. Section VII of the act prohibited discrimination in hiring and promotions by race, color, national origins, religion, or sex. A southern legislator added sex at the last minute, hoping that the addition would help to defeat the bill. The bill became law as amended, and a major part of the litigation and confusion since 1964 has focused on sex discrimination, what it is and is not.

Wielding the power of huge federal defense contracts, the government was able to exert pressure on the industry to change its hiring practices. Under government scrutiny, the steel mills began to hire many more women as well as African Americans.[75] Hugh Henderson had already urged the Ad Hoc to recruit more women at the May meeting at which he resigned the chairmanship. The Philadelphia chapter of the Ad Hoc was the only one led by a woman, Gloria Llorente. She had been on the national steering committee from the beginning. Comer helped recruit Ola Kennedy, the first African American woman in the Calumet Region to join Ad Hoc. Ola Kennedy did not work in basic steel, but at a smaller plant called Hammond Valve. She had hired into the plant in 1959 and established herself as a local union leader. Comer met her at a district conference. Kennedy joined with Llorente and other women, and Ad Hoc was taken to task for its male dominance.[76]

Born in Mississippi like so many of her union brothers, Ola Kennedy was an outspoken single mother of four daughters. She was sent to stay with relatives in Gary in 1942, after she had refused to step off the curb to make way for white folks. "I ain't gettin' off in no ditch to let them walk on by," she recalled. "The Ad Hoc made me feel I wasn't alone," commented Kennedy. Rayfield Mooty took her under his wing, teaching her the ropes and introducing her to black activists throughout the country. "Mooty was my inspiration," she noted.[77] Like Mooty, Kennedy refused "to be muzzled," and turned her back on promotional opportunities in order to speak her mind.[78] "I was supposed to be properly on staff," she commented. "I was too radical and would not join the club. I wasn't made out of the material they wanted. I couldn't do all that twistin' and turnin'. They wanted you to be committed to them."

"That's why we didn't trust the staff," Kennedy continued. "We had reason not to trust them. We were rank and file; we were committed and the staff was feathering its bed. Our motives and dedication were different." Kennedy explained that many newer Ad Hoc members did not want staff reps to participate in the organization. Too many, Kennedy argued, were concerned only with their own careers. An inevitable tension developed between Ad Hoc members and USWA black staff. International staff reps have access to the upper echelons of the union, and to a great deal of information that rarely leaves the Pittsburgh headquarters. Black staff could open doors. That many did not make a way for other African Americans to follow became Kennedy's complaint. She took Mooty's side in a growing, heated debate within Ad Hoc on the role of black staff. Kennedy and Mooty both tried to prevent black staff from joining the Ad Hoc as voting members. According to Kennedy, too many black leaders "wanted to be chief, and we found we did not have enough cohesiveness. You didn't have enough soldiers."

At the next Ad Hoc picket line, held in front of International headquarters in Pittsburgh in 1969, Ola Kennedy took charge. She told the press that Ad Hoc was demanding greater recognition for women, "both black and white. The USW does not have a single woman organizer."[79] Kennedy helped steer the Ad Hoc to support the demands of African American women in the plants and in the union. Under her leadership, the Ad Hoc drafted a resolution calling for "the Restoration of the Women's Auxiliary" and another resolution calling for black women on staff.[80] She sent a letter of protest to the International, stating:

> Women have played an important role in building our Union at the grass roots level, on the picket lines, serving as local union officers, ringing door bells in national elections, serving on community agencies and making other sacrifices. We feel that women should be considered for staff and other meaningful positions within this union. . . .

"Women's experiences and dedication," she continued, "is being ignored by the United Steelworkers of America, this disregard is a loss to the union." A few years down the road, Ola Kennedy became the cofounder of the District 31 Women's Caucus, the first radical protest group of women steelworkers in the union. "Ola raised so much hell in Pittsburgh," said Mooty, that the union started hiring African American women as clericals. "Every office in Pittsburgh got them a black," chuckled Strong.[81]

The International was beginning to see the light. The Ad Hoc movement was not a one-shot deal. I. W. Abel was up for reelection in 1969 and he again needed black support. After the 1968 protest, Abel not only appointed additional black staff but also promised to support an African American for the district director's position in the Baltimore area. In effect, he committed himself to getting an African American on the Executive Board. While Abel still balked at any special position for an African American on the Executive Board, Leander Sims, an African American leader in the Baltimore district, was a subdistrict director and qualified for a director's position. In the 1969 national election, Abel swept the black vote and defeated his opponent, Emil Narick. Abel's support for Sims, however, was not sufficient to defeat the white candidate supported by the previous director.[82]

Ad Hoc returned to the picket lines. They prepared to protest on the boardwalk of Atlantic City in front of the 1970 convention. There were still no African Americans in policy-making positions, without which the union could too easily erase the gains the black activists had made. This time, when the International got wind of the protest, they tried to contact Rayfield Mooty to get him inside to talk. Mooty talked but did not call off the picket. He put Ola Kennedy in charge of setting up the protest. "Don't take but one woman to turn this world around," observed Mooty. "We had one women to lead the picket line in Atlantic City." "This picket got us a hell of a lot of recognition," Mooty stressed. Ola Kennedy was not shy. "People always came to me because they knew I'd be the last one standing."

A number of the black staff reps who came out of Ad Hoc continued to support the work of the group and wanted to use that support as a bargaining chip to keep their membership in the national Ad Hoc Committee. Some of the African Americans on staff, however, never had any association with Ad Hoc and preferred to see their own promotions as rewards for individual merit. Because of the diversity of views and positions among African Americans on the staff, the younger Ad Hoc members did not think that staff belonged in the organization. Curtis Strong, who continued his open endorsement of Ad Hoc, was an exception. He believed that blacks could not have any power unless they organized all blacks as blacks, rank and file, local leadership, and staff.

At a meeting of black staff in Cleveland, Strong advocated this position and convinced the staff men to pay for some rank-and-file Ad Hoc members to attend the Las Vegas convention. According to Strong, the staff asked the Ad Hoc members to come into the meeting to talk about how they could work together. Mooty contradicted him, claiming he was barred from that meeting.[83]

At an Ad Hoc meeting in Youngstown in the spring of 1970, under pressure from black staff, attending members voted to let staff reps pay dues and be members of Ad Hoc nationally. Mooty opposed the measure but was outvoted. A few weeks later Mooty took the flack for the decision; he was bombarded with criticism in Baltimore and Birmingham, where rank-and-file Ad Hoc members were dead set against including staff.

A Return to Radical Alliances

At the 1970 convention, I. W. Abel took the stage as a militant, his strategy for dealing with upcoming bargaining and a shaky economic situation. He advocated so many progressive resolutions and spoke with such a sharp anticompany tongue, the Ad Hoc's miniprotest was pretty much overshadowed. Abel's radical rhetoric reflected a growing militancy among the rank and file and was also an effort to head off the grassroots opposition to him emerging throughout the country. Different protest movements within the USWA began to coalesce around issues of union democracy, the right to ratify contracts, and the right to strike.[84] In locals such as 1010 and 1011 in East Chicago and 1014 in Gary, remaining CIO diehards—including the socialist and communist left—teamed up with younger activists and leftists who had entered the mills during the early seventies. Together they sought to rebuild a national network and the interracial alliances that had existed during the union's first decade, reaching out specifically to the Ad Hoc leaders, to women, and to other minority constituencies within the union.[85] The national network that resulted became known as the Steelworker Fightback in the 1970s. It provided a collective voice for the previously fragmented opposition to various International policies and practices. By 1975 the group had put together a slate to challenge the International's candidates.

In District 31, Ed Sadlowski from U.S. Steel South Works, USWA Local 65, in Chicago challenged Joe Germano's handpicked successor for district director, Sam Evett, in 1972. Evett was declared the winner but the Department of Labor overturned his election due to gross irregularities in voting and in the funding of Evett's campaign.[86] A second election put Sadlowski into office, and almost immediately he began to mobilize a Steelworker Fightback campaign to support his bid for International president. Recognizing the importance of black support, he asked Ad Hoc leader Oliver Montgomery to be his vice presidential candidate in 1975. Montgomery was one of the African Americans moved to staff as a result of the Ad Hoc. The International had assigned him to the Research Department, which limited his ability to travel and, as a result, also his contact with the rank and file. Despite the risk to his job, Montgomery did not flinch when it came to accepting the vice presidential slot on the opposition ticket. In many ways Montgomery and Strong had the same "in-your-face" style of work.

The International could not afford to alienate the black vote completely, so they began a search for another African American candidate to add to the Lloyd McBride slate. Jonathan Comer had no interest, at this point in his career, in staying in Pittsburgh; he was ready to return to Gary and retire. There was no way the International would consider Strong; he was helping to run the Sadlowski campaign. The union turned to Leon Lynch, a hardworking staff rep in Memphis who had not been a part of the black protest movement. A good contract technician, Lynch had demonstrated the commitment and loyalty the International was seeking. What's more, Lynch had no connection to Ad Hoc or its supporters.[87]

Curtis Strong (left) and Rayfield Mooty toast Ad Hoc's achievements at a gathering at Strong's house in Gary, 1971. Photo courtesy of Curtis Strong.

The Ad Hoc at last knew that they would get an African American in a policy-making position; they also realized that it would probably not be someone of their own choosing. The old Ad Hoc members expressed dismay on another count as well. After all its earlier fuss, the International had altered the constitution overnight and created a new position for a token African American, vice president for human affairs. Mooty complained bitterly about this position. "What other union had that kind of vice president, not a general one, not a vice president per se, just over one specific thing, human rights?" As far as people such as Strong, Kennedy, and Mooty were concerned, the union had invented yet another form of segregation. "It was like adding a back porch to the house," argued Mooty.

"That was the end of our mission," Mooty observed. "It was better than nothing, because at least the International integrated to a certain extent." "We did take on the International union," Ola Kennedy confirmed. "The Ad Hoc is responsible for all kinds of changes. If it weren't for Ad Hoc we would not have had the Consent Decree in 1974." The Consent Decree, signed by the industry and the union, enabled workers to transfer out of dead-end jobs and departments and bring their plant seniority with them. The decree fi-

Ola Kennedy with leading activists at an event to honor Strong. From left to right: Curtis Strong, Bayard Rustin, and William "Buddy" Todd. Photo courtesy of Curtis Strong.

nally made it possible for African American workers to bid on jobs in other departments based on their full length of service with the company. The Consent Decree is discussed more fully in chapter 9.

Kennedy continued to describe the legal protests that led to the signing of the decree. "All those workers who filed suit in Birmingham, they were all Ad Hoc-ers. And I'm still here," she said. "It takes a radical person who sees the need for justice and is committed to fight in this organization. Mr. Mooty was the pioneer," Kennedy concluded, respectfully. "He was Mr. Ad Hoc."

"Ad Hoc was one of the greatest things I've ever done in my life," Mooty told Strong and Kennedy at the end of a private video session in 1985. Rayfield Mooty solemnly told the camera, as it closed in on his face: "It's up to me to pass this on to Ola Kennedy and Curtis Strong. This is history. Younger people don't know our sacrifice." Then he picked up a copy of an article by George Kimbley, "The Negro in Organized Labor"—one that had angered Director Germano when it was published in 1948—and locked eyes with Strong and Kennedy. "George Kimbley wrote down all the names he could remember of blacks who helped to build this union. Now I turn this over to you." Then he reached for another document, an article written by Boyd Wilson upon his retirement that also paid tribute to the blacks who had built the Steelworkers Union. "I know Boyd gave this to you, too, Curtis, so I hand this down to Ola, so that you can preserve it and hand it down." They sat in silence for a moment. "We achieved our mission, Ad Hoc did. We made a difference. We know the people who do things don't ever get the credit. And that is why we submit this history, lest we forget."

Following the dissolution of Ad Hoc, local committees and caucuses continued the fight, but they lacked the power of a national movement. A District 31 Black Caucus remained for a while, and a number of activists joined the Coalition of Black Trade Unionists (CBTU). "My dream," said Strong, "was that the rank and file, the leaders, and the staff could form one organization and work together. Pockets of resistance just won't change things. And that's what we have now. Pockets of groups around the country, but no power." "We thought those first black staff men would pull other black steelworkers up behind them, but that didn't happen," observed Mooty. The International saw no need to respond to pressure from a handful of black staff. With an African American on the Executive Board, the USWA had, in its view, met its obligation.

As black staff reps retired in District 31 and in the International, few blacks took their place. Lynch has remained on the International Executive Board as the first and only black International leader. In fact, African American steelworkers never again achieved the voice and power that they had attained during the days of the National Ad Hoc Committee. "I guess they did succeed in buying off the movement by co-opting its leaders," Strong mused to himself. "We probably never should have disbanded the Ad Hoc," concluded Jonathan Comer.

CHAPTER 7

Between a Rock and a Hard Place

Taking a Job on Staff

No greater dilemma faced African American union leaders than deciding whether or not to accept—if offered—a staff position. From the first debate, in 1937, over who should be the first black staff rep in the Calumet Region down to the present, African Americans have moved between painful soul-searching and conscious jockeying for position.[1] What concerned white leadership primarily was an African American's ability or willingness to be a "team player" and to fit into the union culture. For some black leaders, the offer could not come soon enough; for others, the offer was a mixed blessing. The performance pressures on an African American staff representative were weighty; the visibility enormous. For a few African Americans, staff jobs were "hot potatoes" that they would not touch. Yet the struggle for black representation always included the demand for African American staff positions, and those positions were important.

"Whatever the program is," explained Walter Mackerl, "you've got to follow the program. I don't think I would have taken a staff job, not at that time [1937] nor another." He was committed to the union, but his life's work revolved around his people and their freedom struggle. Mackerl was a Garveyite.[2] For a while in the late 1940s, he accepted a position as a statewide legislative coordinator with the CIO. In that position and within labor's Non-Partisan League, he could focus his energies on antilynching initiatives and support for the Fair Employment Practices Committee (FEPC). Like many of his peers, he would also get involved in the Progressive Party's campaign for Henry Wallace for president.

Bill Young dismissed the idea of being a staff rep. "I never wanted the staff job and never tried to get a staff job. I know who I am and I know how I am, and I couldn't keep a staff job. I can't take anybody telling me what to do." In Young's view of unionism, power resided in the hands of the rank-and-file members. He had fought every battle from the bottom up, and he scorned hierarchy, top-down authority, and bosses. In Young's thinking, if he left his local for a district job, he would no longer be representing the interests of the rank and file. As staff, he argued, "you had no protection whatsoever. You had to do what the district said, white or black."

For African American workers who had made the union their weapon in the black freedom struggle, accepting a staff job meant, in part, putting the freedom struggle in second place. Their obligations to their job were demanding and time-consuming. Union work was—and still is—a twenty-four-hour-a-day commitment. Their primary accountability was also to the union. If assigned by the union to work with civil rights or other organizations, their responsibility was to represent the USWA and to work in the union's interest. Given what the union could do for black workers, the challenge and the time commitment were worth the sacrifice.[3] It did not mean that they could no longer support the struggle and remain active in community affairs, but it changed their relationship to the black community and the civil rights organizations. International unions required loyalty of staff to the leadership and adherence to the union's program. Conflicts of interest were resolved in favor of the union and its position. In addition, as a staff rep, a black unionist spoke for the International, not the black members or the black community. Likewise, assigned as a staff rep to work in a civil rights organization, African Americans had to advocate the union's position, even if it was at odds with their own civil rights agenda.[4]

There was little disagreement on this point; every African American who went on staff understood the chain of command, and accepted—on some level—the requirements of the job. For African Americans who rose through the ranks as skilled trade unionists, without a direct connection to an independent black workers' struggle, the decision to go on staff was not as problematic. They saw it as the culmination of their careers as unionists. They did not feel that they owed anything more to the black membership than to the membership as a whole. They would be judged and often criticized, however, by black members and organizations, based on their performance as African Americans.

The debate within the Ad Hoc Committee over whether or not to allow black staff in the caucus reflected the workers' awareness of the inherent conflicts black staff faced. By virtue of their positions, Ola Kennedy had argued, African Americans on staff had different interests and priorities than the rank and file. Their job security depended on doing the work as assigned, and reporting back to the leadership. That was why Rayfield Mooty and Ola

Kennedy felt so strongly that black staff should *not* be voting members of the caucus, even though the staff in question, had, in fact, been some of Ad Hoc's strongest leaders. There was, in their view, no way to serve on staff without serving "the man."

Yet why battle for representation on staff unless black leaders were willing and able to use those positions to the advantage of the freedom struggle? One of the three Ad Hoc demands was that more blacks be appointed to staff and slated for leadership positions. If the most outspoken, radical blacks refused to leave the comfort of their power base to stand between a rock and a hard place, then why fight for those positions? How would black individuals on staff benefit the movement, if those individuals had not been a part of the movement? The goal had never been to gain a few plum positions for a handful of black unionists.

Union leadership preferred African American staffers who would assimilate into the existing culture, people such as George Kimbley. He was a dedicated union man but socialized to view white supremacy as a fact of life. He believed he could advance the struggle for black equality by showing white leaders how non-threatening he could be, and how useful in increasing membership. His visible presence drew black workers into the union and gave the union more legitimacy in the black community and with civil rights groups. His participation helped to prevent the disastrous divisions and race-based strikebreaking of earlier decades. Kimbley believed that his subtle exposures of racist attitudes and practices were effective and appropriate for the times. Above all, Kimbley loved the union and wanted to build a strong, cohesive organization.

John Howard, in some ways, was caught between two generations, the older school of those who put unity ahead of black equality and the emerging circle of rebels who advocated unity based on race equality. Howard never doubted that he himself was equal in ability and stature to his white coworkers, and tried to operate as if race were not an issue at all. From a young age, Howard believed he had more in common with northern whites than fearful southern blacks or overassertive northern ones. The younger generation of black staff, thrust forward by the movement, saw themselves as raising black workers to an equal position, representing an underserved constituency in the union. They were also in a stronger position to exact change because of the existence of the National Ad Hoc Committee. Militancy and broad-based pressure at the bottom created more leverage and space for African Americans at the top. The increased numbers of black unionists in leadership succeeded in challenging the culture. There were never sufficient numbers, however, to change the culture or break through the limits of tokenism. Black freedom fighters who knocked down segregation in the mill and at the local union faced new barriers when they assumed staff positions in a white-dominated union movement.[5]

All African Americans who served in union staff positions had to bear the cross of tokenism.[6] Tokenism had nothing to do with individual qualifications, competence, or integrity. It had to do with lines of accountability and with relative numbers. The International officers made the rules, issued the directives, and evaluated the work. From 1937 to 1976, there were only white males on the USWA International Executive Board. Since 1976, only one African American male has had a position on the board. Black staff at the International level functioned under a constant spotlight; they never gained the safety and invisibility of numbers.[7]

This spotlight meant that African Americans on staff were used to measure the potential of the entire race. Their minority status subjected black leaders to an intolerable level of scrutiny and set impossible standards on all sides; their toughest critics were other African Americans.[8] No white male staff rep was ever considered the voice and incarnation of all white men in the union; the reverse was true, of course, for African Americans. The failures of any one white staff rep were never used to judge the character or abilities of all white workers. The actions of black leaders, in contrast, were so judged repeatedly.

George Kimbley: "Bleeding Inside"

In the eyes of most steelworkers in the Calumet Region, George Kimbley was a *black* staff man. Nick Fontecchio referred to him as "one of our best niggers." White southerners accepted Kimbley as the kind of "good Negro" they were accustomed to in the South. Curtis Strong did not call him an ineffective staff rep; he called him an Uncle Tom. No matter what George Kimbley did as a leader, he was not seen as an individual; he was a token. Kimbley knew this to be true. In the name of helping black workers, he internalized rivers of insult, hid his feelings, and kept focused on what he considered primary: getting more black workers into the union. In his eyes, the union was the best thing that had ever come along for African Americans. Kimbley believed that his personal sacrifice was part of what the job of staff rep required. He thought he was serving the long-term interests of black workers and of the union. He could not understand how his African American peers could consider him an obstacle to their struggle, which they did.[9]

During the late 1940s and the 1950s, after white southerners had captured

George Kimbley participated in a subdistrict meeting in Gary. Standing, George Kimbley (far left), staff rep Lucious Love (center), Local 1014 President John Mayerick (second from right). Seated (from right to left), Pat Riley, Local 1014, and Orval Kincaid, subdistrict director. Photo courtesy of Calumet Regional Archives, Gary, Indiana.

many of the leading district positions, Kimbley frequently faced degrading situations such as Fontecchio's telling a group of black workers Kimbley had assembled, "We've got some of the best niggers in any union!" A subdistrict director in southern Illinois, for example, asked Kimbley to address one of his local meetings in the early 1950s. He wanted to see if Kimbley's presence would attract more black members to the union hall. "I went down there," Kimbley recounted, "and wasn't a black worker to show up. I got up and made an average union talk to the white." When he was finished, he sat down next to the podium. The subdistrict director thanked him for his words and said, according to Kimbley:

> "I want these white workers to know we got some colored workers in these mills and in our union, and they are mighty fine people. The trouble with many of you workers, you think these black people all want social equality." He said black people don't want social equality. "Why if they got it, they wouldn't know what to do with it." I was sitting up there just bleeding on the inside. There wasn't nothing for me to do but to take it. And I said to myself, I'm going to wash this S.O.B.'s face good and clean.

Kimbley's idea of revenge was to retell the whole story to the entire District 31 staff. "Everybody just hooped and hollered and laughed, all the staff men." Then Kimbley looked me in the eyes and asked, "Now, how many people would do that? It takes experience to do a thing like that. Now many blacks would have gotten mad and tried to do some harm or make some bad statements. I never do that. I try to get the truth to men." Then he added, "They'd just push me around any way they want to. I'd just take it. I'd know that there's another side to the coin, see, and that's the side I'd use."

Kimbley's concept of the moral high road was not shared by his union contemporaries. They argued that Kimbley was exactly what the white leadership wanted on staff, someone who would never rock the boat. Again, Kimbley would not have disagreed. Given the immense oppression of African Americans in Kimbley's time, in the North as well as the South, Kimbley maintained that white people were incapable of understanding their own racism, let alone changing it. He did not believe that the union could have promoted or retained on staff any African American who could not put up with racial abuse. After all, Kimbley predated Jackie Robinson by a decade.[10] The union advocated a gradual—actually glacial—pace of integration and change, and the leadership worried primarily about the comfort and continued support of white members, not the rights of black workers. So George Kimbley grew accustomed to "bleeding inside."

Kimbley's first servicing assignment after the 1942 founding convention was to his home local at Gary Sheet and Tin, USWA Local 1066. According to rumors in the local, its first president was a member of the Ku Klux Klan. He was a southerner, and Klan membership was widespread among the recently arrived southern white population.[11] According to Kimbley, the local would not allow him to participate in union-management meetings and would not notify him of any meetings whatsoever. Eventually his assignment was reduced to representing the canteen workers at U.S. Steel, a small, powerless local made up mainly of minority workers. He had the responsibility of negotiating their contract, one of the worst in the district. He was never given other regular assignments. From time to time, District Director Germano would ship him out to another district to help on organizing campaigns.[12] He would always make sure Kimbley served on welcoming committees so that he could keep his black representative visible.[13]

Kimbley was tightly reined in other ways. For example, in 1952 Kimbley wrote an article for *Info,* a local black newspaper, on the contributions of African Americans to SWOC and the union.[14] He tried to name each person he knew, so that there would be a record of the earliest activists. Joe Germano called him into the office, demanding to know who had authorized him to write anything on the union for *Info.* Kimbley had entered radicals and communists into the historical record.[15] Kimbley apologized and agreed not to write any other articles or make speeches without prior consent; he thought it was a reasonable restriction. When Kimbley retired in 1958, he returned to Frankfort, Kentucky, to fulfill the promises he had made to God in the trenches in World War I. He had spent twenty years as a staff man for the USWA and was tremendously proud of his contributions to the union.

Boyd Wilson: Prototype Token

How the International selected the first African American for a union position was indicative of what became the union's early approach to hiring black staff. At the founding convention of the USWA in 1942, black activists, including a handful of staff and local officers, formed a caucus to push for black representation in the union's leadership.[16] George Kimbley, Walter Mackerl, Bill Young, and Rayfield Mooty were present at the discussion. Mackerl made it clear they were talking about a top and not symbolic position; they wanted a black district director. Black leaders active for the preceding five years in SWOC had discussed the importance of making such a breakthrough at the founding convention. They had worked hard building the union, and they expected to be recognized and rewarded. The CIO's promise of black equality led the activists to believe they would succeed in their effort.

Philip Murray and his closest associates had decided that the International Executive Board (IEB) would be made up primarily of district directors, modeling their organization's structure on that of the United Mine Workers, their home union. The directors up to that point had all been appointed. Now they were to be elected in district referenda. The directors, along with four officers, would then constitute the IEB, the most powerful body in the union. Philip Murray and the directors did not prepare for or expect any contested elections. They had chosen to centralize the union through the director positions, and controlling those positions was a top priority for the leadership.[17] Murray knew district elections in a newly formed organization would crown the incumbents, and all the incumbents (close to twenty) were white. Philip Murray's slate for the top four officers was no different. Yet Murray was committed to the CIO's principle of inclusion. He decided to appoint a black special assistant to the president, an advisory position without decision-making authority.

When word reached the black caucus that they would get no more than an advisor, the black activists unified behind Joe Cook, a local president out of Chicago with a radical history and a reputation as a fighter for black rights. The District 31 director, Joe Germano, thought Cook was too militant. He had used his political connections to get information on Cook from the FBI, and he used FBI reports to portray Cook as a communist.[18] Murray looked instead to Boyd Wilson, on staff in Saint Louis, Missouri, out of Scullin Steel Company, a plant that was 60 percent black. SWOC had put Wilson on the organizing staff to help win certification at Scullin. Unfortunately, the effort failed. Boyd Wilson was one of the very few rank-and-file African American steelworkers on staff in SWOC. He had no links to active blacks in other districts and no black base in his own.

In an interview done after his retirement in 1967, Boyd Wilson expressed disagreement with the procedures used in 1942. "I attended the Steelworkers' first constitutional convention with a fixed determination to establish a beachhead from which the battle could be carried on for improved status of the Negro worker," explained Wilson. Being young and inexperienced, he "counseled the support of an older and more experienced delegate named Joe Cook, who was president of his Steelworker local, whose membership had a white majority."[19]

Boyd Wilson was tipped off that he was Murray's top choice, yet he remained silent at the convention. Only decades later did he claim: "I was quite unhappy about this turn of events. This was still the time when Uncle Toms were quite popular, and often became the secret weapon in dealing with aggressive, impatient Negroes in the union. I knew many Negroes of first-class performance who were being discarded because of the use of the vicious 'red rumor' whenever other trick charges failed in the job of 'getting' any aggressive or fearless Negroes."

Boyd Wilson fabricated his own version of history.[20] In 1942, he made no move to turn down the appointment. In fact, he defended Philip Murray's right to select whomever he felt "most comfortable with." This would become the established pattern for promoting African Americans into key positions. For as long as they could, the leadership avoided outspoken, independent-minded African Americans. Wilson and Kimbley both would work hard, but they would never be able to influence general policy or practice. They would be kept in subordinate positions, given marginal assignments, and be sent around from place to place to avoid their building any long-term relationships with black members.

One of Wilson's jobs was to represent the USWA Civil Rights Director Thomas Shane at civil rights and black community events. At more important meetings, Thomas Shane assigned his brother Francis, his executive secretary, to represent him. Wilson would go along as an aid. His position was similar on the CIO Committee to Abolish Discrimination (CARD), which later evolved into the Civil Rights Committee of the CIO. Boyd Wilson attended CARD meetings and events but did not have a voting position. Other African Americans on CARD—Ferdinand Smith and George Weaver, for example—represented their organizations and had a vote. CARD, chaired by cold warrior James E. Carey, focused on lobbying in support of civil rights legislation and supporting anticommunist propaganda within the labor movement and black community.[21]

Wilson's main responsibility, however, was to give a black stamp of approval to USWA policies and practices.[22] Murray described him as his special envoy "in the field of developing the proper kind of relations that ought to exist between colored and white workers." In his first Executive Board meetings, Wilson tried to call attention to problems but rarely was given the floor to address the IEB.[23] Often, he dismissed charges of discrimination, finding some other explanation, like "unfounded sensitiveness" on the part of black members.[24] At an IEB meeting in May 1944, Wilson explained how he had responded to a complaint by a senior black worker over seniority. "It is just one of those things that you have been overlooked, no particular intention to sidetrack you or anything of that sort."

Adding Numbers, Keeping Control

Around 1948, Walter Mackerl grew impatient with the exclusion of blacks from meaningful positions in the district. He saw Kimbley as a friend but did not regard him as effective. He knew that Germano kept Kimbley busy with errands in the district and sent him on the road for long stretches of time. Mackerl called together a small group of African American activists from his local (1066), and they decided to approach Germano about appointing a second black staff rep. Soon after, Germano appointed Lucious Love, from Chicago. Replacements would follow but the quota had more or less been filled. Johnnie Howard from Local 1014, Gary Works, stepped into Kimbley's shoes, and later, Jim Baker from Local 1011, Youngstown Sheet and Tube, replaced Love. Neither Howard nor Baker had an open association with the known black radicals in the Eureka Club, nor had they advocated independent black organization within the union.

John Howard: "The Union Was My University"

John Howard was thrilled about his staff appointment. He welcomed the challenge and the status. He saw his promotion as proof of his abilities as a skilled and knowledgeable union man and set about his work with a professional attitude. He dressed immaculately, met with management as an equal player, and based his arguments and decisions on the letter of contract law.

As a union rep in the workplace, Howard had served the members as their advocate and protected them from wrong-minded foremen. He had, how-

In his second year on staff, John Howard served on a welcoming committee for presidential candidate John F. Kennedy, 1960. From left to right: John Ricard, financial secretary, Local 1066; Senator John F. Kennedy; George Hrnjak, Subdistrict 1 USWA Community Services rep; and John L. Howard, staff representative, Subdistrict 1. Photo courtesy of David Howard, Calumet Regional Archives, Gary, Indiana.

ever, a different perception of his role as a staff member. His concern shifted to enforcing the contract and demonstrating his professionalism by exacting from members the same accountability that he exacted from the company. Play by the rules or pay the consequences was his modus operandi. "I took no prisoners. I made no deals. People would get in trouble and expect me to intervene. 'What do you think I am, a magician? If you promise to straighten up, I'll talk to management.' But then I reamed him out. You have to be willing to reprimand those you represent," he insisted.

Howard's easygoing nature and warm smile, his cautious, reasoned approach to his work, enabled him to build good relationships with other staff men as well as with the management he faced. Some of his peers thought those relationships with management were a bit too friendly. Like Kimbley, he wanted to get along with everyone and rejected confrontational politics. Howard had opposed Strong's Eureka Club back in the local, and on staff, he strongly criticized the Ad Hoc Committee. "You see," he explained, "I wanted to get along with everybody, and they [Ad Hoc] didn't like that. There was envy and jealousy," he believed.

It is important to understand that no African American became a leader or was promoted to a staff position without demonstrating first-rate union skills. Kimbley could organize African Americans into the union. Johnnie Howard, educated in Gary, learned contract administration on the shop floor. Howard was entrusted with more nuts-and-bolts work than Kimbley ever was. But the pressure on African Americans to prove their worth led to somewhat self-serving comparisons; some black leaders lifted themselves by denigrating those who went before. There was a fairly common tendency to label the earlier position as ceremonial. Howard, Strong, and Comer fell prey to that characterization. Howard clearly differentiated himself from his predecessors. "They didn't do anything," he said. "They just carried the title. I gave some substance to the job."

As a staff representative, Howard handled grievances and arbitrations for three locals, Gary Works 1014, his home local; American Bridge local; and the canteen workers' local. "Kimbley never went to arbitration. Boyd Wilson never went to arbitration. Alex Fuller never went. I did fourth steps and arbitrations. The International gave them what they wanted. A status and pay, and a privilege to travel at the expense of the International union. That's the way I saw it! I told Germano, 'I want responsibility and I want to be paid the same as white staff.' "

Howard did not think that Boyd Wilson and George Kimbley wanted responsibility. In fact, they never received training or any opportunities to exercise authority. John Howard also underestimated the degree to which he was a beneficiary of earlier black struggles. He was convinced that being black was not a factor in his promotion, because he was so good at trade union work.

"The union was my university," he stated with pride. "The union played a magnificent role in making individuals understand that there is a legitimate place for everybody in society." On dealing with racist attitudes or behaviors among other staff and leaders, Howard took an approach somewhat similar to Kimbley's. He chose never to expose publicly his white coworkers' shortcomings in the area of race relations. Airing dirty laundry outside the organization, he thought, damaged the union's reputation and ability to function effectively before management.

Howard did not have the same reservations about criticizing his African American brothers, especially Curtis Strong, everyone's favorite target. He recounted:

When they told me they were going to have a meeting of black staff, I said, "You going to have a meeting of black staff? Why not all staff?" I had a relationship with staff, not color. I went to that meeting. Boyd Wilson had a suite over there on the boardwalk. I took a couple of fellows with me. This guy opens the door slightly, like they're selling drugs, and asks, "Who are you?" Boyd knew me. Told me to come in but said the other fellows couldn't come in. I said if they can't come in, I won't. They let us all in. In the meeting I told them what I thought about them. I didn't believe in any kind of clandestine operation behind the backs of the International officers. "Have it out in the open!"

He continued:

Oh, yes. They didn't like me. This was an exclusive group of people who did nothing for the membership. I hate to say it. They drew a nice salary, but they didn't do anything for the rank and file but agitate. They would use the influence of an organization to either make a person or kill a person. I didn't like that at all. You see that's what that organization [Eureka Club] was all about. "We decide who the next black is to do this or that." I didn't buy it. It seemed to me no matter what I did I was always running into a storm!

Howard's last decade in office was his toughest, because the declining state of the industry intensified the political strife in the union. As union participation contracted and dedication flagged, Howard placed the blame on black workers and union opportunists as well as bad economic times. Younger workers, he observed, had inherited too many benefits without enough struggle. "When the younger people came in the mill, they were working double time. The table was just overflowing with goodies that they didn't sweat an ounce of perspiration for. They didn't appreciate the union." He accused black leaders of "only going halfway for selfish reasons." He did not connect the rise of opportunism or careerism among some African Americans with its simultaneous increase among some white leaders. Nor did he associate the growing disillusionment among unionized black workers with the USWA's decreasing support of—even resistance to—the African American push for equal rights. "I would say that blacks had a role to play, but they didn't stick their necks out any further than anyone else. They were recipients of the results," Howard argued.

Johnnie Howard ended his union days believing that everything came down to the skill of the individual, and that most problems could be solved through discussion. "The management people in Industrial Relations were human beings; if they recognized that something was wrong," he maintained, "they dealt with you one on one, on the basis of your intellectual response. We never had people representing our union in the past who were on a par with their counterparts in management. We gained that. In dealing with me, if they recognized something was wrong, they changed it." He then explained his own relationship with management, pointing out, "It's not a fight! It's an exchange of ideas between reasonable people. You can't just condemn management. We got to look at our own inabilities."

John Howard, of course, had the advantage of enforcing the contract during the years that the union wielded power. Most of the domestic steel industry was unionized, and the major corporations were flush with profits. Competition from abroad did not seriously erode the USWA's leverage in bargaining until the late 1970s. Steel executives underwent a transformation in attitude toward the union once they had to deal with global competitiveness in the 1980s. When Howard assumed his staff responsibilities, the union was making consistent economic gains in contracts with the steel industry, so much so that it grew complacent and discouraged member involvement and activism. Two decades later, as Howard entered retirement, the USWA recognized the error of its ways when hit with demands for concessions and plant closings.

For Howard, nothing mattered more than education, and he took responsibility for his own. "I speak for myself," he said proudly. He valued competence, and judged it one individual at a time. Howard declared himself and his union color-blind in a period when no one else around him was. Howard belonged to the first generation of CIO union stalwarts, "union crazy," just like Kimbley. "We were conscientious. We were servants of the people. We were at their disposal twenty-four hours a day. They'd call me two o'clock in the morning with a problem in the mill. I'd get out of bed and go right there. We sweated blood. We suffered." Howard was a twenty-four-hour staff man.

When Howard retired in 1979, he felt the union insiders regarded him "as a stone in their craw." They had forced him to resign when he turned sixty-five, and he was very resentful. "I had twenty-one years of service as a staff rep. I had endured all of the experiences. I'd been to arbitration a thousand times. I was in their way." He regretted the changes he saw in the character and integrity of union leadership. John L. Howard remembered the union he had joined in the 1930s, and wondered what had happened to make it change so dramatically. "We considered it a privilege to serve the membership," he noted sadly. "That was our philosophy." Without a broader historical perspective, Howard saw the decline in union power in terms of individual failures or shortcomings.

Curtis Strong: The Rebel Generation

In the 1960s the National Ad Hoc Committee for the first time forced the International leadership to promote one of its own. Curtis Strong was one of the first Ad Hoc members appointed to staff, shortly after Abel's election.

Abel selected Alex Fuller, more of an establishment figure from Detroit, to head the Civil Rights Department, and Strong was assigned to work with Fuller. I. W. Abel knew he had to make a few concessions to the Ad Hoc, and he was indebted to Strong. Strong's work in District 31 had given Abel 85 percent of the black vote there, which had put him ahead of McDonald nationally. Strong, he recognized, was a hard and effective worker.

Nonetheless, no one was appointed to the International staff without the agreement of the district director, and Joe Germano did not like Curtis Strong. Over thirty officers and grievers from three locals in District 31 signed a petition demanding that Curtis Strong be put on staff.[25] An accomplished politician, Germano agreed to the appointment on one condition: that Strong be removed from and kept out of the district. Germano got only half his wish. Curtis Strong was appointed to the International Civil Rights Department in Pittsburgh in 1966 but remained in Gary for a number of years. Then he returned regularly—like a political homing pigeon—every time there was any controversy afoot.

Within a newly established Civil Rights Department, Curtis Strong's job description focused on two chief tasks: first, to "implement the Civil Rights program of the United Steelworkers of America." The second duty was to be the eyes and ears of the International: "Make exhaustive and systematic analyses of Civil Rights problems and race relation[s] in the Steelworkers Union, the factories and the communities. Make complete and analytical reports and recommendations to the Director of the department of Civil Rights."[26] The terms "complete," "systematic," "exhaustive investigation," and "analysis" appear in one form or another eight times in the job description.

Strong's approach was to do exactly what he was directed to do, and he produced a stack of reports on interracial problem areas in the union. His political sophistication was a real asset to the International. Strong was familiar with most of the groups in the civil rights area, and he understood political differences from left to right. This understanding enabled him to do insightful political analyses and recommend effective strategies for the union. Strong turned out to be an excellent staff rep for the USWA in a time of civil rights turmoil and internal union conflict. Any time he was sent into a difficult situation, his reports to Fuller itemized the people he consulted, the political forces in play, and a summary of his own course of action. He generally concluded with recommendations.[27] At the same time, however, Strong made a habit of doing more than he was asked and not bothering to report on his extracurricular activities. Strong held many "unofficial" conversations with workers and encouraged the formation of black caucuses everywhere he went. From Strong's point of view, he did his job to the letter, and then a little more.

Strong's earliest assignments were a combination of tests and punishments. For example, Germano arranged for Strong to work in Cicero, Illinois, the white community in southwest Chicago where Dr. Martin Luther King Jr. had been pelted with rocks by white protestors. He was also sent to distant towns with no black population and into locals run by ex-Klansmen. At one point, Strong was sent to Texas to help in an organizing campaign among Spanish-speaking workers. Strong did not feel personally singled out. He believed all staff went through a hazing period; black staff faced some additional hurdles.

Five months after his appointment, still residing in Gary, Strong wrote the director of the Civil Rights Department requesting an air travel credit card and a telephone credit card. His only comment: "I am sure you understand, the reason is obvious." African American staff faced continual obstacles of this sort—no office, no phone, no credit card, and no resources.[28] Strong was crisscrossing the United States and spending half his time getting travel approvals one by one.

Once established on staff, Curtis Strong took the tough assignments. He was sent into Buffalo, New York; Sparrows Point, Maryland; and Birmingham, Alabama, where black workers were up in arms against the racist practices in the mills and the unions. Strong referred to his job with sarcasm as "putting down the restless natives." These cities were the areas with the strongest Ad Hoc local chapters, the largest black union membership, and the most militant community support. The International had grown concerned with liability, given the increasing number of lawsuits being filed by black steelworkers against the union with the support of the NAACP. "My first big assignment," Strong recounted, was "to find out what the problem was in Baltimore. My orders," he explained, "were to calm down the natives. The blacks there were fixing to take the building down brick by brick."[29]

Curtis Strong's conscience made it difficult to carry out some of his staff assignments, like the one in Sparrows Point. There he had to take on black activists in the union and the community. Leaders from the Congress for Racial Equality (CORE) were attending meetings with black union members and, in Strong's view, taking over the meetings. He argued that union members had to take the lead in union struggles and pushed to hold closed union meetings. He did not view himself as selling out the black cause, although he admitted that blacks at Sparrows Point "not only called me an Uncle Tom, they threatened me bodily harm."

Strong functioned on a tightrope, collecting information and mediating disputes, yet trying not to undermine the black rebellion. He represented the International at a time when the International itself was the target of black protests. Strong paid a price for going on staff; the perks did not make the job any easier. At one point, he acknowledged that had "a Curtis Strong" come into Gary Works to mediate the problems there, he and his caucus would have run him out of town. Strong believed, however, in the necessity of the union for black workers, and believed that black workers should assume ownership of the union and build it as their own. In addition, Strong had years of union experience and knew how to negotiate and play insider, machine politics. Like every other staff rep, he knew he had to stick to the hierarchical structure of authority, to written procedure and, sometimes, to the unwritten rules of the organization.

For example, Joe Germano assigned Curtis Strong primary responsibility for assisting the mayoral campaign of Richard Gordon Hatcher in 1968. Neither the district nor Strong had supported Hatcher in the Democratic primary. The union had backed the incumbent Mayor Katz's man, and Strong did not particularly like Hatcher, who had no union track record and no political indebtedness to Strong's power base among African Americans.[30] When Hatcher won the primary, Curtis took the assignment and did what he had to do. That job required substantial footwork among black as well as white steelworkers. Strong noted in his summary report that 75 percent of the members attending union rallies were African American. His report detailed every meeting he called with area politicians, local unions, and civil rights organizations, including receptions in the homes of white and Latino union members. Despite his lack of enthusiasm for Hatcher, Strong was an organization man and did not shirk his assignments.[31]

Curtis Strong drew his own lines, however, in establishing where his staff job ended and his civil rights activism entered. In 1968 Strong took a leave from his staff job with the USWA to travel to Mississippi with his wife, Jeannette Strong, president of the Gary NAACP, to work on voter registration.

A good example of Strong's separation of powers came at a 1969 civil and human rights event cosponsored by the Gary and East Chicago Human Relations Commissions and the USWA. Strong attended the banquet as chair of the Labor and Industrial Committee of the Gary NAACP, not as a staff rep. Pete Calacci, district loyalist and former president of Local 1010, now on staff, attended, representing Joe Germano and the district. In the middle of the keynote address, Curtis Strong stood up and accused the speaker of promoting racist views. Calacci turned on Strong and ordered him to sit down. "Who gives you the right or the authority to order me to do anything?" Strong shouted back. "I was not on union business," he explained to me, with a sly shrug. "You don't tell me what to do in my community." When the speech continued, Strong stood up and called on the entire Gary NAACP delegation to leave, which they did dramatically and noisily. Calacci was fuming. He called Germano and demanded that he fire Strong. "Not possible," Germano responded, because Strong did not work for the district.[32]

Very few African Americans ever got away with wearing two hats and switching them at will, once on staff. Two acted in defiance of certain leadership: Curtis Strong and Oliver Montgomery. Montgomery had been placed on staff, like Strong, as a result of Ad Hoc pressure; he was the leader of African American workers in District 26. Since Montgomery had a college education, the International placed him in the Research Department. Montgomery committed the ultimate union sin as a staff man; he ran as the first black candidate for the IEB with Ed Sadlowski, opposing the International slate. Strong challenged the International as well by openly supporting Montgomery on the Fightback slate.[33] Without mass rank-and-file organization in the USWA at that time—not just among African Americans but also political reformers—neither Strong nor Montgomery would have survived the challenge. If not fired, they would have found themselves sorting envelopes in Alaska.

Strong recognized that the union had put him in a compromising position because he was black and militant. The leaders had learned that they needed someone with credibility to represent them among black militants. The union stood to gain if Strong carried out his work effectively.

Jonathan Comer: The Diplomat

When Germano offered a staff job to Jonathan Comer for a second time in 1969, Comer accepted. The first offer had come as an attempt to stop Comer's leadership of the 1968 demonstration; Comer had too much commitment and integrity to walk away from the struggle at that point. In fact, Jonathan Comer was thinking that he would like to run for the presidency of his local union, 1011. He thought he had demonstrated the skills and character needed for the job. At the local and in the district, various forces began to mount an opposition. Had Comer won the presidency in an open election, he would have been a powerful man. No African American had ever been elected president of a basic steel local, and the International was concerned about the growing black power movement in the country and in the union.

Joe Germano resolved the dilemma by offering Comer a staff job. Having established a record of struggle, proud of the contributions he had made, and convinced that there was constructive work for him to do as a part of the International staff, Jonathan Comer took the job. He wrestled with this decision, as he had with the earlier decision to lead the Ad Hoc demonstration. Comer thought deeply about most things and based his life choices on the values and principles that had been instilled in him as a young man.

Comer was assigned to the Civil Rights Committee, as Strong had been, but worked out of the District 31 office until he was ordered to Pittsburgh by the union in November of 1978.[34] He preferred to be in Gary with his family; he knew his wife Nell would not be willing to follow him a second time, as she had in 1948 from New York City.

During his first decade on staff, Comer was a troubleshooter, a mediator, and an educator. He was sent into locals from Gary to Baltimore to Birmingham to deal with racial as well as gender conflicts between members and local leaders and also among members. His main assignment was in the South, reporting to the district director in Birmingham, Howard Strevel. Comer did not make the International nervous, the way Curtis Strong and Oliver Montgomery did, because Comer did not agitate unless every other tactic had failed. "Fussin' and cussin' " was his last resort, not his usual method of operation. He was careful not to raise unwarranted expectations among complainants, at the same time that he pushed the leadership to clean up the problems in the local.

A good example is the work Comer did at Bethlehem Steel Local 6787 in Burns Harbor, Indiana, in 1975. Two African American women had filed complaints against the local for failure to represent them in their fight against discrimination.[35] Comer participated in a series of meetings, carried out an investigation, and worked to rectify not just the immediate problem but also the racist and sexist practices he identified overall.

In his report to Alex Fuller, Comer noted:

> The question of the local union's role in this matter is that the union has "see-no-evil," "hear-no-evil," or at least, is not sensitive to some of the problems our members must face in the work place each day. . . . It was brought out that when a black person, male or female, or women in general, talked to the department representative or griever about an alleged violation, they are sent almost automatically to the civil rights committee for action and solution. In fact, more than 6 complaints I investigated were in no way [about] civil rights complaints. They were clear and precise violations of the agreement and should have been handled by the grievance committee.

What Comer was able to do so successfully was handle egregious examples of discrimination without sending local union officers into a defensive tailspin. His recommendations addressed the need for better and more consistent communications and cooperation among leadership bodies in the local. He suggested that all civil rights and grievance representatives be introduced to members and that their names and phone numbers be posted throughout the mill. He called for an evaluation of the servicing reps, and better education in the local on Title VII. Finally, he shared what the members had confided in him privately. "A number of blacks and women," he wrote, "especially black women, say they do not feel welcome when they come to their local union office. They expressed the fact that there are no minorities, particularly blacks, in office. This is a fact."[36]

In retrospect, Comer complained: "I got more done in Alabama than I did in Michigan, Ohio, Indiana, and Illinois together. Here I had to go back three or four times on the same foolishness. In Alabama I got a settlement." He contrasted his experiences during the U.S. Pipe hate strike in Alabama in the mid-1970s with some of his dealings with northern white union officials. In response to a black's promotion at U.S. Pipe, white workers had walked off the job. "We're down there with the Klan. The Klan is circling the union hall with the gun racks on their pickups, each with two guns. For four hours they rode around the hall blowing their horns and shouting racial insults. When I finally got into that meeting hall, those folks were sitting up in the windows everywhere. I thought, 'I'll never get out of here! But I'll be takin' a couple of those union brothers with me if I go!' "

Comer continued:

The president down there surprised me. He stayed up front, letting them hoot and holler and make catcalls for an hour. Then he got up, walked out front and said, "Okay, you've had your say. By God I'll tell you what I'm going to do. Tomorrow morning, if you're not back on that job, the company and the union has agreed to start hiring folks." Now I really thought we'd never get out. Took ten minutes to quiet them down again. Then he turned to one of the ringleaders: "Hey Jake. I hear you led this strike. I'm going to put this black man with you to work. If he fails, you fail." Well, he settled that strike. Up here, you couldn't do it that quickly.[37]

Comer believed that people could change, and spent an enormous amount of time on educational work. When he began on staff in 1969, fall-out from the enforcement of Title VII of the 1964 Civil Rights Act was reaching a crisis point. Women entering the mills were facing unspeakable hostility; black workers had turned to the NAACP and the courts, fed up with union foot-dragging. Comer worked closely with the NAACP's Herbert Hill, the labor secretary responsible for pursuing many of the suits black steelworkers were filing against their union. "What made me really like Herb," Comer explained, "was he reorganized that NAACP Labor Committee, made it a department, and put teeth in it."

Comer and Hill spent long hours discussing steelworker problems and became close friends during these years. Hill had known Comer for some time and had been an ally during the planning days of the 1968 protest. "Herb was even more valuable to me on staff," Comer noted. "When I had questions, I called on Herb and we talked and talked and talked." During the contentious negotiations leading up to the Consent Decree, the USWA denounced the NAACP and Herbert Hill almost daily. Comer maintained his close relationship with Hill and his support of the work Hill was doing. "Alex Fuller might have asked me to tone Herb down. He was strictly an organization man. But if he had said, 'You need not fool with Hill,' I would not have listened to him." Jonathan Comer took his stands, just more quietly than Curtis Strong.

Comer's grassroots educating and networking inspired hundreds of rank-and-file black workers and equipped them to battle discrimination on the job and in the union. Comer spoke at leadership institutes, civil rights workshops, and NAACP events.[38] His greatest strength was his ability to get people to look at problems differently, to step back from racial conflicts and address the issues from a unionwide perspective. He always claimed to know less than everyone else, so that they would not feel threatened by him. He often prefaced his words with "You know more about this than I do."

When the International wanted advice on appointments and promotions among blacks, they turned to Comer. He disliked being caught in the middle but always felt it was his duty to advise the union, based on the union's objectives and needs. He felt he knew what kind of activist could function effectively on staff, and he knew that those people were often workers who had not risked their jobs or futures by participating in the black struggle. He regretted that folks such as Ola Kennedy would not tow the line long enough to get appointed to staff. But he also knew that he could not recommend for a leadership position someone who would constantly antagonize those in the driver's seat. Comer did not choose to talk publicly about his specific recommendations. While on staff, Comer remained loyal to the leadership and its decisions. For example, Comer did not back Ed Sadlowski and the Fightback.[39]

In 1972, the International assigned Jonathan Comer to work with unions in the Virgin Islands, which, along with Puerto Rico, was part of Director Howard Strevel's region. If Comer felt exiled, he would not have said so, to the union or to me. He welcomed the opportunity to help train black activists and leaders throughout the Caribbean, and responded to every assignment as a gift, a chance to do good, to advance rights, to make the world better. Comer, however, was a family man, and did everything he could to get back to Nell in Gary as often as he could. The constant commute back and forth wore him and, perhaps, his patience down.

Although his assignment was training union leaders in the Virgin Islands, Comer was quickly pulled into organizing. Never having done any organizing before, he relied on his people skills and his union know-how. "Now I won over 90 percent of my campaigns, twenty-one out of twenty-three. But no sooner did I start winning than the International sent down the Organiz-

Jonathan Comer worked to develop officers among workers he organized in the Virgin Islands, 1973. Photo courtesy of Jonathan Comer.

ing Department from Pittsburgh. Well, I called Howard Strevel and read him the riot act. 'Get those suckers out of here. I don't want none of their foolishness, all their charts and bullshit, messing with our work.' " Strevel took them out of there and Comer kept on winning.

Growing up in Comer, Alabama, he had never dreamed he could be part of so many transformational social movements. Now that he was in a position to push change, he worked incessantly and without complaint. On July 19, 1979, Jonathan Comer was promoted to assistant director of the Civil Rights Department.[40] The new position brought prestige but did not reduce the amount of travel Comer was required to do; he needed a home base. "I was tired of maintaining two homes, one in Gary and one in Pittsburgh." Above all, Comer missed the support and advice of Nell, his family, and his friends. Comer chose to retire early in 1983. No sooner had he returned home that he became executive secretary for the NAACP, Indiana State Conference of Branches. He retired from the NAACP in October 1990, only to accept an appointment as executive director of the Gary Human Relations Commission.

What did retired black staff such as Comer and Strong do after decades of struggle against racism in the workplace and perseverance in building the union? They returned to the trenches, to the grassroots freedom struggle. They continued to be active in the NAACP and to serve as representatives on dozens of task forces, councils, campaigns, and mobilizations. They became members of the Steelworkers Organization of Active Retirees (SOAR) and stayed connected to the union and union activists.

Organizational change would not have occurred if African Americans had not stepped into leadership positions. Racism was too deeply entrenched in all the institutions of society to go away without being attacked from all sides, inside and out. Yet no African American leader in a majority white union or movement acted without restraints. Curtis Strong had a lot more leeway than George Kimbley did; he would not have accepted the job without that space. Jonathan Comer did not want to buck the system like Strong, although in some ways he accomplished more than Kimbley or Howard without bringing the house down on his head. Through their years as International staff, Kimbley, Howard, Strong, and Comer made enormous contributions to the United Steelworkers Union. Had it not been for their work, the union would not have had the active participation of so many African American members. The training and education they carried out—formally and informally—raised the awareness of leadership, staff, and workers of the character of discrimination in the mills and union, and on the importance of the anti-racist struggle. Equally significant, these four men were first-rate staff representatives. They were union builders first and foremost and served under some of the toughest conditions.

Every one of these men, however, expressed concern and regret that so many of their contributions had been forgotten or reversed. They spoke with grave disappointment about the setbacks of the past twenty years, in the union and also in the African American community. Jonathan Comer and Curtis Strong, still active and committed, put their energy and hours now into firing up a future generation of black union freedom fighters. Comer still signs his letters, "Yours in the longest struggle."

CHAPTER 8

"Diplomats and Rabble-Rousers"

Black Radicalism and the Union Movement

Debates among the five freedom fighters over strategies for doing union work reflected significant political differences. Although none of the men developed a coherent philosophical framework for their beliefs and actions—they were not intellectuals—they did a lot of thinking and reflecting on the black condition.[1]

The environment in which they moved had become ideologically charged during the depression years, and many unemployed or barely employed workers in the region had adopted a language of class struggle. From the early 1930s through World War II, labor insurgency overshadowed race organizations and movements. The working-class base of the race-conscious Universal Negro Improvement Association turned to the militant Unemployed Councils and other action-oriented coalitions for leadership. They were less drawn to the cooperative movements and the "don't shop where you can't work" campaigns within the African American community. Their involvement in the labor movement coincided with a period of increasing class consciousness among all industrial workers. Even many radical black intellectuals found themselves more at home in the class-based organizations of the left during this period than in nationalist circles. Such intellectuals included poet Langston Hughes and W. E. B. Du Bois, the most outstanding black intellect of the century.[2]

The specific historical circumstances affecting Kimbley, Young, Howard, Strong, and Comer contributed to how each of the five articulated his views and how each functioned within the union. George Kimbley flirted with Garveyism and communism, but he was, in the end, a pragmatist. His horizons were limited by his upbringing, and he favored a short-term "what works" approach. Above all, he took precautions to avoid retaliations against himself, not from capitalists but from white workers. Bill Young, in contrast, had a fairly sophisticated political worldview. He not only counted the leftists as his best friends but also identified himself as a socialist and put the class struggle first. He was a self-educated man with a great capacity for intellectual analysis. Johnny Howard began and ended his life believing in the American dream of equal opportunity and individual advancement. He valued and collaborated with the radical activists of the 1930s and 1940s but placed more faith in professional competence than in collective struggle as a trade unionist.

Curtis Strong turned to his trusted mentor, Arthur Adams, for guidance in his political formation. Adams's ideas had been shaped during his younger years in the left-led Mine, Mill and Smelters' Union. Most likely he was a communist. He schooled Strong to oppose the capitalist system as the source of oppression for African Americans as well as workers. He helped Strong over his early anti-unionism and convinced him of the importance of class unity. But Adams also promoted black organization and never tried to dissuade Strong from his nationalist beliefs. Strong advocated a radical black nationalism as the basis for interracial and class unity.[3]

Jonathan Comer mixed and matched according to context and constituency; his impulse was egalitarian. He resisted subordinating or merging identities and movements, because he believed that race, class, and gender inequities existed throughout the system, and that each required special attention and special measures. His concept of class was inclusive of race; at the same time, his commitment to racial equality crossed class lines. The "fine-tuning" of his black awareness took place in the army during the war. Northern blacks instilled in Comer a sense of entitlement and opened his eyes to the benefits of protest.

To some degree, all five men had an awareness and understanding of the broader political debates common among black intellectuals. In a general way, they knew the differences between Booker T. Washington and W. E. B. Du Bois, between the black nationalism of Marcus Garvey and the nationalism of the African Blood Brotherhood or what would become the nationalism of the Nation of Islam. They did not confuse the socialism of A. Philip Randolph with the socialism of the Communist Party. Their engagement in workplace and community struggles in the 1930s and 1940s brought them into close contact with communism and anticommunism, and their assessment of ideological tendencies mirrored their personal experiences. With the exception of John Howard, they harbored few illusions about the promise of upward mobility based on hard work or individual merit. None of them had witnessed change happening without an uphill struggle.

The five men's participation in the labor movement strengthened the African American freedom struggle by bringing working-class issues and alliances to the forefront. In Gary and East Chicago, Strong and Comer helped to transform the NAACP into a popular organization with working-class leadership. With the USWA's support, Young, Howard, Strong, and Comer, along with their peers, held positions on the Fair Employment Practices Committees, became precinct committeemen in the Democratic Party, and influenced local elections more than the black middle class. They carried out their civil rights activism as unionists, integrating the restaurants, movie theaters, and stores of northwest Indiana.

At the same time, their leadership in both union and civil rights work expanded the base of organized labor and provided the movement with unrelenting fighters. Without the ingenuity, sacrifice, and hell-raising of African American workers such as these five, the industrial union movement overall, and particularly in steel, would not have achieved the level of economic prosperity and security that workers experienced in the decades following World War II.

Black, working-class activism and antiracist CIO leadership turned the potential for broad unity into an effective and powerful alliance.[4] African American workers helped define the basic character of U.S. unionism.[5] One pioneer member of this multi-generational and ideologically diverse group, Oris Thomas, referred to his peers as "diplomats and rabble-rousers." "They were warriors," he recalled. Whether the five African Americans accepted or challenged racist union culture, whether they settled for gradual integration or fought for black power, their struggles for representation came to define the standards for democratic unionism in the region's mills. Their push for equal treatment set the measure for fairness, and their persistent efforts to forge racial unity breathed life into working-class solidarity. It is tragic that the gains they helped secure for American workers never reached the majority of black workers, and never benefited black workers as much as white workers. This reality never caused the men to abandon their fight.

The Meaning of Radicalism

In spite of their differences, all five men considered themselves radicals, and for their times, they were. African Americans who stood up for unionism in the first half of the twentieth century, or who fought for antiracist unionism any time in the twentieth century, were taking radical stands. They challenged the status quo, and put themselves out in front of the struggle. Their radicalism, however, was not the same as the radicalism of union activists or of the left. In a sense, in their resistance to oppression, they drew on traditions of struggle learned in the South, through slavery and beyond.

Black radicalism had a character of its own. In *Black Marxism*, Cedric Robinson describes African American resistance in terms of a broader and deeper legacy. "The Black Radical Tradition," writes Robinson, "was an accretion, over generations, of collective intelligence gathered from struggle." Freedom fighters such as Kimbley, Young, Howard, Strong, and Comer rediscovered this tradition and added to it the wisdom they developed from their industrial, working-class experiences.[6] This perspective helps explain how an accommodationist like Kimbley and a militant confrontationist like Strong could both be radicals.

Their radicalism had the mark of "union crazy" thinking, to use George Kimbley's phrase. Although they accused each other of self-serving careerism, and sometimes fought each other for the token opportunities made available to African Americans, they battled together as well. They shared a powerful belief that the union represented the best hope for black workers in their struggle for economic and social justice, and that the challenge of their generation was to gain union rights for black workers.

In a recent conversation I had, an African American steelworker took issue with my use of the word "radical." In his view, radicals are people who make a conscious decision to support someone else's struggle. In particular, he associated radical with white, and suggested that black people fighting for their own freedom and equality were not radical but "righteous." The distinction deserves consideration, because it seems to reinforce Robinson's view of a special heritage shaping the black liberation fight. In part, it is a rejection of the idea of radicalism defined in terms of political extremism, or opposed to humanistic values. For many white as well as black activists, the radicalism of the 1930s and the 1940s was characterized by an intense passion for justice. African American freedom fighters expressed their outrage at the system with a powerful sense of righteousness, rooted in centuries of oppression and driven by a moral and spiritual force.

Shifting Ideological Loyalties

The battle for ideological leadership of the black freedom struggle underwent a dramatic change in northwest Indiana with the emergence of an African American working class after World War I. The region was home to as many factions and views as every other center of black life in the century.[7] Gary, after all, had the highest density of African Americans of any northern city during the period covered by this study, and, in relative numbers, it also had a much larger black working-class than professional population. The region nurtured major black and labor movements in the country, from the

National Ad Hoc Committee in Steel to the National Black Political Assembly, which brought eight thousand African Americans to Gary in 1972, five years after the election of the city's first black mayor, Richard Gordon Hatcher.[8]

The role of African Americans in the 1919 steel strike in many ways defined the uniqueness of black activism in northwest Indiana. African American workers stepped forward as agents of change, and rejected self-identification as strikebreakers or victims. From the beginning, an important section of African American leadership in the Calumet Region grasped the link between race and class oppression and fought an interconnected battle for freedom. Louis Caldwell and C. D. Elston, for example, played a pivotal role in 1919 in winning black workers to the union campaign and preventing racial violence. That they were also given the opportunity to address all the rallies of mainly ethnic workers reflected the Steel Council leadership's commitment to black-white unity. The spirit of solidarity that reigned in northwest Indiana prior to the declaration of martial law, in retrospect, seems unique at that time.

The number of African American member organizers in the CIO campaign was also remarkable. That Gary steelworkers were able to sign up in the first months of the campaign more African Americans than any other ethnic group reflects the strength of their working-class networks. More than fifteen African American steelworkers served at one time on USWA District 31 staff, and the region produced more black USWA national leadership than any other area in the country.[9]

The Universal Negro Improvement Association (UNIA), founded by Marcus Garvey, infused life into the first movement among African Americans in the Calumet Region. With its emphasis on black pride, rallies, and marches, the UNIA served as a cultural magnet for the poor, the working-class, and new migrants to the north.[10] As Cedric Robinson characterized the movement: "Its dominant ideology was eclectic: incorporating elements of Christianity, socialism, revolutionary nationalism, and race solidarity."[11] Garveyism fostered community, and black Garyites wanted to be part of this community. George Kimbley met Walter Mackerl in the course of UNIA activities, and they both made the acquaintance of Jesse Reese in the same way. Curtis Strong's activist wife, Jeannette, was raised in the Garveyite movement by her father, one of its local leaders. Leonides McDonald, the first black staff organizer in East Chicago, was a former official of the UNIA.[12] The first black freedom celebrations and community traditions in the region emerged in conjunction with UNIA events.[13] The *Gary Sun* and later the *Gary American*, Gary's most important black newspapers, advocated black pride and black organization.[14]

"Soon after I come here, I joined the UNIA," noted union pioneer Walter

Mackerl. It was the organization's program that attracted him. "We knowed we were discriminated against. No question about that," he observed.

But Marcus Garvey had blacks to do something for themselves. It was bringing blacks together. It was the first organization that ever made me know who I was. Marcus Garvey's slogan was "Man know thyself." We didn't know ourselves. We were always told we were nothing. We didn't have no black history then. Garvey did more than the NAACP was doing, because he was training and teaching you who you was, what blacks could do and should do.

Older activists such as Mackerl and Ad Hoc leader Rayfield Mooty traced their roots to the Garvey movement. Although much younger, Oliver Montgomery traced his interest in black activism to his UNIA-loyal uncle.[15]

From Garveyism to Communism

The high unemployment and oppressive housing conditions for most black migrants in central Gary during the Great Migration period triggered strong support for a variety of protest organizations. In 1921, for example, the Communist Party began to have a visible presence in northwest Indiana. According to Elizabeth Balanoff's study of Gary's black community, the Communist Party found support in the region early on and focused its efforts in the African American community. "As early as May 1921," she writes, "Communists from the Calumet Region had traveled to Indianapolis to demand aid for the unemployed. Gary's delegation of nine included three unnamed Negroes."[16] Party speakers visited Gary regularly and the communist newspaper the *Daily Worker* covered incidents of racial discrimination in the mills.[17] Communist events in the black community often drew a crowd, with more recently arrived southern migrants being especially well represented. Faced with overcrowding, dangerous jobs, and frequent unemployment, these migrants sought vehicles for and allies in their struggle. An estimated three hundred blacks in Gary, for example, had joined the left-affiliated International Labor Defense by 1931.[18] The emerging black working class had much less interest than the small, but also growing, professional classes in courting acceptance among white leaders in the community or the mill.

With the UNIA's decline from the late 1920s into the Great Depression, Garvey supporters such as George Kimbley and Walter Mackerl looked for another vehicle to fight for black employment and housing; they found it in the Unemployed Councils formed by the left in the early 1930s.[19] There

Walter Mackerl as young man, c. 1928. Photo courtesy of the Mackerl family.

black activists learned about the Communist Party. George Kimbley, Walter Mackerl, and Jesse Reese sealed their friendship in these years. "We had a way of playing cards, every Friday night," Kimbley said. "Reese was a devout. He came out in the open and tell everybody, 'I'm a communist.' He didn't bite his tongue about it. And he was a very smart fellow, and he wasn't altogether illiterate; he could write his name. But the King's English; he'd tear it up."[20]

Jesse Reese had migrated to Gary sometime in the 1920s from Mississippi; his father was a minister. Reese had been put to work on a chain gang. When he escaped, he fled to northwest Indiana.[21] He hired in at Youngstown Sheet and Tube in Indiana Harbor in 1929.[22] According to Reese, they had "a skeletal union there called the Amalgamated Association. It had only three or four people in it." He said a Communist Party organizer came to his house one afternoon and asked him to become active in the Amalgamated as his party assignment. Reese had probably joined the party shortly after arriving in Gary. "I want you to build that union," he was told. "You're going to meet many difficulties. You're going to meet Jim Crow; they're going to throw it in your face," the organizer warned him. " 'Well,' I said. 'I have a few other things on my mind. Freedom,' I said, 'Tom Mooney, the Scottsboro boys—nine young Negro boys framed for rape in Scottsboro, Alabama.' " Reese, like many others, had been attracted to the party's political work against racism. He agreed to do the trade union work at the party's request.

"I went in," he explained, "and the first thing I met was old Jim Crow. They intended to run me out. So they said to me: 'Well, we don't take colored people in here, we haven't been taking colored people. But since you're a steelworker and we need the trade union built, we'll give you a chance. But remember one thing. You'll have to organize to stay here.' " Reese explained how he soon became president of the Youngstown Lake Front Lodge of the Amalgamated Association of Iron, Steel and Tin Workers. "I met a brother here in this union," Reese recounted. "He told me he liked colored people, but he liked them to stay in their place. I said, 'Brothers, I agree with him. The place of Black people is in the labor movement and officiating in their place. Every working man should know his place. . . . My place is in the labor movement.' "

A few days later, according to Reese, he was warned to keep his distance from the communists. The next time he took the floor at a meeting, he announced, "I didn't come here to tell you how good communism is, I came here to help you build a union." It wasn't long before four white men approached Jesse and told him they wanted to make him president of the Amalgamated. "You're the man for it; you can do a good job." When Reese explained the development to the party organizer, he said, the "man grabbed me and kissed me." Reese declared, "First time I'd ever been kissed by a man in my life, but it was a true kiss. It wasn't a Jim Crow segregation kiss."[23]

"Now I have seen Jesse Reese in a meeting," Kimbley observed, "after the union began to build up. I seen him get up before a crowd, four or five hundred or even a thousand and take the roof off the house. 'We've got to 'cruit the workers! We got to 'solidate the union!' Now isn't that some English." Kimbley continued: "And I mean the crowd would just raise the roof off the house. And on a picket line, nobody could beat him, handling a bunch of pickets with his whistle. He'd tell them when to stop, when to move and they'd stand there just like it was law," Kimbley added, waving his arms as if he were directing a crowd. "He just had that much power over people. Everybody thought a lot of him."[24]

Jesse Reese was not a large man but he was imposing. Of medium height, he had the broad, muscular build of a farmer. A contemporary praised his perceptiveness. "He was full of folk wisdom." As a communist educator, Reese was the best: "He'd always bring up the obvious that everyone else didn't see!"[25]

Walter Mackerl lived with Jesse Reese during the depression. "We rented a house together," he said. "I knowed him even before that. We had the UNIA." According to Kimbley and Mackerl, Reese was the point man for SWOC's work in the black community. Jesse Reese organized the organizers and left the community work to them, especially meeting with members of the Ministerial Alliance. He was not one to mince words or defer to religious leaders. Reese signed up Kimbley and Walter Mackerl. Mackerl used to drive Reese to secret communist meetings in East Chicago and later to SWOC meetings, at which Reese picked up the cards he would deliver to the volunteer organizing committee in Gary. Although Jesse Reese was the main communist spokesperson among black steelworkers, the party had other very strong advocates in people such as Bill Young, Arthur Adams, and Jacob Blake.

When asked who built the USWA in the Calumet Region, Kimbley responded, "Who really built the union? I'm going to tell you the truth, if you want to know. Honkies, niggers, and communists built the union." What they had in common, according to Kimbley and other African American activists I interviewed, was a commitment to social justice and an understanding of the importance of interracial unionism. Mackerl's account of the role of communists echoed Kimbley's. "I'm going to tell you something," he said, "whether you believe it or not. I can tell you the truth. We never could have got a union organized here if it don't be for them communist peoples. They were the only people that could get black and white together. There were a lot of whites that wanted to do it, but they was scared."

Mackerl also described Reese as "a diehard." Reese tried to get Mackerl to join the party, but according to Mackerl, "he couldn't make me a real communist. The only organization I was really on was UNIA. But I worked with them. The communist people were the only ones that would put up the big fight." He explained: "People were hoodwinked by the big shots who was using both sides. The communists taught them, made them understand and see what was being done. At first they couldn't see that. Just like our people can't see certain things. But the big shots was using them. That old slogan the English had was true: 'divide and conquer.' That's what was happening."

Bill Young shared their assessment. "Anybody that even stood up for their rights and was against racial discrimination, was against burning and hanging of black people, anybody that spoke out was called a communist. In the South they were jailed or killed." Inside the union, the communists had helped make Young a top union leader; they gave him friendship and support.

Many leading unionists in the early SWOC and USWA years associated closely with the Communist Party because of the party's success in building working-class organization. The early SWOC organizing team sent into northwest Indiana included at least three leftists and two African Americans.[26] Even Jonathan Comer, who did not arrive in the region until 1947, said the first man who helped him out in the union was a leftist. "I didn't know and I didn't care. He was a good union man."

Class Identity and Radical Alliances

During the 1930s and 1940s, anticapitalist ideology allowed African Americans to combine black nationalism, Christianity, and militant trade unionism with an array of socialist visions. The Communist Party's embrace of the demand for self-determination for African Americans and its continual antiracist emphasis were at the heart of the party's work in places such as Alabama and northwest Indiana.[27] Although few in the black community had any clear idea what the party meant by "the national question," they did understand the party's emphasis on antiracist work. Antilynching, anti-poll tax, Fair Employment Practices Committee, and public housing resolutions far outnumbered any pro-Soviet proclamations.[28] John Howard's son, David, indicated that, for his father in those early union days, "there was very little middle ground. The bad guys and good guys were better defined; my father's radicalism came from the events themselves."

One of the most important efforts to reach out more broadly to the black community, supported by the CIO and African American labor activists, was the establishment of the National Negro Congress (NNC). Robert C. Weaver, Ralph Bunche, and John P. Davis, three black intellectuals who had known each other since the early 1930s, were the driving force in the founding of the NNC. Walter Mackerl, George Kimbley, and Bill Young attended the first NNC meeting, in Chicago in February of 1936,[29] and were energized by the strong commitment to union-building among the black delegates. According to reports on the gathering, "the only ideology that dominated the meeting was support for organized labor," and the delegates voted unanimously for "working-class unity and mass pressure."[30]

The NNC represented one of the broadest coalitions of national black leaders, from its first president, A. Philip Randolph, of the Sleeping Car

Porters, to founding sponsor and black, communist spokesman James Ford. Participants came not only from unions but also from churches; community, civic, and women's organizations; fraternal societies; and youth groups.[31] Two community leaders from northwest Indiana (seven from the Chicago area) served on the Executive Council: Jacob Reddix and Reverend Marshall Talley. Local black labor activists corresponded with the council's executive secretary, John P. Davis; these included George Kimbley, Leonides McDonald, Pat Riley, Joe Cook, and Hank Johnson.[32]

In 1937, the National Negro Congress recommended that special committees be set up in regions such as northwest Indiana to support the mass recruitment of black steelworkers. In a letter to Philip Murray dated March 31, 1937, Davis called attention to "proposals on our Committee of Negro Steel Workers." "I have just received responses," he wrote, "indicating a favorable shift of attitude on the part of a large number of Negro steel workers. They indicate as well an improvement of opinion on the part of Negro community leaders throughout the whole steel area."

In 1938, Kimbley wrote Davis urging the congress to provide more support and coordination for organizing work in the region. "We are tirelessly building the principles and policies of our Congress in to the life of the white workers as well as the Negro workers," he argued. "We feel the need for closer co-operation and assistance in the building of labor committees of the National Negro Congress." In typical Kimbley fashion, he then named a few black activists whose work had been essential up to that point: "Brother Joe Cook, Brother William Young and Brother Stanley Cotton."

Although the Calumet Region's black steelworkers continued to participate in the NNC until its dissolution, its effectiveness was affected by A. Philip Randolph's resignation in 1940; he charged that the Communist Party was maneuvering to control the organization. In fact, between 1940 and 1947, when the NNC dissolved, the party did increase its control. In 1940, for example, party leader Max Yergen assumed the national presidency.

Left Activists in Northwest Indiana Chart Their Own Path

While the national offices of the NNC had an impact on events and relationships in the Calumet Region, the approach of local leftists demonstrated considerable autonomy from those offices and, even more so, from the Communist Party. The left activists in the mills focused a lot of their energies on encouraging other workers to step forward and assume leadership positions. They were, perhaps, better at united front work. The NNC officers from the region represented a broader political spectrum of the community. Arthur Adams, at Local 1014, was also a good example. Although he was very involved, he was pushing Curtis Strong into the more visible posi-

activists were turning from integrated to black organizations to carry forward the civil rights movement.

None of the five black activists went along with the ardent anticommunism that gripped this country in the postwar years. Some remained guarded but recognized that red-baiting, like race-baiting, threatened to reverse the union-based, antiracist struggle. Whether these activists thought primarily in terms of class or race, they understood the impact of McCarthyism on black-white labor alliances.[39] Bill Young championed communist coworkers and socialist ideology throughout his life, but still found it necessary to disclaim any direct organizational ties to the party. Doing so enabled him to defend his socialist views and preserved his credibility among blacks in the union. Both he and Kimbley made the argument that they could never have been members because of their strong Christian beliefs. Back in the 1930s and 1940s, of course, many activists found ways of embracing both God and communism.[40]

The Spread of Independent Black Organizations

Curtis Strong and Oliver Montgomery, leaders of the National Ad Hoc Committee, considered leftists to be their natural allies but never surrendered their independence. They rejected any move to subordinate race to class, or civil rights to workers' rights, because they had seen their cause set aside in the name of political expediency by white unionists on the left and the right. Montgomery, more than Strong, looked to the example of A. Philip Randolph, who had influenced so many black trade unionists.[41] They applauded Randolph's initiatives to build separate black organization while disregarding to a large degree his denunciations of the communists.

The intensity of state and right-wing terrorism aimed at black activists and organizations throughout the 1950s and 1960s required a circling of the wagons. If black organizations had carried the red label along with their demands for racial equality, many of their leaders concluded, they could not have survived the repression nor been able to function effectively in the African American community.[42] There were, in Gary as well as other places, examples of black nationalists who became communists but later returned to all-black organizations. The struggle was more important than the organization, and activists shifted their loyalties to the organizations that were influencing masses of black workers. In one sense, the activists' loyalty was to the radical black tradition. Some of their peers and white, leftist allies regarded these shifts as opportunistic, but for many black leaders, it was a question of flexibility in tactics, not bending of principles. They were committed to the antiracist struggle and supported it across the ideological lines drawn by the white majority. Within the black community, the lines were different.

Sectarianism and paternalism, on the left as well as the right in the trade unions, also pushed African Americans toward their own organizations. The progressives at USWA Local 1010, for example, made a political principle of protecting black leaders from charges of racial preference by assuming the leadership of antiracist work, not only among white workers but also in civil rights and community campaigns into the 1940s. The generation of African Americans that emerged after Bill Young saw this as a usurpation of their leadership.

In contrast, the organized African Americans at Youngstown and Gary Works developed their own leadership structures and lines of accountability among African American steelworkers from the beginning. As a result, they accomplished more for black workers and strengthened the support of African Americans for the union. They resisted the subordination of black issues to so-called class issues and argued that, in the long run, the good of the union would be better served by standing up for racial equality and justice. By building a basis for antiracist unionism through their independence and initiative, they also achieved stronger black-white cooperation and working-class solidarity. At Gary Works, perhaps due to the strength of the black caucus, the left responded to separate black organization by supporting it.

The situation in the Youngstown union, Local 1011, led to the emergence of an independent core of black activists. The activists were an influential voice in local politics but did not produce a caucus or formal organization. The Big Five, as they called themselves, had an extensive network of black leaders in departments throughout the mill. Their alliances with leftists were not as strong as those of the black activists at Inland or U.S. Steel. First of all, the Big Five leaders all hired into the mill after World War II. The relationships with white leftists were not as old or as personal. The more fluid structure of the black network, with multiple centers, and the absence of a pivotal figure like Curtis Strong fostered a more dispersed leadership. Because of his leading position on the Grievance Committee, Frank Perry worked much more closely with leftists in office than Jonathan Comer did. By the time Comer took on responsibilities outside of his department, in the mid- to late 1960s, many of the leftists had retired or withdrawn—men such as Jesse Reese, Chuck Fizer, Joe Norrick, and Fred Stern.

Black Power

One of the most important lessons learned from the 1919 strike was the necessity of maintaining black independence. African American iron and steelworkers in Gary had seen the white workers turned against them in the aftermath of the strike. They had seen the unions collapse and do nothing as the big steel corporations reduced their workforce and closed their semi-skilled and craft jobs to African Americans. The fact that unions were racist was nothing new to black workers. In order to limit white supremacy in the union, black workers increasingly turned toward self-organization and self-protection in the 1920s. Walter Mackerl's departmental organization, the Brotherhood of Hewers, is an example of the kind of mutual aid societies developed in the mills, even before the revival of the Amalgamated lodges, and long before the Sentinel League. Radical black activism ebbed and flowed but seemed always to be the foundation for interracial alliances in the labor movement.

George Kimbley, Bill Young, Walter Mackerl, John Howard, and Curtis Strong put their energies into building a labor movement because they were convinced that black workers could not survive in industrial America without unions. Equally important, they recognized that black workers could not gain union protection without an alliance with white workers. Initially all but Young focused their organizing wizardry on black workers and the black community. Kimbley walked the streets and fought the Ministerial Alliance. Walter Mackerl and his wife carried out "chain recruiting," from house to house. Howard partnered with Pat Riley to fight for promotions in long-bar storage. Strong and Arthur Adams zeroed in on the black coke plant workers.

These activists' methods, according to Elizabeth Balanoff, "seemed geared toward tapping into a network of trust that already existed in the black community and that was based on personal friendship and favors done in time of trouble."[43] Their different approaches captured family and community support for the union and enabled the network to grow more rapidly than in the white community.

African American women also played important activist roles in their community. Except for a handful of jobs in the tin mills during World War II, black women did not enter the mills until the late 1960s. Nonetheless, they did assume leadership in civic society, church life, and professional circles.[44] Equally important, they worked as political supporters in the union struggle. Organizers such as Bill Young, Walter Mackerl, Curtis Strong, and Jonathan Comer relied heavily on their wives in their union work, and not just for advice and comfort. Bill Young's wife was a community leader. Walter Mackerl's wife engaged wholeheartedly in the SWOC campaign. Jeannette Strong was active in the USWA long before she met Curtis Strong. Nell Comer consulted regularly on union business and was the backbone of her husband's campaign for Democratic Party precinct committeeman. With the exception of Kimbley and Howard, the black leaders picked outspoken and activist women as partners. From the earliest days of SWOC up through

Bayard Rustin (left) was the keynote speaker at a testimonial dinner for Curtis Strong, 1971. Photo courtesy of Curtis Strong.

the 1960s, however, there were few examples of black and white women organizing together. Black women activists remained rooted in the black community.[45] Ola Kennedy broke that barrier with her work in the District 31 Women's Caucus in the 1970s.

African American leaders had not quarreled much over building the union; their differences emerged over how to work in the union. These differences reflected national controversies over the role of unionism and black-white relationships in the postwar period. Out of necessity, African Americans advocated inclusive unionism. They had learned that if any group were to be left out, it would be African Americans. Their double struggle for unions and within unions placed them on the side of social unionism rather than business unionism. They argued for union support for antilynching legislation, open housing, and school desegregation, and later turned to sections of organized labor for support of the civil rights movement.

One Struggle, Many Strategies

No one approach to the freedom fight within the labor movement made the difference. The effectiveness of any strategy relied to some degree on the existence of the others. Kimbley and Young came at racist problems from to-

Jonathan Comer involved himself actively in mainstream politics. Here he spoke for civil rights legislation at a Gary city council meeting in 1960. Photo courtesy of Jonathan Comer.

tally different perspectives, as did Strong and Comer, but different times, different situations called for different approaches. Kimbley could not have accomplished what he did were it not for Young, Adams, Mackerl, Howard, and others. Kimbley did not challenge the white supremacists, but he exposed white supremacy. Howard demanded that his race not count for him or against him; and even though neither his idealism nor his abilities erased the impact of race, both were employed to advance the cause of black workers in unions. Kimbley and Howard helped make a place for African Americans in the union by bringing them in at the ground floor and by accepting leadership responsibilities under extraordinarily difficult circumstances.

At the close of every interview, I asked the men what advice they would give to African American workers just coming into the workplace and the union. Their responses varied, but each spoke to the importance of fighting racism and building working-class unity.

Curtis Strong reflected:

> If I'm leaving any tracks, if anything about what happened in the Steel-workers Union was because of me, it's my ability to instill in some blacks

the necessity of organizing a caucus. This was our strength. I helped organize caucuses from California to Maryland. I organized caucuses from Canada to Birmingham. If I've left anything, that's what I'd like to be remembered by. I think I made some tracks. And that would be my advice still: "Coalesce, but do it from a position of strength. Organize yourselves first and then coalesce." I believe it is as important today as it was then.

Bill Young's emphasis was different. "The union changed everything," he noted. "It gave you rights you never had before; it gave you the right to stand up and fight for your rights. It gave you the right to be paid what your job was worth." The advice he offered for the next generation of union activists reflected his own internationalist stand. "Number one: be loyal to your fellow workers and fight for their rights. See that discrimination is completely eliminated, and be loyal to all working people, all over the United States and the world." Finally, he added, always remember: "You can't live without unions."

Part Three

"THE LONGEST STRUGGLE"

Upheaval in Steel

From the Consent Decree to Global Restructuring

The rank-and-file struggle in steel opened opportunities for African American workers and made the United Steelworkers a stronger and more democratic organization. Black activists helped to change job and promotional structures in the mills, from the bottom up, and broadened membership involvement. These "diplomats and rabble-rousers" made some important inroads for African American workers nationally. But the advances did not eliminate the widespread segregation of jobs in the industry. Even as the Ad Hoc Committee disbanded national operations, Ad Hoc members and regional black caucuses were filing lawsuits against the industry and the union under the Civil Rights Act of 1964. With more than four hundred discrimination cases pending before the Equal Employment Opportunity Commission, the USWA signed a Consent Decree in April 1974 with nine steel companies and the federal government.[1]

The 1974 Consent Decree was the union's response to the demands for reparations for past discrimination as well as for affirmative hiring and promotional opportunities for African American workers. The aim of the decree was to broaden seniority rights from unit- or department-based calculations to a plantwide system and, in this way, reduce segregation in the mills. Hammered out in the context of Title VII of the Civil Rights Act, which required fair employment practices, the Consent Decree in basic steel facilitated the transfer of black workers out of dead-end sequences and low-paid ghettoes. African Americans hoped it would erase the very idea of a white man's job. Every integrated steel corporation except for Inland signed on to the agreement.

The controversy at the heart of the decree had to do with addressing the effects of past discrimination. Civil rights organizations and black workers were seeking compensation for all the losses they had suffered because they had been excluded from better-paying and safer jobs in the mill: back pay and special promotional opportunities with job security. The courts, under Title VII, had opposed retroactive remedies that would provide an opportunity to a black worker at the expense of a white worker already established in a position. In other words, those white workers who had benefited from past discrimination in their own promotions would not be penalized for company practices. They would not lose the jobs they obtained under a discriminatory bidding system that removed African American competition.

Under the Consent Decree, African American workers could transfer into new departments, retain their pay rate for two years, and use their plantwide seniority to bid on higher-level jobs that opened up in the unit. Workers would still come in at the bottom of a sequence, but, in the event of a subsequent job opening, they could advance based on their plantwide seniority. Once in a department, they could leapfrog over lower-seniority workers in the bidding process for vacated, higher-paying jobs. They could not bump lower-seniority workers out of the jobs they already held. What black activists such as Bill Young, Johnny Howard, Curtis Strong, and Jonathan Comer had battled for locally—integration of sequences and promotions from within the workforce—now became industrywide policy.

The rules and procedures, however, were complicated and contested. Jonathan Comer traveled to locals all over the United States, trying to educate local unions on civil rights laws and Consent Decree requirements. But lessons on how the Consent Decree should work did not make it work, at least not in the way that many workers hoped it would. Protest groups began to form among white as well as black workers. White workers argued that under the decree they were now being denied long-awaited promotions in their departments, by higher seniority black workers who had only recently bid into positions in their area. Curtis Strong, ambassador to the black workers, had to increase his visits to places such as Birmingham, Alabama; Sparrows Point, Maryland; and Buffalo, New York, where black workers decried the limits of the Consent Decree and the union's refusal to make amends on past discrimination.

Wage rate retention was an important feature of the Consent Decree. In the past, most African Americans had not taken advantage of bidding rights into new departments for two reasons. First, they would have lost their seniority rights for purposes of promotion. Second, by leaving their higher-classification and higher-paid jobs, they would have taken a wage cut. Since most African Americans started out in the dirty end of the mill (in steelmaking)—in the coke plant, blast furnace, and open hearths—few were willing to start again at the bottom in a finishing mill. If they transferred, their lower unit seniority would make them more vulnerable to layoffs. Their lower wages would translate into lower pension benefits upon retirement, since pensions were calculated based on average wages over the five years prior to retirement.

The Consent Decree acknowledged past discrimination by awarding affected black workers monetary compensation. It was pitiful compensation in the eyes of most African Americans, who, unlike their white counterparts, had not been able to buy homes in the suburbs, send their children to college, or support their families on one income between the end of World War II and 1974. Although millions of dollars were distributed to some fifty-five thousand women and minority workers, the checks averaged three hundred dollars, a sum that many African Americans considered yet another insult. What's more, by signing and cashing their check, black workers gave up the right to sue over any past discrimination. Some of the activists refused to cash their checks and tried to convince African American steelworkers throughout the country to do the same. Their efforts brought minimal results, because so many workers had given up any hope of future reparations and decided to take what they could get.

The lawsuits and actions filed against the steel corporations and eventually the union sought affirmative action plans, measures that could gradually reverse the results of a century of segregation and discrimination in the mills. The union balked at the idea of offering black members anything that could not also be offered to its majority white membership, so the Consent Decree offered the same transfer opportunities to white workers. They, too, had often been locked into the sequences or departments in which they were first placed, but there had never been an across-the-board racial employment policy directing white workers into the worst departments and jobs. What the USWA offered as an even-handed approach appeared to many African Americans as another version of so-called color-blind policy that carried over white advantages of the past. It was another way of denying the union's racialized history.

Negotiations for the Consent Decree were carried on by top union and corporate staff, which meant that the African American workers who had filed the complaints and the civil rights organizations that represented them were not included.[2] After years of working toward an alliance with African American organizations such as the NAACP, the USWA criticized civil rights groups locally and the NAACP nationally for their advocacy work supporting the black complainants.[3] African American union representatives were assigned to the implementation committees for the decree, but not afforded adequate resources or training to carry out its complex dictates.

The union had every reason to be concerned about racial divisions in its ranks. Companies and politicians took advantage of racial tensions in order to advance their own agendas. George Wallace, for example, cashed in on the backlash against black power activism in the industrial Midwest when he took his presidential campaign to Indiana, Michigan, and Wisconsin in 1964. He appealed to disgruntled white workers by relying on racial stereotypes and exploiting their fears. He won 30 percent of the total vote in Indiana, and every precinct in Gary with a white majority.[4]

The implementation of the Consent Decree complicated existing hostilities among workers in northwest Indiana—hostilities that dated back to 1920 and the Great Steel Strike. A growing number of white supremacist groups argued that black workers were making gains at the expense of white workers, and that the real problem had become reverse discrimination. Their literature started appearing in some of the region's mills.

Along with most of organized labor, the Steelworkers union was reluctant to criticize or contest reverse discrimination allegations. The union maintained it needed a "biracial approach" because it had to protect all its members, white as well as black. A policy of so-called race neutrality unfortunately perpetuated inequalities and downplayed the racist content of white protests against affirmative action. It would have been difficult to lessen racial divides with any amount of education, because white workers already had promotional expectations based on the advantages secured through decades of segregation. The union did little, however, to try to educate the white membership. Jonathan Comer's seminars on behalf of the USWA Civil Rights Department protected the International's image as proactive on civil rights but did not guarantee change. It took decisive action and intervention by leadership—as in Birmingham—to change the practices of the locals.

In the late 1970s, the union was forced to tackle the issue of affirmative action when a white worker, Brian Weber, filed a reverse discrimination suit against the union and Kaiser Aluminum. Known as the Weber case, the suit dealt with a voluntary affirmative action plan for apprenticeships. The USWA clearly opposed Weber's suit, and the union's position was upheld by the Supreme Court in 1979.[5]

Opening Jobs, Closing Doors

Under pressure from Title VII of the Civil Rights Act and the Consent Decrees of 1974 and 1975, the steel corporations increased the number of women and minorities hired into the mill. The companies opened jobs and apprenticeship programs that had previously been off-limits to African Americans. The United Steelworkers Union also continued to add minorities to its staff. In 1976 Leon Lynch, out of Local 1011 at Youngstown Sheet and Tube, became the vice president for human rights. In 1974 the first woman organizer, Melena Barkman, was hired onto the International staff.[6]

Meanwhile, in District 31 and nationally, opposition reform candidates were mounting a challenge to the incumbents in the International elections. Just as the civil rights movement inspired social justice groups among women, Latinos, environmentalists, and gays, black militancy in the USWA helped reawaken oppositional movements in the union. In some ways the Ad Hoc Committee laid the groundwork for other rank-and-file reform groups, such as the national Fightback. The Steelworker Fightback, headed up by Ed Sadlowski out of Chicago's South Works, challenged Lloyd McBride in 1976 for the International presidency. Sadlowski selected Ad Hoc leader and staff man Oliver Montgomery for his vice president, the first African American to be slated for a top Executive Board position. Old reform caucuses linked up with Ad Hoc groups and recently hired younger radical activists of the new left to rebuild a grassroots prodemocracy movement.[7]

Along with the national Steelworker Fightback, a militant and effective District 31 Women's Caucus emerged in the region. Its founding cochair, not surprisingly, was Ola Kennedy from the Ad Hoc; she brought dozens of African American women into active participation in the caucus. Kennedy's cochair, Roberta Wood, was a young radical with roots and allies that dated back to the old left movements in the district.[8] The mid-1970s were tumultuous times, as grassroots caucuses sprang up around the country and joined forces to fight for democracy and equality in the union.[9] Their main demands included the right to strike over contracts and the right to ratify them as well.

The economic downturn in the late 1970s plunged the steel centers into a recession, triggering the massive and long overdue restructuring of the steel industry. By 1982, Calumet Region steel mills were closing old and obsolete departments on the hot end of the mill—where the steel was made—and modernizing and downsizing every department, laying off tens of thousands of workers. By the mid-1980s, one-half of the Calumet Region's steel workforce had been eliminated. The union dropped by 50 percent in membership and resources, and even union staff representatives were being laid off. The good times had ended, and the last hired, the last promoted, the last put on staff, became the first to go. African Americans began their return to marginality and invisibility.

Global Restructuring

In the absence of any job opportunities, affirmative action policies amounted to nothing. The Inland Steel Company, for example, had 25,460 jobs at its employment peak, in 1979. By 1985 there were fewer than 15,000

Staffer Curtis Strong (left) defied the International and supported the Steelworker Fightback. Here he stands with Fightback leader and District 31 Director Jim Balanoff (center), 1976. The person on the right is unidentified. Photo courtesy of Curtis Strong.

jobs, a 34-percent decline. By March 2002, the number of union workers had fallen to just over 6,000. Youngstown Sheet and Tube, bought by LTV, went from a high of 11,704 in 1959 to 4,700 jobs in 1985. By the end of the 1990s, LTV had entered bankruptcy for the second time in two decades and had fewer than 3,000 bargaining unit employees. In December 2001 LTV shut down its furnaces, and in February 2002 the company ceased to exist, leaving former workers and retirees without health benefits and with reduced pension payments. U.S. Steel's employment declined by 68 percent, from 25,000 jobs in 1959 to 7,000 in 1984. Union jobs were cut to about 4,000 by the end of the century, although U.S. Steel maintained profitability, while nineteen other steel companies declared bankruptcy in 2001. Bethlehem Burns Harbor, the newest and last integrated mill to be built on the lake, dropped from 8,700 employees in 1979 to 6,300 in 1984. In October 2001 Bethlehem also declared bankruptcy, reporting 4,800 employees.[10] In January 2003, Bethlehem went out of business, purchased by International Steel group (ISG).

Even though many African American workers had longevity in the mills, they often worked in the first departments to be shuttered. Open hearth furnaces disappeared completely in steel producing.[11] More efficient furnaces, known as basic oxygen furnaces (BOF), have taken their place. Very few coke plants remain in operation anywhere in the United States. In place of ingot-casting that fed into the blooming, billet, and plate mills, a process of continuous casting now allows the steel to be processed into coils without reheating or moving bulk steel. The elimination of so many middle steps in steelmaking have dramatically reduced energy costs and workers.

The new technology has also opened the door to mini-mills, small operations that melt scrap or recycled steel in a direct reduction process that rolls out a finished product. Mini-mills employ 200 or so workers and are almost

Black activists provided key support to the Fightback, 1976: Bill Gailes, Local 1010 (far left); William "Buddy" Todd, Local 1014 (third from left); Jack Smith (standing, center); and (?) Dixon, Local 1014 (far right). Dorothy Gaines is seated in the middle. Photo courtesy of William "Buddy" Todd, Calumet Regional Archives, Gary, Indiana.

all non-union. The competition from mini-mills have made the large steel-making integrated mills financially unfeasible. More and more, steel mills are purchasing materials from foreign competitors—from coke and scrap to steel plates—for a cheaper price that they can produce them at home. The USWA has mobilized tens of thousands of steelworkers in a fight for fair trade to keep the integrated mills working, but they cannot stop U.S. companies from continuing to acquire foreign-made steel.

The impact of plant closings, new technology, foreign imports, and restructuring on the Calumet Region, and especially on the African American communities, has been devastating. It had taken black workers almost a century to lay claim to their rights to equal opportunity and treatment. The legacy they hoped to pass down to the next generation vanished. Their children and grandchildren would not even have access to low-paid, dirty jobs in the mills.[12]

It was not uncommon to find black workers with over twenty-five years of seniority on layoff at the same mill that still employed workers with less than five years, frequently white skilled tradesmen. The apprenticeship programs have disappeared. The effects of departmental, sequential, and unit seniority systems survived the Consent Decree, because African Americans

District 31 Women's Caucus activists, c. 1978. Standing, from left to right: unidentified, Alice Brody, Sarah Slaughter, Ernestine Mitchell, Cochair Ola Kennedy, Cochair Roberta Woods, USWA Local 65 President Alice Peurala, and Dorreen Carey, editor of the caucus newspaper. The woman in front on the right is Gloria Kelly. Photo courtesy of William Carey, Calumet Regional Archives, Gary, Indiana.

tended not to leave the jobs and departments they had known for decades. They went out the door with the old, dangerous, and obsolete machinery. Of course, thousands of white workers did as well but not in the same proportion.

Many African American workers viewed their fate in steel as the result of a corporate conspiracy; some, as betrayal by the union as well. Adhering to so-called color-blind policies after forty years of race discrimination, the union would not support special measures to remedy the injuries of the past. Its avoidance of affirmative steps was not a response to shrinking employment, because the union did not respond to the gradual erosion in jobs until disaster hit in the 1980s. By then, the union saw no way to stop the job loss and wage concessions. The mobility of capital made corporate announcements of possible closures or divestment real options, not threats. The new technology has helped to accelerate the dismantling of integrated mills.

Efforts of African Americans, and especially women, to find protection against the injuries of past discrimination to keep their jobs confronted a new backlash culture of reverse discrimination. Attempts to gain staff, Executive Board, or top leadership positions in a shrinking union triggered accusations that black workers were seeking preferential treatment. Echoes of past debates haunted USWA conventions, where union officers argued again that decisions had to be based on seniority and ability without reference to race or gender. Once again, blame was directed at black workers and civil rights groups for being divisive and undermining class solidarity. The USWA never claimed that discrimination had not existed and did not still exist in the organization. Its opposition, however, was primarily to retroactive settlements, quotas, and guidelines that might be perceived as advantaging African Americans at the expense of white workers.

The implosion of the steel industry at the dawn of the twenty-first century has wrought incalculable devastation on the African American and Latino communities of East Chicago and Gary. These cities have lost millions of dollars in tax revenues; their budgets can barely support garbage collection, public transportation, and drastically increased demands for social welfare payments. LTV was the second largest employer next to Ispat/Inland in the Indiana Harbor area. Across the board, steel corporations reported even greater losses in 2001 than in previous years.

As seasoned black freedom fighters such as Curtis Strong and Jonathan Comer retired, they were not replaced by activists of the same militant caliber. Fewer African Americans remained on staff, and those who did lacked the kind of race- and class-consciousness that had shaped the attitudes of the

Workers protested concessions on wages, work rules, and apprenticeship changes at a Local 1014 meeting, 1979. Photo courtesy of Dorreen Carey, Calumet Regional Archives, Gary, Indiana.

earlier generations. Without Ad Hoc or other radical black organizations, African Americans promoted into staff positions once again found themselves isolated and limited in their ability to voice the concerns of black members. New staff in the Civil Rights Department, for example, were hired from outside the union. They handled complaints and provided educational services, but they had not experienced the struggles of rank-and-file members. The departure of the early freedom fighters, with their passion and resilience, left a vacuum in the union.

Unfortunately, the passing of these activists went almost unnoticed. When Walter Mackerl died in December 1999, just a month after his ninety-ninth birthday, Curtis Strong and Bill Gailes stood for the union at his funeral. From his home Local 1066, which he had founded and served as its first vice president, the only representative was Glen Dowdell, a rank-and-file activist and labor studies student who had interviewed Mackerl for a class. When Bill Gailes died a year later, Ad Hoc activists from as far away as Pittsburgh, as well as Local 1010 leaders and members, did attend the funeral. It became an occasion for reminiscing.[13] On November 23, 2001, I sat by Curtis Strong and Joe Gyurko at the funeral of John Mayerik, first president of the Gary Works local. There were a handful of retirees and labor studies students but no representative of the union leadership.

What would Curtis Strong or Jonathan Comer think about the increased racism and discrimination in the country's workplaces today? How might they address the disappearing opportunities and jobs? Are there black activists in the USWA today carrying on their legacy of struggle? In the next chapter, Comer and Strong explore their current views in a dialogue with three other African American leaders from the Calumet Region. Their discussion, both practical and philosophical, reflected the humor and spirit that have kept them fighting for so many decades.

CHAPTER 10

"Fire in the Belly"

A Conversation among Black Labor Leaders

"**H**ow are black folks faring today in the workplace and the union?" The question produced a momentary silence, as five African American steelworker leaders—past and present—looked to each other to see who would speak first. In the room with Curtis Strong and Jonathan Comer were three black activists, a generation or two behind them in the struggle. The five gathered on November 30, 2000, to examine the status of African Americans in the Calumet Region, the USWA, and the labor movement in general.[1]

Josephine Brooks, a recently retired staff representative from District 31, had been union president of USWA 3008, the clerical and technical local at the Sheet and Tin, at U.S. Steel Gary Works.[2] Mary Elgin is the financial secretary at USWA Local 1010 at Inland, the first woman to hold that position in a basic steel local. Her activism began with the District 31 Women's Caucus in 1975.[3] Fred Redmond was working on the International staff in Pittsburgh with the Membership Development Department when this discussion took place. Prior to that job, Redmond worked as casual staff in District 31, and before that, was the president of Rayfield Mooty's old local in Chicago representing aluminum workers. In 2002 Redmond became the assistant director of District 7 (formerly District 31).[4] My colleague, Thandabantu Iverson, a seasoned labor and civil rights activist turned labor educator, served as moderator. Together they brought a couple centuries of union experience to the table, layered with equal amounts of reflection, anger, and humor. At times the room sounded like a Sunday morning sermon, with lots of "Amen's". At other times, raised, emotional voices bounced off the walls, mixing chal-

215

Curtis Strong standing in front of U.S. Steel Gary Works, 2000. Photo courtesy of Curtis Strong.

lenges with recriminations. Passion for the struggle, for freedom, had been and still is the wellspring of the five participants' activism.

When the five first sat down, the conversation moved back and forth like a tennis match. Brooks had compiled a list of African Americans who had served on District 31 staff. Had she left anyone out? Each person started throwing out names, trying to reconstruct black labor activism since the days of George Kimbley. "I think there were four or five on the Illinois side at one time in the late 1970s," Brooks observed. There were more than fifteen names on her initial list. "Easier to count them today," someone remarked. "There aren't that many."[5] They all expressed disappointment with the current status of African Americans in the industry as well as in the union; they attributed that status to economic bad times, union back-pedaling, and declining black participation in labor struggles. Since all five activists came out of the steel or aluminum industry, where wages and benefits have outpaced those in most other industrial and service jobs held by black workers, their comments reflected their advantaged position within organized labor.[6]

The dialogue revolved around a few central questions. Why isn't African American involvement in organized labor as widespread today as it once was? What are the issues important to African Americans and how has the union addressed them? What could the union and black leadership do better? And, finally, what approaches have proven effective in increasing black union activism and representation? In the course of the conversation, indi-

Jonathan Comer, 1986. Photo courtesy of Jonathan Comer.

Josephine Brooks, 1995. Photo courtesy of Josephine Brooks.

vidual perspectives changed and merged into a more collective, nuanced reflection on the problems facing African American unionists.

Why Aren't Black Workers More Active?

"Most African American members today don't understand the struggle that brought them inclusion under the collective bargaining agreement," observed Fred Redmond. "They have equal pay, protection under the federal laws and under the contract. They pay their dues and receive representation in the workplace. As a result, there's complacency. I've heard some people even argue that we have representation in the union in proportion to our activism, that we don't get involved enough on the local level. The economic success of people in the mill," continued Redmond, "has led to apathy. Back in the '50s and '60s when my father was active, African Americans held the union accountable."

Mary Elgin, still a local union activist, focused more responsibility on herself and other black leaders, on their reluctance to take unpopular stands. "When our leaders say, 'We don't want to talk about that; we don't want to get involved in that,'" referring to issues in the black community, "we give in to the pressure not to take a position. We've fallen down on the job. We have set the tone and not given direction," she stressed. "There are too many issues that sidetrack us. Now people want more money; they want retirement money so they can get out of the mill, and they want overtime. We're not talking about the kind of issues that really matter to us in our lives and communities."

Josephine Brooks looked for a broader context. "What we are talking about here is not just about unions or blacks," she reminded the others.

It's a societal problem that comes with the times. I've been active since the late '60s, and when we had union meetings, mayors and state legislators used to come. We were an organization to be reckoned with. Today when you look at the NAACP, at the churches, at other organizations, they're all losing people too. We have made fat cats out of folks. They have nothing left to struggle for in their minds. They've got it made. People feel that it's just too hard to struggle. But this system is making sure that black faces are disappearing from leadership positions. I think it's deliberate.

"I see it a little different," interrupted Strong. "There's apathy, but it's the leadership that causes apathy, especially the lack of leadership among black trade unionists." Elgin agreed that blacks deserve part of the blame but not the primary responsibility. "Unions have not been about activism like they used to be," she pointed out. "It's more about control, and we have been controlled and controlled and controlled right out of the picture." "You said it, sister!" "You got that right!" "Amen!" came the choral response. "Leadership has been more interested in controlling the union in terms of resources," continued Elgin, "than in building the union, and bringing in people who have been disenfranchised. The unions are afraid to support black issues because of their white membership. The union does not speak to African Americans today like it did in the past. Black voices are not speaking for themselves as much, and when they are, who's listening?"

The conversation moved from finger-pointing to a recognition that various factors were at work, and that blame could not explain or resolve the problems. The participants struggled to formulate context and analysis. "This is not the 1960s," Brooks pointed out. "We can't go back to the 1960s and apply those same tactics to the year 2000. It just won't work. People are living differently." "And where are those social movements?" asked Mary

Mary Elgin at a reunion for the District 31 Women's Caucus, 2001. Photo courtesy of Dorreen Carey, Calumet Regional Archives, Gary, Indiana.

Elgin. The group explored the increasing stratification and economic polarization of the black community, a growing divide between a fraction of rich and the impoverished majority. The once expanding black middle class is getting smaller. Some black workers thought they had it made, the group agreed, but unemployment, underemployment, and low wages still plagued the majority. Some black leaders had grown complacent and reluctant to stir up the pot, but others were still "cussin' and fussin.'" Many of labor's top leaders had put control first and wanted foot soldiers rather than militant activists. But many unions were searching for ways to rebuild their ranks.

Talking Union

Comer leaned forward, anxious to put his views on the table.

Well, we figured out early in the game that you got to go up to the union hall and get involved. When I started out, there might be 150 people out of

Fred Redmond (left) with Local 1010 active retiree, Joe Gyurko, 2002. Photo courtesy of Ruth Needleman.

ten thousand at a meeting, and not more than ten of them were black. Our strength lies in our attending meetings. Back then, we were primitive in East Chicago. Curt was doing a better job than we were doing. They were organized at 1014. So we started a campaign to get blacks out to the local meetings. At one meeting, the local passed a motion giving two thousand dollars to support skeet shooters. But when a brother jumped up and asked for two delegates to be sent to the NAACP conference, all hell broke loose. "Well, we'll filibuster this skeet shoot thing down because you guys out on the lake shooting skeet think you're out there shooting black folk."

An ability to laugh at the blatant racism of the past had a lot to do with early activists' longevity in the union.

"Is it apathy or have African Americans become disillusioned?" interjected the moderator. "No question," Comer jumped back in. "Why the heck go to the hall if they're not dealing with your issues? I had no fortune there, so why go? But then I got hurt. I started hollerin' until I got attention. Then I felt some inclusion. We used to have hotly contested elections, and fierce debates. Folks came out over issues they really cared about."

"Don't tell me there aren't any issues!" Strong countered. When unions put social justice concerns aside in the name of business unionism, he argued, many black activists lost interest in the unions. Black participation started its downward slide. "Unions are supposed to be about civil and

Thandabantu Iverson, 2001. Photo courtesy of Ruth Needleman.

human rights in the community, not just the workplace," concurred Redmond. "Labor was another venue for addressing civil rights issues. There are still civil rights issues in the black community. Take reparations for African Americans. What organization would you think is more qualified to sit down and discuss reparations than unions? We talk about compensating people for their labor all the time.

Redmond continued:

Let's look at racial profiling. We're talking about harassing people because of the color of their skin. Organized labor has not recognized this as a labor issue. People don't see any link between organized labor and the civil rights movement as a whole. They look at them as two separate entities, and for that reason, black workers are not drawn to the labor movement as an organization that would not only protect their rights on the job but also as a social organization that would protect their social and political rights.

Let me give you an example. A few years ago—I was still local president—our district director, Jack Parton, was arrested for marching against apartheid. African Americans in my local held up newspapers, saying they were proud that their union was in the fight against apartheid. Workers knew that Parton led an anti-Klan rally a few years back. The director's position caught the attention of black people in the district. When organized labor stands for social justice issues that affect African Americans then African Americans get connected to the union.

Mary Elgin shared his views but questioned the union's commitment to social activism. "Unions have to be connected to the movements around them. Even more important, black leaders have to be connected to those organizations and movements which give them energy, spirit, and motivation to take back and fight for in the union. Too often," she continued, "the union forces its leaders not to take positions in other organizations, not to support their issues. It is because we have not been connected to social movements that we cannot provide leadership. Those organizations help us to bring social change and energy back into our union. The problem is not apathy." Both Comer and Strong made sounds of agreement. Throughout their lives, they had maintained their activism in African American civil rights and community organizations, at times in defiance of their union. Strong, in fact, had flaunted his dual affiliations during his years on staff.

How important, then, is the connection or lack of connection between black trade unionists and civil rights organizations? "Do black trade unionists, especially those on staff," asked Iverson, "feel that they have to stop being involved in the NAACP or the Coalition of Black Trade Unionists or anything that is overtly for black self-determination?"

"We are influenced by our coworkers," responded Mary Elgin.

They tell us, "Why do you need black organization when we're all one?" "We're one union, you don't need the black thing anymore." Most of us buy into that, rather than accepting that until we have parity, until we are equal, we need that black organization in our society for checks and balances. We need black organization just to ensure that we stay as equal as we are. But we listen to that kind of dialogue among the white folks around us that say we don't need it anymore. Even our civil rights committees. You find the civil rights committees being merged with the women's committees. We both are looking for something and in that sense there's a similarity. But we're not looking for the same thing. We want racial parity and respect.

Women are still fighting just to find a place. It's a dual fight and I feel it on both sides, as an African American and as a woman. As women we find ourselves still being challenged to prove that we are part of the trade union movement. I can be a better trade unionist if I can bring in my social needs and my political needs. When it comes to working on African

American issues today, the only way our unions feel obligated to do anything is to buy some banquet tickets from the NAACP.

Coalitions Make the Difference

"It's all about coalition-building," noted Redmond.

Mary Elgin during the Newport News strike of 1979. Photo courtesy of Mary Elgin.

Unions know about coalition building. For example, our union is engaged in a struggle against unfair trade. We have entered into relationships with students who are vigorously fighting against sweatshops. We have a common agenda. Organized labor must work harder to build coalitions with traditional civil rights and community-based organizations that are trying to address issues of reciprocity for African Americans and others who have been disenfranchised. We have to ask ourselves the question: Are they not being built because our leadership feels that the white membership is not going to accept such coalitions? That would be my guess why we are not in coalitions against racial profiling.

"It is troubling that the leadership is not trying to form these kinds of coalitions," observed Brooks, "when the statistics tell us that the people out there who are not organized, especially in the South, are African Americans." "If the leadership is taking a back seat because of the white membership, then what is the future of unions?" Iverson's question refocused the conversation. Fred Redmond returned to his previous point about the importance of social issues.

We cannot go into the shop—we do it and it don't work—telling folks they have to come to union meetings, that we got issues. They still don't show up because at the end of the day, they're still being included in the seniority scheme and the wage scheme. We have those because Curtis and Jonathan fought for them and got us included in the economic piece. If we're going to get African Americans involved in the union today, leadership is going to have to be pushed beyond the collective bargaining issues

Josephine Brooks (left) prepares a local activist for an organizing meeting, c. 1995. Photo courtesy of Josephine Brooks.

that we deal with day-to-day. You folks were successful. We already got that. If African Americans on the floor know that my union stands against racial profiling, that there's been a public commitment made by organized labor to stand for social issues that affect African Americans, then I think African Americans will become more interested in getting involved in the movement as a whole. Why isn't more leadership moving in that direction? We have to answer that question.

Self-Organization

"Well, we have to start talking more about the black issues, what is happening now," insisted Comer. "When we leave the union hall, we have to talk one-on-one. We have to pattern ourselves after the Eureka Club. We have to work with the black churches and the black community; that's a step in the right direction." "That's what they're afraid of," asserted Strong.

That's what the white leadership was afraid of in the formative days of protest. David J. McDonald always said to us, "You guys, you're gonna destroy the union from within." We knew better. We said, "We will coalesce with you, as long as we can coalesce from strength. We refuse to coalesce with you when you got all the horses! When we are equal politically, then we'll coalesce." McDonald always thought "those blacks don't have anywhere else to go."

"You mean the Democratic Party syndrome," laughed Redmond. "That's the Democratic Party's argument to the union. 'You ain't got no place else to go.'" "Are we saying that you don't have to make the union attractive to African Americans because they don't have any other place to go?" asked Iverson. "What kinds of things should or could the union do, that you don't see the union doing, to bring in African Americans?" Josephine Brooks responded. "I don't feel that our union is trying to be inclusive. It seems to me that the things the union is doing are designed to kind of push people away. When you don't see people who look like you—our color—in leadership positions, you are a little leery about getting involved." "Or you don't see your own agenda," Strong added. Brooks nodded in agreement.

"When I was at Youngstown Sheet and Tube," Jonathan Comer broke in, taking a lesson from history, "I had the feeling the white folks were saying to me: 'If it ain't broke, don't fix it.' That was the attitude at that time of the union leadership. 'It ain't broke.' What we did in our protest was we broke it, so that something had to be done. It seems to me you got that same attitude today. White folks don't see the problem." "Or they think the problem is reverse discrimination!" offered a more cynical voice.

"Any move to advance black leadership is going to have to come from the local level, not from the staff. The staff reps are political animals," observed Elgin. "It's their job to keep the International informed and deliver the vote. It's going to take local union activists, who make demands. We want parity. We want sufficient numbers of leaders to represent us! The problem is that the movement is not taking place today."

"Now the women in the workplace, they have spoken," acknowledged Elgin.

They came to the convention in 1996 and spoke. They had resolutions and demands. They came back to the convention in 1998, and now we have a woman who's going to be an assistant to the president for women's affairs.[7] Then they come back again in 2000 and made another move. "We want a spot on the International Executive Board." "Well, wait a minute," answered the leadership. "We can't do that because we have a democratic process and within that process we just can't go and appoint a woman. We have to elect people."

"Why that's the same thing they told us thirty-five years ago," Strong recalled. "There's that control mechanism that exists, and the only way it's going to be penetrated and changed is through some kind of organized resistance. The rank and file is going to have to say, 'Wait a minute!' Like we did." "You know that back in 1942 every one of those white district directors were appointed first time around," pointed out Comer. "Then they ran for election as incumbents."

Rebuilding Interracial Unionism

"How do we as African Americans workers," questioned Iverson, "get our white coworkers to push with us?" "You coalesce, like I've been saying all along," Strong stated.

> Politically you can do it, and politically they count the votes. We coalesced with hillbillies and Polish workers, whoever we could get to support our issues. We said "if you will advocate what we want, we'll do the same for you." But first, before you do that, you have to have strong black leadership. And it's not like there aren't any strong black leaders. I look at folks like Mary. But it's not all connected and pushing in the same direction.

"Curtis hit the nail on the head," Comer said, referring to the black caucus groups and the need for national leadership. "That's how we did it too. The blacks got together and worked with progressive white folks. We formed a coalition so that we could clean house. Some of our brothers, you know, are more conservative than the white folks. They're not going to rock the boat. 'Don't talk to me,' they'd say if I came up to them. You form a caucus and a coalition. You can make change. When you have to fuss and cuss," he added, "we know how to do that, too!"

"You have to appeal to the white progressives in our union," Fred Redmond suggested.

> We have to say, "This is what we bring to the table, but we need your support." We have organizations. We could build the union through the South. We could coalesce with the NAACP. We could coalesce with the black churches. This is where the people who are un-unionized are. These are their venues. We have the capability to go into these venues. The only way you're going to get some agreement on that is to approach progressives who want to see the union grow, and they exist in our union.

Josephine Brooks recounted the way in which she built the black-white coalition that put her into office.

In 1960, when they hired me in the accounting office at Sheet and Tin, I was the first African American hired. It was more than two years before they hired another one. Something happened to me, like Jonathan said, "I got hurt," and I decided to go to a union meeting. You know what I saw there? I saw twenty-three white men. Right then and there I made up my mind that I'm not paying dues to this organization if they're not going to listen to me. I came right back to the people in my department—and they were mostly white women—and I said, "I'm not going back to another union meeting unless you come with me. I'm not going to be embarrassed again going by myself." I arranged for us all to have dinner together and then eleven of us, ten white women led by a black woman, marched into that next union meeting. All hell broke loose. We were a force, and they had to reckon with us. They couldn't turn those white women against me because we worked together. I became a union activist and the majority white folks in my local elected me financial secretary and then president.

Fire in the Belly

"You have to have that burning desire for change," stressed Brooks. "You have to take risks and you can't be afraid of losing. I don't see that desire today." "I don't see the desire either, the fire in the belly," agreed Strong. "How you put it there I don't know."

Mary Elgin had some ideas. "I don't think we take the time to talk to the membership as leaders. I don't think we take the time to make it known what we really believe and make it known what we really need. We have to give them reasons. We have to talk about issues. 'This is the issue we need to address.' At a recent Women's Conference," she recounted:

African American sisters got upset because they didn't think we were sufficiently represented in leadership. We just got together and took a room; two of our staff sisters also came in and closed the door behind them. But we didn't know how to agree on what we needed and how we were going to get it. We need to get ourselves organized. If they put a woman on the International Executive Board, it's not going to be one we want unless we are organized. We have to redo what has already been done.

"Yes," Brooks repeated, "we have gone full circle back to the same thing we demanded in the past. Not just what the Ad Hoc demanded, but women too. In 1976 women organized and demanded representation in leadership. Now they're asking again but it looks different this time." "The difference,"

Elgin said with a chuckle, "is who is doing the asking. Now it's more main-stream white women. We were blacks and radicals back then. That's why they're perceiving this movement today as a whole new idea."

"We as African Americans do not demand enough," countered Brooks. "In fact we demand very little. We got a problem with a dirty hallway; we complain to each other, but do we put together a group? I think it takes too little to satisfy some of us. I am on the school board in Gary, and when I started in 1992 I did a tour of all the buildings, forty-two buildings. Eight years later and they look the same. How is it we can't demand that some-thing be done? They patch a roof here and a wall there; it's all patchwork!"

"They ignore our demands in this city," explained Elgin, "by saying that it's all political. That we're all just playing politics." African Americans have always had to deal with allegations of using race for political or personal gain. "They're just playing the race card," continues to be a common re-mark by white folks. "Blacks are just fighting for their own piece of the pie." "Everyone just wants to be 'the man.'" How many times had the five ac-tivists had to respond to accusations such as these? "Trivializing your most basic demands for equality," Comer shook his head sadly, "now that makes you tired." "Mary's right," Strong concluded. "Black workers don't under-stand the structure; they don't know what exists. We're not telling them. We're not getting to them."

"You speak up," Brooks reminded everyone, throwing ice over the heated discussion, "they'll make life rough for you." "But they can't fire you unless you do something wrong," stressed Strong. The discussion turned to per-sonal experiences, a recounting of the added hardships the activists had to put up with while on staff, and how they dealt with them. "My wife was sick in Gary, and they sent me to New Orleans," said Strong. "Well, they sent me to Alabama," retorted Brooks. Comer recalled his assignments face-to-face with the Klan. "If leadership had spoke up and stood together," Elgin rea-soned, "maybe the situations wouldn't have been so bad. All the African Americans I know," she added, "left angry. You do not leave a situation like this," she emphasized. "You got to make it known, put your complaint out there, put it on the table."

Josephine Brooks shared the story of her Fairfield, Alabama, assignment. "I'd been raisin' hell, so they told me I had to go to Alabama and get a con-tract for this hospital. They told me: 'We've been trying to get a contract for eight years. Nobody's been able to get a contract. You have the unique skills and qualities to do this job down there,' I was told. 'How long do you expect me to stay down there?' I asked. 'Until you get a contract.'"

"You have to have the intestinal fortitude for the job," commented Strong. "You have to be very careful because a lot of people buckle down under pressure. We had a black staff caucus too, and we had a few who would loosen up. We knew they were going back and telling Abel everything we were doing. We didn't give a damn. To build a caucus," he said, "you got to have some people who will not take pressure. When they told me they were going to fire me, I said 'Fine. I'll see you in court.' "

"It's not that easy," Comer broke in. "I know somebody to stick his neck out, and I mean all the way out there. Here come the folk behind him, helping him until it get hot. Then he turn around and there ain't nobody there. How do you feel, you look around and there ain't nobody else there?" Jonathan Comer was familiar with being in that position.

"That's part of the risk," answered Mary Elgin. "What does a person do? Sit down and go in the corner? If you go out and fight like there's a whole bunch of people there, well, who knows. Once you've taken on the responsibility, whether there's someone with you or not, once you put yourself out there, you've decided you're going to go the distance. It doesn't matter who's behind you."

"The International co-opted the Ad Hoc Committee," Brooks suggested hesitantly. "Gave them all staff jobs and shut them all up. That's usually what happens." "And you know that's the truth," Curtis Strong echoed her. "Right after you folks retired," Brooks stepped back in, "they write up this little book, a code of conduct, to tell you how to act, what you got to do to promote, and if you don't do this, well they'll take care of you. That's why today people are afraid." Jonathan Comer and Curtis Strong did not think too much of a code of conduct. They had never had to follow one, although they had known when they were breaking the rules of the game.

"You can't build the kind of coalition you need with paid representatives of the Steelworkers," volunteered Strong. "I think there are three elements needed in coalition building," offered Redmond.

> You have to have some people on the inside, and there are people at the International willing to build constructive partnerships. Then you have to go to the local unions. That's going to be the major component, the key. You need people who are willing to stand up for a change in the status quo. Then the third key is people like Curtis and Jonathan and Oliver Montgomery. Fifteen years down the road this experience they have is going to be lost. We need them to come in and work with folks.

"Trust and truth," asserted Mary Elgin. "That's what you need in individuals. So what if it comes time to stand up, and people are for you but not with you, there's stress and disappointment. But I've always seen more to gain than to lose. So you miss out on an appointment, an invitation to a Christmas party. You're not allowed to sit with the inner circle. If you don't ask permission, then they can't tell you not to do it. You can do what you

CONCLUSION

"Ask Harriet Tubman!"

Reflections and Lessons

Why did George Kimbley, William Young, John Howard, Curtis Strong, and Jonathan Comer commit their entire lives to the freedom struggle? Why did they choose to wage that fight through organized labor? Jonathan Comer's response captured the spirit of their commitment: "Ask Harriet Tubman!" The factors that influenced their decision to rely on the union had to do with their own experiences and the historical moment. Like Harriet Tubman, they needed to free themselves from the yoke of slavery—wage slavery and the factory plantation system. Individual uplift ideology held no hope for the African American working class. Neither African American nor white workers could choose as a group to rise above their class status. They had to fight for economic security collectively in whatever arena offered them the most leverage. The local workplace and the new urban working-class communities afforded black workers a point of access and a place of concentration. Worksite industrial unionism was the best vehicle for their struggle.

The deepest traditions of resistance among African Americans are rooted in black communities and extended families and grew out of common experiences of oppression based in race, gender, and class.[1] Family and church networks moved into the Calumet Region during the Great Migration, recreating communities from Mississippi, Alabama, and other southern states. Gary, with its dense African American and overwhelmingly industrial, blue-collar population, provided a favorable environment for grassroots organization and black working-class leadership. Within Gary's black community, the working class gained ascendancy during the 1920s with the expansion of the steel industry. Garveyism provided the cultural fabric within which migrants were woven into a community. Industrial unionism served as a platform and training ground for black workers who took on increasingly influential positions in local politics and the black community.

The NAACP, for example, began with a handful of black professionals and white allies but drew increasingly from the unions for membership and leadership. At the local and state levels, leaders emerged from the industrial union movement, especially from the USWA in northwest Indiana. Steelworker and attorney Louis Caldwell brought the NAACP behind the steelworkers' strike of 1919. Local NAACP chapters welcomed the CIO in the Calumet Region, and gained membership and financial stability through their alliance with the union. Curtis Strong ran the Labor and Industrial Committee in Gary; the East Chicago NAACP chapter was in the hands of USWA Local 1010 and Local 1011 black activists, men such as Gary Glover, Clarence Royster, and Jonathan Comer. Jeannette Strong went from the USWA to NAACP Gary chapter president, and then to Indiana state director for the NAACP. Jonathan Comer took over as state director when he retired from the Steelworkers.

"The union was my university," proclaimed Johnnie Howard. The same was true for hundreds of African Americans throughout the country. Bill Young saw the union as his path from slavery. Kimbley was "union-crazy." Jonathan Comer and Curtis Strong have continued their participation in union activities for more than half a century. Jonathan Comer still attends conventions and speaks at special conferences as a retired assistant director of the Civil Rights Department. In 2001 Curtis Strong became vice president of SOAR at Local 1014, the Steelworkers Organization for Active Retirees.

The African American union leaders in northwest Indiana combined their labor, civil rights, and religious activism, taking the union to church every Sunday and bringing their faith and traditions into the labor movement. Their numbers and their organization gave them power and a sense of ownership of the union; it was always *their union* too. As the preceding dialogue suggests, the younger generation of African American workers does not seem to view the union as its own nor do these workers turn to the union as an instrument in the struggle for equality. The African American USWA veterans do not place blame on any one factor or group; they see the responsibility for this alienation as shared by USWA leadership, black union and community leadership, and rank-and-file membership. Yet the participants in this discussion agreed that, under the current economic conditions, bringing the African American community back into the union coalition is absolutely critical.

Reflecting on History's Lessons

There are many lessons to be learned from the lives and stories in this historical narrative. Clearly no one fought harder and more consistently for interracial unionism than African American workers. Their survival economically depended on building those social and political alliances. Despite significant obstacles and dramatic political changes, black activists labored to sustain working-class coalitions. The CIO's recognition of the importance of black-white unity made a difference. CIO leaders had seen unions weakened and undermined by racism and company "divide and rule" control tactics, and took special measures to include and promote black workers. It took *special and deliberate measures* to overcome the well-founded skepticism among African Americans. It also took *tough, uncompromising stands by CIO leaders* to force some white workers to accept integration.

Throughout the nineteenth century and well into the twentieth, early craft unions and skilled white workers had argued for a strategy of exclusion: control wages by limiting access to labor markets. As a result, they made race a central factor in defining U.S. trade unions. The legacy of this approach continues to influence the thinking of organized labor, in its tendency to regard white, male experiences as universal, and then to hold so-called universal class issues above the race and gender components of class in developing union programs.

Historically there has always been a battle between ideologies and organizations in the labor movement, between those who favored inclusion and others who sought to restrict membership. Changes in the organization of production in the last quarter of the nineteenth century forced changes in union structures. The concentration of corporate ownership and production played a role in the formation of industrywide unions such as the United Mine Workers, the American Railway Union, and the Ladies' Garment Workers' Union. The expansion of mass production industries and the proliferation of new production technologies made craft principles of organizing irrelevant for the vast majority of workers. In response the labor movement transformed itself, opening its doors to previously marginalized groups. Outreach to the unskilled, women, African Americans, Mexicans, and other immigrants became the only viable strategy for securing jobs and standards of living for all workers, including the more privileged core of white, native-born workers.

Once established and accepted as an American institution, however, the AFL-CIO focused primarily on taking care of its own, and practiced a trickle-down approach to wages and benefits for the vast majority of American workers. The emphasis shifted in the 1950s from organizing new workers to improving the lives of established union members, raising the ceiling instead of the floor. John L. Lewis, the voice for industrial unionism, openly opposed this stratagem back in 1937: "Raise the valleys," he argued, "and the peaks will also rise!"[2]

Internally, unions allowed second-class citizenship status to continue for minority members. The devastating wave of corporate restructuring, downsizing, and capital mobility in the 1980s eliminated tens of thousands of industrial jobs and pulled the rug out from under unions based in manufacturing. The unions tried to hold the line on concessions, but they had already lost too much power with dispersed production, the shift of jobs into the service sector, globalized operations, and the move from workplace to cyberspace. New conditions required new approaches.

Inclusion as a Labor Principle

The current unregulated globalization of the economy has reminded the U.S. labor movement how interconnected all workers are. The United Steelworkers survived a frontal attack beginning in the 1980s, as the U.S. steel industry closed obsolete facilities, downsized its workforce, introduced labor-saving technologies, diversified out of steel, and confronted increased competition from mini-mills in the U.S. and integrated mills abroad. Half its basic steel membership was eliminated by 1986. The majority of USWA members no longer work in basic steel; many work in service and health care sectors. Like many other unions, the USWA has broadened its mission and strengthened its resources for reaching women and minority workers. The Calumet Region, now District 7 of the USWA, has demonstrated a renewed commitment to fighting for equality and social justice. The district's response to recent bankruptcies and job loss has been to take to the streets with protests and marches. The USWA District 7 staff has its largest representation of minorities and women to date.[3]

Throughout the country, we see the labor movement reaching out to part-time, temporary, contingent, immigrant, and home workers. Multiracialism and diversity are to the unions today what interracial unionism—black plus white—was to the labor movement of the 1930s. Efforts at cross-border organization and global solidarity have gained prominence in the twenty-first century.

It should not surprise U.S. trade unionists, however, that workers throughout the world, including the United States, regard the U.S. labor movement with apprehension, if not distrust. If the U.S. labor movement advocates global solidarity without specifically addressing its long history of national chauvinism, discrimination, and exclusion, it will not succeed in establishing the foundation of trust required for international coalitions. There is still a tendency for U.S. unions to argue for workers of the world coming to the defense of U.S. workers who are losing their jobs. Targeting unfair trade or working to keep financial investment at home needs to be linked at every point to the fight for international labor standards and union rights and protections for workers worldwide. The United Steelworkers has stumbled in some of its efforts at internationalism, but has taken a positive step by sending numerous delegations to the U.S.-Mexican border in support of Mexican union organizing. Union activists have also visited Columbia to investigate the repression against trade unionists there.[4] In Canada, the USWA has established the Humanities Fund that finances hemispheric exchanges and support for Latin American workers and others worldwide.

The Union as a Coalition

The African American activists in this story learned through experience that a call to unity sometimes meant the subordination of their own concerns to those of an illusory majority, the universal worker. Curtis Strong's warning—"Do not coalesce unless you can coalesce from a position of strength"—has no less relevance to minority or marginalized groups today than it had in the 1940s. Interracial unionism, built on a foundation of equality and social justice, requires *internal coalition building* so that all interests have organized advocates and a place at the leadership table. Perhaps the clearest lesson to be drawn from this history is the need for *independent self-organization* by groups with common issues within the labor movement and within individual unions.

Unions have always been forged as coalitions; the broadest coalitions historically emerged in the post-depression years within the industrial union movement. SWOC in northwest Indiana was in no way a top-down organization, even if Philip Murray and John L. Lewis preferred to run it that way administratively. Black brotherhoods, ethnic clubs, community organizations, women's clubs, religious networks, and mutual aid societies were galvanized into coordinated activity during the latter years of the Great Depression. SWOC stood on the foundations built by the Universal Negro Improvement Association, the Unemployed Councils and leftist organizations, and by the radical circles of the old Amalgamated Association of Iron, Steel and Tin Workers. The union movement was not a melting pot; it did not grow by erasing constituent groups and interests. It was a coalition of those groups, with separate ways of organizing and special forms of representation.

The phrase "the house of labor" offers a useful image for understanding how the union at its most effective—locally as well as nationally—functions as a coalition of organizations.[5] In the early decades of the labor movement, workers built small enclosures for themselves as carpenters, shoemakers, or cigar rollers, based on craft, location, or work site. When larger combinations of employers undermined these small and isolated associations, workers combined as well, creating larger structures. In steel, for example, the craft unions of heaters, rollers, and puddlers merged into the Amalgamated Association of Iron and Steel Workers in 1876.

At the turn of the century, labor unions were coalescing into federations, but each chose different principles of organization. The American Federation of Labor favored craft-based unions, and most of their affiliates were craft or trade unions. In response to industrialization, the American Federation of Labor accepted unskilled workers into what were called federal unions. They also set Jim Crow locals to accommodate black workers. The federal and Jim Crow locals, however, had second-class status and were separate appendages, similar to servants forced to use a back-door entrance. Rayfield Mooty's metaphor to describe the special vice-presidency created for an African American—"adding a back porch to the house"—could apply here. Other labor organizations sought greater geographical concentration, such as the Knights of Labor, rooted in cities and political districts. The Knights advocated a political and electoral approach. Industrialization encouraged the Wobblies, miners, and others to coalesce based on class and industry.

Despite the fact that U.S. business favored exclusive trade union organizations of the privileged, skilled minority, vast changes in technology and production gave an advantage to industrial forms of organization. Yet the pressure for inclusion did not lead to the construction of one gigantic house of labor.

The CIO did better by insuring special positions for and partnerships with these marginalized groups. In 1938 every basic steel local union in northwest Indiana had an African American vice president, and by the early 1940s every local had an Anti-Discrimination Committee. Throughout the country the CIO worked hand in hand with NAACP youth groups, the National Negro Congress, and other black coalitions. As long as those groups continued to draw in their people and advocate for their issues, the union maintained roots in the communities, solidarity in its ranks, and power in the face of capital.

A New House for Labor

Southern black activist Bernice Reagon Johnson, in an address on coalition building, cautioned against confusing "home and coalition." "Home," she explained, "should be a nurturing space where you sift out what people are saying about you and decide who you really are."[6] The UNIA was a home to working-class African Americans, as were the Sentinel League and the Eureka Club. In the same way, the Ad Hoc Committee represented a nurturing space for black steelworkers.[7] It made sense for the house of labor to have many rooms, some reserved for specific purposes, while maintaining and expanding communal spaces. Some of labor's early leaders, however, confused coalition with home and treated the union like a private club, with membership restrictions and closed rituals. "You don't do coalition work in your home," Reagon Johnson warned. "It is some of the most dangerous work you can do. And you shouldn't look for comfort."

The committees within the union were effective only insofar as they too were built as coalitions. Under the CIO, the Anti-Discrimination, Wage Rate, and Civil Rights committees in the USWA in northwest Indiana were formed as representative bodies, not as homogeneous groups or majority-group bastions. USWA Local 1010 might have been known as the red local, but the early radical leadership chose activists from different constituencies, women and men, blacks and whites, skilled and unskilled, left as well as right, to serve on internal committees. Whatever political battles had to be fought were fought internally and through the union's official structures. The USWA Local 1010 minutes attest to the dynamic dissent within the local through the 1940s. USWA Locals 1010, 1011, 1014, and 1066 all had black vice presidents because they did not depend on popular elections to provide for fair representation. They slated representatives from different groups, departments, and skill levels. They appointed white leaders to the Anti-Discrimination Committees to make sure that the committees had access to key decision-makers and were not marginalized.

This coalition approach broke down as union caucuses became polarized and more sectarian during the cold war, as union jobs became full-time careers and volunteerism turned into union business with a paycheck attached.[8] The union rewarded loyalty and conformity, usually at the expense of democratic and distributed representation. For example, when Don Lutes became president of Local 1010 after the Power and Steam blow-up in 1952, he appointed only his supporters to the committees, which forced debate outside the structured channels for discussion and broke the union into insiders and outsiders. "Us and them" came to signify internal differences among union members rather than those between workers and employers.

The use of committee assignments as repayment for support also changed the committees from deliberating coalitions to private clubs, where like-minded people socialized. For example, Lutes "gave" the Civil Rights Committee to the African Americans who had supported him, and the committee became sidelined, serving as a "home" or, better, a ghetto, for African Americans. Women's committees would be used in the same manner, allow-ing women to talk to each other while excluding them from grievance and bargaining committees, where the power resides.

What was meant to provide African American workers with visibility and at least token leadership, the vice presidency, became a one-man, dead-end unit like the one Jonathan Comer complained of in the mill. There was no promotional ladder from vice president to president. Rayfield Mooty called for a National Ad Hoc Committee of Black Steelworkers because African Americans could never rise above the vice presidency or the local union level. Every time black activists demanded representation higher up in the union, they were told that if blacks were given a position, then Greek and Polish and Serbian workers would demand one as well. They were also cautioned that it would take a constitutional amendment to add a position to the International Executive Board.

When the International officers saw that the Steelworker Fightback had slated an African American for vice president in 1976, overnight they created a new IEB position: International vice president for human affairs. Rayfield Mooty objected vigorously to the new title.

When the United Steelworkers of America was founded in 1942, every district director was appointed; they were all white men. When African Americans and, later, women began to demand top leadership positions, they were reminded that theirs was a democratic, color-blind union, where special appointments based on race or gender would not be tolerated. The union opposed what became termed "reverse discrimination," but its existing structures, policies, and practices had already institutionalized society's caste system. Without special organization, special positions, and special advocacy for minorities and women, white, male union leaders passed their advantages from one generation to the next. They perpetuated past inequalities at the same time that they worked against racism in housing, education, and employment.

When unions opened their doors again to previously excluded constituencies, beginning slowly in the 1960s but accelerating into the 1990s, these groups entered as guests in the house of labor, without the same rights of ownership. A few were asked to pull up chairs at decision-making tables but cautioned to play by the rules. Efforts to renovate the house of labor by marginalized groups historically were labeled disloyal, disruptive, and sometimes antiunion. Many labor leaders still regard minority caucuses with suspicion, because the union leadership does not control them. Adding diversity to the table through tokenism is very different from sharing power.

Many unions today have clearly committed themselves to organizing, to inclusion, and to membership involvement. Allocating more money and resources to organizing campaigns, sponsoring an activist labor movement, and allying with grassroots and community-based organizations are important top-down steps. Top-down support is necessary; central coordination facilitates the strategic deployment of grassroots activists and actions. Without the John L. Lewises and financed CIOs of the 1930s, the rank-and-file groups could not have coalesced into such a mighty national movement. But without a vast network of independent grassroots organizations to promote their own leaders into top office, tokenism will persist. Outspoken and intelligent rank-and-file leaders such as Jonathan Comer and Curtis Strong, emerging from strong African American networks and caucuses, fostered social unionism. They broadened labor's appeal by making union democracy and social justice central issues. It is crucial to respect the emphasis that the roundtable participants of the previous chapter placed on social issues such as racial profiling and employment opportunity. The CIO, the SWOC, and the early Steelworkers Union embraced demands for antilynching and anti–poll tax legislation, for fair employment practices, for fair housing, and for voting rights. That commitment attracted tens of thousands of African Americans to unions, even though in the workplace unions had barely challenged segregation and Jim Crow practices.

Without rank-and-file initiative and organization, without debate and opposition, unions lose the spirit and substance that makes them work. The labor movement needs people such as Kimbley, Young, Howard, Strong, and Comer, who refused to be "colored brothers," who stood up and forced their union to address discrimination and inequality. Jonathan Comer was absolutely right when he observed that some union leaders today remind him of those he knew in the 1950s and 1960s, who kept insisting, "If it ain't broke, don't fix it!" "If the white folks today don't see that it's broke," Comer said, "then the rest of us should do as we did back then. Break it so that we can all fix it together." Within the USWA today that joint effort is underway.

There were not five but hundreds of freedom fighters in steel, in every mill and community throughout the nation. Their stories are both inspirational and disturbing. The most significant story, a veritable epic of courage, is the one they wrote collectively. The African American struggle was key to the establishment of seniority rights, promotional opportunities, and whatever fairness still exists in the U.S. workplace. Like the black soldiers in both wars, they fought on two fronts and raised the sign of the double *V*: victory at home and abroad. In the case of steelworkers, the double *V* stood for victory against racism, in the workplace and in the union. Curtis Strong's explanation of how "if we fought the company by day, we fought the union by night" describes their extremely complex and exhausting, ongoing battle.

George Kimbley, Bill Young, John Howard, Curtis Strong, and Jonathan Comer were extraordinary men but not different from many others. They questioned the effectiveness of their efforts and never imagined themselves as agents of social change. Yet, they were. Not one of them let doubts or fears stop them in their tracks, and in the end their character and courage made history.

Abbreviations

CHS   Chicago Historical Society
CRA   Calumet Regional Archives
IHS   Indiana Historical Society
LC   Library of Congress Manuscript Division
NA   National Archives
PS   Penn State Labor Archives
SC   Schomberg Center for Research in Black Culture
WPR   Walter P. Reuther Library

Notes

Introduction: Black Steelworkers Fight for Unionism

1. The most complete story of the CIO is found in Robert H. Zeiger, *The CIO, 1935–1955* (Chapel Hill: University of North Carolina Press, 1995). For a focus on black workers and race relations during the CIO period, see Horace R. Cayton and George S. Mitchell, *Black Workers and the New Unions* (Chapel Hill: University of North Carolina Press, 1939); Philip S. Foner, *Organized Labor and the Black Worker, 1619–1973* (New York: International Publishers, 1974); John Hinshaw, *Steel and Steelworkers: Race and Class Struggle in Twentieth-Century Pittsburgh* (Albany: State University of New York Press, 2002); and James D. Rose, *Duquesne and the Rise of Steel Unionism* (Urbana: University of Illinois Press, 2001).

2. I use the term "radical activist" to include organizers from left or socialist groups as well as from militant formations within organized labor. I am not distinguishing between syndicalists, socialists, Trotskyists, and communists under the grouping of left. When the differences are significant, I note them. For general purposes, "radical" means challenging the status quo in the name of fairness, equality, and justice.

3. See Emma Lou Thornbrough, *The Negro in Indiana before 1900: A Study of a Minority* (Bloomington: Indiana University Press, 1985); Elizabeth Balanoff, "A History of the Black Community of Gary, Indiana, 1906–1940" (Ph.D. diss., University of Chicago, 1974); and John Foster Potts, "A History of the Growth of the Negro Population of Gary, Indiana" (M.A. thesis, Cornell University, 1937), copy located in CRA.

4. Among the more recent books on the Great Migration, see Joe William Trotter Jr., ed., *The Great Migration in Historical Perspective: New Dimensions of Race, Class, and Gender* (Bloomington: Indiana University Press, 1991); James R. Grossman, *Land of Hope: Chicago, Black Southerners, and the Great Migration* (Chicago: University of Chicago Press, 1989); also James R. Grossman, "A Chance to Make Good: 1900–1929," in *To Make Our World Anew: A History of African Americans,* ed. Robin D. G. Kelley and Earl Lewis (New York: Oxford University Press, 2000), 345–408; and Nicholas Lemann, *The Promised Land: The Great Black Migration and How It Changed America* (New York: Vintage, 1991).

5. Between 1984 and 2001 I interviewed more than two dozen African American steelworkers who had hired into the mills before 1950. This book could easily have had ten biographies instead of five. I also interviewed Leon Lynch, the first African American to serve on the International Executive Board of USWA, at length. I did not include him as one of the five, or as a sixth, because he continues to be an active leader of USWA. He has served on the Executive Board since 1976. In 2002, he was reelected at the USWA convention and announced that this would be his final term in office.

6. For an overview of African American thought in the twentieth century, see Robin D. G. Kelley, *Freedom Dreams: The Black Radical Imagination* (Boston: Beacon Press, 2002); Manning Marable, *Black Leadership: Four Great American Leaders and the Struggle for Civil Rights* (New York: Penguin, 1999); Manning Marable, *Race, Reform and Rebellion: The Second Reconstruction in America, 1945–1990* (Jackson: University Press of Mississippi, 1991); Cedric Robinson, *Black Marxism: The Making of the Black Radical Tradition* (Chapel Hill: University of North Carolina Press, 1983); August Meier, *Negro Thought in America, 1880–1915* (Ann Arbor: University of Michigan Press, 1963); August Meier and Elliott Rudwick, "Attitudes of Negro Leaders toward the American Labor Movement from the Civil War to World War I," in *The Negro and the American Labor Movement*, ed. Julius Jacobson (Garden City, N.Y.: Doubleday Anchor, 1968); Scott McLemee, ed., *C. L. R. James on the "Negro Question"* (Jackson: University of Mississippi Press, 1996); Kevin K. Gaines, *Uplifting the Race: Black Leadership, Politics and Culture in the Twentieth Century* (Chapel Hill: University of North Carolina Press, 1996); V. P. Franklin, *Living Our Stories, Telling Our Truths: Autobiography and the Making of the African American Intellectual Tradition* (New York: Scribner, 1995); and Carol Polsgrove, *Divided Minds: Intellectuals and the Civil Rights Movement* (New York: W.W. Norton, 2001).

7. Public address by Alessandro Portelli, Youngstown University Conference on Working Class Studies, Youngstown, Ohio, May 16, 2001. See also "What Makes Oral History Different?" in *The Oral History Reader*, ed. Robert Perks and Alistair Thomason (New York: Routledge, 1998).

8. Alessandro Portelli, *The Battle of Valle Giulia: Oral History and the Art of Dialogue* (Madison: University of Wisconsin Press, 1997), 65. In the same essay he writes: "The responsibility to interpret, of course, does not extend to claiming for our interpretation exhaustive and exclusive access to truth." The subtitle of this essay is "The Ethics of Interpretation." I relied on Portelli's work as I labored to piece together each of my interviews/biographies.

9. I began working on the Swingshift College Program in 1992, after ten years in university labor education and two years as the education director for the Service Employees International Union. I had been inspired by contact with popular educators in the United States and Canada, followed by two meetings with Paolo Freire, one in New York and one in São Paulo, Brazil. My model for worker education was the Highlander School established by Myles Horton. His autobiography, *The Long Haul* (New York: Doubleday, 1990), and his written dialogue with Freire, *We Make the Road by Walking: Conversations on Education and Social Change* (Philadelphia: Temple University Press, 1990), have served me as philosophical guides. Also on oral history work, see Ron Grele, ed., *Envelopes of Sound: The Art of Oral History* (Chicago: Precedent Publishing, 1985), especially Grele's essay, "Movement without Aim: Methodological and Theoretical Problems in Oral History," 127–54. I relied as well on Alessandro Portelli, *The Death of Luigi Trastulli and Other Stories: Form and Meaning in Oral History* (Albany: State University of New York Press, 2001), and Robert Perks and Alistair Thomason, eds., *The Oral History Reader* (New York: Routledge, 1998).

10. My two years with the Service Employees International Union helped me to un-

derstand union building from the top down; I had personally experienced it from the bottom up. These years were crucial to my understanding of change in unions as an interconnected process that must be pushed from above and below. See Ruth Needleman, "Space and Opportunities: Developing New Leaders for Labor's Future," *Labor Research Review* 12, no. 1 (spring/summer 1993): 5–20; "Women and Union Leadership," in *A Labor Movement for the 21st Century*, ed. Greg Mantsios (New York: Monthly Review, 2000), 151–170; and "Women Workers: A Force for Rebuilding Unionism," *Labor Research Review* 11 (spring 1988): 1–14.

Chapter 1: "Oh, That Kimbley, He's Union Crazy"

1. Interview with George Kimbley. Kimbley read the transcription of the interview and sent me a letter with suggestions, mainly giving even more detail (March 15, 1989). In addition, I interviewed his close friend Walter Mackerl and many others who knew him. My introduction to George Kimbley came through USWA staff representative James Baker, whom I also interviewed. There were countless references to Kimbley in the *Gary American* newspaper, the *Chicago Bee,* and in CHS, USWA District 31 Papers, boxes 40 and 41. PS, USWA Collection, also had numerous references—see, for example, box 4. I also found letters from Kimbley to the National Negro Congress (SC, NNC microfilms); articles published in a local black newspaper, *Info*; and writings in a number of collections at CRA, including the George P. Kimbley and SWOC Correspondence collections. I have a few copies of articles, letters, and flyers from Mr. Kimbley. The interview lasted six hours, but I spent the entire day with Mr. Kimbley, looking at scrapbooks and listening to more stories.

2. The interview with George Kimbley was the first one I did with someone I had read about but never met. It was a dark, rainy day, and we were in the wood-paneled living room of his nephew's house. Mr. Kimbley seated himself on the couch, almost invisible against the dark wall, and started his story. He had done this before, and he had a pace and rhythm of his own. He talked for long periods without a break.

Given that racism was the subject of my research, I was aware that we would be discussing controversial and painful experiences. I tried to give him the option of talking or not talking about any subject he chose. I also expected Mr. Kimbley to adjust his narrative based on his perception of me—a younger, white educator and unionist. I have taken this into account in analyzing the transcript, keeping in mind historian Earl Lewis's advice to interpret oral histories and not just repeat them. See Earl Lewis, "Connecting Memory, Self, and the Power of Place in African American Urban History," in *The New African American Urban History*, ed. Kenneth W. Goings and Raymond A. Mohl (Thousand Oaks, Calif.: Sage Publications, 1996).

In all comments taken from oral histories, I have tried to remain faithful to the spoken language. To maintain the flow of the stories, I do not use "sic" to denote spoken or textual inaccuracies. I do not provide citations for materials from the interviews.

3. In his interview, Kimbley traces back his entire family history to Africa.

4. Kimbley traveled and worked best alone. He had four or five very short marriages. He had buried his feelings so deep inside, it is doubtful he could make space for intimacy of any kind. According to him, he picked out very needy or "lost" women, married them to save them, but then could not maintain the marriage. He worked with other blacks in the union campaign and in the union but never had a close friend in his work.

5. The fact that Gary and northwest Indiana were largely controlled by the Klan during the 1920s must have made it a difficult, if not fearful, time for Kimbley.

6. Kimbley provided the following account:

My mother was well known among the whites, and she did quite a bit of work helping students and people that needed help. She would find help for them. And she almost had an unemployment office in her house. . . . She did a little welfare work too.
There were many poor whites with a lot of pride, wouldn't beg for nothing, but they
would contact my mother when they got in need of coal or food. And she would go
among the welfare people here and beg money for help for these people and they accepted it. . . . But if the poor people didn't know you, they wouldn't ask you for anything. They'd rather put salt on their finger and suck that, as we've often said, rather
than to ask for a crumb of bread. I can recall one time, I was on my way home, and
just as I got there, I saw a lady come out of the house with a bag and she said, "George
Preston, I got a package for your mother. You give it to her when she comes in." So, I
took the bag, and I looked in the bag and there was my mother's shoes and stockings
that my mother had loaned to this poor white woman to go to a funeral.

7. For a discussion of resistance behaviors among African Americans, see Robin
D. G. Kelley, *Race Rebels: Culture, Politics, and the Black Working Class* (New York: The
Free Press, 1994), and also his article " 'We Are Not What We Seem': Rethinking Black
Working-Class Opposition in the Jim Crow South," in *New African American Urban His-
tory*, ed. Goings and Mohl.

8. Kimbley clearly had a phenomenal memory. No one I interviewed was able to talk
about the past with as many details. He even remembered names of people from his
childhood.

9. Kimbley "never had a dream" about future employment. He hoped for a job, knew
he would have to work, but did not spend his youth thinking about what he could be.

10. George Kimbley's tale has uncanny similarities with early picaresque genre literature, such as the Spanish work *Lazarillo de Tormes*, from the sixteenth century. The *pi-
caro* traveled through all levels of society unseen because of his lowly status and was
thereby able to report on social customs, political intrigue, and society as a whole. Lazaro
narrates his own story and begins by saying that he has assessed his condition, accepted
his limitations, and decided to live the best he can under the circumstances. First-person
narratives by other, more recent writers follow in the picaresque tradition in style and the
satirical exposure of society's failures. See, for example, Piri Thomas, *Down These Mean
Streets* (New York: Alfred A. Knopf, 1967); Malcolm X with Alex Haley, *The Autobiography of Malcolm X* (New York: Grove, 1965); and James Baldwin, *The Fire Next Time* (New
York: Dial, 1963). Kimbley told his story as a picaresque novel, with touches of epic irony
also characteristic of the genre. For fascinating use of literature in analyzing society, see
George Lipsitz, *The Possessive Investment in Whiteness: How White People Profit from
Identity Politics* (Philadelphia: Temple University Press, 1998).

11. Kimbley's trajectory was similar to that of many African Americans who traveled
north on a chain migration from one place to another. See James R. Grossman, *Land of
Hope: Chicago, Black Southerners, and the Great Migration* (Chicago: University of
Chicago Press, 1989); Farah Jasmine Griffin, *"Who Set You Flowin'?" The African Ameri-
can Migration Narrative* (New York: Oxford University Press, 1995); Nicholas Lemann,
The Promised Land: The Great Black Migration and How It Changed America (New York:
Vintage, 1991); Joe William Trotter Jr., ed., *The Great Migration in Historical Perspective:
New Dimensions of Race, Class, and Gender* (Bloomington: Indiana University Press,
1991); and John Bodnar, Roger Simon, and Michael P. Weber, *Lives of Their Own: Blacks,
Italians, and Poles in Pittsburgh, 1900–1960* (Urbana: University of Illinois Press, 1982).

12. Hod carriers were organized and had already admitted blacks into the union.
David Witwer (untitled paper presented at National Endowment for the Humanities
seminar, Binghamton, New York, July 1986).

13. Most of the southern blacks I interviewed felt the same way. Jonathan Comer emphasized this point when he recounted his staff experiences in the 1970s. Problems got solved in Alabama with one visit, he noted. In the Midwest it took three or four.

14. See James C. Scott, *Domination and the Arts of Resistance: Hidden Transcripts* (New Haven: Yale University Press, 1990).

15. See James R. Grossman, "A Chance to Make Good: 1900–1929," in *To Make Our World Anew: A History of African Americans*, ed. Robin D. G. Kelley and Earl Lewis (New York: Oxford University Press, 2000), 399–400. Grossman discusses the role of African Americans fighting alongside the French. According to him, four national guard units fought with the French. Army troops loaned black workers as replacements for French soldiers killed at the front. Grossman notes that "42,000 [African Americans] served in combat units."

16. Pershing wanted to use black army regiments to cook meals and do the clean-up work for the expedition forces. Kimbley's unit refused and was not the only black unit to fight side by side with the French. Kimbley told me he was assigned to the 157th Red Hand Division. "That's one of the crack divisions of France," he added. According to him, their unit received training from the French and then, two weeks later, was sent into combat against the Germans.

17. It was clear to me that his belief in God was his safe harbor. Nothing meant more to him than his faith, and he drew unbelievable strength from it. Unfortunately, I asked very few questions about his religious beliefs, because, at the time, I was not planning on writing his story.

18. Kimbley even recalled his address as 1744 Monroe. He probably would have named his neighbors had I asked.

19. Raymond A. Mohl and Neil Betten, *Steel City: Urban and Ethnic Patterns in Gary, Indiana 1906–1950* (New York: Holmes & Meier, 1986), 48–90.

20. Oris Thomas, interview by author, August 6, 1990. Thomas described how "the Little Calumet used to overflow every spring and it would come all the way to 25th. So that meant we had to have boats to go in and out and the water would come in our house that deep [he raised his hand more than a foot]. We were out there under water, just like New Orleans." Thomas was born in New Orleans and came to Gary as a child in 1921.

21. Isaac Quillen, "Industrial City: A History of Gary, Indiana, to 1929" (Ph.D. diss., Yale University, 1942), 397; Elizabeth Balanoff, "A History of the Black Community of Gary, Indiana 1906–1940" (Ph.D. diss., University of Chicago, 1974), 164.

22. Mohl and Betten, *Steel City*, 52.

23. Balanoff, "History of the Black Community," chapter 5, table 18.

24. African Americans had made up about one-third of the construction work force. Balanoff, "History of the Black Community," 8. On the efforts to remove blacks, see Balanoff, 20–25; "Black Belt Due for a Clean Up," *Gary Daily Tribune*, November 10, 1911; *Gary Evening Post*, January 20, 1913, August 11, 1913, November 17, 1913. See also Mohl and Betten, *Steel City*.

25. Balanoff, "History of the Black Community," 33. Table 7 details black employment at Gary Works, beginning in 1909 with 66; 1910—105; 1913—316. Black employment then dropped to 189 in 1915. By 1919, there were 1,325 black workers at Gary Works.

26. Nelson Ouellet, "African American Migration and Family Strategies in Gary, Indiana, 1906–1925" (unpublished manuscript in author's possession), 4–5.

27. Ibid., 4–6.

28. Balanoff, "History of the Black Community," 50–69. The first black church was founded in June 1908. Clubs and organizations included the Strangers Aid Society, the

Home Literary Society, the Gary Colored Commercial Club, the Rain or Shine Club, fraternal lodges such as the St. Luke's Lodge of the Colored Masons, the Odd Fellows, and the Knights of Pythias.

29. Although much has been written about the 1919 strike, few historians have followed the events in northwest Indiana. My main sources of information on African American participation were Balanoff, "History of the Black Community," and the *Gary Evening Post*. Balanoff researched the newspaper accounts more thoroughly than any other scholar I know of. She also interviewed the son of Louis Caldwell. See also Neil Betten and Raymond A. Mohl, "The Evolution of Racism in an Industrial City, 1906–1940: A Case Study of Gary, Indiana," *Journal of Negro History* 59 (January 1974): 51–64; Raymond A. Mohl, "The Great Steel Strike of 1919 in Gary, Indiana: Working-Class Radicalism or Trade-Union Militancy?" draft article, CRA 242, Raymond Mohl Papers, 1st scr.

30. For detailed information on the 1919 steel strike, see David Brody, *Labor in Crisis: The Steel Strike of 1919* (Urbana: University of Illinois Press, 1987), and his *Steelworkers in America: The Non-Union Era* (New York: Harper and Row, 1960); William Z. Foster, *The Great Steel Strike and Its Lessons* (New York: B.W. Hoebsch, 1920); Commission of Inquiry, Interchurch World Movement, *Report on the Steel Strike of 1919* (New York: Harcourt, Brace and Howe, 1920), and also *Public Opinion and the Steel Strike* (New York: Harcourt, Brace and Howe, 1921). I also interviewed John Mayerick, a steelworker who as an eleven-year-old participated in the Gary strike with his father. Paul Dremeley was also an observer. His account is in CRA 310, Paul Dremely Papers.

31. The *Gary Evening Post* had the most complete coverage of labor issues in the steel strike in Gary and quoted extensively from the speeches made daily at the major rallies. It also announced the many special meetings held for "colored iron and steel workers." In "History of the Black Community," Balanoff includes information on Louis Caldwell. It is important to note that the situation in northwest Indiana differed in major aspects from the strike back east. Historians have tended to lump the Indiana strike in with the national situation, but there were multiple factors that distinguished black-white relations and the character of interracial organizing in the region. The new immigrants had not yet been educated to adopt the prevalent racist views of the society. Many lived side by side with the black workers in the Patch. Caldwell and Elston had delivered the support of the African American community for the union and prevented widespread scabbing. Together with white leaders of the Steel Council, they had addressed the immigrant workers directly on the importance of unity among all workers. The numbers of blacks imported to cross the lines were not sufficient to carry on production. It was, in fact, the demoralization that came with martial law that forced an increasing number of white workers to return to the mill. They turned their anger and sense of failure against black workers in response to media accounts and the constant agitation by foremen in the mill, even though very few blacks had benefited as strikebreakers.

32. As one observer noted: "The strike was always blamed for these [racial] troubles. Lots of them [white workers] said it [the strike] didn't work because the colored people came in the mills in boxcars. But the colored just laughed. They knew it was the white people who went back in the mills to work themselves that made the strike flop." CRA 310, Paul Dremeley Papers.

33. March 23, 1993. An article in the *Hammond Times*, dated June 17, 1969, notes: "Because of the unions, the steel mills gave Negro workers their first chance of jobs in the industry. They hired them as strikebreakers." The article continues: "In 1919, when the Gary mills were struck, labor lost the battle because the black workers would not leave their jobs." CHS, USWA District 31 Papers, box 29, file 1.

34. Mohl and Betten cover this period quite well in *Steel City*, as does Balanoff in "History of the Black Community." The Gary experience illustrates the centrality of

racism to the process of Americanization. The immigrants had to be taught that it was wrong to live intermingled with blacks, and that to be accepted as Americans, they had best identify as whites. See George Lipsitz, *The Possessive Investment in Whiteness: How White People Profit from Identity Politics* (Philadelphia: Temple University Press, 1998); David Roediger, *The Wages of Whiteness: Race and the Making of the American Working Class* (New York: Verso, 1991); Alexander Saxton, *The Rise and Fall of the White Republic: Class Politics and Mass Culture in Nineteenth-Century America* (New York: Verso, 1990); Bruce Nelson, *Divided We Stand: American Workers and the Struggle for Black Equality* (Princeton, N.J.: Princeton University Press, 2001); and Lizabeth Cohen, *Making a New Deal: Industrial Workers in Chicago, 1919–1939* (Cambridge: Cambridge University Press, 1990).

35. Mohl and Betten, *Steel City*, 55–58. See also Ronald D. Cohen and Raymond A. Mohl, *The Paradox of Progressive Education: The Gary Plan and Urban Schooling* (Port Washington, N.Y.: Kennikat, 1979) and, by the same authors, "Blacks and the Schools of Gary, Indiana, 1908–1930," *Review Journal of Philosophy and Social Sciences* 1 (1976): 160–81.

36. I interviewed Walter Mackerl several times; one of my students, Glenn Dowdell, also interviewed him and shared the tape with me. Mackerl wrote his own story. I have a copy in my possession. It was difficult to leave Mackerl's full story out of this book, because he is such an important figure. I refer to him often, and may publish a full life story at a later date.

37. Oris Thomas stood in the same bullpen.

I stayed in that bullpen, I bet you, for two long months. There was a superintendent to walk through every morning, and he walked with his head down on the side. Never will forget it. He walked by me for two months. Then pretty soon he called me and give me a job. In later years, he told me he hadn't hired me because I looked like I did not want to work . . . then he told me, I put you on a job and I give you the toughest job we had. Loading scrap with tongs. On the shears they would cut that steel off the rolling metal, and shear it up. Then they had little benches where people would open it up. Stand up and open that up. They made good money. But we were making forty cents an hour, four dollars and forty cents a day. That was in 1927 working straight days.

38. Garveyism, the black nationalist movement named after Marcus Garvey, played an important role in bring working-class activists together in Gary. Balanoff, "History of the Black Community," 410–22. According to Balanoff, "Compared to the outpouring of emotion aroused by the Universal Negro Improvement Association [UNIA], all other Negro organization in Gary in the '20's seemed limited." The publisher of the black newspaper the *Gary Sun*, for example, received a personal visit from Mrs. Garvey. Garvey himself appeared in Gary in October 1923 and again in 1924. Balanoff identifies dozens of meeting places for the UNIA in Gary. The records of the Gary UNIA no longer exist, but attendance at its meetings and events was always high. For more on Garveyism, see chapter 8.

39. Many had never even lived in Mexico. See James B. Lane and Edward Escobar, eds., *Forging a Community: The Latino Experience in Northwest Indiana, 1919–1975* (Chicago: Cattails, 1987); and Paul S. Taylor, *Mexican Labor in the United States: Chicago and the Calumet Region*, University of California Publications in Economics, vol. 7, no. 2 (Berkeley: University of California Press, 1932).

40. Balanoff, "History of the Black Community," 200–204.

41. In Staughton and Alice Lynd, eds., *Rank and File: Personal Histories by Working Class Organizers* (Princeton, N.J.: Princeton University Press, 1973), there is an interview with Jesse Reese; see chapter 8 for more information on Reese.

42. Quite a bit is now known about Henry "Hank" Johnson. Stephen Brier published a Works Progress Administration interview done with him in 1937, "Labor, Politics and Race: A Black Worker's Life," *Labor History* 23, no. 3 (summer 1982): 416–21. Johnson was later sent to Chicago to work on the CIO's Packinghouse campaign, and recent studies include additional information on him. See Rick Halpern, *Down on the Killing Floor: Black and White Workers in Chicago's Packinghouses, 1904–54* (Urbana: University of Illinois Press, 1997); Rick Halpern and Roger Horowitz, *Meatpackers: An Oral History of Black Packinghouse Workers and Their Struggle for Racial and Economic Equality* (New York: Twayne, 1996); and Roger Horowitz, *"Negro And White, Unite And Fight!" A Social History of Industrial Unionism in Meatpacking, 1930–90* (Urbana: University of Illinois Press, 1997).

43. Brier, "Labor, Politics and Race," 417. The IWO was organized by the Communist Party in 1930.

44. The members were: Theodore Vaughn, Stanley Cotton, John Spillers, Arthur Adams, Earl Gordon, Walter Mackerl, Robert Bell, Ernest Johnson, Raleigh Smith, Ivory Wright, Thomas Cameron, and Kimbley. See Balanoff, "History of the Black Community," 224; Kimbley's article, "The Negro in Organized Labor," *Info*, undated, in author's possession.

45. The *Gary Sun* and *Gary American* opposed the views spread by the Negro Press Association and both supported the NAACP position in favor of black-white unity. See Balanoff, "History of the Black Community," 222. Ouellet, "African American Migration," gives a history of the *Gary Sun*. Also see James B. Lane, *City of the Century: A History of Gary, Indiana* (Bloomington: Indiana University Press, 1978), 182–207; and Edward Greer, *Big Steel: Black Politics and Corporate Power in Gary, Indiana* (New York: Monthly Review, 1979).

46. The company took out a full-page ad in the *Gary Post Tribune*, July 1, 1936. It read: "The Steel Industry will use its resources to the best of its ability to protect its employes and their families from intimidation, coercion, and violence and to aid them in maintaining bargaining free of interference of any sort."

47. The Amalgamated Association had been involved in the 1919 steel strike but had not been the main force behind the movement. After the strike, many lodges of the Amalgamated disappeared. By the mid to late 1920s, they began to reemerge as secret organizations in the mills. According to notes for a draft speech for Joe Germano, around 1969, the Amalgamated lodges included: Lake Front Lodge No. 53 (Youngstown Sheet and Tube), Rubicon Lodge No. 55 (Gary Works), Inland Lodge No. 56 and Inland Lodge No. 66 (merged into one local later on). There is no listing for Sheet and Tin, which Kimbley and Mackerl told me was called the New Deal Lodge. The notes refer to the New Deal Lodge as belonging to Clayton Marks, predecessor to Youngstown. See CRA SWOC Correspondence.

48. Most of Gary's blacks came from five southern states, the largest number from Mississippi. The one-on-one approach of the days of slavery and post-Reconstruction, when absolute secrecy was needed, was used effectively by black organizers in the SWOC campaign in the black community. For a discussion of the Mississippi organizing tradition, see Charles Payne, *I've Got the Light of Freedom: The Organizing Tradition and the Mississippi Freedom Struggle* (Berkeley: University of California Press, 1995).

49. Walter Mackerl, interview by Elizabeth Balanoff, July 14, 1970.

50. My interviews with Walter Mackerl, George Kimbley, John Mayerik, Reno Mussat; interviews conducted by Elizabeth Balanoff with Walter Mackerl (July 14, 1970), George Kimbley (July 20, 1970), and William Young (June 17, 1969). See also LC, National Urban League Collection, ser. A, boxes 2 and 3; CRA 187, Sam Evett papers, box 1, files 4 and 5; Cohen, *Making A New Deal*, 291–321; also Horace R. Cayton and George S.

Mitchell, "Blacks and Organized Labor in the Iron and Steel Industry, 1880–1939," in *Black Workers and Organized Labor,* ed. John H. Bracey Jr., August Meier, and Elliott Rudwick (Belmont, Calif.: Wadsworth, 1971).

51. Balanoff stresses this part of her discussion with Mackerl. She notes that she herself joined the Women's Auxiliary of USWA Local 1010 in the late 1940s, and that white women were often concerned that black women would not attend their meetings. On the other hand, they were often surprised by the enormous turnout of black women during strikes and other community struggles.

52. See Ouellet, "African American Migration," and Balanoff, "History of the Black Community."

53. Kimbley demonstrated incredible patience with white folks but was much less patient with his own, especially those he thought should stand up or those he thought were unreachable. Kimbley was most comfortable talking to working-class strangers.

54. In 1937 SWOC held a special conference in Pittsburgh. "When they had their first conference in Pittsburgh," Kimbley recounted, "and you can ask Walter Mackerl about this, we all stood up and held up our hands and swore to fight to build the union or die in the attempt. I'm one of them that stood up and held my hand up."

55. Kimbley attributes most of his strength to his spiritual upbringing. "My parents gave me a spiritual basis never equaled by anything else that I had done. They gave me God. I came here believing in God. My grandparents used to pray over me before I was born. They believed I had a destiny. They could see something. And all my life I felt that God was leading me, giving me guidance. I've done things that nobody else could have lived through."

56. Let me mention that this story not only stunned me but made Kimbley in many ways inscrutable. Every other black steelworker to whom I told the story was equally stunned but reacted with more anger than surprise.

57. According to records of the NNC, local committees were quite active in the Calumet Region. Three letters from George Kimbley appear on microfilm in SC (13:0845; 27:0466; 30:0298). There is also correspondence from Joe Cook in Chicago and information on meetings in Indiana Harbor (11:0492). Pat Riley, an activist at Gary Works, wrote four letters that have been archived (23:0001; 24:0591; 26:0803; 34:0720). I also found correspondence from the Lake County Council and the CIO Indiana Council.

In a letter dated March 18, 1938, Kimbley wrote to John P. Davis at the NNC: "We are very proud of the activities of the National Negro Congress that is carrying on an extensive fight for the freedom and equality of the Negro people. Such efforts shall not be in vain for the very spirit filtrates into the minds of the Negro workers throughout these United States. In Gary, Ind. where we are tirelessly building the principles and policies of our Congress in to the life of the white worker as well as the Negro workers, we feel the need for closer co-operation and assistance in the building of the labor committees of the National Negro Congress." He goes on to thank local activists Joseph Cook, William Young, and Stanley Cotton.

58. Balanoff, "History of the Black Community," 225. Jacob Reddix was vice president of the business section of the NNC; Stanley Cotton worked with the industrial section, and a Mrs. H. J. Redd, a leading Gary Garveyite, was on the resolutions committee. Mrs. Lena Harris, active in one of Gary's women's clubs, was in the civil liberties section. Reverend Delaney, a leading activist among black ministers, and Mackerl were delegates. SC, NNC microfilms, part 2: Records and Correspondence, 1943–47.

59. The reader will find a fuller discussion of Kimbley's experiences on staff in chapter 7.

60. Germano had refused to take a staff job in the first couple of years because of what he termed the communist influence in the district. He helped maneuver the firings of al-

leged communists Rusak and Webber after the Memorial Day Massacre and then came on staff. He was president of his local, but his power came even more from his links to the Chicago Democratic Party bosses.

From the moment Germano became district director, the district became more centralized and authoritarian. Every decision went through Germano. Germano wanted to see the union get established and tried to appoint good trade unionists, but he was often motivated more by his anticommunism. He promoted some leaders who were later embroiled in union embezzlement schemes and found to have used wholly undemocratic procedures. Germano also worked with the FBI and other intelligence agencies to identify communists in the district. His own files at the Chicago Historical Society have FBI reports on black activists alleged to have been communists, including leaders such as Joe Cook. He consistently kept files on his opposition, and worked to get them fired, drafted, or unelected. Kimbley, however, had no trouble working with Germano. Germano rarely gave him assignments of substance but kept him on staff and prevented him from moving to any other district. PS, USWA Collection, interview with Joe Germano, Alice Hoffman, parts 1 and 2.

Chapter 2: "Slavery Never Ended at Inland"

1. The interview with William Young was done in East Point, Georgia, on February 15 and 16, 1989. Part of the interview on the first day was videotaped by the Labor Archives at Georgia State University. All quotes from Young, unless otherwise noted, are from my interview.

2. Interviews with Bill Young were also done by Elizabeth Balanoff for "A History of the Black Community of Gary, Indiana 1906–1940" (Ph.D. diss., University of Chicago, 1974) and by Alice and Staughton Lynd for *Rank and File: Personal Histories by Working-Class Organizers* (Princeton, N.J.: Princeton University Press, 1973). USWA Local 1010 has been one of the more studied local unions in the country. Jack London wrote "Decision-Making in a Local Union" (Ph.D. diss., University of Chicago, 1952) and "Factionalism and Rank-and-File Participation" (M.A. thesis, University of Chicago, Industrial Relations Center, 1949). Along with Jack Barbash and Bernard Karsh, London used the 1010 materials to publish a number of articles and a book on local unions. See Jack Barbash, *Labor's Grass Roots: A Study of the Local Union* (New York: Harper, 1961). USWA Local 1010 has the most complete documentation of its own history in the Calumet Regional Archives. Joel Seidman sent a chapter he wrote on Local 1010 to then-president Peter Calacci (March 1, 1957), a copy of which can be found in CHS, USWA District 31 Papers, and in CRA 115, USWA Local Union 1010 collection. Edward Zivich wrote "Fighting Union: The CIO at Inland Steel, 1936–1942" (M.A. thesis, University of Wisconsin-Milwaukee, July 1972). He interviewed Bill Young on November 16, 1971. In CRA 115, there are minutes of Local 1010's Executive Board, Grievance Committee, and local membership meetings from 1938 through 1970. Bill Young was also interviewed by CBS in 1978 for a documentary on Local 1010 called *Inside the Union, CBS Report* (copy in author's possession).

3. Many of the people I interviewed knew Bill Young personally, including James Balanoff, Elizabeth Balanoff, Curtis Strong, George Kimbley, Bill Gailes, and Joe Gyurko.

4. Young was elected vice chairman of the Grievance Committee when the union was established. He held that position for decades with a few breaks. During the war, he took over the responsibilities of the chair, who joined the U.S. Army. CRA 115, USWA Local Union 1010, Grievance Committee and general meeting minutes, 1939–1954.

5. I borrow the term "oppositional consciousness" from sociologist Aldon Morris,

"Political Consciousness and Collective Action," in *Frontiers in Social Movement Theory*, ed. Aldon D. Morris and Carol McClurg Mueller (New Haven: Yale University Press, 1992), 363. The label "red local" was not applied in a pejorative sense and was commonly used by politically active steelworkers in the region.

6. Young was brought up on charges as part of the administration under Don Lutes in the early 1950s, although he had no involvement with that administration and was never a member of the Lutes caucus. In the 1970 election African Americans organized by Bill Gailes and others ran a disastrous all-black slate. It lost every position, thereby removing blacks from union leadership for the term.

7. During the interview, he insisted repeatedly that he was "his own man" and especially that he would never have taken a staff job. He knew staff worked for the district director and Young chose to stay in an elected position, where he had more power and his accountability was to the membership. There is no question that William Young would never have been considered for a staff job during the 1930s or 1940s because of his radical ways. As far as the record shows, his name was never mentioned for consideration.

8. I asked few questions about his family, anxious as I was to jump into fifty years of unionism. As a result, there are many missing pieces. He never told me his father was involved in the 1919 steel strike, but he did tell that story to CBS in *Inside the Union*.

9. Young told me he had remained in Mississippi until 1922, but interviews done when he was younger put him in East Chicago with his father around 1914. I credit the earlier accounts with accuracy.

10. Powell Moore, "East Chicago," in *The Calumet Region: Indiana's Last Frontier* (East Chicago: Indiana Historical Bureau, 1959), 216–57, describes the early history of the city.

11. Ibid., 344–99. Paul S. Taylor's study of Mexican labor in the Midwest during the first decades of the last century includes extensive information on nationality distribution in the major steel mills of the Calumet Region. Between 1912 and 1928, for example, the numbers of Mexican workers rose from 0 to 4,081 at the three major mills. In contrast, African Americans accounted for 266 workers in 1912 but only 2,716 in 1928 (46, table 7). During the 1919 strike, according to Taylor's interviews with a labor agent, Inland Steel's main recruiting was among Mexicans. In 1918, Inland had 90 Mexican employees; by 1919, the number had jumped to 945. "The companies sent me to get our Mexicans to work for them," the agent reported. "I got some at Chicago, others at Omaha, Kansas City, a few at St. Louis. I even went down to El Paso and some cities in Texas. . . . My steel company got about two or three thousand that year" (117). Paul S. Taylor, *Mexican Labor in the United States: Chicago and the Calumet Region*, University of California Publications in Economics, vol. 7, no. 2 (Berkeley: University of California Press, 1932).

A later study of the Calumet Region notes that in 1920 there were only 1,424 blacks in the city of East Chicago out of a population of 40,000 or more. When Bill Young returned to Inland in 1924, 26.4 % of the workforce was of Mexican descent. Julian Samora and Richard A. Lamanna, "Mexican Americans in Midwest Metropolis: A Study of East Chicago," *Mexican American Study Project*, Advance Report 8 (Los Angeles: University of California, 1967).

12. By the late 1920s the Mexican community would be very well established, and therefore would become a focus for attacks during the depression. Around 1919, there was no real community infrastructure. See Taylor, *Mexican Labor in the United States* and James B. Lane and Edward Escobar, eds., *Forging a Community: The Latino Experience in Northwest Indiana, 1919–1975* (Chicago: Cattails, 1997).

13. Young was not the only African American involved early on in union organizing. According to Balanoff, there were blacks involved in the 1920s with the Amalgamated in

Gary and with the Communist Party and its Trade Union Unity League. It is significant that a white worker invited Young into the most secret of places. It supports the argument that the tensions were not mainly black versus white, but pro-union versus anti-union. Young must have made his sympathies known to some of the men he worked with every day.

14. Young included the following names as the pioneers: William Thomas, O. H. McKensie, E. C. Johnson, Patty Faulkner, and Miguel Arredondo. Thomas had been the president of the Amalgamated in 1919 and continued to head up the meetings; he became the first president of the SWOC Lodge.

15. Young could not put a specific date on this incident, but he said it was long before the SWOC period.

16. The repatriation drives, as they were called, began in May 1932. In that year alone, 1,800 Mexicans from East Chicago—mostly American-born—were dropped on the Mexican side of the border. From Gary, the trains carried another 1,500 Mexicans in 1932. Julian Samora and Richard A. Lamanna, *Mexican American Study Project*, Advance Report 8 (Los Angeles: University of California, 1967), 6.

17. Young remembered George Kimbley, Walter Mackerl, Stanley Cotton, and Jesse Reese from those early SWOC years, so he was aware of black participation at the other mills. He also knew black staff organizers Hank Johnson and Leonides McDonald. Young's relative isolation from organized groups of African Americans affected his relationships with other blacks. It was not uncommon for a black activist drawn into leftist circles to not maintain contacts in the black community. Most of Young's work was done through integrated, though largely white, groups.

18. In addition to union records, there are company histories. For example, see W. A. Perry, *A History of Inland Steel Company and the Indiana Harbor Works*, CRA 12, Inland Steel Corporation, box 1. See also Brian Apelt, *The Corporation: A Centennial Biography of United States Steel Corporation, 1901–2001* (Pittsburgh: Cathedral Publishing, 2000), chapter 7. For an excellent account of the emergence of steel unionism in the East, see James D. Rose, *Duquesne and the Rise of Steel Unionism* (Urbana: University of Illinois Press, 2001).

19. Open hearths one and two had been in full operation before 1929. This incident probably occurred between 1929 and 1935. W. A. Perry, *History of Inland Steel*, 75.

20. There are many firsthand and secondary accounts of the 1937 Memorial Day Massacre. The film series *The Great Depression* has excellent footage of it and interviews with participants. All the papers had coverage. On the union's tenth anniversary, member Joseph Chandler wrote a piece for *Steelworker News*, May 30, 1947. See also Donald G. Sofchalk, "The Chicago Memorial Day Incident," *Labor History* 6, no. 1 (winter 1965): 3–43; and Daniel Leab, "The Memorial Day Massacre," *Midcontinent American Studies Journal* 8 (fall 1967): 3–17.

21. See Alessandro Portelli for a discussion of how memories merge different events in *The Battle for Valle Guilia: Oral History and the Art of Dialogue* (Madison: University of Wisconsin Press, 1997).

22. Wage rates at the Gary mill tended to be higher on the whole than those at Inland. The large number of blacks in Gary also helped secure them better conditions. During the first years of contract negotiations, Inland grievers would go over to Gary Works to compare wage rates and classifications in order to force Inland to meet "area standards." It is doubtful that Gary steelworkers had any privileges before the union.

23. At a grievance meeting years later, January 17, 1952, Grievance Chair Don Lutes pointed to dissension in the transportation department caused by the company's demoting a supervisor who "in 1937 was a strike breaker." CRA 115, USWA Local Union 1010, box 2, file 19, p. 201. The union never forgot scabs, and Young was probably its main source of memory.

24. The files included minutes from a meeting between the Grievance Committee and Inland Steel management, Wednesday, March 8, 1939. This was clearly not the first meeting. Many of the points made referred back to previous discussions. See CRA 115, USWA Local Union 1010, box 2, file 16.

25. Zivich, "Fighting Union," 29–50.

26. Beginning in 1937, Young served on the board of the National Negro Congress, attending meetings regularly. He was also a delegate to the Indiana Industrial Union Council. The general union minutes in the CRA collection include an account of all delegates sent to any labor or related events. See also SC, NNC microfilms.

27. Elizabeth Balanoff, interview by author, June 4, 1985, and July 19, 2000.

28. Zivich, "Fighting Union," 37–39.

29. There were open communists at Youngstown and Gary Works, but at Inland the Communist Party members had very widespread support in their departments, and the circle of "fellow travelers" or sympathizers was quite large.

30. CRA 115, USWA Local Union 1010, minute books, December 7, 1939.

31. CRA 115, USWA Local Union 1010, minute books, February 1, 1940; April 11, 1940; April 25, 1940; August 8, 1940. In these meetings Young advocated special drives "among new men," representation for temporary employees, and equal pay for women.

32. George Kimbley's article "The Negro in Organized Labor," in *Info* (undated, in author's possession), mentions his own and Young's participation on the first Wage Policy Committee.

33. He studied job evaluation methods and took a primary role in dealing with wage inequities and the reclassification of jobs, helping to break down the isolated sequences reserved for blacks and Mexicans.

34. USWA 1010 had the first woman officer of any basic steel local, Mary Abramovich. She would later marry griever Joe Gyurko and retire. The woman elected after her, Helen Kelley, was probably the best note-taker the local ever had. The delegate lists were included in the union's minutes; integrated delegations were consistently chosen to represent the local.

35. Nick Migas was an open spokesman for the Communist Party at Inland. Sargent and Maihoffer were associated with left politics. It is important to note how long the effects of McCarthyism have lasted. Almost every person I interviewed tiptoed around who was and who was not in the Communist Party. I have chosen not to make a list of party members, to respect the wishes of those I interviewed. One person I interviewed would not let me tape the interview or take notes. Another used hand signals to help me figure out political affiliations. Some of Young's peers insisted that he had been a party member. There is no evidence, and he himself denied it vehemently. He did say he attended at least one party event in New York. He also read and appeared in the *Daily Worker*.

36. For an overall description of work organization in the steel industry, see Katherine Stone, "The Origins of Job Structures in the Steel Industry," in *Labor Market Segmentation*, ed. Richard Edwards, Michael Reich, and David Gordon (Lexington: D.C. Heath, 1975), 27–84.

37. See minutes of the Grievance Committee. The ability to transfer from one department to another and bring your seniority with you was not established until the Consent Decree in 1974. See chapter 9.

38. Young used this wording in our interview. I also found the phrase attributed to Young in the minutes for December 6, 1951. Young could not label every practice or attitude as racist and maintain his leadership position, so he used the term "discrimination" to describe racial and other biases. This was part of his class approach, seeing every worker issue as a class issue, whether the worker was black or white or female or Mexican.

39. It would take two decades to establish the right under the law to union representa-

tion, now known as Weingarten rights. Bill Young instinctively demanded rules and procedures that over time became the most basic union standards.

40. Tommy Mills, interview by author. Mills worked in the department with Jim Balanoff, who helped him gain a promotion to the trades. His foreman refused to promote him, saying, "You're too qualified to do the job you're doing. We need you to stay there."

41. In already integrated departments, promotions sparked initial protests, but workers were used to working interracially. The worst protests always came in areas that had been previously all white. Hate strikes were more common in the auto industry, because African Americans were being moved out of segregated departments or even plants into new work areas. See August Meier and Elliott Rudwick, *Black Detroit and the Rise of the UAW* (New York: Oxford University Press, 1979). See also NA, Record Group 211, War Manpower Commission.

42. Grievers did lose elections because of their efforts to integrate sequences. Joe Gyurko was voted out of office in the open hearth for one term in the late 1940s after forcing the company to promote a black worker into a semiskilled job.

43. Local 1010 minutes in CRA 115 record numerous examples of white workers' resistance to integration. Grievance Committee minutes: December 6, 1951; February 8, 1957, problems in the yard department. General minutes: November 9, 1944, "unauthorized shutdown staged in the number two open hearth on the promotion of a Negro brother"; February 15, 1945, "non-cooperation of Inland in regard to track labor and other depts."; December 16, 1945, "transfer of Negro worker from sheet mill to field forces"; March 7, 1946, investigation of discrimination in the coke plant; November 6, 1947, protests "against the barring of Negroes in transportation"; November 20, 1947, on "barring negroes and Mexicans" in some departments; November 15, 1951, resolution on integrating employees; January 17, 1952, incident in power and steam; February 21, 1952, mechanical department in the coke plant.

44. Then, as now, job evaluation criteria embody institutionalized racism and sexism. They give higher value to skills characteristic of male or white jobs. Danger was not, in those days, an accepted factor, and often, unrelated educational requirements were adopted to protect white and male jobs from competition.

45. The minutes include many references to the Anti-Discrimination Committee. The CIO in general spoke out directly against discrimination. See the files of the CIO Secretary Treasurer James Carey in WPR, Committee Against Race Discrimination (CARD), boxes 1, 136, 149, 180, 192, 193, 196.

46. For a discussion of CIO practices on housing issues especially, see Thomas J. Sugrue, *The Origins of the Urban Crisis: Race and Inequality in Postwar Detroit* (Princeton, N.J.: Princeton University Press, 1996), and "Labor, Liberalism, and Racial Politics in 1950s Detroit," *New Labor Forum* 1 (fall 1997). The union leadership supported building public housing in white areas and not just black, which led, in part, in Detroit to mass white flight and the election of a Republican mayor in a union town.

47. Grievance Committee minutes, February 28, 1947, CRA 115, USWA Local Union 1010, box 2, file 18.

48. Manuel Trbovich was the first chair. Nick Migas might have been the second one. In June 1947 African American Al McClain gave the Anti-Discrimination Committee's report at the general meeting, but Eugene Blue was the first black named in the records as chair, in February of 1951. By 1950 the Anti-Discrimination Committee had been renamed the Civil Rights Committee.

49. Al McClain went from the Anti-Discrimination Committee to chair the Safety and Health Committee. Clarence Royster was on the Civil Rights Committee and soon would be the local's vice president. Grover Gary was chair of the Industrial Section of the East Chicago NAACP.

50. *Labor Sentinel* 2, no. 2 (July 10, 1946): 6; CRA 115, USWA Local Union 1010.

51. Nick Migas and Joe Gyurko fought the battle in the open hearth. Nick Migas took on Inland's discrimination against the Puerto Ricans brought into the mill as part of Operation Bootstraps, a U.S.-backed plan to reduce unemployment in Puerto Rico by moving the jobless to fill labor demands on the East Coast and in the Midwest. Migas also organized delegations for NAACP and other civil rights conferences. Hugh McGilvery put together a scathing indictment of discrimination in an article published in the *Labor Sentinel*, August 28, 1946. "Point by point exposure of deliberate discrimination," McGilvery wrote, "would require volumes." For example, "Frank Borzaro, heater foreman of the coke ovens, openly boasts that no Negro is permitted to stay on the job of heater helper." When Grievance Committeeman Buster Logan was put in that position, "no older heater helpers were permitted to show Logan the intricate workings of a heater helper's duties." McGilvery added examples of black women being kept out of jobs. He also was a frequent progressive voice at union meetings. CRA 115, USWA Local Union 1010, General minutes, August 15, 1946; December 5, 1946; May 15, 1947; October 2, 1947; October 16, 1947; and November 20, 1947.

52. CRA 115, USWA Local Union 1010, General minutes, September 21, 1950, and October 5, 1950. Maihoffer tried to convince members by pointing to the request of the Women's Auxiliary for money for a bowling team. He wanted to know if the local should deny the request because all the women who wanted to bowl were white. The Women's Auxiliary was headed up by Maihoffer's wife, and he did not address the problem of segregated bowling leagues. The auxiliary came under attack two years later, accused of being a communist front group by Recording Secretary Helen Kelley herself. IEB Hearing on the 1010 Administratorship, transcript, CHS, USWA District 31 Papers, box 168, file 7, Appeal's Case, 1955.

53. CRA 115, USWA Local Union 1010, General minutes, November 2, 1950. Bill Gailes took on the role of exposing discrimination every chance he got during this period. For example, he denounced the sudden requirement of high school diplomas by Inland for new employees (February 16, 1950); he criticized the union's support of businesses that discriminated against blacks (April 5, 1951); he attacked the local paper for accepting ads from businesses that discriminated (May 3, 1951); he pointed to problems in the Machine Shop and the Cold Strip (December 6, 1951); he castigated the local for holding its Christmas party too far away from Indiana Harbor, probably in a predominantly white area (January 3, 1952); and he brought up discrimination at the Hiawatha restaurant (July 17, 1952). Bill Gailes and Clarence Royster were the first blacks to repeatedly challenge the local over its own discrimination.

54. Recording Secretary Helen Kelley took such thorough minutes that it would be safe to assume that if Young had spoken, she would have quoted him. In fact, the minutes of the next meeting show that some members were criticizing her for her thoroughness. She replied that "the L.U. membership is entitled to know the pro and con arguments on questions affecting their Union and who takes various stands on these questions." CRA 115, USWA Local Union 1010, General minutes, November 2, 1950.

55. This incident appears in many documents. The most extensive firsthand report was done by Jack London in his 1952 Ph.D. dissertation, "Decision-Making in a Local Union." London interviewed all the key players in USWA Local 1010 and quoted from a long written account provided to him by Clarence Royster. The union gave London access to all internal documents and meetings, and he kept daily field notes. In the dissertation, London does not identify the local and refers to all participants by their initials. The Grievance Committee minutes tell the same story, in sketchier form. Through the use of the union records I was able to identify all the participants mentioned in London's work.

56. Local 1010 held two union meetings every month, on alternate Thursdays. For a

brief period in the early 1940s, the local called for weekly meetings to better involve members. The low turnout, however, ended that practice. Meeting attendance was generally not high unless there was a contract or controversy to discuss.

57. Jack Metzgar, *Striking Steel: Solidarity Remembered* (Philadelphia: Temple University Press, 2000); John Herling, *Right to Challenge: People and Power in the Steelworkers Union* (New York: Harper and Row, 1972).

58. Philip Murray had to ask, reluctantly, for the resignation of his general counsel, Lee Pressman, because Pressman would not denounce communism and the party. Germano had been an avid red-baiter from the beginning, and the Taft-Hartley loyalty oath gave him the opportunity to complete the work he had begun years earlier. Germano had actually blamed the Memorial Day Massacre on communist staff and fired two staff members as a result, Jack Rusack and Joe Webber. In District 31, Germano saw his main adversary as Local 1010 and systematically cultivated an opposition to remove the leadership of the local.

59. In his address at this gathering, Randolph went on to say: "While the Negro American Labor Council rejects black nationalism as a doctrine and the practice of racial separation, it recognizes the fact that history has placed upon the Negro and the Negro alone the basic responsibility to complete the uncompleted civil war revolution through keeping the fires of freedom burning in the civil rights movement." Philip Foner, *Organized Labor and the Black Worker, 1619–1973* (New York: International Publishers, 1974), 334.

60. International Executive Board trial minutes indicate that Murray had agreed to give Migas the microphone if he would abide by the rules. The party, however, flooded the convention with anti-International flyers the next morning, and Murray arranged for Migas's removal.

61. When I interviewed Nick Migas in his Florida home, he shared his scrapbooks with me. He had copies of articles from the Boston and Indiana papers on his removal from the convention. I took notes on and pictures of his material but he was not willing to have it removed from his possession for copying.

62. The petition is cited in the transcript from the Trial Committee hearing, CHS, USWA District 31 Papers, box 169, file 2, pp. 10–15, exhibit D. Elizabeth Balanoff also had a copy of the transcript, now in the CRA.

63. Trial Committee hearing, CHS, USWA District 31 Papers, box 169, file 2, p. 17, August 9, 1948.

64. A transcript of the proceedings appeared in the International Executive Board Minutes at PS and in the USWA District 31 Papers at the CHS. I asked Bill Young about Nick Migas's trial and he said he recalled very little. He did not mention he had been Migas's advocate.

65. Elizabeth Balanoff explained that Young visited her house repeatedly for political and social purposes. She knew Bill Young's wife socially. Interracial socializing was fairly common among 1010 activists.

66. There were many financial schemes going on at 1010 under Don Lutes, but the biggest outright theft was perpetrated by staff rep Joe Jeneske with the help of Financial Secretary Tom Conway. They had written large checks out to nonexistent arbitrators and then cashed them for themselves. The International at this hearing had already decided to clear Jeneske and transfer him to another staff job, under the advice of Joe Germano. Conway would be slapped on the wrist. Young was not naive at the time. Right after Young's testimony, the IEB introduced a former USWA staff rep who had gone over to the company as the head of the Labor Relations Department, Herb Liebman. Young referred to the department as a goon squad. After Liebman's testimony, the IEB committee met behind closed doors. District Director Whitehouse pointed out that the lack of action on the part of the IEB had opened the union up to attack by the communists in the local.

About this situation, he said, "We were playing right into their hands and feeding them a lot of propaganda. . . . Feeding the Communist party and our enemies. It was a situation that we just had to do something about."

67. Transcript of the appeals proceedings, CHS, USWA District 31 Papers, box 168, file 7, pp. 255–57.

68. I heard this story from Al Samter, who was also called before the House Un-American Activities Committee and was standing next to Bill Young when this incident occurred. During his testimony before HUAC, Joe LeFleur volunteered the information on Bill Young. "William Young was another man that was a Commie," he reported. The chair questioned him, and he continued: "Yes, sir. He was also——well, he had been an old-line party member for a long time, for the good part of the war and up to '50; and he was instrumental in reporting at closed Communist meetings about things that went on in the union, the complete proposals and plans of the union, and so on and so forth, the policy committee plans, wage committee plans, and so on" (2017). LeFleur also referred to griever Joe Gyurko as "Comrade Joe." LeFleur had been sent to Gary by the Federal Bureau of Investigation to identify leftists. "Communist Infiltration in Basic Industry," HUAC hearings, February 10 and 11, 1958, Gary, Indiana, microfilm synopsis and transcript in possession of Fran Malis, Gary.

Chapter 3: "The Only Race That Mattered Was the Human Race"

1. For a description of Gary in the 1920s, see James C. Kollros, "Creating a Steel Workers Union in the Calumet Region, 1933–1945" (Ph.D. diss., University of Illinois-Chicago, 1998). Johnnie Howard's neighborhood in central Gary was characteristic of most central Gary neighborhoods. Immigrants and African Americans shared blocks, even buildings, until the end of the decade. Segregation was largely the result of the Americanization campaigns supported by most public and private institutions, from social service agencies to the public school system under William Wirt. See Ronald Cohen, *Children of the Mill: Schooling and Society in Gary, Indiana: 1906–1960* (Bloomington: Indiana University Press, 1990).

2. Clarence Currie worked with Howard on the Gary School Board. He was quoted in Howard's obituary, *Post Tribune*, March 23, 1993.

3. He attributed this statement to Paul Robeson, whom he admired and had met in Gary.

4. David Howard, interview by author. Four of John Howard's children still live in Gary, and they reviewed the manuscript for accuracy. David Howard described his father with reverence, using words such as "integrity," "honesty," and "good-intentioned."

5. "Friends and Co-Workers Throw Farewell Party for John Howard," *Info*, copy in his son's possession.

6. I did two long interviews with John Howard, one at his house on November 6, 1989, another videotaped at the Indiana University Northwest studio in front of a class on January 13, 1990. Howard told many of the same stories in the second interview he'd told in the first, often using the exact same expressions and details. I asked much less about his personal life during the class interview and explored his union experiences in more depth. Howard was also interviewed, after our discussions, for the public television special *The Great Depression*, produced by Lyn Goldfarb. He appears in the segment "Mean Things Happening," which was written by Steve Fayer and directed by Dante J. James in 1993. I take all the quotations here from my interviews. In addition, his peers spoke about him quite a bit, and the black newspaper *Gary American* mentions his role on a number of occasions.

7. For example, he named his first supervisors in the mill, his childhood playmates, the names of second cousins and in-laws.

8. When activists, especially, retell a story that has become legendary among their peers or has entered the public domain—a story often retold at the union hall or family gatherings—it is common for them to mix the many accounts of the story into one personal memory or to revise their story based on later information or experience. See Alessandro Portelli, *The Battle of Valle Guilia: Oral History and the Art of Dialogue* (Madison: University of Wisconsin Press, 1997).

9. Oral historians James B. Lane and John Bodnar warned me before I started interviewing that repetition often produced a standard story made up from various experiences and retellings. They advised me to rely on my first interviews for the freshest account.

10. N. L. Sayres, *Gary American*, October 21, 1949, p. 1.

11. Walter Mackerl told of a very similar train experience in relating his 1927 migration north from Pine Bluff, Arkansas.

12. Elizabeth Balanoff, "A History of the Black Community of Gary, Indiana, 1906–1940" (Ph.D. diss., University of Chicago, 1974), 156.

13. According to 1941 data gathered for "The Current Housing Situation in Gary-Hammond, Indiana," Mexicans made up no more than 3.5 percent of the population in Gary, although they accounted for 9.8 percent of East Chicago's population. African Americans made up to 18 percent of the population in Gary. NA, Record Group 183, box 110, file Gary-Hammond, Indiana, 24. See also Balanoff, "History of the Black Community," and Kollros, "Steel Workers Union," for demographic information during this period.

14. The Howards owned a home in the Froebel area, which was what enabled Johnnie to attend the mostly white school. As a craftsman and seasoned steelworker, Johnson Howard had advantages.

15. The steel industry came under severe pressure to end the twelve-hour shift after the publicity on the 1919 strike. By 1924 only a small percentage of steelworkers still worked seven twelve-hour shifts with one day off every other week. There is no way to know how long Johnson Howard remained on that work schedule.

16. Balanoff, "History of the Black Community," 186–88.

17. *Gary Sun*, August 15, 1924.

18. See Alessandro Portelli's description of Kentucky mine wars in *Battle for Valle Guilia*.

19. According to Kollros, there were over five thousand industrial gardens in Gary and another twenty thousand private ones, with about thirty-five thousand people working on them. U.S. Steel did more than many other companies in providing stopgap measures for its workforce. The company maintained wages until 1931, when U.S. and Bethlehem cut wages by 10 percent, followed the next year by a 15-percent cut. Kollros notes that workers' "basic wage rate, which had been 40 cents an hour, fell to 30.5 cents an hour." The severest cuts came in the company welfare programs. U.S. Steel's group insurance plan dropped disability benefits and cut death benefits in half. Yet the company continued to collect insurance premiums. Kollros, "Steel Workers Union," 90–91.

20. Balanoff, "History of the Black Community," 198–99.

21. For more detailed information on the industry and the welfare plans at U.S. Steel, see Kollros, "Steel Workers Union," 85–109; Brian Apelt, *The Corporation: A Centennial Biography of United States Steel Corporation, 1901–2001* (Pittsburgh: Cathedral Publishing, 2000), chapter 7; also Powell Moore, "Politics, Prohibition and Depression," in *The Calumet Region* (East Chicago: Indiana Historical Bureau, 1959), 533–70.

22. David Howard, interview by author.

23. Secretary-Treasurer of SWOC David McDonald sent regular letters to local finan-

cial secretaries with the new password. In May 1938 it was "consolidate"; in January 1939, it was "fortify," then "integrity." In September 1941, it became "forward." I could not find the letter that named "expansion," so I cannot date Howard's first meeting. Most likely, he joined in 1937. CRA, SWOC Correspondence, District 31 letters dated May 25, 1938; December 22, 1938; February 8, 1940; and August 26, 1940.

24. A copy of the first agreement can be found in CRA, SWOC Correspondence, and CRA 187, Sam Evett Papers.

25. In "Steel Workers Union," Kollros provides an excellent overview of the development of unionism in the region. See also Robert Brooks, *As Steel Goes . . . Unionism in a Basic Industry* (New Haven: Yale University Press, 1940).

26. Robert H. Zieger, *The CIO, 1935–1955* (Chapel Hill: University of North Carolina Press, 1995), chapter 7.

27. The Department of Labor wrote a series of letters to Director Fontecchio to find out the causes of a series of strikes in steel, particularly at Youngstown Sheet and Tube. Many were instigated over wage issues. CRA, SWOC Correspondence.

28. When John Howard died, the medical records listed the cause as heart failure, according to his son.

29. Arthur Adams and Curtis Strong ran the coke plant through a rank-and-file caucus. This story is told in the next chapter. For more information on the wartime strikes, see Nelson Lichtenstein, *Labor's War at Home: The CIO in World War II* (Cambridge: Cambridge University Press, 1982), and *The Most Dangerous Man in Detroit: Walter Reuther and the Fate of American Labor* (New York: Basic Books, 1996).

30. Many historians have detailed the fight for shop floor control. See, for example, David Montgomery, *Workers' Control in America* (Cambridge: Cambridge University Press, 1979); Harry Braverman, *Labor and Monopoly Capital: The Degradation of Work in the Twentieth Century* (New York: Monthly Review, 1974); and Lichtenstein, *Labor's War*.

31. According to records of the War Manpower Commission, Gary Works had 18,782 production workers, including 4,202 nonwhites. NA, Record Group 228, Administrative Division Reports, Region 5–8, box 259, file April–December 1944.

32. NA, Record Group 228, Regional Files, Region 6, Closed Cases, box 721, file Carnegie Illinois Steel—Gary Works. The letter of complaint, signed by Howard, is dated August 24, 1944.

33. National Urban League, "A Study of the Social and Economic Conditions of the Negro Population of Gary, Indiana," conducted for the Gary Council of Social Agencies, December 1944, CRA 160, Clifford Minton Papers, box 3, file 3, 8–15. Walter Mackerl, John Howard, and George Kimbley served as sources of information for the study.

34. The small number of hate strikes in steel was not related to the union's intervention. The United Auto Workers also opposed such strikes firmly and quickly. In steel, the black workers fighting for advancement usually worked in the department promoting them, and already had developed relationships of some kind with the white workers. In steel quite a few of the strikes took place in the sheet and tin inspection departments when African American women were first sent in to work with white women. The only hate strike investigated by the War Manpower Commission was in 1944 at Youngstown Sheet and Tube, in the sheet and tin inspection department. Information on hate strikes and government intervention can be found in NA, Record Group 228, boxes 163, 175, 204, 241, 259, 372, 409, 465, 721; NA, Record Group 183, box 110.

35. WPR, CIO Collection, Office of the Secretary Treasurer, box 204, file FEPC: Field Letters, 1945, Field Letter No. 47, Division of Field Operations, 47–54. See also Joy Davis, "Tension Reports," NA, Record Group 228, Division of Review and Analysis, boxes 404 and 405; NA, Record Group 228, Administrative Division Reports, Region 6, 1–99, and box 241C.

36. Grievers who fought for upgrades and integration were often labeled leftists. This was the case at Gary Works, Youngstown, and Inland. White workers who tried to force the integration of washhouses and locker rooms, for example, also became targets of vicious red-baiting. In fact, almost any white worker who assumed an advocacy role in fighting racism was labeled a leftist whether or not it was the case.

37. National Urban League, "Study of Social and Economic Conditions."

38. At the same time, some black informants stressed that the inactivity of black workers, their failure to attend union meetings, was a factor in their second-class status in the union. "They content themselves with paying dues," remarked one USWA 1066 activist, cited in National Urban League, "Study of Social and Economic Conditions." An African American Gary Works official, most likely John Howard, remarked: "Many of our Negro workers who have recently joined the union are from the South. They have an inferiority complex. Some feel the Superintendent and the boss' word is law. Our union is playing a great part in letting them know just how we work in their behalf."

39. According to Walter Mackerl, there were 6,426 black members of SWOC in Gary in 1943. Not all their struggles, however, bore fruit. According to the records of the Fair Employment Practices Committee and War Manpower Commission, many complaints were dismissed as nondiscriminatory. In March 1944, for example, a black worker struck a foreman at Gary Works in response to abusive language. Not only was the case dismissed but the investigating committee refused to recertify the man for other employment through the U.S. Employment Service, claiming that in the absence of racial discrimination, the government had no jurisdiction. There was widespread evidence that African American women were being refused jobs throughout northwest Indiana in the war industries. The companies openly resisted hiring black women, according to a September 1944 report. One woman, Rose Aldridge, sent her complaint directly to President Roosevelt on May 4, 1944. "I know I can qualify for any number of war essential jobs . . . which though available I am refused because of my nationality." The SWOC lodges at Gary Works did not come to the defense of minority women as the lodge had at 1010, under the leadership of Bill Young.

40. After twenty-seven years at the company Johnson Howard fell victim to mill speedup and overwork. It was the very end of his long shift—he was working overtime—a night Johnnie had asked him not to work in order to attend his wife's father's funeral. "He was of that old school. If he'd had two legs cut off," John Howard recalled, "he would have tried to go to work."

> He worked in the 160-inch mill but during the war they were rolling oversized, up to 175 inch. . . . My father was the shear man. He was standing in a little place and you have a lever there. And if the plates are narrow you can stand there and press the lever. If they're wider you have to stand outside. My father was standing in the normal place. When he pushes the red light, the operator sends down the next plate. The operator couldn't see him. They're working for incentive, and he made good incentive. He was making his last cut. He hits the red light and it flashes white and the operator sends down the plate. It was too wide and cut him in half.

41. The CIO backed away from Henry Wallace's presidential campaign and then associated any remaining supporters with the left. The Communist Party's support of Wallace put some distance between it and its former allies in the CIO. According to people such as Al Samter, a leftist at U.S. Steel, the decision drove a wedge between leftists and some of their close friends. Al Samter and Ed Yellen, interviews by author.

42. The Unity Council had representation from the Ministerial Alliance, League of Women Voters, Optimists' Club, Urban League, CIO, Froebel Alumni, International Workers' Order, United Council of Negro Organizations, First Methodist Church, Na-

tional Council of Catholic Women, Parent-Teachers Association, and the American Veterans' Committee. *Labor Sentinel* 3, no. 21 (March 6, 1946): 1–2.

43. See James B. Lane, *City of the Century: A History of Gary, Indiana* (Bloomington: Indiana University Press, 1978), 232–39.

44. *Labor Sentinel* 3, no. 5 (August 28, 1946): 1. As chair of the resolutions committee for an alliance of thirty organizations, Howard presented five resolutions against the KKK, lynching, and racism, including support for a "petition of the National Negro Congress asking the United Nations to investigate the conditions of the American Negro." By this time, A. Philip Randolph had denounced the NNC as a front for communists, but Howard did not sever his ties with left organizations and initiatives. See *Gary American*, December 19, 1947; April 8, 1948; July 30, 1948.

45. There is much debate around the Henry Wallace campaign due to the role of the Communist Party. For John Howard and others, foreign policy, the Marshall Plan, and the red scare took a back seat to the fight against racism. See Zieger, *The CIO*; Thomas Borstelmann, *The Cold War and the Color Line: American Race Relations in the Global Arena* (Cambridge: Harvard University Press, 2001), 45–84.

46. *Gary American*, May 27, 1949; September 29, 1949; August 26, 1949; September 2, 1949. The black newspaper criticized the *Gary Post Tribune* for "red-baiting and race-baiting." Jacob Blake, an African American radical in Local 1014, in a letter to the editor, wrote: "We, as Negroes, have learned and are learning, that any move by any organization, group or individual, to help secure first-class citibzenship [*sic*] for negroes, or any fight for negro rights, is labeled 'red,' in an attempt to keep us divided and unorganized." The NAACP was against the march to the beach because of its confrontational character. Chapter leader Edna Morris called for people to try again to go to the beach as individuals, even though the violent incidents had been going on for a year. Even the Urban League report pointed to the situation at Marquette Park beach as one of the main sources of racial tensions in Gary. The *Gary American* editorial observed: "The story carried in Wednesday's daily on the Young Progressive's proposed picnic at Marquette beach was the most vicious piece of red-baiting which we've seen in many a day" (August 26, 1949). In a 1951 editorial, the *Gary American* was still discussing the Marquette beach segregation: "Another summer is upon us, and again it's time for our yearly gripe—the beach situation. One day maybe someone will lend an ear to the plea of Gary's forty thousand Negroes" (May 18, 1951).

47. Part of the debate centered on a definition of tokenism. For Howard, tokenism meant workers' taking jobs for which they were not qualified. He thought he was qualified to be vice president, in contrast to his predecessors. The Eureka Club members saw tokenism differently, as an issue of numbers and lines of accountability, as discussed in chapter 7. For further analysis of tokenism, see Rosabeth Moss Kantor, *Men and Women of the Corporation* (New York: Basic Books, 1977); Charles Lawrence III and Mari J. Matsuda, *We Won't Go Back: Making the Case for Affirmative Action* (New York: Houghton Mifflin, 1997); Ruth Needleman, "Space and Opportunities," *Labor Research Review* 12, no. 1 (spring/summer 1993): 5–20; Ruth Needleman, "Women in Union Leadership," in *A New Labor Movement for a New Century*, ed. Greg Mantsios (New Jersey: Garland Press, 1998), 175–96; and Ruth Needleman, "Comments" in *Women and Unions*, ed. Dorothy Sue Cobble (Ithaca, N.Y.: ILR Press, 1993), 406–13.

48. Chestovich also beat Curtis Strong in 1958 for the vice president position. Divisions and competition among black workers eliminated the once-sacred token position in the leadership. Pat Riley challenged Steve Bazin for Treasurer, also in 1958, and lost to the white opposition. African Americans survived only as outer guards and trustees that year. CRA 377, USWA District 31 Collection.

49. The next chapter covers Curtis Strong's story and that of the Eureka Club.

50. It's a great story, but it is unlikely that it is true, although David Howard said he heard it many times from Germano and his father. I did find petitions asking that Strong be promoted to staff in the early 1960s, but I found no petitions that said, "We want this one, not that one." I doubt that Curtis Strong was interested in a staff job in 1958; he was a powerhouse in the local, head of the Eureka Club, and ran the coke plant. Sylvester Palmer was too militant to have been considered for a staff job in 1958. Oris Thomas was interested in a staff job, and felt overlooked when this one went to Howard. That may account for the negative portrayal of Howard by Thomas in his interview with me.

51. Germano had put a second African American worker on the staff in the late 1940s. Lucious Love, from Chicago, remained on staff for only a brief time due to an early, sudden death. Howard believed that Love and Kimbley were not given substantial responsibilities because they were not qualified for staff positions.

Chapter 4: "Get Your Horses"

1. Oris Thomas, interview by author, February 7, 1989.

2. I have interviewed Curtis Strong more than a dozen times. Formal taped interviews were done on September 10, 1985; January 27, 1989; April 1, 1997; September 8, 1998; July 13, 2000; and October 25, 2000. He has been a guest speaker in my labor history classes at least eight times over the past ten years. On Labor Day 1995, I appeared with Strong on a Channel 56 public television program, and we have had personal discussions regularly over the past eighteen years. I have relied on formal interviews for all the substantive information in this book. Information on Curtis Strong is also available in the CRA and CHS USWA District 31 collections. The USWA International Executive Board and Civil Rights Committee files at PS include references, letters to and from Strong, and his reports to the Civil Rights Committee chair, Alex Fuller, for over ten years. See also John Herling, *The Right to Challenge: People and Power in the Steelworkers' Union* (New York: Harper and Row, 1972), chapter 18. Judith Stein also draws from Strong's reports to the Civil Rights Department in *Running Steel, Running America: Race, Economic Policy, and the Decline of Liberalism* (Chapel Hill: University of North Carolina Press, 1998), 94, 140. Curtis Strong is a public figure in northwest Indiana because of his many leadership roles in the Gary NAACP, the USWA District 31, the National Ad Hoc Committee in Steel, and currently the Steelworkers Organization of Active Retirees. He has been equally active in community efforts such as the Sickle Cell Foundation and church activities.

3. The *Gary Post Tribune* of September 21, 1956, carried the headline "Murder Attempt Charged by Injured Worker." "First they beat him; then he was thrown from the window and fell three floors." Strong had been one of thirty-six region delegates to the USWA International Convention that year, chosen because of his participation in the dues protest movement. For information on the dues protest activities, see Herling, *Right to Challenge*, 48–69; and Philip Nyden, *Steelworkers Rank-and-File: The Political Economy of a Union Reform Movement* (New York: Praeger, 1984), 39–41, 49–52.

4. Pete Calacci, International staff rep and close ally of District Director Joe Germano, did not mince words. After labeling Strong a Mussolini, he explained: "I hated him." White and black steel activists I spoke with expressed more hatred and fear or admiration and respect for Curtis Strong than of any other black leader.

5. Curtis Strong resented being called a colored brother more than almost anything else. It was not an unusual expression at the time, and Strong's local union president during the 1940s and 1950s, John Mayerick, used it. Strong and Mayerick worked much more closely after they retired than before. Although Strong never forgave Mayerick for

the use of "colored brother," he had tremendous respect for him. In fact, on November 23, 2001, Curtis Strong was one of only a handful of steelworkers who attended a memorial service for John Mayerick.

6. It was common for migrating African American families to make various stops on the way. Kimbley settled first in Indianapolis, then Detroit, and finally Gary. On chain migration, see James R. Grossman, *Land of Hope: Chicago, Black Southerners and the Great Migration* (Chicago: University of Chicago Press, 1989), 89–94.

7. Strong is referring to other African Americans who were willing to accept the status quo and leave the white union leaders in charge. He chose not to name anyone.

8. Adams was known as a socialist or leftist. Even those who knew him at the time would not comment on whether or not he had Communist Party affiliations. He never spoke to Strong about the party, but it was known that Adams worked in close association with party members. The impact of red-baiting and McCarthyism on the black freedom struggle is not past history, so no one would speak freely about membership in the Communist movement.

9. USWA Local 1014 did not keep its records, as USWA 1010 did. Contested politics and changes in leadership account for the destruction of some of the records. Information here on internal 1014 affairs comes from the District 31 collections in CHS and CRA and from interviews.

10. His opponent was Sam Ivey, who had been appointed by the local leadership to finish Moses Brown's term. Leaders at the USWA and other unions often retire early so that they can appoint their choice of successor. The Sentinel League demanded and won an election, which put Strong into office.

11. Curtis Strong has told many generations of steelworkers about the importance of building relationships before you build an organization. I had a similar view, although I was able to develop my analysis with the help of Curtis Strong. See, for example, Ruth Needleman, "Building Relationships for the Long Haul between Unions and Community-Based Organizations," in *Organizing to Win,* ed. Kate Bronfenbrenner et al. (Ithaca, N.Y.: ILR Press, 1993), 71–86.

12. The approach that African Americans took in organizing was rooted in a tradition of community-based organizing. Charles Payne describes many parallels in *I've Got the Light of Freedom: The Organizing Tradition and the Mississippi Freedom Struggle* (Berkeley: University of California Press, 1995), chapter 8. That a majority of blacks in Gary came from Mississippi and Alabama was a factor in the organizing styles in their community.

13. George Kimbley, for example, explained that he used to go to meetings to stay "close to Curtis," because he didn't trust him or agree with him.

14. There are a number of studies that confirm Strong's description of segregation in the coke plant, as well as plantwide segregation of jobs. See Edward Greer, *Big Steel: Black Politics and Corporate Power in Gary, Indiana* (New York: Monthly Review, 1979); Elizabeth Balanoff, "A History of the Black Community of Gary, Indiana, 1906–1940" (Ph.D. diss., University of Chicago, 1974); Horace R. Cayton and George S. Mitchell, *Black Workers and the New Unions* (Chapel Hill: University of North Carolina Press, 1939); and Dennis Dickerson, *Out of the Crucible: Black Steelworkers in Western Pennsylvania, 1875–1980* (Albany: State University of New York Press, 1986).

15. All the mills maintained segregation but not always with the same departmental and promotional systems. Gary Works and Youngstown Steel had seniority units. Inland had a very elaborate system based on sequences and separate lines of progression. The effects, however, were similar. Jobs for blacks were dead-end jobs. Where a worker was assigned upon hiring determined lifetime promotional opportunities. This situation continued until the Consent Decree allowed for transfers based on seniority, but the racial

distribution of workers in today's steel mills clearly reflects the past. See Judith Stein, *Running Steel*; John Hinshaw, "Steel Communities and the Memories of Race," *Pennsylvania History* 60, no. 4 (October 1993): 510–18; Dennis Dickerson, *Out of the Crucible*; Bruce Nelson, *Divided We Stand: American Workers and the Struggle for Black Equality* (Princeton, N.J.: Princeton University Press, 2001); and James D. Rose, *Duquesne and the Rise of Steel Unionism* (Urbana: University of Illinois Press, 2001).

16. Reports of wildcats in the coke plant appeared in the local newspapers, including the *Gary American, Gary Post Tribune,* and *Chicago Bee.* Tom Higgins was a reporter at that time for the *Gary Post* and covered many walkouts. He talked about his experiences on the Channel 56 television program he hosted with Strong and myself.

17. NA, Record Group 228, Division of Review and Analysis, box 364, file Studies 2. This report discusses two industrial strikes at Gary Works involving racism. The first one, in June 1943, involved nine hundred workers. The second was the strike Strong discussed with me. The report noted "a strike of 200 colored workers at the Gary Coke Plant of the Carnegie Illinois Corporation after a fist fight with a white waitress in the plant's cafeteria." Another memo pointed to the "recent heavy influx of Southern White and Negro people" as a cause of tension. "There is great possibility for war production to be hampered through interracial tension and possible violence." The report also commented on "tension felt even between Southern Negroes and Northern Negroes." NA, Record Group 228, Division of Review and Analysis, Tension Files, Idaho–Indiana, box 446, file Gary.

18. The coke plant at Gary Works had black maintenance workers and black foremen years before the other mills because of Eureka's power base and use of direct action.

19. Many studies of the black power movement in unions support this view. See, for example, Eric Arnesen, "Charting an Independent Course: African American Railroad Workers in the World War I Era," in *Labor Histories: Class, Politics and the Working-Class Experience*, ed. Eric Arnesen et al. (Urbana: University of Illinois Press, 1998), 284–308; Nelson, *Divided We Stand*; Bruce Nelson, "CIO Meant One Thing for the Whites and Another for Us: Steelworkers and Civil Rights, 1936–1974," manuscript in author's possession; Dan Georgakas and Marvin Surkin, *Detroit: I Do Mind Dying—A Study of Urban Revolution*, rev. ed. (Cambridge, Mass.: South End, 1998); and James Geschwender, *Race, Class, and Worker Insurgency* (Cambridge: Cambridge University Press, 1977). On understanding organizational issues of accountability, Charles R. Lawrence III and Mari J. Matsuda do a very good job in *We Won't Go Back: Making the Case for Affirmative Action* (New York: Houghton Mifflin, 1997), 120–41.

20. Oliver Montgomery, Jim Davis, and Curtis Strong, interview by Michael Olszanski, January 7, 2000. They had gathered for William Gailes's funeral and testimonial.

21. Strong saw tactical advantages in being second. The African American at the top was under constant pressure to be a team player, to go along with the majority, and to speak for the majority. There was pressure down the line as well, but the spotlight focused on the top leader. Also, Strong did not want ultimate responsibility for decisions and policies that he had to endorse but did not like.

22. See *Gary Post Tribune*, February 1958, for local coverage of the HUAC proceedings. Ed Yellen is working on a study of the hearings as well. On February 10 and 11, 1958, HUAC held hearings in Gary on "communist techniques and tactics of infiltration." Microfilm synopsis and transcript in possession of Fran Malis, Gary, pp. 1953–2208.

23. *Chicago Bee*, May 14, 1944, p. 7. The caption under a picture of the delegates names George Kimbley, Walter Mackerl, Manuel Taylor, Ellis Cochran, Benjamin Ridgeway, and Jeannette Strong, identified as the secretary of 1014.

24. The UNIA chapter in Gary was not that large. According to Judith Stein, the membership stayed at about 185. Nonetheless, the support for Garveyism and for many other cultural and political movements was substantial. Judith Stein, *The World of Marcus Garvey: Race and Class in Modern Society* (Baton Rouge: Louisiana State University Press, 1986), 242–47; Balanoff, "History of the Black Community"; Raymond Mohl and Neil Betten, "The Evolution of Racism in an Industrial City, 1906–1940: A Case Study of Gary, Indiana," *Journal of Negro History* 59 (January 1974): 61–64; and Isaac Quillen, "Industrial City: A History of Gary, Indiana, to 1929," (Ph.D. diss., Yale University, 1942).

25. See CRA 79, Jeannette Strong Papers.

26. A growing body of literature explores how race and class interconnect. For example, see David R. Roediger, *The Wages of Whiteness: Race and the Making of the American Working Class* (New York: Verso, 1991); also by Roediger, *Towards the Abolition of Whiteness: Essays on Race, Politics, and Working Class History* (New York: Verso, 1994), and "What If Labor Were Not White and Male: Recentering Working-Class History and Reconstructing Debate on the Unions and Race," *International Labor and Working Class History* 51 (spring 1991): 72–95; Alexander Saxton, *The Rise and Fall of the White Republic: Class Politics and Mass Culture in Nineteenth-Century America* (New York: Verso, 1990); Robin D. G. Kelly, "Identity Politics and Class Struggle," *New Politics* 6 (winter 1997): 84–96; Robin D. G. Kelley, " 'We Are Not What We Seem': Rethinking Black Working-Class Opposition in the Jim Crow South," in *The New African American Urban History*, ed. Kenneth W. Goings and Raymond A. Mohl (Thousand Oaks, Calif.: Sage Publications, 1996), 187–239; Dana Frank, "White Working-Class Women and the Race Question," *International Labor and Working-Class History* 54 (fall 1998): 80–102; and Ruth Frankenberg, *Displacing Whiteness: Essays in Social and Cultural Criticism* (Durham, N.C.: Duke University Press, 1997).

27. See Nelson, *Divided We Stand*; Dickerson, *Out of the Crucible*; Philip S. Foner, *Organized Labor and the Black Worker, 1619–1973* (New York: International Publishers, 1974); Michael Goldfield, "Race and the CIO: The Possibilities of Racial Egalitarianism in the 1930s and 1940s," *International Labor and Working Class History* 44 (fall 1993): 1–32. The fall 1993 issue of *International Labor and Working Class History* has a special debate and discussion on race, "Thematic: Race and the CIO," 1–63. See also Herbert Hill, "Lichenstein's Fictions Revisited: Race and the New Labor History," *New Politics 7* (winter 1999): 148–63; Herbert Hill, "Mythmaking as Labor History: Herbert Gutman and the United Mine Workers of America," *International Journal of Politics, Culture and Society* 2, no. 2 (winter 1988): 132–200; Joe William Trotter Jr., *Coal, Class, and Color: Blacks in Southern West Virginia, 1915–32* (Urbana: University of Illinois Press, 1990); also Trotter, *Black Milwaukee: The Making of an Industrial Proletariat, 1915–1945* (Urbana: University of Illinois Press, 1988).

Oral histories done with African American workers tell similar stories. Unions support the integration of leadership by promoting African Americans one at a time, forcing them to accommodate or adopt the customs and rules of the white majority. It is a form of absorption more than it is integration. See Michael Honey, *Black Workers Remember: An Oral History of Segregation, Unionism, and the Freedom Struggle* (Berkeley: University of California Press, 1999); Rick Halpern and Roger Horowitz, *Meatpackers: An Oral History of Black Packinghouse Workers and Their Struggle for Racial and Economic Equality* (New York: Twayne, 1996). I read the oral histories of black workers George Crockett, Rev. Charles Hill, Hodges Mason, Horace Sheffield, and Shelton Tappes in WPR. At PS, I reviewed oral histories of Boyd Wilson and Asbury Howard.

28. See N. L. Sayles, "As I Was Saying . . ." *Gary American*, March 29, 1946. See also April 27, 1945, p. 1.

29. Was Curtis Strong a black nationalist? I think he values the label. Strong is not an idealogue and does not seek a theoretical explanation for the positions he takes. As a result, he does not see a conflict or analyze the tension between race and class issues. The discussion in chapter 8 on black radicalism explores the activist synthesis African Americans have developed in this country. See especially Cedric J. Robinson, *Black Marxism: The Making of a Black Radical Tradition* (Chapel Hill: University of North Carolina Press, 1983), and Robin D. G. Kelley, *Freedom Dreams: The Black Radical Imagination* (Boston: Beacon Press, 2002).

30. Chapter 7 looks more closely at the problems black staff men had operating within a white union culture and hierarchy. In the absence of a caucus, black workers were forced to rely on white allies to include them on election slates in the majority caucuses. If blacks in 1010 or in the district wanted a black representative, the union leadership or district director would decide who would hold that position. At 1014, the Eureka Club decided.

31. Thomas never did learn to play the game right, however. Thomas felt he owed his position to the white workers in the merchant mill, so he rarely opposed them, even on certain discriminatory practices. He also never got the position he most wanted—on staff with the district. But Oris Thomas was also a path-breaker and a freedom fighter. Thomas, like Kimbley, liked to tell his story and told it well. Born in 1909 in New Orleans, Thomas witnessed lynchings in the South and participated in Garveyite rallies and steelworker strikes in the North; he married one of the few black women to be hired at Gary Works during World War II.

32. Strong referred to the Green Slate as "the foreigners," because it had support among a majority of immigrant and second-generation workers. John Mayerik headed this slate for decades; Mayerik's father was a Czech immigrant steelworker, involved in the 1919 strike. Strong also referred to the slate as "the Polish slate." The other slate was identified more closely with southern whites; it was known in the mill as the hillbilly or redneck slate, clearly pejorative labels.

33. In the 1952 struggle in power and steam at Inland, it was the leftists who cautioned moderation, to protect themselves in the next election. At USWA 1014 the leadership came more from the black caucus than from the leftists. Interestingly, a number of the early African American SWOC organizers at U.S. Steel Gary Works were Communist Party members, although none of them openly so, like Jesse Reese at Youngstown.

34. The Ad Hoc Committee leaflets give the same numbers. Jonathan Comer shared a packet of information on the Ad Hoc Committee in northwest Indiana with me.

35. Herling, *Right to Challenge*, 9–32. Many of the old-timers I interviewed provided anecdotes about McDonald's lack of character and commitment.

36. See Herling, *Right to Challenge*; Nelson, *Divided We Stand*; Stein, *Running Steel*; and Paul F. Clark, Peter Gottlieb, and Donald Kennedy, eds., *Forging a Union of Steel: Philip Murray, SWOC, and the United Steel Workers* (Ithaca, N.Y.: ILR Press, 1987).

Chapter 5: "Plain Old-Fashioned Discrimination"

1. I have been interviewing Jonathan Comer since 1986, formally and informally. The first interview took place on January 21, 1986, in the office of the Human Relations Commission, where he was serving as director. Since that time, he has spoken at seven of my college classes and has been an outspoken student in two. Taped interviews were also done on August 17, 1999; September 22, 1999; and November 29, 2000. I am assisting him in writing an autobiography, so I have a number of his written papers. Among our many informal discussions was a six-hour talk we had driving to and from Madison,

Wisconsin, in August 2000. Comer was a guest speaker at the retirement program honoring Herbert Hill. Jonathan Comer and his wife, Nell, have reviewed manuscript chapters with me and shared many personal stories that inform but do not appear in this book.

2. October 2001, class on leadership development at Indiana University Northwest, Gary.

3. On June 22, 1995, Jonathan Comer received the State of Indiana Council of the Sagamores of the Wabash Award from Governor Bayh, along with the Freda Dawkins Civil Rights Award from state and human rights agencies. The day before, on June 21, he had been named honorary lieutenant governor of the state of Indiana.

4. Comer has a different generational version of this art of resistance than Kimbley. Comer was never willing to overlook insults. He knew how to declare his total ignorance at the same time that he exposed the ignorance of the people with whom he was talking. Afterward, they must have realized they'd been had, but Comer outsmarted his opponents by covering his intelligence with modesty. I would call it exaggerated modesty because of his thoughtfulness and cleverness, but Comer embodies modesty in his presentation of self, and there is no pretense in it.

5. Nell Comer often sat in on interviews I did with Jonathan. On March 22, 2001, I did an extensive interview alone with Nell. Most of the information I have on her life comes from that interview.

6. For general background on black experiences in World War II, see Nat Brandt, *Harlem at War: The Black Experience in WWII* (Syracuse, N.Y.: Syracuse University Press, 1996); Andrew Edmund Kersten, *Race, Jobs, and the War: The FEPC in the Midwest, 1941–46* (Urbana: University of Illinois Press, 2000); and Joe William Trotter Jr., "From a Raw Deal to a New Deal? 1929–1945," in *To Make Our World Anew: A History of African Americans,* ed. Robin D. G. Kelley and Earl Lewis (New York: Oxford University Press, 2000), 409–44.

7. Philip S. Foner analyzes the effects of World War II experiences and their aftermath in *Organized Labor and the Black Worker, 1619–1973* (New York: International Publishers, 1974), 238–74. Harry Haywood describes his experiences in the merchant marine in *Black Bolshevik* (Chicago: Liberator, 1978), 490–528. The War Manpower Commission issued many studies on the status of blacks during the war, especially in the homefront industries. See, for example, "Employment of Negroes in War Industries," Bureau of Program Requirements, War Manpower Commission, NA, Record Group 228, Division of Review and Analysis, box 364, file Releases and Clippings 1; National Urban League, "Performance of Negro Workers in 300 War Plants," NA, Record Group 228, Division of Review and Analysis, box 371; Julius A. Thomas, "The Negro in Industry and Labor," a series of National Urban League reports, LC, National Urban League Collection, ser. 4, box 14. George F. McCray wrote a series of articles under the theme "Industry and Labor," published throughout the war in black newspapers, including the *Gary American* and the *Indianapolis Recorder,* IHS, microfilm.

8. In an article titled "Disillusionment II," published in the *Gary American,* April 12, 1946, the author wrote: "America has thrown about the cause of race relations an iron curtain of intimidation and laisses [*sic*] faire that is disheartening to serious minded interracialists throughout the nation. If interracialism cannot help in this cruel period of the Negro's disillusionment II, then we may as well close shop!"

9. NA, Record Group 183, USES reports by region. "The primary problem in the local office," notes one report, dated December 1947, "has been the in-migration of nonwhite job seekers, on the one hand, and a curtailment in the hiring of transients on the other hand." NA, Record Group 183, USES 209A, box 110.

10. See James P. Comer, M.D., *Maggie's American Dream: The Life and Times of a*

Black Family (New York: Penguin, 1988). James Comer came to East Chicago with his cousin Hugh Comer. Hugh Comer was Jonathan's father. They both hired in at American Steel Foundries, but Hugh Comer was seriously injured and returned to Comer, Alabama, in 1913. Jonathan's brother O. C. Comer worked at Inland. He used the initials O. C. because he hated his name, Othellus Cornelius. With encouragement from his parents, Jonathan had given him that name.

11. The USES reports for the Gary-Hammond area explain that local residents could get jobs in steel at this time. "It is their sisters, and their cousins and their uncles from distant places who create surpluses in a labor shortage area." NA, Record Group 183, box 110, file Gary-Hammond, Indiana, December 1947–January 1948, p. 1.

12. A second USES report, dated April and May 1948, added: "The labor market in Gary continues to present a lop-sided picture; namely a strong demand for workers, this demand being 90% white, while 55% of the available applicants in the files are non-white." All the help wanted signs were misleading, since they really were meant for white workers only.

13. Nell had lived with her mother in Jacksonville but had been raised by her grandparents until she left Alabama in 1939 at the age of fifteen. She did not want to be separated from her mother, and her mother did not want to lose the chance of raising her grandchild, after having given up Nell. In the end, Nell would allow her mother to keep her first son in New York and raise him, while she moved to Indiana.

14. Frank Perry was born in 1920, in Alabama, and grew up in a boarding house in the mainly white neighborhood in which his mother worked. He dropped out of high school and held a series of jobs for an ice and coal company, then for the Alabama Water Company, at about ten cents an hour, a dollar a day. Perry left the South during the war and started working at a war plant in East Chicago, Indiana, in 1942. He moved around during the war and spent over a year working at California shipyards. As soon as the war ended, he returned to East Chicago and hired in at Youngstown Sheet and Tube. In all his previous jobs, when there had been a union, he had been excluded from membership. At Youngstown he became active almost immediately. In his words, "Maybe some people would have turned thumbs down on the union, saying they want no part of the union, but I felt more inclined to break that barrier and to get involved with the union. I felt I could do more within than I could without." He went into the tin mill in 1945. He said out of a thousand workers, there might have been a hundred blacks. Frank Perry became the first black representative in the tin mill, then in 1949 he became the tin mill's first black Grievance Committeeman. Shortly afterward, like Bill Young over at Inland, he became the first African American vice chairman of the Grievance Committee in his local, USWA 1011. Perry claimed to have been the first real black activist, but he came in way after Jesse Reese. Nonetheless, when Comer arrived, Perry was a recognized union activist. Frank Perry, interview by author, March 3, 1989.

15. Comer and Perry still see each other regularly. They take long morning walks and argue! Perry, like Comer, continues to be very active. In the spring of 2002 he decided to run for city council. He had no campaign staff and just went door to door. He lost the election, although he garnered about one third of the votes.

16. Red-baiting and trials, expulsions and denunciations were as common at 1011 as 1010. Charles Fizer, who had served in many leading positions during the first decade of the local, was hounded by the International and disqualified from running for office after 1948. Joe Norrick was also disqualified, and activist Fred Stern faced red-baiting attacks as well. See correspondence and reports on communist activities in the local, CHS, USWA District 31 Papers, box 173, file 2.

17. Information on Jesse Reese appears in Staughton and Alice Lynd, eds., *Rank and File: Personal Histories by Working-Class Organizers* (Princeton, N.J.: Princeton Univer-

sity Press, 1973). Reese was the one who signed up Kimbley and Mackerl in 1936. Reese's activities are discussed in chapter 8.

18. The Youngstown local maintained minutes and other records during the 1940s. I was able to consult the Executive Board and Stewards Council minutes from 1946 through 1959, and occasional issues of the Local 1011 newspaper, *The Record*, in CRA 121, USWA Local Union 1011. The CHS USWA District 31 Papers also had materials from and on USWA 1011.

19. I interviewed Frank Perry, Basil Pacheco, Henry Rowsey, Jim Baker, Charles Fizer, Reno Mussat, Bill Scoggins, Leon Lynch, and Fred Stern from Local 1011. The information on black activism and Comer is drawn from all of these interviews.

20. Frank Perry was vice chairman and then chairman of the Grievance Committee for some time. Clelon Hobson, also African American, was vice president of the local after a series of black vice presidents, including Jesse Reese, Frank Breckenridge, and Chatman Wailes. Lawrence Hall was treasurer. Leroy Love held a trustee position; Jim Baker became a griever in the pipe mill and Hank Rowsey a griever in the rolling mills. There were more black officials in USWA 1011 during the 1950s and 1960s than at other locals, including 1014. USWA 1011 had a broad circle of equally skilled activists. Black workers did run against other blacks, but the black vote generally went as a block with the progressive slate until the 1960s. Jim Baker and Leon Lynch from USWA 1011 eventually went on international staff. CRA 121, USWA Local Union 1011, Stewards Council minutes, 1946–1959; Executive Board minutes, 1947–1953; *The Record*, USWA Local 1011 newspaper, incomplete runs; also CHS, USWA District 31 Papers, boxes 173 and 174; and interviews.

21. The CHS USWA District 31 Papers include extensive reports on this strike.

22. CRA 121, USWA Local Union 1011, Stewards Council minutes, 1946–1959. On April 9, 1952, the minutes read: "Bro. Christy spoke on situation developing in transportation regarding working with Negro Bro's. Bro. Kokot made a motion that the body go on record to support our Negro members in their fight for their just rights." The motion carried. At this same meeting the body passed a motion that "if the company pulls Negro Bro. off of job, the mill will be struck." This motion also carried. In June 1952 the local leadership lectured the white switchmen: "Bro Christy gave a talk on meeting concerning colored Bro. promoted to switchman. Bro Kokot gave a talk on how present administration fought for switchmen to get their raises. And then turn their backs on the present administration because a Negro Bro. was promoted to their dept."

23. Comer became active within months of hiring in but did not act on a localwide level until later. The local union records between 1946 and 1960 make very few references to him. In contrast, Frank Perry spoke at almost every meeting, and Jesse Reese continued to make speeches into the 1960s. Ben Coleman was also a frequent contributor. The antiracist struggle at USWA 1011 paralleled that of Local 1010. The Stewards Council minutes mention many work situations involving race discrimination and white resistance. For example, see the minutes of August 10, 1946; August 25, 1946; October 20, 1949; March 16, 1950; May 18, 1950; June 19, 1950; January 4, 1951; January 12, 1951; February 15, 1951; March 9, 1951; April 5, 1951; April 19, 1951; August 16, 1951; October 18, 1951, and November 1, 1951. From 1949 to 1951 at Local 1011, the struggles were intense, because the district leadership was supporting opposition candidates to rid the local of its radicals.

After 1951 the fight against race discrimination took a back seat to the anti-communist fight at the local, much as it had at Local 1010. The next references in the Stewards Council minutes to race discrimination came in August 1957. As late as June of 1965 Fred Nunn, chair of the Civil Rights Committee at 1011, wrote in *The Record*: "The Civil Rights Committee of Local 1011 has reached an impasse in the investigation of hiring practices of the Youngstown Sheet and Tube Company. The Company does not recognize the Civil Rights Committee as an integral part of Local 1011. As a result, no information requested is given the committee. This includes the employment of minority groups."

The underlying issue behind many of the disputes at Local 1011 and 1010 between 1948 and 1958 was anticommunism. In the battle between right and left, both sides took some advantage of race issues to make their arguments. Comer was not involved in these debates. During December 1951, for example, a dispute arose over the hiring of a black woman as a secretary in the union office. The progressives on the Finance Committee tried to interview and hire an African American woman to help on year-end accounts. The financial secretary of the union, George LaBrow, one of the most outspoken red-baiters, claimed only he could do the hiring and opposed the committee. An International auditor found in favor of George LaBrow. CHS, USWA District 31 Papers, box 173, file 2, letters 1951.

24. The National and Gary Urban League pointed to the same discriminatory practices affecting job opportunity. A report on Gary, dated April 12–26, 1945, from the Community Relations Project of the Gary Urban League, identified four problems. The first was "the upgrading of Negro workers in local industries"; the second, "introduction of Negroes into departments of local industries in which they are not now employed." LC, National Urban League Collection, ser. 6, box 25, file CRP Gary, Correspondence 1944. Joseph Chapman, executive director of the Gary chapter, wrote a regular column in the *Gary American*, "Not for the Meek." On May 14, 1948, he listed nine goals, including: "Remove discriminatory hiring practices, widen the occupational distribution of Negroes, secure upgrading for eligible workers, and encourage active union membership." On December 24, 1946, Chapman wrote to the National Urban League: "I quite agree that we should engender more interest on the part of labor." LC, National Urban League Collection, ser. 6, box 24, file Correspondence. As was the case in Local 1010, the postwar period in Local 1011 was very embattled all around. Leaders such as Dan Kokot and William Christy went out of their way to denounce company discrimination. They generally argued in the 1940s and early 1950s that "we should inform the Company that we do not want double standards of qualifications." CRA 121, USWA Local Union 1011, Stewards Council minutes, February 13, 1953. Black grievers who sided with white craftsmen had resolutions passed against them. These battles took place during the same period as the power and steam dispute at Inland.

25. From 1948 to 1954, Comer was a departmental representative; from 1954 to 1967, Grievance Committeeman. From 1959 to 1965 he was an International Wage Policy Committeeman. In 1967 he became vice president. Comer papers in author's possession.

26. Comer served twelve years as precinct committeeman in Gary. Later Mayor Richard Hatcher would appoint him to the Human Relations Commission. Biographical assignment Comer completed for one of my labor studies classes, paper in my possession.

27. CHS, USWA District 31 Papers, boxes 173 and 174, election results, files 1 and 2, 1950–1962.

28. Observation and interviews with peers and friends, including Herbert Hill, who worked with Comer during the 1960s and 1970s, when he [Hill] was in charge of the Labor Department of the NAACP.

29. The Steelworkers Improvement was an informal caucus within the local that provided black workers with some leverage in elections.

30. The problems never did go away. USWA 1011 had an active core of African Americans, Mexicans, and Puerto Ricans, but tensions among the groups, embattled caucuses, and competition for union positions interfered with unity. On December 7, 2001, when the plant known as LTV closed, everyone lost, but the minorities were especially hard hit. East Chicago, home to many Mexican and African American workers, has been devas-

tated; they lost more than twenty-five million dollars in back taxes alone. There were about fifteen hundred workers left at LTV, formerly Youngstown Sheet and Tube, when it closed. A new buyer, the International Steel Group, has assumed control of the plant, but the number of jobs has been greatly reduced.

31. Not all the positions were ceremonial, and the original SWOC organizers in the mill included politically conscious black activists such as Jesse Reese and Ben Coleman, and Mexicans such as Basil Pacheco. But from the point of view of most of these freedom fighters, "history" began with them. No matter how hard African American workers struggled, each step forward brought on a backlash, and gains made in one year had to be fought for again and again in later years. Perhaps it seemed like those who went before were ceremonial, but my interviews with the George Kimbleys, Walter Mackerls, and Johnnie Howards confirm that the struggle never seemed to get easier.

Chapter 6: "Change This Segregated System!"

1. My information on Ad Hoc comes from multiple sources. Among the Ad Hoc members I interviewed are: Curtis Strong, Sylvester Palmer, Jonathan Comer, William Scoggins, Ola Kennedy, and Oliver Montgomery, all of whom played leadership roles. Activist member Sidney Dent read the chapter for accuracy. Jonathan Comer gave me his· personal papers, including flyers, minutes, notes, constitution, and bylaws. Ola Kennedy gave me her collection, also rich in handwritten minutes, receipts, and notes. Rayfield Mooty had passed some of his materials on to Ola Kennedy. Kennedy also provided me with a two-hour video on the history of the Ad Hoc Committee, done by Rayfield Mooty, Curtis Strong, and Ola Kennedy in Rayfield Mooty's Chicago apartment. The video was made in 1985; copies with Ola Kennedy, one copy in author's possession. A number of other people I interviewed had had contact with or some firsthand knowledge of Ad Hoc: James Baker, Hubert Dawson, John Howard, Tommy Mills, and Al Samter.

2. Ad Hoc Committee history, Comer papers in author's possession.

3. Ibid.

4. Mooty, Strong, and Kennedy, Ad Hoc video.

5. Philip Foner, *Organized Labor and the Black Worker, 1619–1973* (New York: International, 1974), 332–424.

6. Oliver Montgomery, interview by author.

7. "White Supremacy in Steel Unions," *Muhammad Speaks*, June 27, 1969, 13, 16. PS, USWA Collection, box 21, file 13, Curtis Strong.

8. Letter from Thomas Johnson to Joe Maloney, USWA Vice President, January 14, 1967, PS, USWA Collection, box 12, file 54.

9. Ad Hoc Committee Minutes, April 27, 1968, Comer papers in author's possession. Jackson had the support of a citywide insurgency. See James A. Geschwender, *Class, Race, and Worker Insurgency: The League of Revolutionary Black Workers* (Cambridge: Cambridge University Press, 1977); Foner, *Organized Labor*; Philip S. Foner, Ronald L. Lewis, and Robert Cvornyek, eds., *The Black Worker*, vol. 8, *The Black Worker since the AFL-CIO Merger, 1955–1980* (Philadelphia: Temple University Press, 1984); Dan Georgakas and Marvin Surkin, *Detroit: I Do Mind Dying—A Study in Urban Revolution*, rev. ed. (Cambridge, Mass.: South End, 1998).

10. Following the confrontation with AFL-CIO President George Meany, Randolph decided to let black workers speak for themselves and helped organize the 1963 March on Washington. A. Philip Randolph, president of the Sleeping Car Porters' Union, pioneered many efforts at national organization. The Negro American Labor Council (NALC) he founded in May 1960 brought together a generation of black militants ready

to transform the labor movement. The call for the founding convention stated: "We resent Jim Crow locals; we deplore the freeze-out against Negroes in labor apprenticeship and training programs; we disclaim the lack of upgrading and promotional opportunities for Negroes; we repudiate the lock-out against Negroes by some unions; we, above all, reject the 'tokenism,' that thin veneer of acceptance masquerading as democracy." Foner, *Organized Labor,* 334.

Rayfield Mooty in Chicago, Oliver Montgomery in Youngstown, and a group from Inland Steel—Benjamin Coleman, C. C. Crawford, Otis Chandler, and James Alexander—formed their own local-based NALC chapters. Inland USWA 1010 had an active NALC chapter even though it had not had a black caucus. PS, USWA Collection, box 12, file 31, District 31.

11. Curtis Strong had been involved in organizing for the 1963 March on Washington, according to a *Post Tribune* article, August 21, 1983, C1. The article covered preparations for a second march on the twenty-year anniversary of the March on Washington, called the Twentieth Anniversary Mobilization for Jobs, Peace, and Freedom. Curtis Strong, the article noted, had "solicited people to go to the nation's capital, secured transportation by train and by plane, and sat in on the planning session in Chicago" for the 1963 event. Strong and Ola Kennedy were involved in the 1983 march as well. Gary sent five hundred people to Washington in 1983.

12. There had been an earlier challenge to McDonald by Don Rarick, but he was a local leader with little access to the membership and to the union's resources. John Herling, *The Right to Challenge: People and Power in the Steelworkers' Union* (New York: Harper and Row, 1972), 33–57.

13. Ad Hoc flyer, Comer papers in author's possession.

14. Mooty, Strong, and Kennedy, Ad Hoc video; also *Philadelphia Tribune*, March 23, 1969, 17.

15. Not only had SWOC and the early USWA made more consistent efforts before 1950 but in later years the expectations grew as well. Black steelworkers would not have been satisfied in 1964 with the best efforts of the formative CIO years.

16. See interview with Boyd Wilson, PS, USWA Collection; also interviews with George Kimbley and Walter Mackerl. Bruce Nelson, in *Divided We Stand: American Workers and the Struggle for Black Equality* (Princeton, N.J.: Princeton University Press, 2001), provides an overview of USWA civil rights work (185–250) and analyzes the role of Boyd Wilson (202–3).

17. CRA 115, USWA Local Union 1010 minutes, and CRA 121, USWA Local Union 1011 minutes; War Manpower Commission Reports, NA, Record Group 228.

18. Ellen Schrecker, *Many Are The Crimes: McCarthyism In America* (Princeton, N.J.: Princeton University Press, 1998), "McCarthyism and the Labor Movement: The Role of the State" in *The CIO's Left-Led Unions,* ed. Steve Rosswurm (New Brunswick, N.J.: Rutgers University Press, 1992), and "McCarthyism's Ghosts: Anticommunism and American Labor," *New Labor Forum* 4 (spring/summer 1999): 7–17. See also Robert H. Zieger, *The CIO, 1935–1955* (Chapel Hill: University of North Carolina Press, 1995) and Michael Keith Honey, *Black Workers Remember: An Oral History Of Segregation, Unionism, and the Freedom Struggle* (Berkeley: University of California Press, 1999).

19. See chapter 2 on William Young. Trial minutes and reports were included in IEB minutes. The CHS USWA District 31 Papers includes letters and reports on similar trials in Local 1011.

20. See Jack Metzgar, *Striking Steel: Solidarity Remembered* (Philadelphia: Temple University Press, 2000), for a comprehensive analysis of the USWA and labor in the 1950s.

21. USWA District 31 files in CHS and CRA 377 include clear evidence of red-baiting

beginning in 1937, with the Memorial Day Massacre and Germano's access to FBI reports, right down to the contested 1973 District 31 director's election. CRA 187, Sam Evett Papers, trial materials, includes reports from spies, allegations against all of Evett's opponents, copies of flyers, and more.

22. PS, USWA Collection, Civil Rights Department, box 1, file 1, Negro—Misc., 1945–46.

23. Linda Williams's book, *Playing the Race Card: Melodramas of Black and White from Uncle Tom to O. J. Simpson* (Princeton, N.J.: Princeton University Press, 2001), analyzes the immense impact of stereotypes on the country's understanding of race.

24. Oliver Montgomery, Jim Davis, and Curtis Strong, interview by Michael Olszanski, January 6, 2000.

25. Letter to Philip Murray from Jimmy Jones, undated, WPR, CIO Collection, Office of the Secretary Treasurer, box 176, file Steelworkers, 1944–49. Also PS, USWA Collection, 1968 Convention Proceedings.

26. See PS, USWA Collection, Civil Rights Department: for example, Officers Report 1950, box 1, file 12; minutes of USWA Civil Rights Committee, September 12, 1956, box 7, file 46; minutes of September 12, 1956, meeting, box 7, file 48; minutes of April 9, 1957, meeting, box 9, file 5; minutes of the August 27, 1957, meeting, box 9, file 5. Also see the reports by Boyd Wilson, in PS, USWA Collection, International Executive Board Minutes, Record Group A1: box 1, file 8, September 23, 1943; box 2, file 1, May 24, 1945; box 4, May 12, 1952.

27. Data was commonly manipulated to hide problems. No "serious" problems, of course, meant that the leadership saw no problems it considered serious, or no one in local leadership had reported on the problems in his or her local. Racial incidents were often trivialized, and all-white locals commonly reported no problems with discrimination.

28. A grievance filed by black worker John Brown at Inland in 1969 spoke to the persistence of the problems. Brown had been sent home by his foreman for being "sullen or sulky looking." "Who is he," the grievant wrote on the complaint form, "to judge my facial expression and determine that I am insolent or resentful?" He requested to be "treated as a man and given the same right and opportunity as any other man, regardless of personal conviction. Stop supression [*sic*] because I fight for human dignity as a black man." CHS, USWA District 31 Papers, box 171, file 3.

29. "The Steel Problem on Civil Rights," CHS, USWA District 31 Papers, box 29, file 1.

30. PS, USWA Collection, Civil Rights Department, Correspondence, box 9, file 5, 1957.

31. See Foner, *Organized Labor,* and Herbert Hill, "Black Workers and Organized Labor." See also Hill, "Title VII of the 1964 Civil Rights Act: Legislative History and Litigation Record," in *Race in America: The Struggle for Equality* (Madison: University of Wisconsin Press, 1993), 263–341; and Julius Jacobson, ed., *The Negro and the American Labor Movement* (Garden City, N.Y.: Doubleday Anchor, 1968).

32. See Judith Stein, *Running Steel, Running America: Race, Economic Policy, and the Decline of Liberalism* (Chapel Hill: University of North Carolina Press, 1998); interview with Jonathan Comer, who worked for Strevel in the 1970s, and IEB minutes in PS.

33. See Foner, *Organized Labor*, on other black power groups in labor (397–424). The UAW was very aggressive in opposing DRUM (Detroit Revolutionary Union Movement) and plant-based chapters such as FRUM and ELRUM (Ford and Eldon Avenue Gear and Axel).

34. Herbert Hill has continued to expose racist practices in unions; see, for example, "Chinese Immigrant Workers and the Contemporary Labor Movement," *New Politics* 7, no. 4 (winter 2000): 149–65, and "Race and the Steelworkers Union," *New Politics* 8, no. 4 (winter 2002): 172–205.

35. Herling, *Right to Challenge,* 220. Herling names as delegates at the black caucus meeting at the Atlantic City convention: W. A. Davis of Buffalo, Aaron Jackson of Detroit, Tom Johnson from Alabama, Rayfield Mooty from Chicago, Curtis Strong from Gary, and Hugh Henderson from Youngstown. See also Dennis Dickerson, *Out of the Crucible: Black Steelworkers in Western Pennsylvania, 1875–1980* (Albany: State University of New York Press, 1986), 226–31.

36. Mooty, Strong, and Kennedy, Ad Hoc video; Ad Hoc Committee Minutes, April 27 and 28, 1968, Comer papers in author's possession.

37. Pamphlet on National Ad Hoc Committee with review of the years 1966 through 1968, in author's possession.

38. Mooty, Strong, and Kennedy, Ad Hoc video; Herling, *Right to Challenge,* 220.

39. Constitution, in author's possession.

40. "Discussion," a two-page photocopy outlining the committee's three demands, with explanations. CHS, USWA District 31 Papers, box 29, file 1, undated.

41. Letter from Aaron Jackson to "Brother Steelworker," November 7, 1964, CHS, USWA District 31 Papers, box 29, file 1. Jackson referred to the meeting attended by McDonald, General Counsel Bredhoff and Thomas Shane, chair of the Civil Rights Committee. He names as black participants himself; Roger Payne, Duquesne, Pennsylvania; W. A. Davis, Buffalo, New York; Rayfield Mooty, Chicago, Illinois; Thomas Turner, Inkster, Michigan; and Thomas Johnson, Fairfield, Alabama.

42. Flyer endorsing Abel, undated, Comer papers in author's possession.

43. There are a number of different versions of the Ad Hoc and Abel story. Herling and Dickerson give Alex Fuller credit for starting the Ad Hoc and calling certain meetings, based on interviews. Fuller was president of the Wayne County AFL-CIO and more closely integrated into the union hierarchy. He was also the assistant director of Abel's campaign. Strong and Mooty made it clear that Ad Hoc steered away from automatic endorsement of or complete identification with the Abel campaign. I do not believe there is evidence to support Fuller's pivotal role in Ad Hoc.

44. Herling, *Right to Challenge,* 222.

45. For a more detailed account of the use of race in the campaign, see Herling, *Right to Challenge,* 221–29.

46. McDonald appointed Mark Tencher, the one-term president of USWA 1014, to head his District 31 campaign. Tencher was a white southerner; he had been elected the previous year because of Curtis Strong's decision to ally the black caucus with Tencher against Bazin (see chapter 4). Tencher took advantage of anti-Germano sentiment to rally votes for McDonald. He could not get the black vote away from Strong and the caucus.

47. Herling, *Right to Challenge,* appendix 5.

48. Herling, *Right to Challenge,* 320.

49. "Resolution for Civil Rights Section Embodied into Contract," Comer papers in author's possession.

50. International convention proceedings, PS; also Herling, *Right to Challenge,* 320–23. A couple of black International loyalists also took the floor, complimenting Abel. "I love what is happening here," said Philadelphia black staff man Jimmy Jones. Joe Maloney, who was chairing the convention at that point, realized he had to end on a more self-critical note. He concluded: "Is the judgment of the convention that the chairman has been sufficiently goosed this afternoon?"

51. The officers were: Hugh Henderson, Youngstown, Ohio, chairman; Thomas Johnson, Fairfield, Alabama, vice chairman; Carl Dickerson, Duquesne, Pennsylvania, vice chairman; and Rayfield Mooty, Chicago, Illinois, secretary-treasurer. The Steering Committee also included Thomas Mann, Detroit, Michigan, and Sylvester Palmer, Gary, Indiana. "A Progress Report of Ad-Hoc Committee, 1966–68," Comer papers in author's

possession. Report on the Ad Hoc Committee meeting, September 20, 1966, Kennedy papers on loan to author. Alex Fuller reported at this meeting on the new setup of the Civil Rights Department. He explained that Brother Curtis Strong had been assigned to his department as a full-time staff man. "Much legwork," the minutes from that meeting continue, "has been done to lay the foundation for action in the field of Civil Rights, and Equal Rights, within the Union, the Community, the Mills, and Factories."

52. Program, July 29–30, Birmingham, Alabama, PS, USWA Collection, box 12, file 54, Misc., 1967.

53. Education Coordinator Larry Keller accused Strong and Alex Fuller of holding a secret meeting in the district for black activists. Fuller responded, explaining that Jonathan Comer and his local had called the meeting, that Fuller had agreed to attend and requested Strong's participation. "The only role played by Curtis," he wrote, "was to take notes, which I asked him to do." Alex Fuller to Joe Germano, December 29, 1967, CHS, USWA District 31 Papers, box 29, file 1.

54. Letter from Rayfield Mooty to Ray Pasnick, Director, Public Relations, July 17, 1970. CHS, USWA District 31 Papers, box 29, file 1.

55. Letter from Rayfield Mooty to Alex Fuller, May 28, 1968. "I was instructed by this group," Mooty wrote, "to solicit support from your office to secure a meeting with Mr. I. W. Abel." Comer papers in author's possession.

56. Undated, mimeographed flyer, urging black members to get their directors' support for a constitutional change. It is an early document; it relies on information from the 1964 audit presented at the Atlantic City convention, and its wording resembles that of other early literature. Kennedy papers on loan to author.

57. A copy of the letter provided by Comer to the author.

58. Besides Comer, Leon Randall, Martin Cotton, Ora Lee Flagg, William Scoggins, and Sherman Ford attended the meeting. Minutes, February 2, 1967, CHS, USWA District 31 Papers, box 29, file 1. John Hopkins wrote a piece in 1969 for the *Hammond Times*, based on interviews with Young, Strong, and Comer. "Comer," he wrote, "although he has a good union job, believes unions could do more about minority group members. He and other black steelworkers are trying to pressure the international headquarters to hire more Negroes on its staff" (June 17, 1969). In an interesting aside, Hopkins says of Young, "Young won't talk now about his experiences in the labor movement, but to show how the black man makes it in the union he points to Jonathan Comer."

59. Minutes, February 2, 1967, CHS, USWA District 31 Papers, box 29, file 1, five pages of discussion.

60. Handwritten minutes dated December 1, 1967, Comer papers in author's possession. An undated mailing list for Gary and East Chicago included thirty names. Kennedy papers on loan to author.

61. Handwritten minutes dated December 1, 1967, Comer papers in author's possession. The same page continues: "We were told by the director not to invite his Staff to any meetings without his permission. When Negroes have problems we will invite Negroes if they happen to be Staff. We do not feel that we have to get permission from anyone to invite Negroes to discuss our problems."

62. Constitution as adopted at a conference in Birmingham, Alabama, 1967, after the reorganization of the Civil Rights Committee into a department. Mimeographed copy, Comer papers in author's possession.

63. Minutes for Ad Hoc meeting, April 27, 1968, typed copy, Comer papers in author's possession.

64. In fact, when Hugh Henderson announced that he was resigning as chairman of the Ad Hoc, Comer recommended that Gloria Llorente, the only woman to chair a chapter, take his place. The motion carried by a standing vote, and Llorente took office.

65. His wife and children were threatened during the week of the convention, and special police patrols were arranged for his house. Comer did not know about these threats until after the convention.

66. Comer claims that the bulk of support in the region came out of his own Local 1011, and that the other locals did not participate in many of the preparatory meetings in the district. The main flyer circulated in the district—"ATTENTION! BLACK BROTHERS"— was signed by Comer (1011), Mooty (3911), Sylvester Palmer (1014), and Lester White (1010). "It may be necessary," announced the flyer, "to dramatize the plight of the Blacks within the USW by demonstrating at the United Steelworkers Convention to be held in Chicago. Join the effort to upgrade THE BROTHER by assisting in this action." Mooty, Strong, and Palmer described their role as working with local chapters nationally to broaden support. "We had to convince black steelworkers throughout the country that this was something that had to be did. We went to Philly, Baltimore, Birmingham, Cleveland, we traveled all over the country," detailed Strong. "There was black awareness in the country at that time." Mooty and Strong agreed that the International had misjudged their power.

67. Letter from the Pick Congress to Rayfield Mooty confirming reservation. Kennedy papers on loan to author.

68. This is Comer's version. Mooty probably played an equal or greater role in the arrangements.

69. A final Ad Hoc meeting was called in Dayton, Ohio, on July 19 to "outline strategy and methods to stimulate participation in the demonstration." Methods included "membership cards, and Buttons, Car Stickers, Picket Signs, Appointment of different Committees to make the demonstration effective." Kennedy papers on loan to author. This action was approved at a meeting held in Gary, Indiana, on August 2. At this meeting, the minutes detail, "volunteer pledges were from many members to finance the project." Then at a subsequent meeting in Hammond, "it was decided that a Public Relations man was needed. Bro. Mooty was instructed to contact Mr. Augustus Savage of Chicago. First meeting with Mr. Savage, August 15, second meeting, August 16." The elaborate preparations reflected the sophistication and seriousness of Ad Hoc. Gus Savage volunteered his services because "we were fighting for a Just cause." Kennedy papers on loan to author.

70. These rather dramatic minutes were written by Rayfield Mooty after the event. Ad Hoc held a black caucus meeting on Monday night before the demonstration, attended by five hundred to a thousand people. Kennedy papers on loan to author.

71. From August 20 through August 27, local newspapers gave extensive coverage to the black protest. See *Chicago Tribune, The Times,* and *Gary Post Tribune. U.S. News and World Report* used its "Labor Week" column on September 7, 1968, to examine the demonstration and its impact.

72. Quoted in Herling, *Right to Challenge,* 359.

73. Ibid. On September 7, 1968, *U.S. News and World Report* quoted Jones as saying: "Don't tell me there is no possibility of getting a Negro elected. . . . I say to my black brothers: Get yourself nominated in your District and get yourself elected. Then you can stand up like a man—not as somebody appointed by President Abel." Jones held an appointed position. Comer described how Jones had to be escorted out of the convention hall through a rear door to be protected from his black brothers and sisters.

74. The use of black manhood images appeared in all the Ad Hoc's materials until Ola Kennedy became a leader. Hazel V. Carby has done an excellent analysis of the social constructions of manhood among blacks in *Race Men* (Cambridge: Harvard University Press, 1998).

75. The federal government was able to apply more pressure through the Office of

Federal Contract Compliance than through the Equal Employment Opportunity Commission (EEOC) that oversaw Title VII complaints. Executive Order 11246 had required companies with federal contracts to abide by affirmative action hiring procedures. The hiring changes did not occur immediately, but by the end of the decade (1968–69) large numbers of women began to enter the mills. The companies had done nothing to prepare the work force for the dramatic demographic shift, which led to an epidemic of harassment and discrimination problems. African American women ended up in the worst departments and jobs, although almost all of the women faced resistance and resentment from the foremen and their coworkers.

76. Minutes from 1969 describe a protest that happened because women were not allowed to vote at a meeting. Kennedy papers on loan to author.

77. Testimony from Ola Kennedy comes from three sources: the Ad Hoc video, an interview done by James Lane in Gary (CRA, Indiana University Northwest, Record Group 13.1, James B. Lane Papers) and an interview done by the author, August 24, 2000.

78. Comer tried to tone her down, because the International was considering her to be the first woman appointed to staff in District 31. Kennedy, however, flaunted her radicalism by attending a World Federation of Trade Unions conference (led by the Soviet Union) and then holding a press conference in New York when she returned. Yvonne "Sugar" Porter from Local 1010 was given the staff position instead.

79. The first woman to be put on staff as an organizer was Melena Barkman, in 1974. She led a small local of nurses (Local 6981) at Jones & Laughlin Pittsburgh Works. Today Barkman is one of the highest-ranking women on the International staff. She is director of the Membership Services Department, which oversees all education and leadership development programs. Melena Barkman, interview by author, June 27 and 28, 2000, Linden Hall Training Center, USWA, Dawson, Pennsylvania.

80. Resolution, Comer papers in author's possession. I also found a letter signed by Ola Kennedy to the International demanding equal rights for women, dated March 22, 1970. CHS, USWA District 31 Papers, box 29, file 1.

81. "Blacks Picket USW, Seeking Top-Level Jobs," *Pittsburgh Post-Gazette*, July 14, 1970. See Ruth Needleman, "Women of Steel: From Keeping a Job to Building a Movement" (paper presented at the North American Labor History Conference, Detroit, Michigan, October 2000). Also James B. Lane, "Feminism, Radicalism, and Unionism: The Calumet District Women's Caucus and Its Fight against Sex Discrimination in American Steel Mills," CRA, Indiana University Northwest, Record Group 13.1, James B. Lane Papers, 541–48.

82. There are numerous references to the Sims campaign in Kennedy's papers. District 31 Ad Hoc contributed eighty dollars to the campaign. Curtis Strong, Sylvester Palmer, and Jonathan Comer all contributed individually. A handwritten, partial set of minutes (undated) indicates that the International was "making an effort to get bro. Sims elected. We agreed to support the nomination of the incumbent officers." Comer said he had found that "white folks ain't quite ready to listen in the Pitts. Meeting . . . still paternalistic. We straightened them out on Jimmy Jones' performance at the convention." He also made an allusion to Sims as "not our cup of tea."

83. Mooty, Strong, and Kennedy, Ad Hoc video. I could not locate any minutes from the Cleveland meeting.

84. Following the epic 1959 strike that lasted 116 days, the USWA entered into an Experimental Negotiating Agreement (ENA) that voluntarily relinquished the workers' right to strike over contracts. See Metzgar, *Striking Steel,* on the 1959 strike. During the 1960s, the union leadership moved toward a more cooperative stance with the steel companies, while at the grassroots level, workers, women, students, and minorities were driving the social conscience of the country leftward.

85. In the Youngstown/Pittsburgh area there were a number of radical caucuses. See, for example, Philip W. Nyden, *Steelworkers Rank-and-File: The Political Economy of a Union Reform Movement* (New York: Praeger, 1984); Bruce Nelson, *Divided We Stand: American Workers and the Struggle for Black Equality* (Princeton: Princeton University Press, 2001), especially 251–86. See also Staughton and Alice Lynd, *The New Rank and File* (Ithaca, N.Y.: ILR Press, 2000). Mary Margaret Fonow fills in the blanks on women's activism during these years in her forthcoming book *Forging Feminism in the United Steelworkers of America* (St. Paul: University of Minnesota Press, forthcoming). See also James B. Lane and Mike Olszanski, eds., *Steelworkers Fightback: Rank-and-File Insurgency in the Calumet Region during the 1970s*, Steel Shavings 30 (2000).

86. CRA 187, Sam Evett Papers. The materials on the elections were kept closed until January 1, 2000.

87. Comer was asked for a recommendation when he refused the offer, and he suggested Leon Lynch. He knew the International would not tolerate a rabble-rouser, and he thought Lynch would do a good job. For many African Americans, Leon Lynch's selection was a milestone. Leon Lynch still holds the vice president's position and is the most senior executive board member.

Chapter 7: Between a Rock and a Hard Place

1. From the beginning, the decision-making debate took place among top white leaders. In 1937, for example, different District 31 staff reps lobbied for different African Americans. According to Walter Mackerl, "each one of them had their own pick. Johnson wanted me and Jack Rusack wanted Cotton, and Hart wanted Arthur Adams. So they was squabbling over that and they couldn't get together. So finally they had to compromise with George." Kimbley has a different slant on the story (see chapter 1). Curtis Strong, who was not there at the time, thought that Kimbley was supported by the leftists on staff because he was closely allied with them. That's unlikely, since Adams and Cotton were equally, if not more, associated with the left. What is clear is that African American unionists, like all others, spent a lot of time thinking about how selections were made.

2. In chapter 8 I discuss the influence of Garveyism. My last few discussions with Walter Mackerl took place in 1998, a year before his death. He still identified his views with those of Garvey's Universal Negro Improvement Association. He had found a way to use the union as a platform for his political work, focusing his attention on antilynching legislation and voting rights.

3. Black staff members have helped in many ways to provide support, resources, and opportunities for black unionists and the civil rights movement. They have also contributed greatly to building a strong and accountable union. Given the hurdles and standards faced by African Americans, these men proved to be among the best union staff, working tirelessly. At the same time, they held the union to equally high standards of accountability and integrity. Pressure from black grassroots organizations, however, make organizational change possible. Individual staff have only a limited impact on union culture. I base these views on interviews with black staff, including Kimbley, Strong, Comer, Montgomery, Jim Baker, Scott Dewberry, Leon Lynch, Josephine Brooks, and Fred Redmond.

4. In the earliest memos to staff from leadership, even in the SWOC years, staff discipline and loyalty were emphasized. For example, a memo from April 1940 specified: "The duties of the field staff is to devote their time strictly to the affairs of the organization. . . . Every member of the field staff is to take the responsibility of his position in fulfillment of his obligation to the organization. Passing the buck will not be tolerated. . . .

Each member of the field staff is held personally responsible for the delegates in his own respective territory." CRA, SWOC Correspondence.

I also found two petitions from the SWOC staff in District 31 complaining about non-payment of wages. David McDonald responded to Director Nick Fontecchio, in a letter dated September 11, 1940, saying: "I wonder if you have considered the fact that the time has come when we should think seriously about some changes being made. I believe we have pampered some of these people for quite some time. One thing is certain some of them have never delivered." On September 12, Fontecchio responded, writing: "Kindly be informed that the action taken by the field staff was taken without my knowledge and I deeply regret that such a request was made. Rest assured that this very morning I am having a staff meeting in this office and this matter will be thoroughly discussed with the staff members." The International did not want to hear complaints from staff; staff members reported to the director, and bypassing the director was a violation of protocol.

5. See Ruth Needleman, "Space and Opportunities: Developing New Leaders for Labor's Future," *Labor Research Review* 12, no. 1 (spring/summer 1993): 5–20.

6. See Charles R. Lawrence III and Mari J. Matsuda, *We Won't Go Back: Making the Case for Affirmative Action* (New York: Houghton Mifflin, 1997), chapter 5. This is one of the best analyses of the problem of tokenism, because the authors examine context and power relations, and do not connect tokenism to the individual in the position. For a similar analysis of women, see Cynthia Cockburn, *In the Way of Women: Men's Resistance to Sex Equality in Organizations* (Ithaca, N.Y.: ILR Press, 1991). Leading women unionists tell stories similar to those of their African American counterparts in Brigid O'Farrell and Joyce Kornbluh, eds., *Rocking the Boat: Union Women's Voices, 1915–1975* (New Brunswick, N.J.: Rutgers University Press, 1996).

7. See Rosabeth Moss Kantor, "The Impact of Hierarchical Structures on the Work Behavior of Men and Women," in *Women and Work: Problems and Perspectives*, ed. Rachel Kahn-Hut, Arlene Kaplan Daniels, and Richard Colvard (New York: Oxford University Press, 1982), 202–17.

8. See Manning Marable, *Black Leadership: Four Great American Leaders and the Struggle for Civil Rights* (New York: Penguin, 1999).

9. This has been one of the hardest issues for me to analyze. In my own experience, I have seen women leaders acting as "one of the boys," and perhaps even impeding the advancement of other women. Yet George Kimbley taught me how simplistic and unhelpful judgments of any kind are. I have learned from Kimbley, as well as Strong and Comer, how dangerous the waters are and how complex the navigational systems; building coalitions is more important than drawing endless lines of distinction.

10. See Jackie Robinson, *I Never Had It Made: An Autobiography* (Hopewell, N.J.: Ecco, 1995), and Arnold Rampersad, *Jackie Robinson: A Biography* (New York: Ballantine, 1998). Robinson was trained to stand in the outfield and ignore the cans and bottles thrown at him from the bleachers.

11. During the 1920s the KKK controlled many of the local government officials in northwest Indiana, including in Gary. The Klan dominated Valparaiso, and many people from the South joined it as a hometown organization. Kimbley and Mackerl both assumed the president was in the Klan, although they thought he was a decent unionist. They said the same about other SWOC activists who were known Klansmen. An excellent study of the Klan is Betty A. Dobratz and Stephanie L. Shanks-Meile, *White Power, White Pride! The White Separatist Movement in the United States* (New York: Twayne, 1997).

12. He spent quite a bit of time in Milwaukee, assisting in new organizing. The district director there requested Germano transfer him to his district but Germano refused because he liked the role that Kimbley played in District 31.

13. See CHS, USWA District 31 Papers and issues of the *Gary American*. Examples of

his assignments include: sergeant of arms, August 17, 1947, CHS, USWA District 31 Papers, box 40, file 5; sergeant of arms, May 8, 1948, box 40, file 4; reception committee, box 40, file 7, tab 1950; box 40, file 8, 1953; box 40, file 9; box 40, file 10, 1956. Kimbley's staff assignment can be found in box 40, file 3, 1947, listed as "factory stores."

14. George Kimbley, "The Negro in Organized Labor," *Info*, undated, in author's possession. He wrote a column for a short time that focused on naming the black workers who had built the union. He also did radio broadcasts for WJOB.

15. The article reads, in part: "Much of the hard work to organize was accomplished by Leonides McDonald, Staff Representative and a former official of the Universal Negro Improvement Association, also Wm. M Young, Jesse Reese, Lee Tisdale (deceased) and others." He added that Jesse Reese was vice president of the Youngstown local and that he was one of four "colored delegates from Gary and East Chicago at the First Wage and Policy Convention in Pittsburgh, Dec. 1937. They were William M. Young and Jesse Reese of East Chicago and Theodore Vaughn and George P. Kimbley of Gary." Kimbley provided me with a copy of the article.

16. I compiled this story from my interviews with Kimbley and Mackerl; from an interview with Boyd Wilson done after his retirement in PS; from Rayfield Mooty, Curtis Strong, and Ola Kennedy, Ad Hoc video (Chicago, 1985, copy in author's possession); and from IEB and convention materials in the USWA Collection in PS.

17. Districts had the right to elect their own director, but the incumbents ran unopposed the first time, and almost every other time after that. Since the director appointed the staff, and the staff basically worked the elections union by union in the district, it was almost impossible for an outsider to win a contested race for district director. When George Patterson ran against Germano during the war, Germano used his power in the Democratic Party to get Patterson drafted into the army. When John Mayerik ran against Germano after the war, he was fired from staff, and then Germano arranged for him to be discharged from U.S. Steel. Mayerik got reinstated at Gary Works through Philip Murray's own intervention; he then ran for president of 1014 and won. Copies of letters from Germano to the International (February 15, 1945), from Mayerik to McDonald (March 15, 1945), and from McDonald to Mayerik (March 17, 1945), copies in author's possession, obtained from Mayerik's family.

Also see John Conroy, "Mill Town: In the Steelworkers Union They Don't Assassinate Opponents. But They Do Rig Elections," *Chicago Magazine* (January 1977): 114–16. The first successful challenge in the district was Ed Sadlowski's bid for director. Germano's candidate, Sam Evett, won the election with more votes than were cast, so the election was overturned by the Department of Labor and another vote was held. CRA 187, Sam Evett Papers.

18. Most African Americans characterized Cook as a radical; a few thought he was a communist. One thought he may have been an FBI agent. The consensus was that Cook was a strong and skilled fighter within the union, which was how he got elected president in a local with a majority white membership.

I found FBI reports on Cook, obtained by Germano, in CHS, USWA District 31 Papers, box 30, file 6, Communist Activity. There was a full page of information on Cook, including public meetings and parades in which he participated, for example: "Spoke at National Negro Congress held at the Baptist Church 53rd and Michigan Avenue" and "Presided at mass meeting of the Communist Party celebrating the 20th anniversary of the daily worker." The dates covered in the report begin in 1933 and continue through 1946. Mackerl knew Cook well and visited him later in life in a nursing home, where Cook survived in complete poverty.

19. A transcript of the interview is in PS, USWA Collection.

20. Every person I interviewed shared with me a reconstructed story of his or her life,

affected by memory, circumstance, hindsight, and desire. Curtis Strong put it more bluntly: "You know every one of them lied to you." In keeping with historian Earl Lewis's call to interpret, I do not consider the statements in these interviews as lies. All stories call for interpretation and contextualization; dates can sometimes be checked, but perspectives are just perspectives.

21. Ironically, when the USWA Civil Rights Department was set up and Alex Fuller put in charge, Francis Shane sued the union for reverse discrimination. A fairly complete collection of materials on CARD can be found at WPR, CIO Collection, Office of the Secretary Treasurer, boxes 1, 136, 140, 149, 180, 192, 193, and 196. Files cover the entire life of the committee, from 1942 to 1951; they include minutes, speeches, reports, and correspondence.

22. Wilson remained silent on how he had been treated by the union until after he retired. His bitterness was aimed at McDonald, not Murray. For example, in the IEB minutes from 1944, Philip Murray pointed out that "unfortunately for Brother Wilson, he is required, under existing circumstances, to carry his office around in his pocket." Murray concludes: "The time has come when Boyd Wilson should be given an office and a secretary." Wilson's office was set up in the annex building at union headquarters, apart from all the other International officers.

23. In his report on September 23, 1943, Wilson states:

The other day I had a letter from a member of the union, and he told me that in a Union meeting, where there was an attempt to upgrade Negro members of the Union, a member of the Union got up and said, "I will not work with a Negro, nor will I train one." I thought that was a pretty serious thing for a man to say openly in one of our meetings. So I got in contact with the Sub-regional Director of this district, and I asked him if this statement was made. He said, "Yes, it was." I asked him if he knew the man who stood up and who made the statement. Yes, he did. I asked him if any disciplinary action had been taken against the man. He said, "No." Now, I am wondering if this Union is going to continue to maintain the confidence of the people who carry out its programs, unless we who are charged with carrying out these programs do a little more than we have been doing.

In response, Murray lectured the Executive Board: "It is the responsibility of our Directors to protect the interests of the colored workers just the same as it is the responsibility of our Directors to represent the interests of the white workers." He asked that directors do thorough examinations of the facts in cases of discrimination. PS, USWA Collection, International Executive Board Minutes, Record Group A1, box 1, file 8, 319–20, 327–36.

24. Untitled manuscript, PS, USWA Collection, Civil Rights Department, box 1, file 1, Negro—misc., 1945–46.

25. A copy of the petition with signatures can be found at CHS, USWA District 31 Papers, box 174, file 3.

26. PS, USWA Collection, box 21, file 13. Excerpts from the job description follow:

DIRECTION EXERCISED: Advise District Coordinators, Local Union officers, and Local Union Civil Rights Committees on procedure and methods in handling Civil Rights Complaints.

RESPONSIBILITY FOR CONTACTS: (1) Other departments in the International office, (2) District offices, (3) Local Unions, (4) National and local management of various companies, (5) National and local Civil Rights Civil Liberties, Civic and community organizations, (6) Municipal, State and Federal agencies, Commissions and departments.

WORKING PROCEDURES: (1)Make exhaustive and systematic investigations of conditions that may affect the Civil Rights or race relations of the membership, (2) Make exhaustive and in-depth investigations of conditions in communities that may affect Civil Rights or cause disturbances among the membership, (3) Make complete and analytical reports of conditions in plants, Locals or communities. . . . (6) Plan, develop and coordinate programs and meetings of Local Union Civil Rights Committees. . . . (8) Plan, develop, coordinate and participate in meetings between Local Unions and plant management. . . . (10) Negotiate with companies on Local Union Civil Rights Complaints or problems.

27. See his reports in PS, USWA Collection, Civil Rights Department, box 11, file 31, and box 16, file 51, District 31, General Info. Copies of reports related to District 31 are also located in CHS, USWA District 31 Papers, box 16; box 29, file 1; box 11, file 31.

28. This was true for African Americans in many unions. On George Holloway (United Auto Workers), see Michael Honey, *Black Workers Remember: An Oral History of Segregation, Unionism, and the Freedom Struggle* (Berkeley: University of California Press, 1999). I also consulted the oral histories of Shelton Tappes, Horace Sheffield, and others in WPR, Oral History Collection. See Nelson Lichtenstein, *The Most Dangerous Man in Detroit* (New York: Basic Books, 1996); Bruce Nelson, *Divided We Stand: American Workers and the Struggle for Black Equality* (Princeton, N.J.: Princeton University Press, 2001); Needleman, "Space and Opportunities."

29. Strong spent most of 1967 in Baltimore trying to identify and resolve civil rights complaints. His reports provide background information, a list of the people he met with officially, and the content of his findings. For example, his February 21, 1967, report covers the charges filed by the U.S. Labor Department against Bethlehem Steel and the efforts the company had made to date. PS, USWA Collection, box 12, file 64. See also reports dated March 6, 1967; April 11, 1967; May 4, 1967; May 23, 1967; October 3, 1967; and October 12, 1967.

30. See Alex Poinsett, *Black Power Gary Style: The Making of Mayor Richard Gordon Hatcher* (Chicago: Johnson, 1970), and James Lane, *"City of the Century": A History of Gary, Indiana* (Bloomington: Indiana University Press, 1978).

31. Summary report, CHS, USWA District 31 Papers, box 29, file 1.

32. Strong and Pete Calacci told me the same story from very different perspectives in my interviews with them.

33. Like Strong, Montgomery had come on staff with enormous backing from African Americans in his home district. He had helped found the Negro American Labor Council in Ohio, a local chapter of A. Philip Randolph's organization, and he had used that base to fight for black workers' rights in the union. The International had limited Montgomery's influence by assigning him to the Research Department and not letting him travel outside of Pittsburgh. Bruce Nelson interviewed Montgomery several times and covers his story in *Divided We Stand*.

34. Letter from Leon Lynch to Jonathan Comer, November 1, 1978, Comer papers in author's possession.

35. Comer did not know it at the time, but one of the two women was one of Ola Kennedy's daughters, Diane Smith. Smith still works at Bethlehem and has continued to file similar complaints. With a group of other African American workers, she tried to expose Bethlehem's refusal in the 1990s to hire black applicants.

36. Letter to Alex Fuller on the meeting with 6787 on March 12, 1975. The letter is dated March 27, 1975, Comer papers in author's possession.

37. The district director in Alabama, Howard Strevel, had taken a clear stand against

open racism. His support of Comer and his work made it easier to get things done in Alabama.

38. Comer has dozens of letters thanking him for his help and his kindness. One handwritten letter he received pleaded for help. "I need someone that is honest, love people and really know what it is all about, that's why I am writing you. I believe you are all those things and more, would you please help me get this project off the ground." January 3, 1982, Comer papers in author's possession.

39. I spent hours discussing this issue with Comer, and he helped me understand the conflicting pressures and competing loyalties that influenced him. I doubt that he would do anything differently if he could, although I know that he has been deeply disappointed by some developments in the union.

40. Letter from Joseph Jeneske, personnel administrator, to Jonathan Comer. Comer papers in author's possession.

Chapter 8: "Diplomats and Rabble-Rousers"

1. The NAACP's Herbert Hill, for example, characterized Jonathan Comer as "a thinker." He said they would "spend hours on the phone talking. He would think about his work and choices." Interview by author, December 6, 2000, Madison, Wisconsin. Hill saw Strong more as a man of action. Strong presents himself that way as well, although he, too, acted with an awareness of the lessons of history.

2. For an excellent overview of black radicalism in this period, see Robin D. G. Kelley, *The Black Radical Imagination* (Boston: Beacon Press, 2002); Rod Bush, *We Are Not What We Seem: Black Nationalism and Class Struggle in the American Century* (New York: New York University Press, 1999), 121–54; and Cedric Robinson, *Black Marxism: The Making of the Black Radical Tradition* (Chapel Hill: University of North Carolina Press, 1983), 207–40. See also Harry Haywood, *Black Bolshevik* (Chicago: Liberator Press, 1978); Mark Naison, *Communists in Harlem during the Depression* (Urbana: University of Illinois Press, 1983); Faith Berry, *Langston Hughes: Before and Beyond Harlem* (Westport: Lawrence Hill, 1983); William J. Maxwell, *New Negro, Old Left: African American Writing and Communism between the Wars* (New York: Columbia University Press, 1999).

Maxwell lays out his perspective: "The history of African-American letters cannot be unraveled from the history of American Communism without damage to both." He goes on: "The New Negro's entrance onto the Old Left, I hold, was early, voluntary, and key to the formative modern instant in African-American intellectual life" (2, 9). Cedric Robinson, perhaps more accurately, examines the role played by black, radical intellectuals in the African Blood Brotherhood in Harlem and earlier in the UNIA. He argues that these intellectuals formed the basis for the partnership between the "New Negro" and the "Old Left" (218–40). "African Americans had their own unique revolutionary tradition, and their interests were not identical to those of white workers," writes Robin Kelley (49).

3. Strong explained that Adams never tried to recruit him into anything and never spoke openly about the Communist Party. In *We Are Not What We Seem*, Bush makes the point that most black radicals "manifest some degree of nationalist consciousness" (2).

4. See Robert Korstad and Nelson Lichtenstein, "Opportunities Found and Lost: Labor, Radicals, and the Early Civil Rights Movement," *Journal of American History* 75, no. 3 (December 1988): 786–811; also Michael Honey, *Southern Labor and Black Civil Rights* (Urbana: University of Illinois Press, 1993).

5. The initiative did not come primarily from the CIO but equally from both sides. The agency of African Americans has often been underestimated. Mark Naison in his

book *Communists in Harlem during the Depression* makes a similar point about the inter-relationships between blacks and communists. He argues that insufficient attention has been paid to the influence of African Americans on the Communist Party; more writers have investigated the party's influence on the black struggle (xvi–xvii).

6. Robinson's arguments seem particularly relevant to an explanation of the radicalism of these freedom fighters. He contends that the black radical tradition reemerged through intellectuals such as Du Bois and, as he puts it, "began to overtake Marxism." New preface to *Black Marxism: The Making of the Black Radical Tradition* (Chapel Hill: University of North Carolina Press, 2000), xxx–xxxi.

7. For further analyses of black radicalism and differing ideologies, see William L. Van Deburg, ed., *Modern Black Nationalism: From Marcus Garvey to Louis Farrakhan* (New York: New York University Press, 1997); Cedric J. Robinson, *Black Movements in America* (New York: Routledge, 1997); Scott McLemee, ed., *C. L. R. James on the 'Negro Question'* (Jackson: University Press of Mississippi, 1996); and Harry Haywood, *Negro Liberation* (New York: International, 1948).

8. See Alex Poinsett, *Black Power, Gary Style: The Making of Mayor Richard Gordon Hatcher* (Chicago: Johnson, 1970); also William Edward Nelson Jr., "Black Political Mobilization: The 1967 Mayoral Election in Gary, Indiana" (Ph.D. diss., University of Illinois, 1971).

9. The only black Executive Board member, Leon Lynch, came from the region. De Witt Walton, for a few years special assistant to the president for minority affairs, came from USWA Local 1010. Fred Redmond, previously with the International's Membership Development Department, came from Chicago. There have been African American presidents elected in Local 1010 and Local 1014, and both Comer and Strong served on the Civil Rights Department's staff.

10. Robinson, *Black Marxism*, 212–18; Judith Stein, *The World of Marcus Garvey: Race and Class in Modern Society* (Baton Rouge: Louisiana State University Press, 1986); Ted Vincent, *Black Power and the Garvey Movement* (Oakland, Calif.: Nzinga, 1988).

11. Robinson, *Black Marxism*, 213.

12. Kimbley, "The Negro in Organized Labor," *Info*, undated, in author's possession.

13. Elizabeth Balanoff, "A History of the Black Community of Gary, Indiana, 1906–1940" (Ph.D. diss., University of Chicago, 1974), 410–27.

14. The *Gary Sun* did criticize Garvey on occasion and alleged that some of his local supporters were buying votes. April 11, 1924; April 18, 1924.

15. Oliver Montgomery, Ola Kennedy, Curtis Strong, and Jonathan Comer, interviews by author. Rayfield Mooty, Curtis Strong, and Ola Kennedy, Ad Hoc video (Chicago, 1985, copy in author's possession). According to Oliver Montgomery, his uncle had a picture over his sofa of a Black Star Line ship. The UNIA relied on its own Black Star Line operation to carry African Americans back to Africa. Next to this picture his uncle hung a photo of John Brown. "My crazy uncle thought [Garvey] was like a messiah who was going to take us home."

16. Balanoff, "History of the Black Community," 205. In *Black Marxism,* Robinson indicates that the African Blood Brotherhood in New York and Chicago had started to pull black activists from the UNIA into the Communist Party beginning in 1921 (217).

17. The party began by organizing within the American Federation of Labor and Amalgamated Association of Iron, Steel and Tin Workers through the Trade Union Education League. Later in the decade they would use the Trade Union Unity League to organize independently, forming an industrial union to compete with the Amalgamated.

18. *Gary American*, May 23, 1931.

19. Balanoff found reference to an Unemployed and Civic Workers' Council in the *Gary Post Tribune*, November 16, 1934. She speculates that this organization combined

the radical Unemployed Council with the more traditional black organization the Civic Affairs Committee (" History of the Black Community," 206).

20. Jesse Reese embraced the party for its work against race discrimination. See also Nell Irvin Painter, ed., *The Narrative of Hosea Hudson: The Life and Times of a Black Radical* (New York: W.W. Norton, 1994). Intellectuals such as Harry Haywood became critical of the Communist Party's position when it moved away from self-determination after the war. Haywood left the party in the fifties but did not leave the left movement.

21. Lydia Grady, interview by author.

22. Staughton and Alice Lynd, eds., *Rank and File: Personal Histories by Working-Class Organizers* (Princeton, N.J.: Princeton University Press, 1973). Alice and Staughton Lynd interviewed Jesse Reese for their book.

23. Ibid., 99.

24. A few who met Reese later on did not share Kimbley's view. Curtis Strong, for example, referred to him as "a joke in the black community." Strong, however, did not meet Reese until the 1960s. They never worked together.

25. Lydia Grady, interview by author.

26. Hank Johnson from the International Workers' Order and the United Mine Workers headed up the work in Gary for a year or so, until he was transferred to the Packinghouse Workers. John Rusack and Joe Webber, both Communist Party members, were on District 31 SWOC staff until after the Memorial Day Massacre. See Max Gordon, "The Communists and the Drive to Organize Steel, 1936," *Labor History* 23, no. 2 (spring 1982): 254–65; Stephen Briar, "Labor, Politics and Race: A Black Worker's Life," *Labor History* 23, no. 3 (summer 1982): 416–21.

27. See Painter, *Narrative of Hosea Hudson;* Robin D.G. Kelley, *Hammer and Hoe: Alabama Communists during the Great Depression* (Chapel Hill: University of North Carolina Press, 1990); Haywood, *Black Bolshevik;* and Cedric Robinson, *Black Marxism.*

28. Minutes from union meetings at Locals 1010 and 1011 throughout the 1940s include many resolutions against discriminatory practices but very few in solidarity with the Soviet Union or in support of party activities.

29. The complete records of the NNC are at SC; the introduction to part 1 provides a history covering the years from 1933 to 1942. See also John B. Streater Jr., "The National Negro Congress 1936–1947" (Ph.D. diss., University of Cincinnati, 1981).

30. The report indicates that there were 817 delegates representing twenty-eight states and the District of Columbia. SC, NNC microfilms, introduction, part 1, vi.

31. Bush, *We Are Not What We Seem,* 127; Joe William Trotter Jr., "From a Raw Deal to a New Deal? 1929–1945," in *To Make Our World Anew: A History of African Americans,* ed. Robin D. G. Kelley and Earl Lewis (Oxford: Oxford University Press, 2000), 431; Philip S. Foner, *Organized Labor and the Black Worker, 1619–1973* (New York: International Publishers, 1974), 217–21.

32. See SC, NNC microfilms, Correspondence: George Kimbley, 13:0845, 27:0466, 30:0298; Leonides McDonald, 13:0857; Pat Riley, 23:0001, 24:0628, 27:0558, 28:0755, 32:0457; Joe Cook, 9:0158, 12:0495, 23:0907, 27:0466. Hank Johnson, who went to the Packinghouse Workers from the region, wrote frequently.

33. A copy of the petition is in CHS, USWA District 31 Papers. Nick Migas, William Young, Joe Gyurko, and Elizabeth Balanoff also refer to the incident in interviews.

34. Robert Zieger, *The CIO: 1935–1955* (Chapel Hill: University of North Carolina Press, 1995), chapter 9; Honey, *Southern Labor,* chapters 5 and 6.

35. Al Samter, interviews by author.

36. Ed Yellen, Al Samter, William Young, and Elizabeth Balanoff, interviews by author; *Gary Post Tribune,* February 11, 1958. Correspondence between district and locals,

CRA 115, USWA Local Union 1010, box 2, files 13 and 23; also CHS, USWA District 31 Papers, box 169, files 2 and 3.

37. Whatever Samter's political leanings—and he was a leftist—he told me he never talked to Strong about the left or about socialism, only about work-based issues and jazz, a mutual passion. Strong's relationship with Al Samter was and still is very social. It involved wives and children, Sunday dinners, and evenings of listening to jazz. They often did business over lunch, but the only nearby restaurant that allowed them to sit together was the one in the bus station in downtown Gary. "So that's where we always had to go," said Strong.

38. Ed Yellen and Al Samter, interviews by author.

39. See Ellen Schrecker, *Many Are the Crimes: McCarthyism In America* (Princeton, N.J.: Princeton University Press, 1998), "McCarthyism and the Labor Movement: The Role of the State" in *The CIO's Left-Led Unions*, ed. Steve Rosswurm (New Brunswick, N.J.: Rutgers University Press, 1992), and "McCarthyism's Ghosts: Anticommunism and American Labor," *New Labor Forum* 4 (spring/summer 1999): 7–17. See also Kelley, *Hammer And Hoe*; Painter, *Hosea Hudson*.

40. Kelley, *Hammer and Hoe*. Kelley describes party meetings in Alabama that began with prayers and church songs.

41. Books on A. Philip Randolph include Paula F. Pfeffer, *A. Philip Randolph, Pioneer of the Civil Rights Movement* (Baton Rouge: Louisiana State University Press, 1990); Jervis Anderson, *A. Philip Randolph—A Biographical Portrait* (Berkeley: University of California Press, 1986).

42. Oliver Montgomery discussed this issue with me at length. He noted that A. Philip Randolph's advice—"Don't let yourself get branded as leftists or communists"—was taken very seriously. Montgomery made the decision to form a chapter of the Negro American Labor Council in his local instead of forming a black caucus or an open alliance with the Rank and File Team, a leftist opposition caucus. Throughout his life, however, Montgomery allied himself with radicals; his closest supporters and some of his friends were leftists, even open communists.

43. Balanoff, "History of the Black Community," 228.

44. Nelson Ouellet, "African American Migration and Family Strategies in Gary, Indiana, 1906–1925" (unpublished manuscript, in author's possession).

45. The newsletters of the Local 1010 Women's Auxiliary covered the activities of white ethnic women only, in the 1930s. Not until the District 31 Women's Caucus was interracial unity actively built. Mary Margaret Fonow, *Forging Feminism in the United Steelworkers of America* (St. Paul: University of Minnesota Press, forthcoming), and James B. Lane, "Feminism, Radicalism, and Unionism: The Calumet District Women's Caucus and Its Fight against Sex Discrimination in American Steel Mills," CRA, Indiana University Northwest, Record Group 13.1, James B. Lane Papers.

Chapter 9: Upheaval in Steel

1. There were actually two Consent Decrees signed, the first in 1974 and a second in 1975. Both were the result of complicated negotiations and compromises among the three signatories: the union, the companies, and the federal government. For a closer look at the history of the decrees, see Herbert Hill, *Black Labor and the American Legal System* (Madison: University of Wisconsin, 1985). Judith Stein, in *Running Steel, Running America: Race, Economic Policy, and the Decline of Liberalism* (Chapel Hill: University of North Carolina Press, 1998), provides a history of the Consent Decree as well. Stein defends the union and holds the NAACP and the black workers responsible for po-

larizing race relations. A detailed critique of Stein's analysis by Herbert Hill, "Race and the Steelworkers Union: White Privilege and Black Struggle, a Review Essay of Judith Stein's *Running Steel*," was published in *New Politics* 11, no. 1 (winter 2002): 172–205. Hill was involved in the lawsuits through the NAACP's Labor Department. He traces the debate and legal positions of the parties involved. The union, in his opinion, refused to address the demands of black workers and sought a compromise solution that would be acceptable to its white membership. Other analyses of the Consent Decree and race relations in steel can be found in Bruce Nelson, *Divided We Stand: American Workers and the Struggle for Black Equality* (Princeton, N.J.: Princeton University Press, 2001), 279–89; and John Hinshaw, "Dialectics of Division: Race and Power among Western Pennsylvania Steelworkers, 1937–1975" (Ph.D. diss., Carnegie Mellon University, 1995). The heartbreaking story of the effect of the Consent Decree on black steelworkers is told in the full-length documentary film *Struggles in Steel*, by Tony Buba (1996, distributed by California Newsreel).

2. Stein provides the union's argument for excluding civil rights organizations, reasoning that they only represented black workers and not the whole working class (*Running Steel, Running America,* 183–185). "From the very beginning, the USWA was forced to balance because it had a biracial constituency. Thus, its reasoning and its remedies differed from those of the NAACP and LDF [Legal Defense Fund]. Civil Rights lawyers represented a portion of the working class. Their interest in general labor practices was always contingent upon its effect on blacks" (183–84). Bruce Nelson, in contrast, criticized this subordination of race to so-called class, writing: "There are, to be sure, various economic issues around which blacks and whites, and workers of every race and nationality, can unite. But too often scholars and labor activists have sought to envelop race in the language of class, the 'magic bullet' of broad-gauged social-democratic policy agendas, and the invocation of the 'common dreams' that allegedly animated progressive social movements before the emergence of 'identity politics.' These ideological formulas and programmatic blueprints seek to hide race because of its volatility and proven capacity to divide. But given the ways in which race is encoded in working-class identities and definitions of self, there can be no economistic cure for the malady that is 'whiteness.' Nor is there any escaping the basic fact that 'class is lived through race and gender.' " See *Divided We Stand*, 293.

3. See Stein, *Running Steel, Running America,* chapter 7.

4. Nelson, *Divided We Stand*, 290. "In Indiana's Lake County," Nelson writes, "where steel mills dominated the landscape and blue-collar workers made up the bulk of the population, Wallace did not even campaign, but nevertheless it was one of the three counties where he won a majority." Nelson quotes a Gary voter as saying: "We've got Negroes in my union and they're ok, but eighty-five percent of the Negroes in this town are too pushy. It's time for the whites to enjoy some segregation."

5. Herbert Hill, "Race and the Steelworkers' Union" (unpublished manuscript), 56–58.

6. Melena Barkman has since become one of the highest-ranking women in the USWA today, serving as director of the Membership Services Department.

7. The story of this movement is told through the voices of participants in the Calumet Region in James B. Lane and Mike Olszanski, eds., *Steelworkers Fightback: Rank-and-File Insurgency in the Calumet Region during the 1970s, Steel Shavings* 30 (2000).

8. James B. Lane interviews, CRA, Indiana University Northwest, Record Group 13.1, James B. Lane Papers; Mary Margaret Fonow, *Forging Feminism in the United Steelworkers of America* (St. Paul: University of Minnesota Press, forthcoming).

9. See, for example, Philip W. Nyden, *Steelworkers Rank-and-File: The Political Economy of a Union Reform Movement* (New York: Praeger, 1984); and Joseph F. Wilson,

"Cold Steel: The Political Economy of Black Labor and Reform in the United Steelworkers of America (USWA)" (Ph.D. diss., Columbia University, 1980).

10. Data on steel employment can be found in Ann Markusen, *Steel and Southeast Chicago* (Chicago: Northwestern University Press, 1985); USWA, "Steel Crisis Fact Sheet," USWA District 7, Gary, Indiana, September 2001, with cover letter from then director Jack Parton; John P. Hoerr, *And the Wolf Finally Came: The Decline of the American Steel Industry* (Pittsburgh: University of Pittsburgh Press, 1988); *Hammond Times* and *Post Tribune*, October–December 2001; and *Post Tribune*, March 10, 2002.

11. Inland Steel closed the last existing open hearth in 1982.

12. Mill jobs no longer exist as an alternative for black youth in Gary. Willie Richardson's story illustrates the full tragedy. Richardson left Mississippi in the 1960s and hired in to U.S. Steel Gary Works. She raised five children as a single mother on a steelworker's wage. She managed to pay for all her children to attend college by working days as a substitute teacher in a Gary elementary school and nights in the mill as a lab technician. Not one of her children will ever work in the mill. Her two sons were murdered in separate incidents, innocent victims of the crime and desperation that came with the disappearance of jobs in Gary.

13. Mike Olszanski, a former president of Local 1010, seized the opportunity and taped six hours of discussion; among the participants were Oliver Montgomery, Jim Davis, and Curtis Strong, January 6–7, 2000, partial transcript in author's possession.

Chapter 10: "Fire in the Belly"

1. I organized the discussion and taped it. There was no audience, and this chapter has been edited from the original transcript.

2. Brooks was the second African American woman to be promoted to the District 31 staff. The first, Yvonne Porter, spent a relatively short time on staff. Josephine Brooks continues to be very active in Gary politics as an elected representative on the Gary school board. She holds a bachelor's degree from Indiana University Northwest in labor studies and is now an adjunct faculty member in the program.

3. Mary Elgin was elected three times as recording secretary before winning the post of financial secretary. She has been a delegate to many International conventions and to three Democratic Party conventions. In addition, Elgin has served as president of the local chapter of the Coalition of Trade Union Women and the Indiana Coalition of Black Trade Unionists. In 2002 she was elected to serve as the Calumet Township Trustee, winning against the incumbent.

4. Fred Redmond participated in this roundtable on his own time and at his own expense. He speaks here as a civil rights activist and committed unionist. In December 2002, Fred Redmond was asked to return to the Calumet Region as assistant district director by the newly elected District 7 director, Jim Robinson.

5. The USWA District 7 staff in northwest Indiana currently includes the following full-time African American staff members: a servicing rep from Local 1010, Alexander Jacques; Fred Redmond; two African American women, currently casual, or temporary, but on full-time tracks; one servicing representative out of Local 13796, Jo Elaine Robinson, and the other from 650L, a former Rubber Workers' local, Ruth Bloch. The district civil rights coordinator, Ray Jackson, out of Bethlehem Steel Local 6787, is African American also but not a full-time staff member. At the time of this roundtable, the only black staff rep was Alexander Jacques, who was still a casual. There are currently two Latino staff reps as well, Sal Alguilar and Alfredo Martinez, and three white women— Robin Rich, the rapid response coordinator; Sandy Warner, an organizer; and Sue

Maroko-Beckman, also in organizing, who is casual but on track for a permanent position. The new director, Jim Robinson, explained his choices by stressing the union's need for excellence at all levels. "I selected the most competent activists to carry out the union's work" (interview by author, July 20, 2002, Gary). The skill, experience, and diversity of District 7's staff bodes well for the future of unionism in the Calumet Region.

6. The discussion took place before the second major wave of bankruptcies and layoffs in the Calumet Region. Still, the speakers' views on complacency among blacks and their characterization of blacks as living as fat cats reflected their focus on black workers in unionized steel jobs. All the participants recognized how much better off black workers in steel have been in comparison to black workers generally.

7. At the 1998 convention the USWA president, George Becker, announced that Sharon Stiller, a staff representative from District 7, would move to Pittsburgh to be his special assistant. Stiller has acted decisively in that position to organize district women's councils and International women's conferences and to expand the Women of Steel program.

Conclusion: "Ask Harriet Tubman!"

1. Charles Payne, *I've Got the Light of Freedom: The Organizing Tradition and the Mississippi Freedom Struggle* (Berkeley: University of California Press, 1995). Payne's study of the freedom struggle in Mississippi describes in detail the organizing traditions that took root in southern communities during and after slavery, continuing into the civil rights organizing of the twentieth century.

2. John L. Lewis to S. J. Woolf, in the *New York Times*, March 21, 1937, republished in Melvyn Dubofsky, ed., *American Labor since the New Deal* (Chicago: Triangle, 1971), 108.

3. Ruth Needleman, "Women Workers: A Force for Rebuilding Unionism," *Labor Research Review* 11 (spring 1988): 1–14, and "History of Women in Steel" (paper presented at the North American Labor History Association, Detroit, Michigan, October 2000).

4. The USWA, as part of the AFL-CIO, came under criticism for its work to keep China out of the World Trade Organization, because some perceived the union's characterizations of the Chinese government as falling into racial stereotypes. See, for example, Kent Wong and Elaine Bernard, "Labor's Mistaken Anti-China Campaign," *New Labor Forum* 7 (fall/winter 2000): 19–23. The current International president, Leo Girard, a Canadian, faces significant challenges in balancing North American and international interests.

5. See Toni Morrison, "Home," in *The House that Race Built*, ed. Wahneema Lubiano (New York: Vintage, 1998); and Ruth Needleman, "Black Caucuses in Steel," *New Labor Forum* 3 (fall/winter 1998): 41–56.

6. Bernice Reagon Johnson, "Coalition Politics: Turning the Century," in *Race, Class, and Gender: An Anthology,* ed. Margaret Anderson and Patricia Hill Collins (Belmont, Calif.: Wadsworth, 1998), 518–19.

7. In "Coalition Politics," Reagon Johnson goes on to say: "You come together to see what you can do about shouldering up all of your energies so that you and your kind can survive. There is no chance that you can survive by staying *inside* the barred room. . . . But that space while it lasts should be a nurturing space" (519).

8. I asked many interviewees why, in their opinion, the union had started its downward slide in power. Many pointed to money and careerism. John Howard strongly believed that money corrupted the union and union leaders. Mackerl put it this way: "After the union got up and they went to paying these guys, then everybody got greedy, black and white, and that's what made the thing go wrong. Back then nobody was paid noth-

ing. We was all struggling because we wanted to help each other. The money split us up every which way, and so they don't stand for much now." In the late 1940s the union began to pay for time spent on union business. Interviews; CRA 115, USWA Local Union 1010, minutes; and PS, USWA Collection, International Executive Board Administratorship discussions.

Selected Sources

Archives

Calumet Regional Archives, Gary, Indiana

Collection 12, Inland Steel Corporation
Collection 13, United Steelworkers of America (USWA)
Collection 41, U.S. Steel Corporation
Collection 79, Jeannette Strong Papers
Collection 91, Orval Kincaid Papers
Collection 92, George P. Kimbley Papers
Collection 102, International Institute of Northwest Indiana Records
Collection 115, USWA Local Union 1010
Collection 119, John Oglesby Papers
Collection 121, USWA Local Union 1011
Collection 187, Sam Evett Papers
Collection 138, Peter Calacci Papers
Collection 141, John Howard Papers
Collection 144, USWA Local Union 1066
Collection 160, Clifford Minton Papers (Gary Urban League)
Collection 168, John Mayerick Papers
Collection 188, William "Buddy" Todd Papers
Collection 242, Raymond Mohl Papers
Collection 256, Joseph Norrick Papers
Collection 310, Paul Dremeley Papers
Collection 325, E. Thomas Colosimo Papers
Collection 328, USWA District 31, Sub 2
Collection 337, USWA Local Union 1014
Collection 358, Don Lutes Papers
Collection 371, Robert "Bob" Flores Papers
Collection 373, Kerry Taylor Papers

Collection 378, USWA District 31, Sub 1
Collection 391, Dorreen and William Carey Papers
SWOC Correspondence

Chicago Historical Society, Chicago, Illinois

United Steelworkers of America (USWA) District 31 Papers

Indiana Historical Society, Indianapolis, Indiana

Indianapolis Recorder, 1935–38, 1942

Library of Congress Manuscript Division, Washington, D.C.

National NAACP Collection
National Urban League Collection

National Archives, Washington, D.C.

Record Group 183, Office of Employment Security
Record Group 211, War Manpower Commission
Record Group 228, Committee on Fair Employment Practice

Penn State Labor Archives, Penn State University, University Park, Pennsylvania

Oral History Collection
United Steelworkers of America (USWA) Collection
    Civil Rights Department, 1945–1971
    International Executive Board Minutes, 1942–1964, Record Group A1

Walter P. Reuther Library, Wayne State University, Detroit, Michigan

Blacks in the Labor Movement Oral History Collection—Interviews by Herbert Hill
    Joseph Billups, October 27, 1967 (Hill with assistance by Shelton Tappes and Roberta
        McBride)
    George W. Crockett Jr., March 2, 1968
    Edward L. Doty, November 2, 1967
    Nick Di Gaetano, June 17, 1968 (Hill with assistance by Jim Keeney)
    Jack Lever, May 29, 1967
    Hodges Mason, November 28, 1967
    Arthur Osman, July 12 and 13, 1968
Committee for Industrial Organization (CIO), Office of the Secretary Treasurer
    Part I—James Carey, 1935–1955 (chairman, CIO Civil Rights Committee)
    Part II—George Weaver, 1941–1960 (director, CIO Civil Rights Committee)
George Crockett Papers, 1944–1946, UAW, FEPC
Neal Edwards Papers, Indiana CIO Conventions, 1941–1954
Oral History Collection
    Alice Peurala
    Horace Sheffield
    Shelton Tappes

United Auto Workers (UAW)

Education Department—Edward Coffey Papers
Public Relations Department—Frank Winn Papers

Schomberg Center for Research in Black Culture, New York Public Library, New York, New York

National Negro Congress (NNC)

Periodicals

Chicago Defender
Gary American
Gary Evening Post
Gary Post Tribune
Gary Sun
Indianapolis Recorder
Labor Sentinel, vols. 1 and 2, April 1944–1949; vols. 6–9, 1950–1952, CHS, CRA
Latin Times, 1957–1960, CRA
Steel Labor, vols. 1–6, 1936–1941, CHS

Interviews by Author

All locations are in Indiana unless specified otherwise.
Jose "Sosa" Alamillo, November 29, 1988, East Chicago
Jesse Arredondo Sr., February 1, 1989, East Chicago
James Baker, November 15, 1988, East Chicago
Elizabeth Balanoff, June 4, 1985, and July 19, 2000, Hammond
James Balanoff, October 24, 1988, Hammond
Peter Calacci, October 26, 1988, East Chicago
Louis Chickie, March 11, 1988, East Chicago
Jonathan Comer, January 21, 1986, East Chicago; April 7, 1989, Gary; August 17, 1999, Gary; September 22, 1999, Gary; November 29, 2000, Gary
Nell Comer, March 22, 2001, Gary
Hubert Dawson, January 31, 1989, Gary
Charles Fizer, June 22, 1987, Gary
James and Irma Fleming, January 16, 1989, Gary
Robert Flores, November 22, 1988, East Chicago
William Gailes, January 14, 1986, East Chicago
Gavino Galvan, September 12, 1986, East Chicago
Concepcion Gonzalez, March 27, 1989, East Chicago
Lydia Grady, June 9, 1998, Gary
John Gutierrez, November 30, 1988, East Chicago
Joe Gyurko, November 21, 1988, Hammond; February 8, 1996, class presentation, video, Gary; February 18, 1997, class presentation, video, Gary
Lawrence J. Hall, April 4, 1989, Gary
Robert Hoggs, December 1, 1988, East Chicago
David Howard, October 25, 2001, Gary
John L. Howard, January 13, 1986, and October 7, 1989, Gary
Larry Keller, March 10, 1989, East Chicago
Ola Kennedy, August 24, 2000, Gary
George Kimbley, January 14, 1989, Frankfort, Ky.
Nick Koleff, October 31, 1988, East Chicago
Don Lutes Sr., March 3, 1989, East Chicago

Leon Lynch, April 23, 1998, Pittsburgh, Pa.
Walter Mackerl, January 17, 1989, and August 4, 1997, Gary
Chris Malis, June 2, 1986, Gary
Fran Malis, June 2, 1986, Gary; March 1, 2002, Merrillville
John Mayerick, June 4, 1986, Merrillville; February 4, 1997, class presentation, video, Gary; February 18, 1997 class presentation, video, Gary; November 5, 1998, by phone
Al McClain, on his father, Al McClain Sr., July 25, 1985, Gary
Nick Migas, February 17, 1989, and February 18, 1989, New Port Richey, Fla.
Tommy Mills, January 15, 1986, East Chicago
Oliver Montgomery, March 23, 2000, Pittsburgh, Pa.
Ermelina Murillo, March 28, 1989, East Chicago
Reno Mussat, March 2, 1989, Griffith
Sylvester Palmer, April 13, 1989, Gary
Basil Pacheco, May 30, 1986, East Chicago
Frank Perry, March 3, 1989, Gary; October 11, 1989, on video, Gary
Hank Rowsey, March 1, 1989, Gary
Stanley Rygas, February 7, 1989, Griffith
Al Samter, January 10, 1986, Gary; August 11, 1998, Gary; October 5, 2000, Gary
William Scoggins, January 31, 1989, Gary
Fred Stern, January 22, 1986, Gary
Curtis Strong, September 10, 1985, Gary; January 27, 1989, Gary; June 24, 1989, Gary; February 25, 1995, Gary; April 1, 1997, Gary; September 8, 1998, Gary; July 13, 2000, Gary; October 25, 2000, Gary
Curtis Strong and Al Samter, April 1, 1997, class presentation, Gary
Oris Thomas, February 7, 1989, Gary; August 6, 1990, Gary
Arthur Vasquez, March 1, 1989, Whiting
Joe Vasquez, May 28, 1986, East Chicago
Louis Vasquez, November 29, 1988, East Chicago
Jesse Villapando, February 15, 1989, Gary
Ed Yellen, June 12, 1998, Gary
Lamar Young, February 16, 1989, East Point, Ga.
William Young, February 15, 1989, and February 16, 1989, East Point, Ga.

Interviews by Others

William Gailes, February 10, 1999, interviewed by Mike Olszanski, Gary
Joe Gyurko, May 11–May 12, 1983, and May 13, 1983, interviewed by Mike Olszanski, East Chicago
Mary Hopper, October 3, 1983, interviewed by Mike Olszanski, East Chicago
Mary Hopper and Ann Giba, September 21, 1983, interviewed by Mike Olszanski, East Chicago
Walter Mackerl, August 22, 1997, interviewed by Glen Dowdell Jr., Gary
Oliver Montgomery with Jim Davis and Curtis Strong, January 5, 2000, and January 6, 2000, interviewed by Mike Olszanski, Gary
Al Samter, January 21, 1998, and January 28, 1998, interviewed by Jim Lane, Gary
John Sargent, February 14, 1978, interviewed by Mike Olszanski, East Chicago
Curtis Strong, October 1, 1998, interviewed by Jim Lane, Gary
Manuel Trbovich, June 1989, interviewed by Kathy Seale for author, Hollywood, Calif.

Index

Note: Page numbers with an *f* indicate figures.

Washington, Booker T., 185
Weaver, George, 169
Weaver, Robert C., 193
Webber, Joe, 28
Weber, Brian, 208
Welch, Joe, 132
White supremacy. *See* Racism
Whitlock, A. B., 65
Wilcher, Joe, 123
Wildcat strikes, 52
    Jonathan Comer and, 180
    racism and, 49–50
    Curtis Strong on, 97–99
    See also Work stoppages
Williams, Jesse Mae, 128f
Wilson, Boyd, 137
    Ad Hoc Committee and, 160–61
    racism and, 139–41
    union staff job of, 168–70, 172–73
Wirt, William, 24
Women
    Ad Hoc Committee and, 154–57
    community work by, 199–200
    Local 1010 and, 45–46
    Title VII and, 154–55

    union politics and, 50–51, 101–3, 109, 228–29, 239–40
    See also specific individuals
Women's Caucus, 156, 200, 209, 212f, 215
    See also Caucus(es)
Woods, Roberta, 212f
Works Progress Administration (WPA), 115
Work stoppages, 77, 99
    See also Wildcat strikes
World War I, 18–20, 187
World War II, 50–52, 78, 207
Wright, Frank, 79

Yergen, Max, 194
Young, William, 1–6, 36–59, 38f, 47f, 234
    family of, 37–39, 199
    McCarthyism and, 55–59
    Nick Migas and, 57–58, 196
    NNC and, 193
    parents of, 37–39
    racism and, 39–40, 46–55, 103
    Clarence Royster on, 52
    union organizing by, 42–46, 162–63, 185, 193, 202